T0222852

Machine Learning with the Raspberry Pi

Experiments with Data and Computer Vision

Donald J. Norris

Apress®

Machine Learning with the Raspberry Pi: Experiments with Data and Computer Vision

Donald J. Norris
Barrington, NH, USA

ISBN-13 (pbk): 978-1-4842-5173-7   ISBN-13 (electronic): 978-1-4842-5174-4
https://doi.org/10.1007/978-1-4842-5174-4

Managing Director, Apress Media LLC: Welmoed Spahr
Acquisitions Editor: Aaron Black
Development Editor: James Markham
Coordinating Editor: Jessica Vakili

Distributed to the book trade worldwide by Springer Science+Business Media New York, 233 Spring Street, 6th Floor, New York, NY 10013. Phone 1-800-SPRINGER, fax (201) 348-4505, e-mail orders-ny@springer-sbm.com, or visit www.springeronline.com. Apress Media, LLC is a California LLC and the sole member (owner) is Springer Science + Business Media Finance Inc (SSBM Finance Inc). SSBM Finance Inc is a **Delaware** corporation.

For information on translations, please e-mail rights@apress.com, or visit http://www. apress.com/rights-permissions.

Apress titles may be purchased in bulk for academic, corporate, or promotional use. eBook versions and licenses are also available for most titles. For more information, reference our Print and eBook Bulk Sales web page at http://www.apress.com/bulk-sales.

Any source code or other supplementary material referenced by the author in this book is available to readers on GitHub via the book's product page, located at www.apress.com/978-1-4842-5173-7. For more detailed information, please visit http://www.apress.com/source-code.

Printed on acid-free paper

Table of Contents

About the Author

Donald J. Norris is an avid electronics hobbyist and maker. He is also an electronics engineer with an advanced degree in Production Management. Don is retired from civilian government service with the US Navy, where he specialized in acoustics and digital signal processing. He also has more than a dozen years' experience as a professional software developer using C, C#, C++, Python, and Java, and 5 years' experience as a certified IT security consultant.

About the Technical Reviewer

 **Ahmed Fawzy Gad** is a machine learning engineer who holds B.Sc. and M.Sc. in Information Technology. Ahmed is a teaching assistant and a researcher who is interested in machine/deep learning, computer vision, and Python. He is a machine learning technical reviewer and consultant helping others do their projects. Ahmed contributes written tutorials and articles to a number of blogs including Paperspace, Real Python, KDnuggets, Heartbeat, and Towards Data Science.

Ahmed has authored three books titled *TensorFlow: A Guide to Build Artificial Neural Networks Using Python* (Lambert 2017), *Practical Computer Vision Applications Using Deep Learning with CNNs* (Apress, 2018), and *Building Android Apps in Python Using Kivy with Android Studio* (Apress, 2019).

He welcomes you to connect with him through LinkedIn (`linkedin.com/in/AhmedFGad`), Facebook (`fb.com/AhmedFGadd`), and e-mail (`ahmed.f.gad@gmail.com`).

## CHAPTER 1

Introduction to machine learning (ML) with the Raspberry Pi (RasPi)

This chapter will provide you with introductions to both RasPi and ML. The RasPi discussion will be first, which will help you understand the hardware platform that will be used to run all the book's demonstrations. An introductory ML discussion follows, which will provide you with a framework to comprehend what ML is all about and why it is such an exciting and rapidly evolving field of study.

RasPi introduction

You will need to use a RasPi in order to run this book's demonstrations. In the next few sections, I will show you how to set up and configure a RasPi 3 Model B or B+ as a workstation that will run the scripts and programs required for the various ML demonstrations. Figure 1-1 shows a RasPi 3 Model B+, which is used in this book.

© Donald J. Norris 2020
D. J. Norris, *Machine Learning with the Raspberry Pi*,
https://doi.org/10.1007/978-1-4842-5174-4_1

Figure 1-1. *Raspberry Pi 3 Model B+*

There are a few differences between the RasPi 3 Model B and B+. They are basically the same except that the B+ has a slightly faster processor clock speed increase and has some improvements in the wireless functions as compared to the B model. Neither of these improvements will have a significant impact on running this book's projects if you use a B instead of a B+ model.

I will not discuss what constitutes a RasPi single-board computer because that is already adequately covered by many available books and blogs. As mentioned earlier, I used a RasPi 3 Model B+ in a workstation configuration. This setup is where a RasPi is connected with a USB keyboard, USB mouse, and HDMI monitor. In my setup, the RasPi is powered by a 2.2A, 5V supply with a micro USB connector.

The RasPi does not use a mechanical disk drive for implementing a file system which includes an operating system (OS). All recent RasPi versions rely on using a pluggable micro SD card to serve as the secondary storage. While it is possible to connect a traditional disk drive to a RasPi, it will only serve as an auxiliary storage device and not as the primary storage for the OS or as the bootable partition. I will next show you how to download and install an OS on a micro SD card in order to enable the RasPi to serve as a functional ML microcontroller.

Undoubtedly the simplest way to get up and running is to purchase a preprogrammed micro SD card. Such cards are ready to go and only need to be configured to match your particular workstation configuration, including your WiFi network. The WiFi configuration process will be discussed in a later section, but first I would like to discuss how to create your own micro SD card if you so desire.

The micro SD card software to be loaded is known as a Raspbian Image and is available without charge from many online web sites, with my recommended site being the Raspberry Pi Foundation site at raspberrypi.org. The latest OS Image is always available from the Downloads section of the web site. There are two types of the OS Image that you can download. The first type is named NOOBS, which is an abbreviation for "New Out of the Box Software." There are two versions of NOOBS available. One version is named NOOBS, and the other version is named NOOBS Lite. Both versions are identified as v3.0.0 as of the time of this writing. NOOBS has an easy operating system installer which contains the Raspbian OS as well as another popular OS named LibreELEC. Additionally, the NOOBS version provides a selection of alternative operating systems which are subsequently downloaded from the Internet and installed. NOOBS Lite contains the same operating system installer without Raspbian pre-loaded and no LibreELEC option. However, this version provides the same operating system selection menu allowing Raspbian and other OS Images to be downloaded and installed.

The NOOBS and NOOBS Lite Images are just collection of files and sub-directories that can be downloaded either using the BitTorrent application or simply as a raw Zip file. The BitTorrent and Zip downloads are approximately 1.2 GB in size. The extracted Image is 1.36 GB in size, but the final installed size is over 4 GB. This means that you will need to use at least an 8 GB micro SD card to hold the final Image. However, to replicate all the ML demonstrations in this book, I strongly recommend that you use at least a 16 GB, class 10 micro SD card to ensure there is plenty of storage available as well as to maximize the data throughput with the operating RasPi.

The second Image type is a direct OS download. The currently available Image is the Raspbian Linux distribution with a code name of Stretch. This Raspbian version may be downloaded using BitTorrent or as a Zip file with final Image sizes similar to the NOOBS Image.

A micro SD card must be configured after an Image is downloaded. I will only discuss the direct Raspbian download type because I believe the readers of this book are sufficiently experienced with basic computer operations and also with the RasPi so that they will overwhelmingly choose to use the direct downloaded approach.

Writing the Raspbian Image to a micro SD card

The micro SD card does not need to be formatted prior to writing the Image. That portion of the process is automatically done by the application that writes the Image to the card. You just need to set up an appropriate application based on your host computer. For a Windows machine, I highly recommend that you use the Win32DiskImager available from

```
https://sourceforge.net/projects/win32diskimager/files/latest/
download.
```

The download is a Zip file, which will need to be extracted prior to use. Then just run the application, select where the disk Image is located, and also select the micro SD card logical file letter. Figure 1-2 shows my configuration screen for writing the Raspbian Stretch version to a micro SD card on a Windows machine.

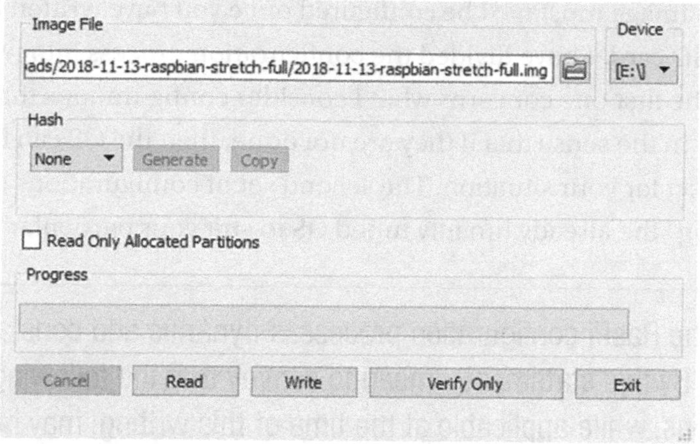

Figure 1-2. *Win32DiskImager screenshot*

If you are using a Mac, I recommend using the Etcher program to write the disk Image. It is available from https://etcher.io/. This application functions in a similar fashion to the Win32DiskImager program. Figure 1-3 is a screenshot of it being run on my MacBook Pro.

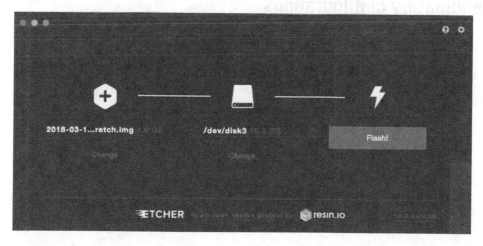

Figure 1-3. *Etcher screenshot*

The OS Image must next be configured once you have written it onto the micro SD card. I have divided the configuration process into two sections. The first one concerns what I consider configurations that are mandatory in the sense that if they are not done, then the OS can function as you expect for your situation. The second set of configurations concern "fine-tuning" the already broadly tuned OS to suit your particular needs.

Note   The RasPi configuration process is dynamic and constantly evolving. By this statement, I mean to convey that the following instructions, while applicable at the time of this writing, may not be applicable when you attempt to replicate the instructions. This fact is simply due to the nature of open source software. However, I am convinced that whatever procedures are in place, they will be clear and simple to follow.

Mandatory configurations

Figure 1-4 shows the opening screen after the RasPi boots.

Figure 1-4. *The initial configuration screenshot*

You must click the Next button to begin the configuration process just as it is stated in the figure. Figure 1-5 will immediately appear showing the defaults for country, language, and timezone.

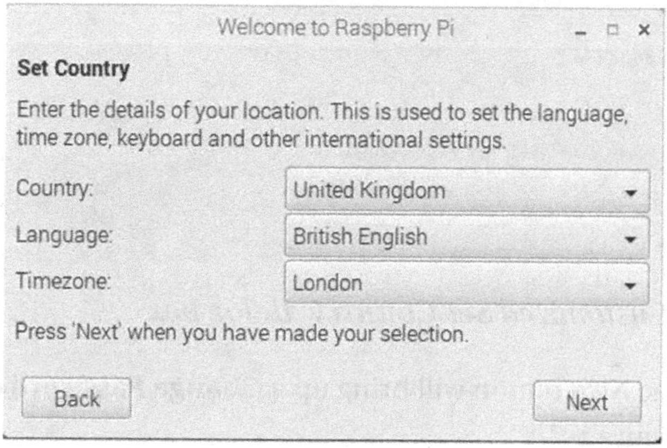

Figure 1-5. *Default **Set Country** dialog box*

It is important for you to at least select the appropriate country and language, or you will have great difficulty in entering any scripts or programs due to conflicts between the way your physical keyboard is set up and the desired characters you wanted to enter. The timezone menu will also be automatically adjusted to reflect the timezones available in the selected country.

Figure 1-6 shows this box after I made my particular selections.

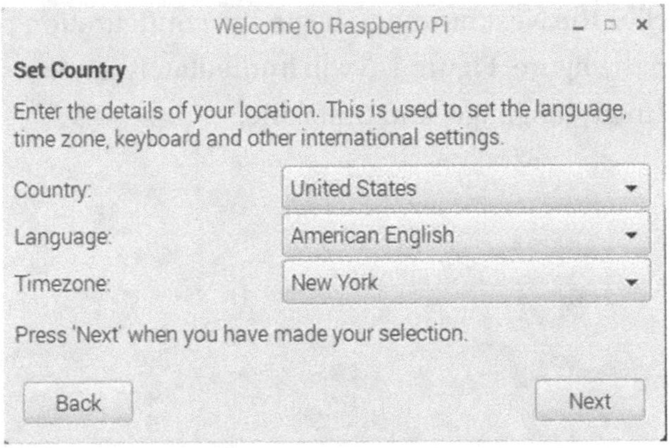

Figure 1-6. *Customized **Set Country** dialog box*

Clicking the Next button will bring up a **Change Password** dialog box as shown in Figure 1-7.

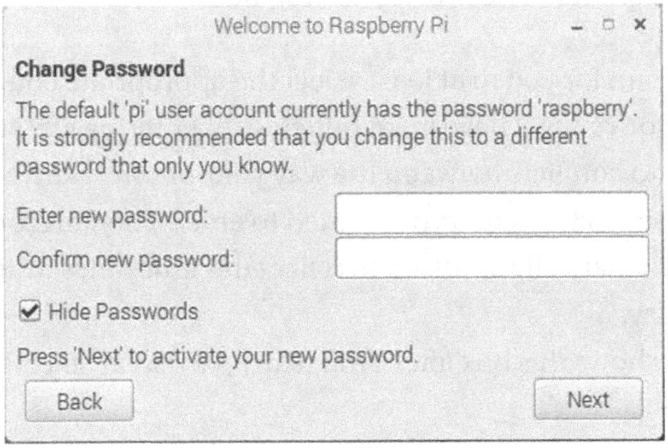

Figure 1-7. *Change Password dialog box*

Changing the default password of raspberry, which is likely universally known, should improve your system's security. This choice is entirely up to you and frankly will have no impact on replicating any of this book's demonstrations. You will just have to remember the password or else you will need to install a fresh Image. I do not believe there is an easy way to recover a forgotten password with the Raspbian OS. If you choose not to change the password, simply click the Next button and the **Select WiFi Network** dialog box should appear. Figure 1-8 shows the dialog box for my situation after I clicked the button.

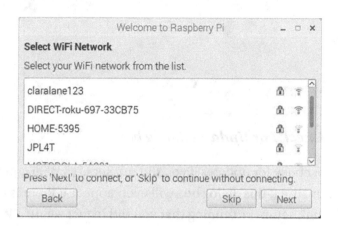

Figure 1-8. Select WiFi Network dialog box

You will need to click the appropriate WiFi network SSID in order to establish a WiFi communications link. Another dialog box will appear prompting you to either press a button on the physical router or enter the passphrase associated with the selected WiFi SSID. I choose not to show this particular dialog box for obvious security reasons. Clicking the Next button will bring up the **Check For Updates** dialog box, which is shown in Figure 1-9.

Figure 1-9.   Check For Updates dialog box

You cannot check for updates if you did not set up a WiFi connection. I am actually unsure if this dialog box will even appear if there is no working WiFi link setup. Presuming that you did in fact set up a WiFi link, then clicking the Next button will cause the RasPi to go out to the Internet and check on the status of the currently installed software contained in the new Image. However, you do not need to run the check at this point in the configuration because I will shortly show you how to do an update using a terminal window command. The choice is up to you. In reality, it will do no harm to do both other than cost you some extra time in the configuration process. If you want to use the manual update process, just click the Skip button; otherwise, click the Next button. Figure 1-10 shows how the **Check For Updates** dialog box changed after I clicked the Next button.

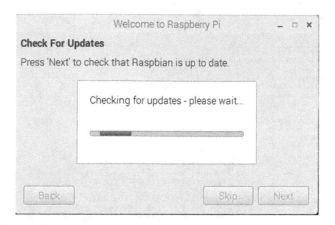

Figure 1-10. Active *Check For Updates* dialog box

The activity bar will remain active for several minutes depending upon how many updates are detected. Once the updates have completed, you will see an information box informing you that the configuration process has almost finished and you will need to click a Reboot button to complete the process. I would suggest you do that and don't forget to enter your new password if you changed it.

I now recommend that you enter the following command into a terminal window to check the status of your WiFi connection:

```
Ifconfig
```

Figure 1-11 shows the result of entering this command on my RasPi system.

```
                              pi@raspberrypi: ~                    _  □  ×

 File  Edit  Tabs  Help
 pi@raspberrypi:~ $ ifconfig
 eth0: flags=4099<UP,BROADCAST,MULTICAST>  mtu 1500
         ether b8:27:eb:bd:e9:c9  txqueuelen 1000  (Ethernet)
         RX packets 0  bytes 0 (0.0 B)
         RX errors 0  dropped 0  overruns 0  frame 0
         TX packets 0  bytes 0 (0.0 B)
         TX errors 0  dropped 0 overruns 0  carrier 0  collisions 0

 lo: flags=73<UP,LOOPBACK,RUNNING>  mtu 65536
         inet 127.0.0.1  netmask 255.0.0.0
         inet6 ::1  prefixlen 128  scopeid 0x10<host>
         loop  txqueuelen 1000  (Local Loopback)
         RX packets 0  bytes 0 (0.0 B)
         RX errors 0  dropped 0  overruns 0  frame 0
         TX packets 0  bytes 0 (0.0 B)
         TX errors 0  dropped 0 overruns 0  carrier 0  collisions 0

 wlan0: flags=4163<UP,BROADCAST,RUNNING,MULTICAST>  mtu 1500
         inet 192.168.0.6  netmask 255.255.255.0  broadcast 192.168.0.255
         inet6 2601:700:8002:5dc0:d6b8:bb1e:6516:f013  prefixlen 64  scopeid 0x0<
 global>
         inet6 fe80::da7e:c0e1:7c6:a750  prefixlen 64  scopeid 0x20<link>
         inet6 2601:700:8002:5dc0::8  prefixlen 128  scopeid 0x0<global>
         ether b8:27:eb:e8:bc:9c  txqueuelen 1000  (Ethernet)
         RX packets 76  bytes 9012 (8.8 KiB)
         RX errors 0  dropped 0  overruns 0  frame 0
         TX packets 101  bytes 18827 (18.3 KiB)
         TX errors 0  dropped 0 overruns 0  carrier 0  collisions 0

 pi@raspberrypi:~ $ □
```

Figure 1-11. The ifconfig command display

You should be able to see in the wlan0 section that a local IP address of 192.168.0.6 was assigned to the RasPi by the home WiFi router. This assignment confirms that the RasPi is able to be connected to the Internet. Check to see that your home router is set up for DHCP in case you do not see an IP address similar to the one shown in the figure.

Optional configurations

The optional configuration process uses a utility named raspi-config. This utility is provided in the initial downloaded Image. You can run the raspi-config utility by opening a terminal window and entering the following command:

```
sudo raspi-config
```

Figure 1-12 shows the opening screen for the raspi-config utility.

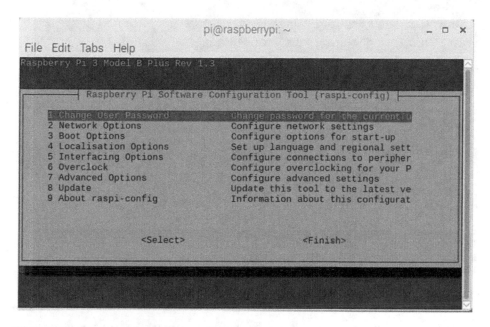

Figure 1-12. *raspi-config opening screen*

Selecting the Interfacing Options from the menu will cause the sub-menu shown in Figure 1-13 to appear.

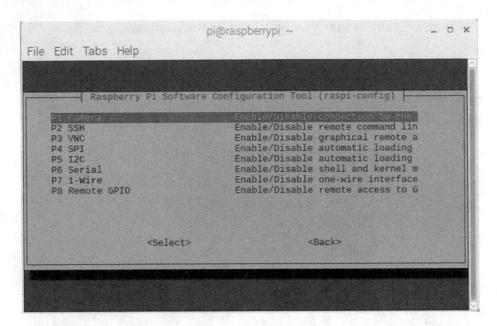

Figure 1-13. *Interfacing Options menu*

This menu has eight selections, as shown in the figure. Which options you enable will depend on the types of devices you employ in your RasPi system. I recommend enabling the following options to match the demonstrations and procedures discussed in this book:

Camera

SSH

SPI

I2C

Serial

1-Wire

You can easily add or subtract interfacing options at any time by rerunning the raspi-config utility. In any case, adding an interfacing option only minimally increases the size of the overall OS. Also note that enabling an interface only invokes the associated driver(s) for that particular device.

You will again need to reboot the RasPi to finish these optional configuration choices. Enter the following in the terminal window to reboot the computer:

```
sudo reboot
```

At this point, you have successfully set up and configured your RasPi system. You next need to update and upgrade your system to ensure that the latest Raspbian OS software is installed.

Updating and upgrading the Raspbian distribution

The Raspbian Linux distribution is always being improved, as mentioned earlier. It is very easy to ensure that you have the latest updated and upgraded distribution once you have established Internet connectivity. Enter the following command in a terminal window to update the installed OS:

```
sudo apt-get update
```

The update action changes the internal system's package list to match the current online package list. It does not actually change any of already installed packages if they are obsolete or outdated. Those changes are effected by entering the following command in a terminal window:

```
sudo apt-get upgrade
```

The update is reasonably quick if that original installed distribution is not too old. However, the upgrade action could take quite some time if a lot of outdated packages are already installed.

Just remember to always update prior to upgrading. All the projects in this book were created using an updated and upgraded Stretch Raspbian distribution. I have found that failing to update and upgrade can sometimes lead to some odd errors and system failures that are unexpected and puzzling.

You should have a completely functional RasPi system at this point in the installation and configuration process. At this point I need to introduce the concept of a virtual Python environment before proceeding to the ML discussion.

Python virtual environment

This section answers two questions:

What is a Python virtual environment?

Why are they needed?

I will initially address the second question. Python, like many similar object-oriented languages, depends on many supporting libraries and routines to function. In Python, these libraries are known as dependencies and are stored in one of two directories depending on their point of origin. The point of origin means those libraries which are considered to be essential or core to the Linux kernel are stored in the System-packages directory. All others, while they may be extremely important for proper Python operations, are stored in the Site-packages directory. Every time there is a new Python language revision issued, the System-packages directory is updated and modified as needed to support the latest revision. Consequently, there is only the version of each of the necessary system libraries stored in this directory. This is not the case for the Site-packages directory. This is because the user typically installs desired software and any and all libraries or dependencies required for that software. It is entirely possible to have one or more versions of the same dependency in the Site-packages directory simply due to multiple software installs. A problem quickly arises due to the fact that Linux installs a dependency based solely on its name and neglects any version checking. It is entirely possible to have Project A require software library X, version 1, while Project B requires software library X, version 2. Linux cannot disambiguate the version inconsistencies, and one or both projects will fail to run properly. Python virtual environments are designed to eliminate this issue.

The primary purpose of Python virtual environments is to create an isolated environment for each Python project. This means that each project will have its own dependencies, regardless of the dependencies required for other projects.

Creating separate virtual environments for both projects A and B would eliminate the version inconsistency issue. Each environment would be able to depend on whatever version of software X that is required, independent of any other project.

One of the nice things about virtual environments is that there are no limits to the number of environments you create, except for any constraints imposed by physical memory. Answering the first question posed earlier is simple. Python virtual environments are just a hierarchical set of directories containing some scripts and symbolic links, nothing more. There is no black magic or black arts involved in creating them. I believe that once you start using them, there will be no turning back. Many developers routinely use them, saving themselves many potential hours of frustration and angst while attempting to troubleshoot unknown errors caused by inadvertent dependency issues.

Installing a Python virtual environment

Please ensure that Python 3 is installed and operating correctly before following these instructions. Also ensure that you have updated and upgraded the Raspbian Stretch Linux distribution as previously discussed in this chapter.

There are six steps in this procedure. Please follow them in order to successfully create a Python virtual environment that you will use to work with the data models:

1. Install pip, which is a Python package manager utility. This utility is very similar to advanced packing tool (apt), but uses a separate distribution repository. Enter the following commands:

```
wget https://bootstrap.pypa.io/get-pip.py
sudo python3 get-pip.py
```

Note   The latest pip version was 19.0.3 at the time of this writing.

---

2. Install the `virtualenv` and `virtualenvwrapper` utilities. The `virtualenv` utility is used to create the virtual environment within Python 3. The `virtualenvwrapper` utility creates the links between the Python language and the Python code to be executed within the environment. Enter the following command:

```
sudo pip install virtualenv virtualenvwrapper
sudo rm -rf ~/get-pip.py ~/.cache/pip
```

3. A hidden file named .profile located in the home directory must be edited to include some initialization data. I recommend that you use the nano editor and append the data as shown here:

```
cd ~
sudo nano .profile
```

The data to be appended follows the last line in the existing file:

```
# virtualenv and virtualenvwrapper
export WORKON_HOME=$HOME/.virtualenvs
export VIRTUALENVWRAPPER_PYTHON=/usr/bin/python3
source /usr/local/bin/virtualenvwrapper.sh
```

Alternately, you may directly enter the initialization data at the command-line prompt using the following commands:

```
echo -e "\n# virtualenv and virtualenvwrapper" >>
~/.profile
echo "export WORKON_HOME=$HOME/.virtualenvs" >> ~/.profile
echo "export VIRTUALENVWRAPPER_PYTHON=/usr/bin/python3"
>> ~/.profile
echo "source /usr/local/bin/virtualenvwrapper.sh" >>
~/.profile
```

4. The `~./profile` file must now be sourced. The source command is used to load functions contained in the named file into the current shell for execution.

```
source ~/.profile
```

Note   You should see the text shown in Figure 1-14 displayed after you run the preceding command for the first time.

```
                              pi@raspberrypi: ~                        _  □  ×

File  Edit  Tabs  Help
pi@raspberrypi:~ $ source ~/.profile
virtualenvwrapper.user_scripts creating /home/pi/.virtualenvs/premkproject
virtualenvwrapper.user_scripts creating /home/pi/.virtualenvs/postmkproject
virtualenvwrapper.user_scripts creating /home/pi/.virtualenvs/initialize
virtualenvwrapper.user_scripts creating /home/pi/.virtualenvs/premkvirtualenv
virtualenvwrapper.user_scripts creating /home/pi/.virtualenvs/postmkvirtualenv
virtualenvwrapper.user_scripts creating /home/pi/.virtualenvs/prermvirtualenv
virtualenvwrapper.user_scripts creating /home/pi/.virtualenvs/postrmvirtualenv
virtualenvwrapper.user_scripts creating /home/pi/.virtualenvs/predeactivate
virtualenvwrapper.user_scripts creating /home/pi/.virtualenvs/postdeactivate
virtualenvwrapper.user_scripts creating /home/pi/.virtualenvs/preactivate
virtualenvwrapper.user_scripts creating /home/pi/.virtualenvs/postactivate
virtualenvwrapper.user_scripts creating /home/pi/.virtualenvs/get_env_details
pi@raspberrypi:~ $ []
```

Figure 1-14. *Initial source command results*

5. This step actually generates a virtual environment
    using the `virtualenv` and `virtualenvwrapper`
    utilities previously installed in step 2. You will need
    to provide a unique name for the environment. The
    one used in this example is py3cv4_1. If you plan on
    generating multiple environments, then a naming
    scheme such as py3cv4_1, py3cv4_2, py3cv4_3, and
    so on might be used. The name py3cv4_1 refers to
    the fact that the virtual environment uses Python 3
    and it also contains the OpenCV 4 software package.
    Additionally, it would be very desirable to document
    the reason for creating each environment or you will
    quickly become confused. Enter the following to
    generate the py3cv4_1 Python virtual environment:

    `mkvirtualenv py3cv4_1 -p python3`

    It takes about 40 seconds to create the virtual
    environment. Figure 1-15 shows the result of running
    this command. You should notice the (`py3cv4_1`)

prepended to the regular command-line prompt. This indicates that a virtual environment is currently in effect.

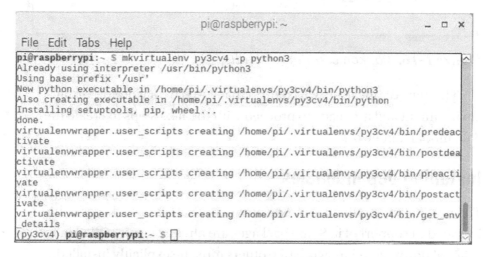

Figure 1-15. *mkvirtualenv command results*

You can easily shut down the py3cv4_1 virtual environment by simply closing the terminal window. I recommend doing that.

6. Open a new terminal window to verify that you can start the py3cv4_1 virtual environment. Enter the following command:

```
source ~/.profile
workon py3cv4_1
```

The workon command is included in the virtualenvwrapper software package. This command allows for the easy and quick startup of any Python virtual environment. Figure 1-16 shows the result of the preceding commands.

```
                          pi@raspberrypi: ~              _  □  ×

 File  Edit  Tabs  Help
 pi@raspberrypi:~ $ source ~/.profile
 pi@raspberrypi:~ $ workon py3cv4
 (py3cv4) pi@raspberrypi:~ $ []
```

Figure 1-16. *workon command results*

This figure appearing will confirm that you have a working virtual environment and are ready to proceed with the next steps to create the data model framework.

Installing dependencies

The next demonstration requires a number of software packages to be installed in support of it. Some packages are already pre-installed in the original downloaded Image, while others must be explicitly installed. The following commands will install all the packages. You will get an informational statement if the package is already installed; otherwise, the full installation will happen. These commands will take some time because the packages can be large and complex to install:

```
pip install numpy
pip install scipy
pip install matplotlib
pip install pandas
sudo apt-get install libatlas-base-dev
pip install -U scikit-learn
```

The following Python script is named checkLib.py and will return the version numbers for all of the software packages loaded. I would recommend you run to confirm that all the dependencies are installed. This script is available from the book's companion web site:

```
# Check library versions
# Python version
import sys
print('Python: {}'.format(sys.version))
# scipy
import scipy
print('scipy: {}'.format(scipy.__version__))
# numpy
import numpy
print('numpy: {}'.format(numpy.__version__))
# matplotlib
import matplotlib
print('matplotlib: {}'.format(matplotlib.__version__))
# pandas
import pandas
print('pandas: {}'.format(pandas.__version__))
# scikit-learn
import sklearn
print('sklearn: {}'.format(sklearn.__version__))
```

Figure 1-17 shows the results after I ran the script.

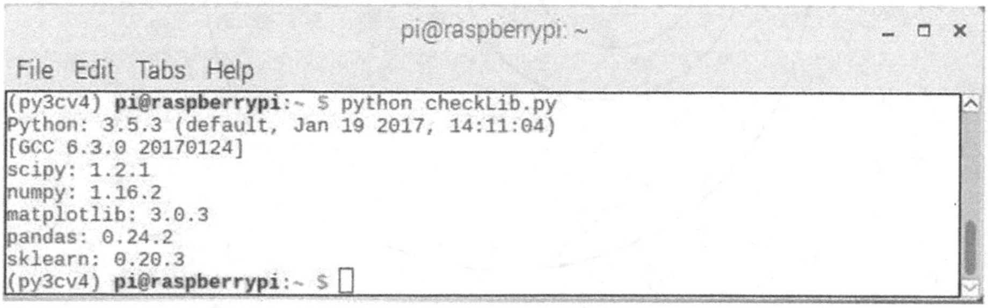

Figure 1-17. *Results for the checkLib.py script*

The versions you display will likely differ from the figures to some degree because open source software is constantly being revised. However, the packages should function in the same way as earlier versions unless some radical and unforeseen changes were made. This is not normally done for consistency's sake.

You will now be ready to tackle the ML demonstration once all the dependencies are installed and operational.

ML facts

ML is a significant sub-topic within the parent field of artificial intelligence (AI). Figure 1-18 is a Venn diagram highlighting the relationships between AI, ML, and deep learning (DL).

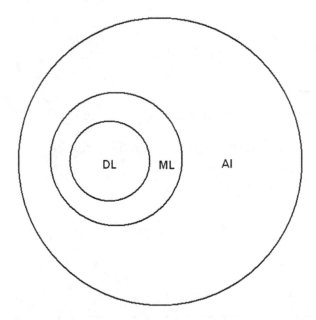

Figure 1-18. *Venn diagram for AI, ML, and DL*

It should be clear from the figure that ML is an important portion of AI and DL is an important portion of ML. In terms of current interest and development, the figure should be inverted with DL receiving the most attention with decreasing importance to ML and then AI in general. The hierarchy of DL receiving the preponderance of attention will also be followed in this book simply because DL is the essential ingredient to implement computer vision, which is currently the hottest topic in AI and ML. I will deep dive into DL in later chapters; however, I must first explore some fundamental ML topics before attempting the more complex DL matters.

ML basics

If you ask a dozen AI/ML researchers what ML is, you would likely get a dozen different, yet mildly similar responses. I have studied many definitions, and I believe the following one I developed is about appropriate as any other one that I have found.

> *Machine learning is the science and art of creating algorithms to enable computers to learn from data without being explicitly programmed.*

Interestingly, I found multiple definitions which used exactly the same phrase "without being explicitly programmed," which confirmed my belief that any pure ML application must exclude all algorithms or systems that encapsulate expert knowledge. Just note that expert systems are a very important part of AI, but just not in ML. However, there are likely to exist hybrid systems which incorporate both ML and expert systems, taking advantage of the best capabilities provided by each of these technologies.

Machine learning was first defined back in 1959 by MIT Professor Arthur Samuel, a recognized pioneer in both computer science and artificial intelligence. Professor Samuel stated in part "...gives computers the ability to learn without being explicitly programmed." What essentially he was driving at was that computers could be programmed with algorithms that both can learn from input data and then make consequent predictions based on that same data. This means these learning algorithms could be completely divorced from any preprogrammed or static algorithms and would be free to make data-driven decisions or predictions by building models based on the input data.

ML models are primarily used for prediction and classification. It is worthwhile to introduce you to some fundamental concepts regarding these operations before discussing more complex ML applications. This introduction will be in the form of a small, but complete ML project.

Linear prediction and classification

This project is based primarily on a June 2016 blog titled *"Your First Machine Learning Project in Python Step by Step"* and written by Dr. Jason Brownlee, who is presently an active ML researcher living in Australia. I would recommend looking at his blog at MachineLearningMastery.com, which contains a wealth of ML information and resources. Jason suggests and I heartily agree that you should start all ML projects with a structured approach consisting of the following steps, which I have paraphrased from the blog:

1. Define the problem.

2. Prepare and cleanse all the relevant data.

3. Evaluate any and all applicable algorithms.

4. Continually improve the results until the point of diminishing returns.

5. Present results in a clear and unambiguous fashion as possible.

This beginning ML project is a famous one concerning Iris flower classification. The Iris flower data is a multivariate dataset presented by the British statistician and biologist Ronald Fisher in his 1936 paper "The Use of Multiple Measurements in Taxonomic Problems" as an example of linear discriminant analysis (LDA). The dataset is sometimes called Anderson's Iris dataset because Edgar Anderson collected the data to quantify the morphologic variation of Iris flowers of three related species. Two of the three species were collected in the Gaspé Peninsula, Quebec, Canada, "all from the same pasture, and picked on the same day and measured at the same time by the same person with the same apparatus" as cited in Anderson's paper. Photographs of the three species of the Iris flower are shown in Figure 1-19.

Figure 1-19. *Three species of the Iris flower*

The dataset consists of 50 samples from each of three species of Iris (Iris setosa, Iris virginica, and Iris versicolor). Four features were measured from each sample: the length and the width of the sepals and petals, in centimeters. Fisher developed a linear discriminant model based on the combination of these four features to distinguish the Iris species from each other. A sepal is a part of the flower of angiosperms (flowering plants) and is usually green. Sepals typically function as protection for the flower in bud and often as support for the petals when in bloom. Petals are modified leaves that surround the reproductive parts of flowers. They are often brightly colored or unusually shaped to attract pollinators, that is, bees. Figure 1-20 shows a flower (not an Iris) with the sepal and petal identified.

Figure 1-20. *Sepal and petal*

Step 1 of the problem solution approach is reasonably simple. Identify the Iris species given four dimensions describing sepal height and width as well as petal height and width. The dimensions should all be in centimeters to match the units in the underlying dataset.

The next step in the solution process is to address the dataset. There are several online sources available to download the original Iris dataset in a CSV format. I used Jason's Iris CSV dataset that he made available on github.com. The first part of this chapter's demonstration will be concerned with becoming familiar with the dataset.

Iris demonstration – Part 1

The following listed Python script is named irisDemo.py and was created to work through a number of the following steps to familiarize you with the data properties and characteristics. Being familiar with the data will help you choose the proper algorithms that will best suit your requirements. These steps are

- Load dependencies.

- Load the dataset.

- Display the dataset dimensions.

- Display the first 20 records in the dataset.

- Display dataset statistics.

- Display dataset classes and associated sizes.

- Univariate and multivariate data plots.

The following script in its entirety is available from the book's companion web site. I discuss the entire script results after the code listing.

```
# Usage
# python irisDemo.py

# Load libraries
import pandas
from pandas.plotting import scatter_matrix
import matplotlib.pyplot as plt

# Load dataset
url = "https://raw.githubusercontent.com/jbrownlee/Datasets/
master/iris.csv"
names = ['sepal-length', 'sepal-width', 'petal-length',
'petal-width', 'class']
dataset = pandas.read_csv(url, names=names)
```

```
# Display the shape
print('Dataset dimensions')
print(dataset.shape)

# Display the first portion of the data
print('Head of the data')
print(dataset.head(20))

# Display data statistics
print('Statistics')
print(dataset.describe())

# Display class distribution
print('Class distribution')
print(dataset.groupby('class').size())

# Visualize data with box and whisker diagrams
dataset.plot(kind='box', subplot=True, layout=(2,2),
sharex=False, sharey=False)
plt.show()

# Visualize data with histograms
dataset.hist()
plt.show()

# Visualize data with scatter plots
scatter_matrix(dataset)
plt.show()
```

Figure 1-21 shows the first portion of the irisDemo script results.

```
                                    pi@raspberrypi: ~                          _  □  ×

 File  Edit  Tabs  Help
(py3cv4) pi@raspberrypi:~ $ python irisDemo.py
Dataset dimensions
(150, 5)
Head of the data
      sepal-length  sepal-width  petal-length  petal-width        class
0            5.1          3.5           1.4          0.2  Iris-setosa
1            4.9          3.0           1.4          0.2  Iris-setosa
2            4.7          3.2           1.3          0.2  Iris-setosa
3            4.6          3.1           1.5          0.2  Iris-setosa
4            5.0          3.6           1.4          0.2  Iris-setosa
5            5.4          3.9           1.7          0.4  Iris-setosa
6            4.6          3.4           1.4          0.3  Iris-setosa
7            5.0          3.4           1.5          0.2  Iris-setosa
8            4.4          2.9           1.4          0.2  Iris-setosa
9            4.9          3.1           1.5          0.1  Iris-setosa
10           5.4          3.7           1.5          0.2  Iris-setosa
11           4.8          3.4           1.6          0.2  Iris-setosa
12           4.8          3.0           1.4          0.1  Iris-setosa
13           4.3          3.0           1.1          0.1  Iris-setosa
14           5.8          4.0           1.2          0.2  Iris-setosa
15           5.7          4.4           1.5          0.4  Iris-setosa
16           5.4          3.9           1.3          0.4  Iris-setosa
17           5.1          3.5           1.4          0.3  Iris-setosa
18           5.7          3.8           1.7          0.3  Iris-setosa
19           5.1          3.8           1.5          0.3  Iris-setosa
Statistics
      sepal-length  sepal-width  petal-length  petal-width
count  150.000000   150.000000    150.000000   150.000000
mean     5.843333     3.054000      3.758667     1.198667
std      0.828066     0.433594      1.764420     0.763161
min      4.300000     2.000000      1.000000     0.100000
25%      5.100000     2.800000      1.600000     0.300000
50%      5.800000     3.000000      4.350000     1.300000
75%      6.400000     3.300000      5.100000     1.800000
max      7.900000     4.400000      6.900000     2.500000
Class distribution
class
Iris-setosa         50
Iris-versicolor     50
Iris-virginica      50
dtype: int64
(py3cv4) pi@raspberrypi:~ $ 
```

Figure 1-21. *Initial portion of the irisDemo results*

The first two lines show the dataset dimensions, which are 150 rows with 5 columns. Following that is the first 20 rows of the dataset. The column headers are clearly shown with all the row data displayed in a tabular fashion. This listing should provide you with a good insight into the data that is to be processed.

Next follows a small statistical display showing classic statistical measures for the dataset columns including means, standard deviations, min/max values, as well as values for the 25, 50, and 75 percentile levels.

Finally, there is a display showing how many items were counted for each class of Iris in the dataset. Unsurprisingly, there are 50 reported in each class, which precisely matches the expected values.

Figure 1-22 shows "box and whisker" plots for each of the four class attributes.

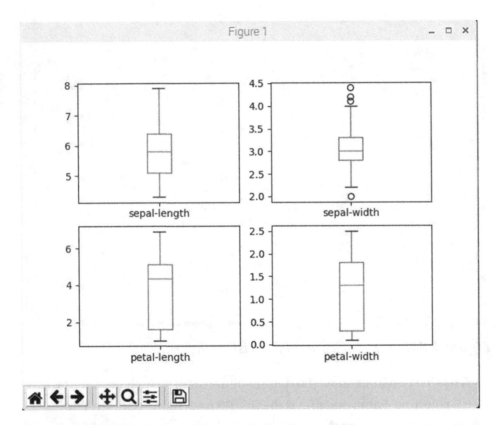

Figure 1-22. *Box and whisker plots for class attributes*

These univariate plots are a useful adjunct to help you understand the numeric distributions associated with each attribute. It may turn out that some models can handle wide numerical distributions while others are more sensitive, which can lead to undesired results. Reviewing the plots indicates a somewhat wider numerical distribution for the petal-length and petal-width attributes as compared to the same sepal attributes. Additionally, there appears to be a few data outliers with the sepal-width attribute, which might cause problems with certain models. These plots are just designed to provide further insight into the data to help explain any strange model results.

Another approach to visualize the data is to create histograms for each input variable. Figure 1-23 shows these histograms for all four Iris attributes.

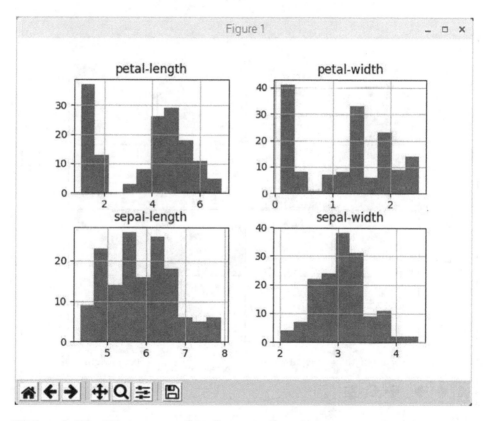

Figure 1-23. *Histograms for class attributes*

It appears that two of the sepal attributes have a Gaussian or near-Gaussian distribution. This information can be useful in selecting an appropriate model or algorithm for prediction purposes. The petal attributes seem to have bimodal histograms, which is an interesting fact that may help in selecting an algorithm such as Otsu's binarization.

Another approach to inspect the dataset is to check for structured relationships between attributes. This approach is known as multivariate analysis. Figure 1-24 shows the scatterplots of all pairs of class attributes.

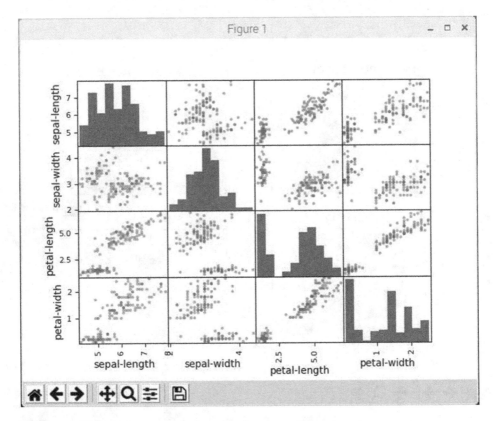

Figure 1-24. *Scatterplots for all class attributes*

These plots are helpful in visualizing relationships not easily detected when only reviewing numerical listings. You should note the diagonal grouping of some pairs of attributes in the figure. This strongly suggests a high correlation between the attributes and that a likely quantifiable relationship exists.

The next portion of the demonstration is where the data will be input into a series of models and predictions run. I must warn you that I will be committing a cardinal sin for technical book writing by simply using the models without a prior introduction. Just know that I will catch up and discuss the model algorithms in detail as part of the book's ML basics in either this chapter or following chapters.

Iris demonstration – Part 2

The following listed Python script is named irisDemoTest.py and was created to test a number of models using the Iris dataset and determine how accurate they are in describing an Iris species given a set of Iris attributes. The tests will be conducted in a series of steps in a manner similar to what was done in part 1. These steps are

- Import all the models.

- Create training and validation datasets.

- Set up a test harness using tenfold cross-validation.

- Use six different models to describe Iris species from attribute measurements.

- Select an accurate model.

The following listed Python script is named irisDemoTest.py and is available from the book's companion web site. I will discuss each portion of the script as it relates to the steps after the listing.

```
# Usage
# python irisDemoTest.py

# Load libraries
import pandas
from pandas.plotting import scatter_matrix
import matplotlib.pyplot as plt
from sklearn import model_selection
from sklearn.metrics import classification_report
from sklearn.metrics import confusion_matrix
from sklearn.metrics import accuracy_score
from sklearn.linear_model import LogisticRegression
from sklearn.tree import DecisionTreeClassifier
from sklearn.neighbors import KNeighborsClassifier
from sklearn.discriminant_analysis import
LinearDiscriminantAnalysis
from sklearn.naive_bayes import GaussianNB
from sklearn.svm import SVC

# Load dataset
url = "https://raw.githubusercontent.com/jbrownlee/Datasets/
master/iris.csv"
names = ['sepal-length', 'sepal-width', 'petal-length',
'petal-width', 'class']
dataset = pandas.read_csv(url, names=names)

# Create training and validation datasets
array = dataset.values
X = array[:,0:4]
Y = array[:,4]
validation_size = 0.20
seed = 7
```

```
X_train, X_validation, Y_train, Y_validation = model_selection.
train_test_split(X, Y, test_size=validation_size, random_
state=seed)

# Set the scoring criteria
scoring = 'accuracy'

# Build all the models
models = []
models.append(('LR', LogisticRegression(solver='liblinear',
multi_class='ovr')))
models.append(('LDA', LinearDiscriminantAnalysis()))
models.append(('KNN', KNeighborsClassifier()))
models.append(('CART', DecisionTreeClassifier()))
models.append(('NB', GaussianNB()))
models.append(('SVM', SVC(gamma='auto')))

# Evaluate each model
results = []
names = []
for name, model in models:
    kfold = model_selection.KFold(n_splits=10, random_
    state=seed)
    cv_results = model_selection.cross_val_score(model,
    X_train, Y_train, cv=kfold, scoring=scoring)
    results.append(cv_results)
    names.append(name)
    msg = "%s: %f(%f)" % (name, cv_results.mean(), cv_results.
    std())
    print(msg)
```

The imports list was changed considerably from the first script. It now includes six models from the sklearn package. The list of models in alphabetical order is

- DecisionTreeClassifier

- GaussianNB

- KNeighborsClassifier

- LinearDiscriminantAnalysis

- LogisticRegression

- SVC

I will not be discussing any specifics regarding the models function as I mentioned earlier.

The dataset is then loaded in exactly the same manner it was done in the first script. It is important to use this exact dataset as I found out by trying an Iris dataset from a different source. I suspect that minor changes in formatting were the issue when trying to use the new dataset.

The next portion of the script deals with the step regarding creating both training and validation datasets. Eighty percent of the original dataset will be used for model training, and 20% will be allotted for validation. During the validation process, a small sub-set of the original data will be input into models that have not been trained with it. The resulting output from the models will then be compared to the species label for each record in the validation dataset. The percentage accuracy will then be calculated as a simple ratio between the number of correctly identified species and the total number of records in the dataset.

The next step in the testing process is to set up a loop that implements a tenfold cross-validation procedure for every model. This means that the input dataset is initially divided into ten parts, with training done with nine of the ten parts and validation done using only the tenth part.

The results are recorded and the dataset is then randomly divided again into ten parts, and the process is repeated for a total of ten times, hence, the name tenfold. I do want to point out something that might be confusing to readers. The dataset being used in the tenfold cross-validation procedure is only the training dataset and not the validation dataset. The validation dataset will not be used until the next script is discussed where a model's prediction accuracy is discussed in detail.

The loop in the script runs cross-validation scores for each of the models. The results are shown in Figure 1-25.

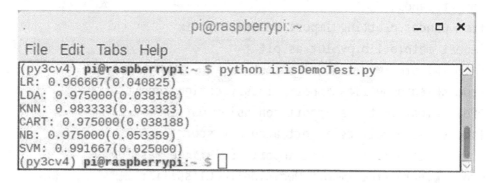

Figure 1-25. *Cross-validation scores for six models*

You can see that they all score in the high nineties, meaning that all likely good describers of Iris species given a set of class attributes. The numbers in the parentheses are the standard deviations for each model's result. You should be able to see that the deviations are relatively small, which means the models are again good describers. Looking at the figure, it appears that the support vector machine (SVM) model has the best result with a score of 0.991667 and a standard deviation of only 0.025. But is it really the best model for our purposes? That will be discussed in part 3 of this demonstration.

Iris demonstration – Part 3

This next discussion compares the accuracy of the six models using box and whisker diagrams. The script used is named irisDemoSelection.py and is essentially the same as the previous script except for the addition of plotting functions as well as a few algorithms used to detail the performance of a selected model. The six models' accuracy display was also eliminated in this script:

```
# Load libraries
import pandas
from pandas.plotting import scatter_matrix
import matplotlib.pyplot as plt
from sklearn import model_selection
from sklearn.metrics import classification_report
from sklearn.metrics import confusion_matrix
from sklearn.metrics import accuracy_score
from sklearn.linear_model import LogisticRegression
from sklearn.tree import DecisionTreeClassifier
from sklearn.neighbors import KNeighborsClassifier
from sklearn.discriminant_analysis import
LinearDiscriminantAnalysis
from sklearn.naive_bayes import GaussianNB
from sklearn.svm import SVC

# Load dataset
url = "https://raw.githubusercontent.com/jbrownlee/Datasets/
master/iris.csv"
names = ['sepal-length', 'sepal-width', 'petal-length',
'petal-width', 'class']
dataset = pandas.read_csv(url, names=names)

# Create training and validation datasets
```

```
array = dataset.values
X = array[:,0:4]
Y = array[:,4]
validation_size = 0.20
seed = 7
X_train, X_validation, Y_train, Y_validation = model_selection.
train_test_split(X, Y, test_size=validation_size, random_
state=seed)

# Set the scoring critera
scoring = 'accuracy'

# Build all the models
models = []
models.append(('LR', LogisticRegression(solver='liblinear',
multi_class='ovr')))
models.append(('LDA', LinearDiscriminantAnalysis()))
models.append(('KNN', KNeighborsClassifier()))
models.append(('CART', DecisionTreeClassifier()))
models.append(('NB', GaussianNB()))
models.append(('SVM', SVC(gamma='auto')))

# Evaluate each model
results = []
names = []
for name, model in models:
    kfold = model_selection.KFold(n_splits=10, random_
    state=seed)
    cv_results = model_selection.cross_val_score(model,
    X_train, Y_train, cv=kfold, scoring=scoring)
    results.append(cv_results)
    names.append(name)
```

```
# Plot model results
figure = plt.figure()
figure.suptitle('Algorithm Comparison')
algPlot = figure.add_subplot(1, 1, 1)
plt.boxplot(results)
algPlot.set_xticklabels(names)
plt.show()

# KNN prediction
knn = KNeighborsClassifier()
knn.fit(X_train, Y_train)
predictions = knn.predict(X_validation)
print(accuracy_score(Y_validation, predictions))
print(confusion_matrix(Y_validation, predictions))
print(classification_report(Y_validation, predictions)
```

Figure 1-26 shows the results for all models in a box and whisker diagram.

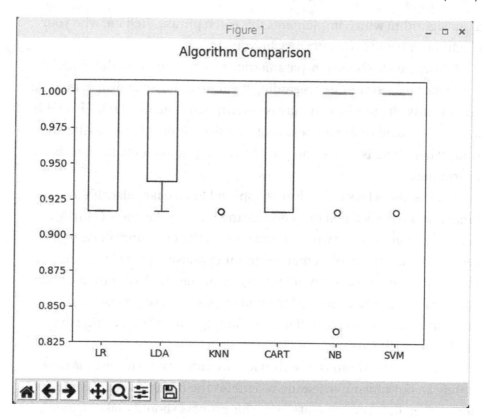

Figure 1-26. *Box and whisker diagram for model results*

You can observe that the box and whisker plots are squashed at the top of the y-axis range, illustrating that half the models is achieved at or near 100% accuracy. Selecting the top performer in this situation is almost impossible; however, I did select the KNN model for a more detailed examination of its performance. The KNN is a simple and accurate model. The formal name for the KNN model is K-nearest neighbors algorithm and is one of the simplest classification algorithms existing and quite likely one of the most widely used ones. KNN is a non-parametric, lazy learning algorithm. It's primarily used with a dataset in which the data points are separated into several classes to predict the classification of a new data point or sample. In simpler terms, KNN has been described as an algorithm which implements this catch phrase, "tell me who your neighbors are and I will tell you who you are."

I described KNN as non-parametric, which means that the model does not make any assumptions regarding the underlying data distribution. In other words, the model structure is determined from the data. Given this fact, KNN probably should be one of your first choices for a classification study when there is little or no prior knowledge about how the data is distributed.

KNN is also a lazy algorithm as opposed to an eager algorithm. What this means is that it does not use the training data points to do any generalization. In other words, there is no explicit training phase or it is very minimal. This implies that any training phase is likely to be minimal in duration, an important point for large datasets. Lack of generalization also means that KNN keeps all the training data. More precisely, no generalization means most, if not all, training data is used during the validation/testing phase.

The KNN algorithm is based on feature similarity. This means how closely an out-of-sample feature resembles the training set determines how a given data point is classified. This process should make clearer by examining Figure 1-27, a graphical example for KNN classification.

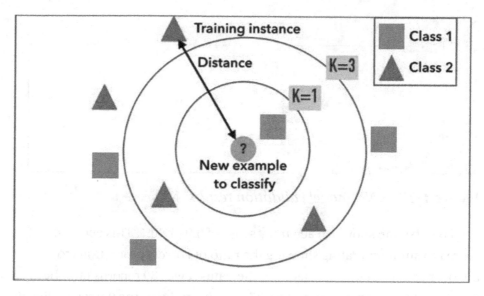

Figure 1-27. *KNN classification*

The test sample (inside circle) can be classified either to the first class of blue squares or to the second class of red triangles. If k = 3 (outside circle), it is assigned to the second class because there are 2 triangles and only 1 square inside the inner circle. If, for example, k = 5, the new sample would be assigned to the first class (3 squares vs. 2 triangles outside the outer circle).

The final portion of the script runs the KNN model directly with the validation dataset. The summary results for a final accuracy score, confusion matrix, and classification report are shown in Figure 1-28.

```
                                    pi@raspberrypi: ~                        _ □ ×
 File  Edit  Tabs  Help
(py3cv4) pi@raspberrypi:~ $ python irisDemoSelection.py
0.9
[[ 7  0  0]
 [ 0 11  1]
 [ 0  2  9]]
              precision    recall  f1-score   support

  Iris-setosa       1.00      1.00      1.00         7
Iris-versicolor     0.85      0.92      0.88        12
 Iris-virginica     0.90      0.82      0.86        11

    micro avg       0.90      0.90      0.90        30
    macro avg       0.92      0.91      0.91        30
 weighted avg       0.90      0.90      0.90        30

(py3cv4) pi@raspberrypi:~ $ ▯
```

Figure 1-28. *KNN model validation results*

The first line shows an accuracy score of 0.9 or 90%. This accuracy score is a summary rating showing the ratio of correct predictions to the overall dataset size. In this case, the dataset was 30 records and the number of correct predictions was 27, which produces the 0.9 result. Recall that this accuracy score is based on using the validation dataset, which was 20% of the original Iris dataset. The accuracy score shown in Figure 1-28 is artificially higher due to the nature of the tenfold cross-validation testing. This lower accuracy score is reflective of real-world conditions and should be considered more trustworthy.

The confusion matrix (error matrix) provides an indication of where the three errors were made. Table 1-1 details the actual classes vs. the predicted classes.

Table 1-1. *Actual vs. predicted classes*

		Actual class		
		Iris setosa	Iris versicolor	Iris virginica
Predicted class	Iris setosa	7	0	0
	Iris versicolor	0	11	1
	Iris virginica	0	2	9

Finally, the classification report provided by sklearn metrics is a breakdown of the class results by precision, recall, F1-score, and support. This report shows very good to excellent results even though the validation dataset was small. I explain each of the metrics in Table 1-2.

Table 1-2. *sklearn learn metrics analysis*

Metric	Iris setosa	Iris versicolor	Iris virginica	Remarks (see notes)
precision	1.00	0.85	0.90	precision = tp / (tp + fp)
recall	1.00	0.92	0.82	recall = tp / (tp + fn)
f1-score	1.00	0.88	0.86	mean(precision + recall)
support	7	12	11	class size

Notes: tp = true positive

  fp = false positive

  fn = false negatives

The precision is intuitively the ability of the classifier not to label as positive a sample that is negative.

The recall is intuitively the ability of the classifier to find all the positive samples.

The f1-score (F-beta) can be interpreted as a weighted harmonic mean of the precision and recall, where an F-beta score reaches its best value at 1 and worst score at 0.

I will refer you to the sklearn documentation to read more about the micro, macro, and weighted avgs. The page is

```
https://scikit-learn.org/stable/modules/generated/sklearn.
metrics.precision_recall_fscore_support.html
```

CHAPTER 2

Exploration of ML data models: Part 1

This chapter will be mostly about discussions and demonstrations of basic data models used in ML. However, before I can get into the heart of data model operations, I need to show you how to install OpenCV 4 and the Seaborn software packages. Both these packages will be needed to properly support the running and visualization of the basic data models. These packages will also support other demonstrations presented in later book chapters.

Installing OpenCV 4

This section is about installing the open source OpenCV software package. I will be using OpenCV for various ML demonstrations including making use of the great variety of visualization utilities contained in the package. OpenCV version 4 is the latest one and is not yet available for direct download and installation from any of the popular repositories. It must be loaded in a source code format and built in place. The following instructions will do this task. It is important to precisely follow these instructions or else you will likely not be successful with the OpenCV install.

© Donald J. Norris 2020
D. J. Norris, *Machine Learning with the Raspberry Pi*,
https://doi.org/10.1007/978-1-4842-5174-4_2

The first step is to install the CMake utility along with three other key utilities. Enter the following:

```
sudo apt-get install build-essential cmake unzip pkg-config
```

Next, install three imaging and video libraries that support the three most popular Image formats, jpeg, png, and tiff. Enter the following:

```
sudo apt-get install libjpeg-dev libpng-dev libtiff-dev
```

For successful execution of the preceding command, make sure apt-get is updated according to the following command:

```
sudo apt-get update
```

Now install three imaging utilities used for common video processing functions. Enter the following command. Similarly, make sure apt-get is updated.

```
sudo apt-get install libavcodec-dev libavformat-dev libswscale-dev
```

Next install two supplemental video processing libraries. Enter the following:

```
sudo apt-get install libxvidcore-dev libx264-dev
```

The next command installs the GTK library. GTK will be used to implement the OpenCV GUI backend. Enter the following:

```
sudo apt-get install libgtk2.0-dev
```

The next command reduces or eliminates undesired GTK warnings. The "*" in the command ensures that the proper modules supporting the ARM processor are loaded. Enter the following:

```
sudo apt-get install libcanberra-gtk*
```

The next two software packages are used for OpenCV numerical optimizations. Enter the following:

```
sudo apt-get install libatlas-base-dev gfortran
```

You will now be ready to download OpenCV 4 source code once all the preceding dependencies have been loaded.

Download OpenCV 4 source code

Ensure that you are in the virtual environment and also in the home directory prior to starting the download. Enter the following command to go to your home directory if you are not there:

```
cd ~
```

Next, use the wget command to download both the latest OpenCV and opencv_contrib modules. At the time of this writing, the latest version was 4.0.1. It will likely be different when you try this download. Simply substitute the latest version wherever you see a version entered in this discussion. The opencv_contrib module contains open source community contributed supplemental functions, which will be used in this book's projects and demonstrations. Enter the following command to download the OpenCV zipped file from the GitHub web site:

```
wget -O opencv.zip https://github.com/opencv/opencv/
archive/4.0.1.zip
```

Enter the following command to download the opencv_contrib zipped file from the GitHub web site:

```
wget -O opencv_contrib.zip https://github.com/opencv/opencv_
contrib/archive/4.0.1.zip
```

The downloads will now have to be extracted and expanded using these commands:

```
unzip opencv.zip
unzip opencv_contrib.zip
```

Next, rename the newly generated directories to the following to ease the access to the OpenCV packages and functions and ensure that the directories are named as expected for CMake configuration file. Enter the following command:

```
mv opencv-4.0.1 opencv
mv opencv_contrib-4.0.1 opencv_contrib
```

You should be ready to start building the OpenCV package once the source code downloads have been completed.

Building the OpenCV software

You will need to ensure that the numpy library has been installed prior to commencing the build. I discussed installing numpy along with several other dependencies in Chapter 1. If you haven't installed numpy yet, then it is easily installed using the following command:

```
pip install numpy
```

The next step set ups a directory where the build will take place. Create and change into the build directory by entering these commands:

```
cd ~/opencv
mkdir build
cd build
```

Upon completing the preceding commands, enter the following to run the CMake command with a number of build options. Note that "\" symbol (backward slash) is required for the command-line interpreter (CLI) to recognize that a single command is spread over multiple lines. Don't overlook the two periods at the tail end of the following complex command. Those periods indicate to the CLI to execute all that was entered before the periods.

```
cmake -D CMAKE_BUILD_TYPE=RELEASE \
    -D CMAKE_INSTALL_PREFIX=/usr/local \
    -D OPENCV_EXTRA_MODULES_PATH=~/opencv_contrib/modules \
    -D ENABLE_NEON=ON \
    -D ENABLE_VFPV3=ON \
    -D BUILD_TESTS=OFF \
    -D OPENCV_ENABLE_NONFREE=ON \
    -D INSTALL_PYTHON_EXAMPLES=OFF \
    -D BUILD_EXAMPLES=OFF ..
```

Note The option OPENCV_ENABLE_NONFREE=ON ensures that all third-party functions are made available during the compilation step. The line

```
"Non-free algorithms:    YES"
```

---

in Figure 2-1 results screen confirms that the condition was set.

```
pi@raspberrypi: ~/opencv/build                    _ □ ×

File   Edit   Tabs   Help
--    OpenCV modules:
--      To be built:                    aruco bgsegm bioinspired calib3d ccalib core
 datasets dnn dnn_objdetect dpm face features2d flann freetype fuzzy gapi hfs hi
ghgui img_hash imgcodecs imgproc java_bindings_generator line_descriptor ml objd
etect optflow phase_unwrapping photo plot python2 python3 python_bindings_genera
tor reg rgbd saliency shape stereo stitching structured_light superres surface_m
atching text tracking ts video videoio videostab xfeatures2d ximgproc xobjdetect
 xphoto
--      Disabled:                       world
--      Disabled by dependency:         -
--      Unavailable:                    cnn_3dobj cudaarithm cudabgsegm cudacodec cu
dafeatures2d cudafilters cudaimgproc cudalegacy cudaobjdetect cudaoptflow cudast
ereo cudawarping cudev cvv hdf java js matlab ovis sfm viz
--      Applications:                   perf_tests apps
--      Documentation:                  NO
--      Non-free algorithms:            YES

--    GUI:
--      GTK+:                           YES (ver 3.22.11)
--        GThread :                     YES (ver 2.50.3)
--        GtkGlExt:                     NO
--      VTK support:                    NO
--
```

Figure 2-1. *Confirmation of non-free algorithms availability*

Having the non-free algorithms available is applicable for non-commercial applications. If you are intending to develop an application for sale or licensing, then you must comply with any and all applicable licensing agreements. There are several patented algorithms contained in the OpenCV software package, which cannot be used for commercial development without paying royalty fees.

You should also confirm that the virtual environment points to the proper directories for both Python 3 and numpy. Figure 2-2 shows the correct directories within the cv virtual environment.

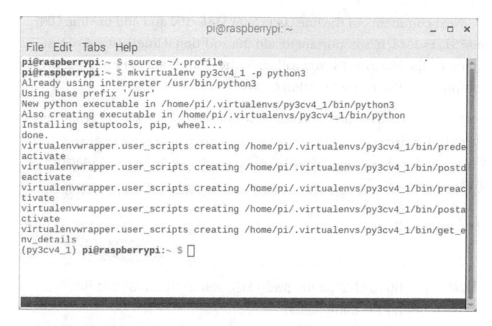

```
                        pi@raspberrypi: ~                    _ □ ✕

 File  Edit  Tabs  Help
 pi@raspberrypi:~ $ source ~/.profile
 pi@raspberrypi:~ $ mkvirtualenv py3cv4_1 -p python3
 Already using interpreter /usr/bin/python3
 Using base prefix '/usr'
 New python executable in /home/pi/.virtualenvs/py3cv4_1/bin/python3
 Also creating executable in /home/pi/.virtualenvs/py3cv4_1/bin/python
 Installing setuptools, pip, wheel...
 done.
 virtualenvwrapper.user_scripts creating /home/pi/.virtualenvs/py3cv4_1/bin/prede
 activate
 virtualenvwrapper.user_scripts creating /home/pi/.virtualenvs/py3cv4_1/bin/postd
 eactivate
 virtualenvwrapper.user_scripts creating /home/pi/.virtualenvs/py3cv4_1/bin/preac
 tivate
 virtualenvwrapper.user_scripts creating /home/pi/.virtualenvs/py3cv4_1/bin/posta
 ctivate
 virtualenvwrapper.user_scripts creating /home/pi/.virtualenvs/py3cv4_1/bin/get_e
 nv_details
 (py3cv4_1) pi@raspberrypi:~ $ []
```

Figure 2-2. *Confirmation for Python 3 and numpy directories within the py3cv4_1 virtual environment*

The default disk swap size of 100 MB must be changed to 2048 MB to have a successful compilation. The swap space will be restored to the default value after the compilation is done. It is important to realize that swap size has a significant impact on the longevity of the micro SD card, which is used as the secondary memory storage for the RasPi. These cards have finite number of write operations before failing. The number of write operations dramatically increases with the swap size. It will be of no consequence to card life by changing the swap size for this one-time process. First use the nano editor to open the swap configuration file for editing as follows:

```
sudo nano /etc/dphys-swapfile
```

Next comment out the line CONF_SWAPSIZE=100 and add the line CONF_
SWAPSIZE=2048. It is important to add the additional line, instead of just
changing the 100 to 2048. You will undo the change after completing the
compilation. The revised portion of the file is shown here:

```
# set size to absolute value, leaving empty (default) then uses
computed value
# you most likely don't want this, unless you have a special
disk situation
# CONF_SWAPSIZE=100
CONF_SWAPSIZE=2048
```

Note   Failing to change the swap size will likely cause the RasPi to
"hang" during the compilation.

After making the edit, you will need to stop and start the swap service
using these commands:

```
sudo /etc/init.d/dphys-swapfile stop
sudo /etc/init.d/dphys-swapfile start
```

This next step is the compilation from source code to binary. It will take
approximately 1.5 hours using all four RasPi cores. You should be aware of
an issue known as a race condition that can randomly occur when a specific
core needs a resource currently in use by another core. The problem happens
due to very tight timing issues where a using core cannot release a resource
and a requesting core does not drop the request for that resource. The result
is the processor simply hangs "forever." A very bad situation. Fortunately,
there is a solution of simply not requesting the forced use of four cores. I do
not know how long a complete compilation would take, but suspect it would
be at least 3 hours. The command to compile using four cores is

```
make -j4
```

The command to compile not using any specific number of cores is simply make.

There is a bit of good news, that is, if the initial compilation hangs while trying the -j4 option, you can redo the compilation using only the make command and the system will find and use all the code already compiled. This will considerably shorten the compile time. I know this is true because I experienced it. My first compilation hung at 100%. I restarted the compilation using only the make command, and it successfully completed in about 15 minutes. Figure 2-3 shows the screen after the success compilation.

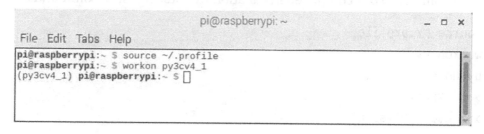

Figure 2-3. *Successful compilation*

Finish the OpenCV 4 installation by entering these next commands:

```
sudo make install
sudo ldconfig
```

This is the last step which has some finishing and verification operations. First restore the swap size to the original 100 MB by uncommenting the line

```
CONF_SWAPSIZE=100
```

and commenting out the newly added line

```
# CONF_SWAPSIZE=2048
```

Next create a symbolic link to OpenCV so that it can be used by new Python scripts created in the virtual environment. Enter these commands:

```
cd ~/.virtualenvs/py3cv4_1/lib/python3.5/site-packages/
ln -s /usr/local/lib/python3.5/site-packages/cv2/python-3.5/
cv2.cpython-35m-arm-linux-gnueabihf.so  cv2.so
cd ~
```

Failure to create the symbol link will mean that you will not be able to access any OpenCV functions.

Finally, test your completed installation by entering these commands:

```
source ~/.profile
workon cv
python
>>> import cv2
>>> cv2.__version__
'4.0.1'
>>> exit()
```

The first two commands start the py3cv4_1 virtual environment. The next one starts the Python interpreter associated with this environment, which is Python 3. The next command imports OpenCV using the symbolic link you just created. This line should demonstrate to the importance of the symbolic link. The next command requests the OpenCV version, which is reported back as 4.0.1 as may be seen in the following line with the version request. The last command exits the Python interpreter. Figure 2-4 shows the py3cv4_1 version verification.

```
                              pi@raspberrypi: ~              _  □  ✕

 File  Edit  Tabs  Help
(py3cv4_1) pi@raspberrypi:~ $ python
Python 3.5.3 (default, Sep 27 2018, 17:25:39)
[GCC 6.3.0 20170516] on linux
Type "help", "copyright", "credits" or "license" for more information.
>>> import cv2
>>> cv2.__version__
'4.0.1'
>>> 
```

Figure 2-4. *py3cv4_1 version verification*

At this point, you should now have a fully operational OpenCV software package operating in a Python virtual environment. To exit OpenCV, simply close the terminal window.

Seaborn data visualization library

Visualizing the data, you will be using an important step when dealing with ML models as I discussed in the previous chapter. There are a number of useful Python compatible utilities and software packages, which will help you in accomplishing this task. Hopefully, you have already installed the Matplotlib library as part of the dependency load described in the previous chapter. The OpenCV package also contains useful visualization routines and algorithms. In this section I will introduce the Seaborn library, which is another useful data visualization tool and is considered a supplement to the data visualization functions in both Matplotlib and OpenCV.

Seaborn specifically targets statistical data visualization. It also works with a different set of parameters than the ones used with Matplotlib.

The first step required in this section is to install the Seaborn software package. That is easily accomplished by entering the following command:

```
pip install seaborn
```

Figure 2-5 shows the results of installing the Seaborn software package. You should notice from the figure that the Seaborn package requires a fair number of dependencies including numpy, Pandas, Matplotlib, scipy, kiwisolver, and several other Python utilities.

Figure 2-5. *Seaborn package installation results*

Once installed, I believe the easiest way to explain Seaborn is to use it to visualize the Iris dataset that was introduced in Chapter 1. One extremely convenient Seaborn feature is the immediate availability of a limited number of datasets contained in the package. The Iris dataset is one of those organic datasets (no pun intended). To use the Iris dataset, you just need to incorporate these statements in your script

```
import seaborn as sns
iris = sns.load_dataset("iris")
```

where sns is the reference to the Seaborn import.

There are 15 datasets available in the Seaborn package. These are listed as follows for your information:

    anscombe

    attention

    brain_networks

    car_crashes

    diamonds

    dots

    exercise

    flights

    fmri

    gammas

    iris

    mpg

    planets

    tips

    titanic

Judging from the titles, the Seaborn datasets are diverse and a bit unusual. They were apparently selected to demonstrate Seaborn package capabilities for analysis and visualization. I will use some of these datasets during the data model discussions, in addition to the Iris dataset.

Table 2-1 shows the first five records in the Iris dataset, which was generated by the following command:

```
iris.head()
```

Table 2-1. *Head command results for the Iris dataset*

Rec #	sepal_length	sepal_width	petal_length	petal_width	species
0	5.1	3.5	1.4	0.2	Setosa
1	4.9	3.0	1.4	0.2	Setosa
2	4.7	3.2	1.3	0.2	Setosa
3	4.6	3.1	1.5	0.2	Setosa
4	5.0	3.6	1.4	0.2	Setosa

Data visualization is an important initial step when selecting an appropriate data model which best handles the dataset. Seaborn provides many ways of visualizing data to assist you in this critical task. I will be introducing a series of scripts that will help you visualize data. The multivariate Iris dataset will be used in all the following scripts.

Scatter plot

Starting the data visualization process with a scatter plot is probably the easiest way to approach the data visualization task. Scatter plots are simply two-dimensional or 2D plots using two dataset components that are plotted as coordinate pairs. The Seaborn package uses the `jointplot` method as the plotting function indicating the 2D nature of the plot.

I used the following script which is named jointPlot.py to create the scatter plot for sepal length vs. petal height. This script is available from the book's companion web site:

```
# Import the required libraries
import matplotlib.pyplot as plt
import seaborn as sns

# Load the Iris dataset
iris = sns.load_dataset("iris")

# Generate the scatter plot
sns.jointplot(x="sepal_length",y="sepal_width",
data=iris,size=6)

# Display the plots
plt.show()
```

The script is run by entering

```
python jointPlot.py
```

Figure 2-6 shows the result of running this script.

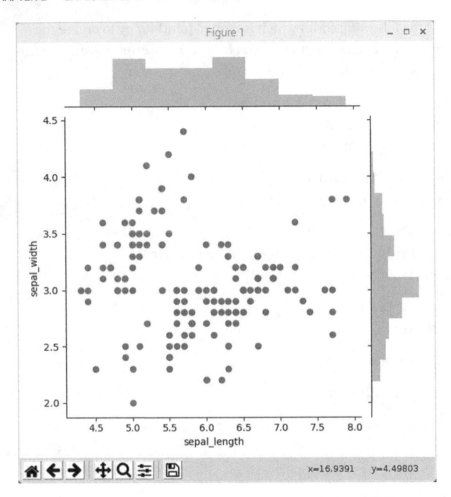

Figure 2-6. *Scatter plot for sepal length vs. sepal height (all species)*

Looking at the figure, you can easily see that the data points are spread out through the plot, which indicates there is no strong relationship between these two dataset components. The histogram at the top for sepal length indicates a broad value spread as compared to the sepal width histogram on the right-hand side, which shows a peak mid-range value of approximately 3.0. Just be mindful that this plot covers all the Iris species and could conceivably be masking an existing data relationship for one or more individual species. Other visualization tools could unmask hidden relationships as you will shortly see.

Facet grid plot

A facet grid plot is a variant of the scatter plot just presented in the previous section. However, all the dataset components are clearly identified in a facet grid plot as opposed to being unclassified and ambiguous in a scatter plot. I used the following script which is named facetGridPlot.py to create the facet grid plot for sepal length vs. petal height. This script is available from the book's companion web site:

```
# Import the required libraries
import matplotlib.pyplot as plt
import seaborn as sns

# Load the Iris dataset
iris = sns.load_dataset("iris")

# Generate the Facet Grid plot
sns.FacetGrid(iris,hue="species",size=6) \
.map(plt.scatter,"sepal_length","sepal_width") \
.add_legend()

# Display the plot
plt.show()
```

The script is run by entering

```
python facetGridPlot.py
```

Figure 2-7 shows the result of running this script.

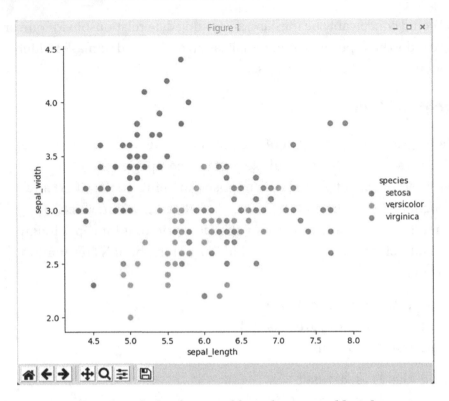

Figure 2-7. *Facet grid plot for sepal length vs. sepal height*

I do acknowledge that the grayscale figure will be hard to decipher in the published book, but you should be able to discern that a group of dots in the upper left-hand side of the plot appear to form a meaningful relationship, wherein a linear, sloped line could be drawn through the dot group to represent the relationship. These dots are all from the Iris Setosa species.

This same dot group was plotted in Figure 2-6, but there was not differentiation between the dots as regards to the species they represented and this relationship could not have been easily identified. Visualizing a probable relationship is an important first step in selecting an appropriate data model. In this case, using a linear regression (LR) model would be a good choice for this particular data sub-set. I will discuss the LR data model later in this chapter.

The remaining dots in Figure 2-7 belong to the remaining Iris species and do not appear to have any obvious visual relationships as far as I can determine. However, I am still proceeding to show you some additional plots which may help with the analysis.

Box plot

Box plots were first introduced in the previous chapter; however, I used the Matplotlib package to generate those plots. The following box plot was generated by a Seaborn method named boxplot. In reality, I suspect that the actual plot is likely created by the Matplotlib software because the Seaborn package has a strong linkage to Matplotlib.

I used the following script which is named boxPlot.py to create the box plot for all sepal length attribute for all of the Iris species. This script is available from the book's companion web site:

```
# Import the required libraries
import matplotlib.pyplot as plt
import seaborn as sns

# Load the Iris dataset
iris = sns.load_dataset("iris")

# Generate the box plot
sns.boxplot(x="species",y="sepal_length", data=iris)

# Display the plot
plt.show()
```

The script is run by entering

```
python boxPlot.py
```

Figure 2-8 shows the result of running this script.

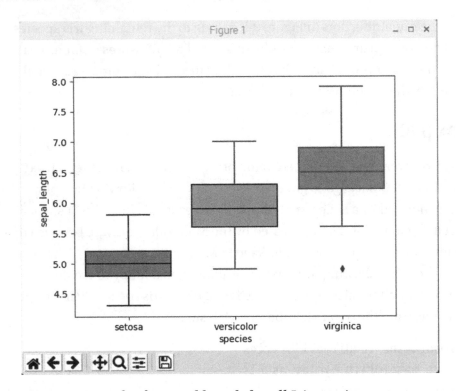

Figure 2-8. *Box plot for sepal length for all Iris species*

Box plots are inherently univariate in nature because they are created from only a single dataset dimension or 1D. Nonetheless, they provide important insights into the dataset attribute ranges, variances, and means. Box plots are useful to identify data outliers which can easily disrupt certain data models, which in turn can cause unpredictable and uncertain results from using those models with disruptive outliers inadvertently included as inputs.

Strip plot

A strip plot may be considered as augmented box plot because it includes an underlying box plot as well as shows the actual data points that go into creating that box plot. The data points would ordinarily be plotted along a single vertical line for each dataset class; however, the Seaborn `stripplot` method has a jitter option that randomly shifts the dots away from the vertical line. This random jitter does not affect the data display because the vertical axis is the only one used to identify a dot's value. This concept should become clear after you study the example plot.

I used the following script which is named stripPlot.py to create the strip plot for all sepal length attribute for all of the Iris species. This script is available from the book's companion web site:

```
# Import the required libraries
import matplotlib.pyplot as plt
import seaborn as sns

# Load the Iris dataset
iris = sns.load_dataset("iris")

# Generate the strip plot
ax = sns.boxplot(x="species",y="sepal_length", data=iris)
ax = sns.stripplot(x="species", y="sepal_length", data=iris,
jitter=True, edgecolor="gray")

# Display the plot
plt.show()
```

The script is run by entering

```
python stripPlot.py
```

Figure 2-9 shows the result of running this script.

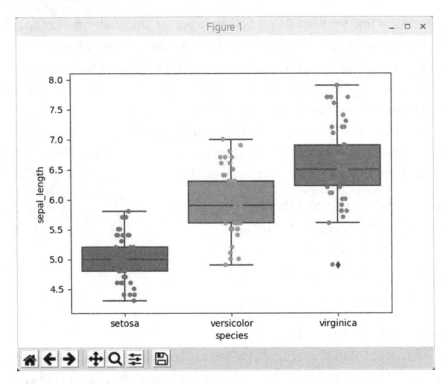

Figure 2-9. *Strip plot for sepal length for all Iris species*

My preceding comments regarding the box plot apply here. The strip plot just provides some additional insight regarding how the data points that go into creating the box plot are distributed throughout the recorded range of values.

Violin plot

A violin plot is similar to a box plot, except it has a rotated kernel density plot on each side of the vertical line that represents class data for the dataset. These kernel densities represent the probability density of data at different values and are smoothed by a kernel density estimator function. The curious name for this plot should be readily apparent after you examine the figure.

I used the following script which is named violinPlot.py to create the violin plot for all sepal length attribute for all of the Iris species. This script is available from the book's companion web site:

```
# Import the required libraries
import matplotlib.pyplot as plt
import seaborn as sns
```

```
# Load the Iris dataset
iris = sns.load_dataset("iris")
```

```
# Generate the violin plot
sns.violinplot(x="species",y="sepal_length", data=iris, size=6)
```

```
# Display the plot
plt.show()
```

The script is run by entering

```
python violinPlot.py
```

Figure 2-10 shows the result of running this script.

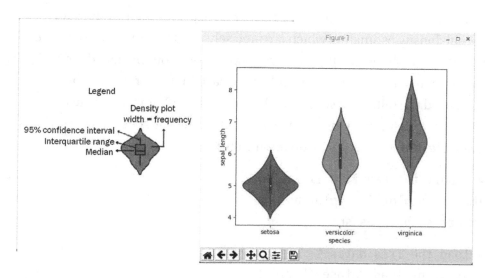

Figure 2-10. *Violin plot for sepal length for all Iris species*

Violin plots overcome a big problem inherent to box plots. Box plots can be misleading because they are not affected by the distribution of the original data. When the underlying dataset changes shape or essentially "morphs," box plots can easily maintain their previous statistics including medians and ranges. Violin plots on the other hand will reflect any new shape or data distribution while still containing the same box plot statistics.

The "violin" shape of a violin plot comes from a class dataset's density plot. The density plot is rotated 90° and is placed on both sides of the box plot, mirroring each other. Reading the violin shape is exactly how a density plot is interpreted. A thicker part means the values in that section of the violin plot have a higher frequency or probability of occurrence and the thinner part implies lower frequency or probability of occurrence.

Violin plots are relatively easy to read. The dot in the middle is the median. The box presents interquartile range. The whiskers show 95% confidence interval. The shape of the violin displays frequencies of values. The legend shown in Figure 2-10 points out these features.

KDE plot

A KDE plot shows only the dataset class density plots. KDE is short for kernel density estimators which are precisely the same plots used in violin plots. A KDE plot is most useful if you simply focus on the data distribution rather than data statistics as would be the case for box or violin plots.

I used the following script which is named kdePlot.py to create the KDE plot for all sepal length attribute for all of the Iris species. This script is available from the book's companion web site:

```
# Import the required libraries
import matplotlib.pyplot as plt
import seaborn as sns

# Load the Iris dataset
iris = sns.load_dataset("iris")
```

```
# Generate the kde plot
sns.FacetGrid(iris,hue="species",size=6) \
.map(sns.kdeplot,"sepal_length") \
.add_legend()

# Display the plot
plt.show()
```

The script is run by entering

```
python kdePlot.py
```

Figure 2-11 shows the result of running this script.

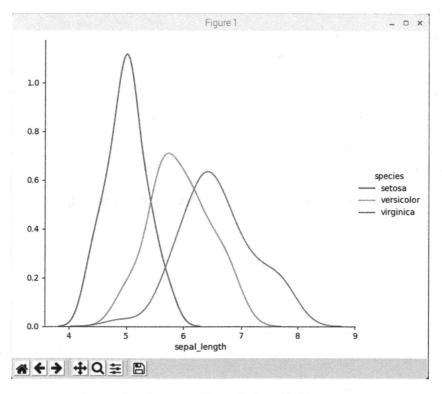

Figure 2-11. *KDE plot for sepal length for all Iris species*

The data distribution plot results were already discussed earlier.

Pair plots

Pair plots are created when joint plots are generalized to large dimension datasets. These plots are useful tools for exploring correlations between multidimensional data, because all data pair values are plotted against each other. Visualizing the Iris dataset multidimensional relationships is as easy as entering the following script, which I named pairPlot.py. This script is available from the book's companion web site:

```
# Import the required libraries
import matplotlib.pyplot as plt
import seaborn as sns

# Load the Iris dataset
iris = sns.load_dataset("iris")

# Generate the pair plots
sns.pairplot(iris, hue='species', size=2.5)

# Display the plots
plt.show()
```

Figure 2-12 shows the results of running the preceding script.

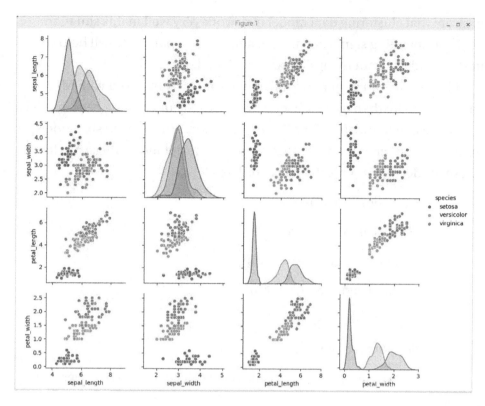

Figure 2-12. *Iris dataset pair plots*

At first glance, this pair plot figure seems to be the most comprehensive and complex plot shown to this point. Upon closer inspection, you will quickly realize that the individual plots shown in the figure are either facet grid or KDE plots, which have already been discussed. The plots on the major diagonal from top left to bottom right are all KDE plots for the same intersecting dataset classes. The non-intersecting plots, that is, those with different classes for the x and y axes, are all facet grid plots. Class attribute relationships should quickly become apparent to you as you inspect the individual plots. For example, the Setosa attributes are clearly set apart from the other species attributes in almost all pair plots. This would indicate that clustering data model may work very well in this situation. I believe spending significant time examining the pair plots will help you understand the underlying dataset to a great degree.

I believe it is an imperative that anyone actively involved with ML should be more than trivially acquainted with the underlying basic models that serve as a foundation for ML core concepts. I introduced six models in the previous chapter without delving into the details for these models. These models were (in alphabetical order)

*Decision tree classifier

*Gaussian Naive Bayesian

*K-nearest neighbors classifier

Linear discriminant analysis

*Logistic regression

Support vector machines

There are four more additional models, which will also be covered in this book:

Learning vector quantization

*Linear regression

Bagging and random forests

Principal component analysis

(* Discussed in this chapter)

Experienced data scientist cannot tell you which of these ten models would be the best performer without trying different them all for a particular problem domain. While there are many other ML models and algorithms, these ten are generally considered to be the most popular ones. It would be wise to learn about and use these ten as a solid starting point for an ML education.

Underlying big principle

There is a common principle that underlies all supervised ML algorithms used in predictive modeling.

ML algorithms are best described as learning a target function f( ) that best maps input variable x to an output variable y or in equation form

$$y = f(x)$$

There is often a common problem where predictions are required for some y, given new input values for the input variable x. However, the function $f(x)$ is unknown. If it was known, then the prediction would be said to be analytical and solved directly and there would be no need to "learn" it from data using ML algorithms.

Likely the most common type of ML problem is to learn the mapping $y = f(x)$ to make predictions of y for a new x. This approach is formally known as predictive modeling or predictive analytics and the goal is to make accurate predictions.

I will start the data model review with probably the most common model ever used for predictions.

Linear regression

Linear regression (LR) is a method for predicting an output y given a value for an input variable x. The assumption behind this approach is that there must exist some linear relationship between x and y. This relationship expressed in mathematical terms is

$$y = b_0 + b_1 x + e$$

where

b_1 = slope of a straight line
b_0 = y-axis intercept
e = estimation error

Figure 2-13 shows a simplified case with three data points and a straight line that best fits between all the points. The $\hat{y}$ points are the estimates created using the LR equation for a given x_i. The r_i values are the estimation errors between the true data point and the corresponding $\hat{y}$ estimate.

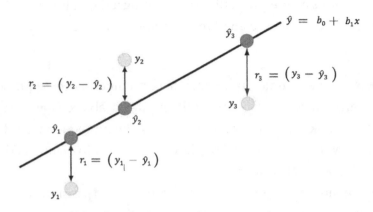

Figure 2-13. *Simple LR case example*

The normal approach in creating an LR equation is to minimize the sum of all the r_i errors. Different techniques can be used to learn the linear regression model from data, such as a linear algebra solution for ordinary least squares and using a gradient descent optimization.

Linear regression has been around for more than 200 years and has been extensively studied. Two useful rules of thumb when using this technique are to remove independent variables that are very similar and to remove any noise from the dataset. It is a quick and simple technique and a good first-try algorithm.

LR demonstration

The following Python script is named lrTest.py and is designed to create a pseudo-random set of points surrounding a sloped line with the underlying equation

$$y = 2x - 5$$

The learn regression method contained in the scikit-learn package uses the pseudo-random dataset to recreate the underlying equation. This script is available from the book's companion web site:

```python
# Import required libraries
import matplotlib.pyplot as plt
import seaborn as sns
import numpy as np
from sklearn.linear_model import LinearRegression

# generate the random dataset
rng = np.random.RandomState(1)
x = 10*rng.rand(50)
y = 2*x -5 + rng.randn(50)

# Setup the LR model
model = LinearRegression(fit_intercept=True)
model.fit(x[:, np.newaxis], y)

# Generate the estimates
xfit = np.linspace(0, 10, 1000)
yfit = model.predict(xfit[:, np.newaxis])

# Display a plot with the random data points and best fit line
ax = plt.scatter(x,y)
ax = plt.plot(xfit, yfit)
plt.show()

# Display the LR coefficients
print("Model slope:     ", model.coef_[0])
print("Model intercept:  ", model.intercept_)
```

The script is run by entering

```
python lrTest.py
```

Figure 2-14 shows the result of running this script.

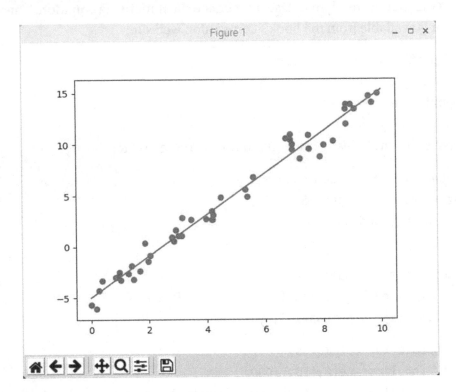

Figure 2-14. *Results for the lrTest script*

It should be readily apparent from viewing the figure that the best fit line is placed perfectly within the dataset as would be expected from the way the data was generated. This is a proper result because the sole purpose of this demonstration was to illustrate how a linear regression model worked.

Figure 2-15 shows the b_0 and b_1 coefficients that the LR model computed. They are extremely close to the true values of 2 and –5, respectively.

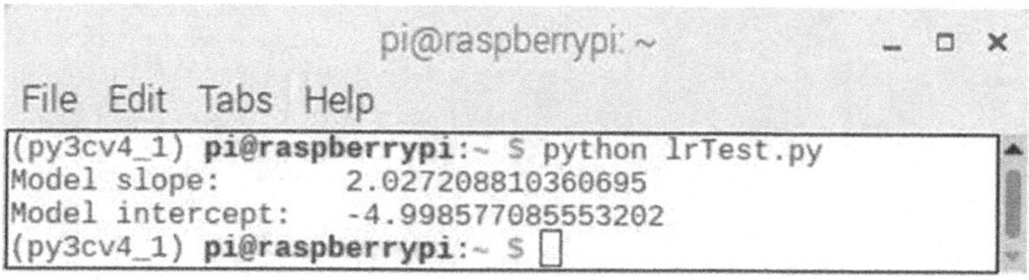

```
                      pi@raspberrypi: ~              _  □  ×
  File  Edit  Tabs  Help
 (py3cv4_1) pi@raspberrypi:~ $ python lrTest.py
 Model slope:        2.027208810360695
 Model intercept:    -4.998577085553202
 (py3cv4_1) pi@raspberrypi:~ $ []
```

Figure 2-15. *Computed LR coefficients*

Logistic regression

Logistic regression (LogR) is often used for classification purposes. It differs from LR because the dependent variable (x) can only take on a limited number of values, whereas in LR the number of values is unlimited. This arises because logistic regression uses categories for the dependent variable. It becomes binary logistic regression when there are only two categories.

In LR, the output is the weighted sum of inputs. LogR is a generalization of LR in the sense that the weighted sum of inputs is not output directly, but passes through a function that maps any real input value to an output ranging between 0 and 1. In LR, an output can take on any value, but for LogR, the values must be between 0 and 1.

Figure 2-16 shows the function which maps the sum of weighted inputs. This is called the sigmoid function and is also known as an activation function.

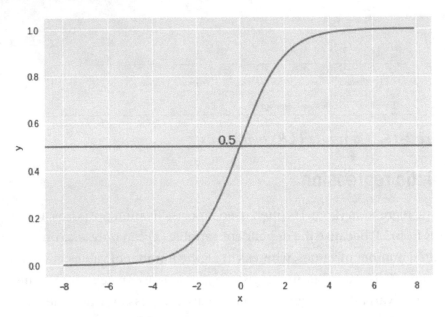

Figure 2-16. *Sigmoid function*

The figure shows that the output value (y) of the sigmoid function always lies between 0 and 1 and when x = 0, y= 0.5. In the case of two categories, if y >= 0.5, then it can be stated that Class 1 was detected; else, it must be Class 0.

Before I delve into the actual data model, it is important to review the two underlying assumptions that must be met for a logistic regression to be applied. These are

- The dependent variable must be categorical.

- The independent variables (features) must be independent.

I will be using Professor Andrew Ng's dataset regarding admission to a university based on the results of two exam scores. The complete dataset consists of 100 records with two exam scores or marks ranging from 0 to 100. Each record also contains a 1 or 0, where 1 means the applicant was admitted and 0 the reverse. The objective for this data model is to predict based on two exam marks whether or not an applicant would be admitted. The raw data is taken from a CSV file named marks. txt, which is available from

https://github.com/animesh-agarwal/Machine-Learning/blob/
master/LogisticRegression/data/marks.txt

The data is loaded into the following script as a DataFrame using Pandas software. The data is also split into admitted and non-admitted categories to help visualize the data and meet the categorical assumption. This script named logRTest.py was used to generate a plot of the original dataset. This script is available from the book's companion web site:

```python
# Import required libraries
import matplotlib.pyplot as plt
import pandas as pd

def load_data(path, header):
    marks_df = pd.read_csv(path, header=header)
    return marks_df

if __name__ == "__main__":
    # load the data from the file
    data = load_data("marks.txt", None)

    # X = feature values, all the columns except the last column
    X = data.iloc[:, :-1]

    # y = target values, last column of the data frame
    y = data.iloc[:, -1]

    # Filter the applicants admitted
    admitted = data.loc[y == 1]

    # Filter the applicants not admitted
    not_admitted = data.loc[y == 0]
```

```
# Display the dataset plot
plt.scatter(admitted.iloc[:, 0], admitted.iloc[:, 1], s=10,
label='Admitted')
plt.scatter(not_admitted.iloc[:, 0], not_admitted.iloc[:, 1],
s=10, label='Not Admitted')
plt.legend()
plt.show()
```

The script is run by entering

```
python logRTest.py
```

Figure 2-17 shows the result of running this script.

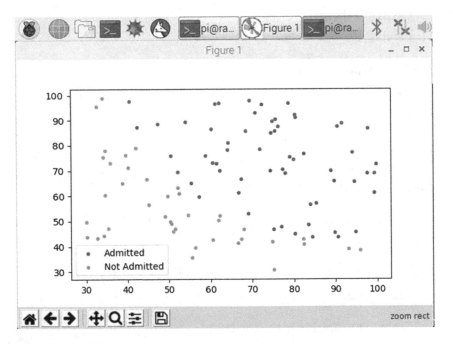

Figure 2-17. *Results for the logRTest script*

LogR model development

By examining this figure, you might be able to Image a straight line drawn from the upper left to the lower right, which would bisect the majority of the data points with admitted students to the right and non-admitted ones to the left. The problem becomes how to determine the coefficients for such a classifier line. LR cannot determine this line, but a LogR data model can.

At this point, I will attempt to explain how the LogR model was developed. However, I will of necessity omit much of the underlying mathematics because otherwise it will devolve this discussion into many fine-grain details that will distract from the main purpose of simply introducing the LogR data model. Rest assured that there are many good blogs and tutorials available, which explore LogR mathematical details.

The fundamental hypothesis for this LogR example is to determine the coefficients θ_i that "best fit" the following equation

$$h(x) = \theta_0 + \theta_1 x_1 + \theta_2 x_2$$

where

$$h(x) = classification \ value \begin{cases} class \ 1 \ if \ h(x) => 0 \\ class \ 0 \ if \ h(x) < 0 \end{cases}$$

$$x_1 = Category \ 1 \ value$$

$$x_2 = Category \ 2 \ value$$

In this binary LogR example, x_1 is the Exam 1 score (mark) and x_2 is the Exam 2 score.

A cost function must be assigned to this hypothesis such that the gradient method can be applied to minimize the cost and subsequently determine the coefficients that are needed for a minimal cost solution. Without proof or a derivation, I will just present the cost function as shown in Figure 2-18.

$$J(\theta) = -\frac{1}{m}\sum_{i=1}^{m}[y^i log(h(x^i)) + (1 - y^i)log(1 - h(x^i))]$$

Figure 2-18. *LogR cost function for the example problem*

The cost for all the training examples denoted by *J(θ)* in the figure may be computed by taking the average over the cost of all 100 records in the training dataset.

LogR demonstration

The following script is named logRDemo.py and will compute the desired coefficients as described earlier. In addition, the script will plot the classifier line overlaid with the training dataset. Finally, the coefficients are displayed in order to obtain a usable classifier equation. I have included many comments within the script to help you understand what is happening with the code. This script is available from the book's companion web site:

```
# Import required libraries
import numpy as np
import matplotlib.pyplot as plt
import pandas as pd
import scipy.optimize as so

def load_data(path, header):
    # Load the CSV file into a panda dataframe
    marks_df = pd.read_csv(path, header=header)
    return marks_df
```

```python
def sigmoid(x):
    # Activation function
    return 1/(1 + np.exp(-x))

def net_input(theta, x):
    # Computes the weighted sum of inputs by a numpy dot product
    return np.dot(x, theta)

def probability(theta, x):
    # Returns the probability after Sigmoid function is applied
    return sigmoid(net_input(theta, x))

def cost_function(theta, x, y):
    # Computes the cost function
    m = x.shape[0]
    total_cost = -(1/m)*np.sum(y*np.log(probability(theta,x))+
    (1-y)*np.log(1-probability(theta,x)))
    return total_cost

def gradient(theta, x, y):
    #Computes the cost function gradient
    m = x.shape[0]
    return (1/m)*np.dot(x.T,sigmoid(net_input(theta,x))-y)

def fit(x, y, theta):
    # The optimal coefficients are computed here
    opt_weights = so.fmin_tnc(func=cost_function, x0=theta,
    fprime=gradient,args=(x,y.flatten()))
    return opt_weights[0]

if __name__ == "__main__":
    # Load the data from the file
    data = load_data("marks.txt", None)
    # X = feature values, all the columns except the last column
    X = data.iloc[:, :-1]
```

```python
    # Save a copy for the output plot
    X0 = X
    # y = target values, last column of the data frame
    y = data.iloc[:, -1]
    # Save a copy for the output plot
    y0 = y
    X = np.c_[np.ones((X.shape[0], 1)), X]
    y = y[:, np.newaxis]
    theta = np.zeros((X.shape[1], 1))
    parameters = fit(X, y, theta)
    x_values = [np.min(X[:,1]-5), np.max(X[:,2] + 5)]
    y_values = -(parameters[0] + np.dot(parameters[1], x_
    values)) / parameters[2]
    # filter the admitted applicants
    admitted = data.loc[y0 == 1]
    # filter the non-admitted applicants
    not_admitted = data.loc[y0 == 0]
    # Plot the original dataset along with the classifier line
    ax = plt.scatter(admitted.iloc[:, 0], admitted.iloc[:, 1],
    s=10, label='Admitted')
    ax = plt.scatter(not_admitted.iloc[:, 0], not_admitted.
    iloc[:, 1], s=10, label='Not Admitted')
    ax = plt.plot(x_values, y_values, label='Decision
    Boundary')
    ax = plt.xlabel('Marks in 1st Exam')
    ax = plt.ylabel('Marks in 2nd Exam')
    ax = plt.legend()
    plt.show()
    print(parameters)
```

The script is run by entering

```
python logRDemo.py
```

Figure 2-19 shows the result of running this script.

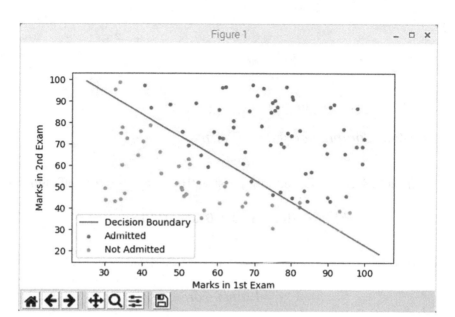

Figure 2-19. *Results for the logRDemo script*

The classifier line appears to be properly placed between the data points separating admitted students from non-admitted students. However, if you closely examine the classifier line, you find five admitted student data points to the left of the classifier line. These points will cause a false negative if the LogR classification model is used because students with those exam scores were refused admission, but should have been admitted. Similarly, there are six non-admitted students either on the line or to the right of the classifier line. These points will cause false positives if the LogR classification model is used because students with those exam scores were admitted, but should have been refused admission. In all, there are 11 either false negatives or false positives, which create an overall 89% accuracy for the LogR model. This is not terribly bad and likely could be improved by increasing the size of the training dataset.

Figure 2-20 shows the θ_i coefficients that the LogR model computed.

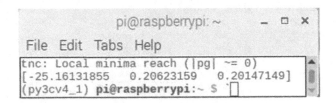

Figure 2-20. *Computed LogR coefficients*

The final LogR classifier equation using the computed θ_i coefficients is

$$h(x) = -25.1613 + 0.2062x_1 + 0.2015x_2$$

where

$$x_1 = Exam\,1\,score$$

$$x_2 = Exam\,2\,score$$

I tried a few random scores to test the classifier equation. The results are shown in Table 2-2.

Table 2-2. *Random trials for LogR classifier equation*

Exam 1	Exam 2	Classifier	Admitted	Not admitted
40	60	−4.825		X
80	60	3.423	X	
50	60	−2.763		X
55	65	−0.7245		X
60	65	0.3065	X	

(*continued*)

Table 2-2. (*continued*)

Exam 1	Exam 2	Classifier	Admitted	Not admitted
80	90	9.468	X	
70	75	4.4835	X	
60	65	0.3065	X	
60	75	2.3215	X	
60	60	−0.701		X
62	63	0.3159	X	
70	65	2.3685	X	
65	70	2.1345	X	
50	55	−3.7705		X
70	48	−1.057		X
56	59	−1.7273		X

The last entry in the table is not random but instead is a false negative taken from the original dataset. I did this to illustrate a potential issue with relying solely on the classifier equation.

Naive Bayes

Naive Bayes is a classification algorithm for both two-class (binary) and multi-class classification problems. The technique best understands using binary or categorical input values.

It is called Naive Bayes because the calculation of the probabilities for each hypothesis is simplified to make their calculation possible. Rather than attempting to calculate the values of each attribute value P(d1, d2|h), they are assumed to be conditionally independent given a target data value and calculated as P(d1|h) * P(d2|h).

This is a very strong assumption which is not likely to hold for real-world data. This assumption is based on a supposition that class attributes do not interact. Nonetheless, this approach seems to perform well on data where the basic assumption does not hold.

Before jumping into a real-world demonstration, I believe it would be prudent to review some fundamental principles regarding Bayesian logic.

Brief review of the Bayes' theorem

In a classification problem, a hypothesis (h) may be considered as a class to be assigned for each new data instance (d). An easy way to select the most probable hypothesis given the new data is to use any prior knowledge about the problem. Bayes' theorem provides a method to calculate the probability of a hypothesis given the prior knowledge.

Bayes' theorem is stated as

$P(h|d) = (P(d|h) * P(h)) / P(d)$

where

- $P(h|d)$ is the probability of hypothesis h given the data d. This is called the posterior probability.

- $P(d|h)$ is the probability of data d given that the hypothesis h was true.

- $P(h)$ is the probability of hypothesis h being true (regardless of the data). This is called the prior probability of h.

- $P(d)$ is the probability of the data (regardless of the hypothesis).

It is plain to observe that the goal is to calculate the posterior probability of $P(h|d)$ from the prior probability $P(h)$ with $P(d)$ and $P(d|h)$.

The hypothesis with the highest probability is selected after calculating the posterior probability for a number of different hypotheses. This selected h is the maximum probable hypothesis and is formally called the maximum a posteriori (MAP) hypothesis. It can be expressed in several forms as

$$MAP(h) = max(P(h|d))$$

or

$$MAP(h) = max((P(d|h) * P(h)) / P(d))$$

or

$$MAP(h) = max(P(d|h) * P(h))$$

The P(d) is a normalizing term which allows for the calculation of a normalized probability. It may be disregarded when only the most probable hypothesis is desired because this term is constant and only used for normalization, which leads to the last MAP equation shown earlier.

Further simplification is possible if there is an equal distribution of instances in each class in the training data. The probability of each class (P(h)) will be equal in this case. This would cause another constant term to be part of the MAP equation, and it too could be dropped leaving an ultimate equation of

$$MAP(h) = max(P(d|h))$$

Preparing data for use by the Naive Bayes model

Class and conditional probabilities are required to be calculated before applying the Naive Bayes model. Class probabilities are, as the name implies, the probabilities associated with each class in the training set. Conditional probabilities are those associated with each input data value for a given class.

Training is fast because only the probability of each class and the probability of each class given different input values are required to be calculated. There are no coefficients needed to be fitted by optimization procedures as was the case with the regression models.

The class probabilities are simply the frequency of instances that belong to each class divided by the total number of instances.

For example, in a binary classification problem, the probability of an instance belonging to class1 would be calculated as

P(class1) = count(class1) / (count(class0) + count(class1))

In the simplest case where each class had an equal number of instances, the probability for each class would be of 0.5 or 50%.

The conditional probabilities are the frequency of each attribute value for a given class value divided by the frequency of instances with that class value.

This next example should help clarify how the Naive Bayes model works.

Naive Bayes model example

The following is a training dataset of weather and a corresponding target variable "Play" (suggesting possibilities of playing).

Table 2-3 shows a record of weather conditions and the Play variable value.

Table 2-3. *Weather/Play dataset*

Weather	Play
Sunny	No
Overcast	Yes
Rainy	Yes
Sunny	Yes
Sunny	Yes
Overcast	Yes
Rainy	No
Rainy	No
Sunny	Yes

(*continued*)

Table 2-3. (*continued*)

Weather	Play
Rainy	Yes
Sunny	No
Overcast	Yes
Overcast	Yes
Rainy	No

The first step is to convert the training dataset to a frequency table as shown in Table 2-4.

Table 2-4. *Frequency table*

Frequency table

Weather	No	Yes
Overcast		4
Rainy	3	2
Sunny	2	3
Total	5	9

The second step is to create a Likelihood table by finding the probabilities. For instance, overcast probability is 0.29 and the overall playing probability is 0.64 for all weather conditions. Table 2-5 shows the Likelihood table.

Table 2-5. *Likelihood table*

Likelihood table				
Weather	No	Yes		Weather probabilities
Overcast		4	4/14	0.29
Rainy	3	2	5/14	0.36
Sunny	2	3	5/14	0.36
Total	5	9		
	5/14	9/14		
Playing probabilities	0.36	0.64		

The next step is to use the Naive Bayesian equation to calculate the posterior probability for each class. The class with the highest posterior probability is the outcome of prediction.

Problem statement: Players will play if weather is sunny. Is this statement correct?

Solve this problem by using the method of posterior probability.

$$P(Yes \mid Sunny) = P(Sunny \mid Yes) * P(Yes) / P(Sunny)$$

Substituting actual probabilities yields

$$P(Sunny \mid Yes) = 3/9 = 0.33$$

$$P(Sunny) = 5/14 = 0.36$$

$$P(Yes) = 9/14 = 0.64$$

Therefore:

$$P(Yes \mid Sunny) = 0.33 * 0.64 / 0.36 = 0.60$$

Next compute the posterior probability for the other Play class value of "No".

$$P(No \mid Sunny) = P(Sunny \mid No) * P(No) / P(Sunny)$$

Substituting actual probabilities yields

$$P(Sunny \mid No) = 2/5 = 0.40$$

$$P(Sunny) = 5/14 = 0.36$$

$$P(No) = 5/14 = 0.36$$

Therefore:

$$P(No \mid Sunny) = 0.40 * 0.36 / 0.36 = 0.40$$

The probability P(Yes | Sunny) is higher than the P(No | Sunny) and is the MAP or prediction. Note, you could have simply subtracted the P(Yes | Sunny) from 1.0 to obtain the complementary probability, which is always true for binary class values. However, that operation does not hold true for non-binary class value situations.

Pros and cons

The following are some pros and cons for using a Naive Bayes data model.

Pros:

- It is easy and fast to predict class value from a test dataset. It also performs well in multi-class predictions.

- When assumption of independence holds, a Naive Bayes classifier performs better compare to other models like logistic regression and less training data is needed.

- It performs well in case of categorical input variables compared to numerical variable(s). For numerical variables, a normal distribution is assumed, which is a strong assumption.

Cons:

- If a categorical variable has a category in the test dataset, which was not observed in training dataset, then the model will assign a 0 probability and will be unable to make a prediction. This case is often known as "zero frequency." A smoothing technique called Laplace estimation is often used to resolve this issue.

- Naive Bayes is also known as a bad estimator, so probability outputs can be inaccurate.

- Another limitation of Naive Bayes is the assumption of independent predictors. In the real world, it is almost impossible that we get a set of predictors which are completely independent.

The scikit-learn library will be used shortly to build a Naive Bayes model in Python. There are three types of Naive Bayes model available from the scikit-learn library:

- Gaussian – It is used in classification and it assumes that features follow a normal distribution.

- Multinomial – It is used for discrete counts. Consider a text classification problem as a Bernoulli trial which is essentially "count how often a word occurs in the document." It can be thought of as "number of times outcome number x_i is observed over n trials."

- Bernoulli – The Bernoulli model is useful if the feature vectors are binary (i.e., zeros and ones). One application would be text classification with "bag of words" model where the 1s and 0s are "word occurs in the document" and "word does not occur in the document," respectively.

Based on your dataset, you can choose any of the preceding discussed models.

Gaussian Naive Bayes

Naive Bayes can be extended to real-valued attributes, most commonly by assuming a Gaussian distribution. This extension of Naive Bayes is called Gaussian Naive Bayes. Other functions can be used to estimate the distribution of the data, but the Gaussian or normal distribution is the easiest to work with because it only needs the mean and the standard deviation to be computed from the training data.

Mean and standard deviation values of each input variable (x) for each class value are computed using the following equations:

$$mean(x) = 1/n * sum(x)$$

$$standard\ deviation(x) = sqrt(1/n * sum(x_i\text{-}mean(x)\wedge 2))$$

where

    n = number of instances

    x = values for input variables

Probabilities of new x values are calculated using the Gaussian probability density function (PDF). When making predictions, these parameters can be entered into the Gaussian PDF with a new input for the x variable and in the Gaussian PDF will provide an estimate of the probability of that new input value for that class.

$$pdf(x, mean, sd) = (1 / (sqrt(2 * PI) * sd)) * exp(\text{-}((x\text{-}mean\wedge 2)/(2*sd\wedge 2)))$$

Where pdf(x) is the Gaussian PDF, sqrt() is the square root, mean and sd are the mean and standard deviation, PI is the numerical constant, exp() is the numerical constant e or Euler's number raised to power, and x is the value for the input variable.

The following demonstration uses the preceding equations, but they are an integral part of the software package and are separately invoked.

Gaussian Naive Bayes (GNB) demonstration

The following Python script is named gnbTest.py and uses the GNB model contained in the scikit-learn software package. A minimal training dataset is contained in the script to have the model "learn" and make a prediction. The dataset may be purely arbitrary, or it could actually represent real-world attributes depending if the data has been encoded. In any case, the predictor will function without any problem because it is based only on numerical data. It is always the user's responsibility to decode the final results. This script is available from the book's companion web site:

```
# Import Library of Gaussian Naive Bayes model
from sklearn.naive_bayes import GaussianNB
import numpy as np

# Assigning predictor and target variables
x= np.array([[-3,7],[1,5], [1,2], [-2,0], [2,3], [-4,0],
[-1,1], [1,1], [-2,2], [2,7], [-4,1], [-2,7]])
y = np.array([3, 3, 3, 3, 4, 3, 3, 4, 3, 4, 4, 4])

# Create a Gaussian Classifier
model = GaussianNB()

# Train the model using the training sets
model.fit(x, y)

# Predict output
predicted= model.predict([[1,2],[3,4]])
print(predicted)
```

The script is run by entering

```
python gnbTest.py
```

Figure 2-21 shows the result of running this script.

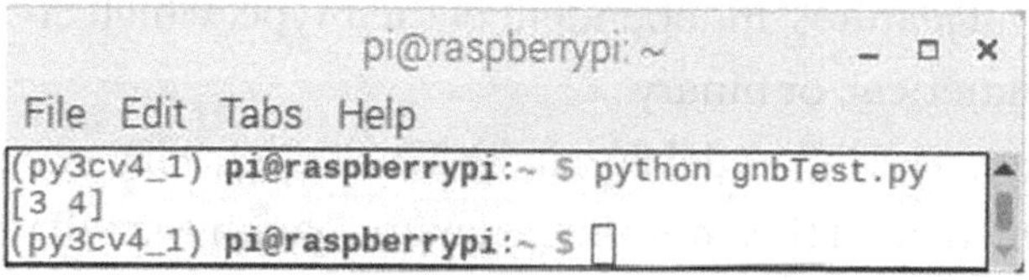

Figure 2-21. *Results for the gnbTest script*

The final results show [3 4] as the prediction. As I mentioned earlier, what this means in the real world would depend on the way the dataset was originally encoded.

k-nearest neighbor (k-NN) model

I introduced the k-NN model in the previous chapter in the Iris demonstration – part 3. However, I didn't mention two major drawbacks to using this model at that time. If neither of them is a problem, then a k-NN model should definitely be considered for use because it is a simple and robust classifier.

The first problem is the performance issue. Since it's a lazy model, all the training data must be loaded and used to compute the Euclidean distances to all training samples. This can be done in a naive way or using more complex data structures such as k-d trees. In any case, it can be big performance hit when a large training set is involved.

The second problem is the distance metric. The basic k-NN model is used with Euclidean distance, which is a problematic distance metric when a high number of dimensions are involved. As the number of dimensions rises, the algorithm performs worst due to the fact that the distance measure becomes meaningless when the dimension of the data increases significantly. Another related issue is when noisy features are encountered. This problem happens because the model applies the same weight for all features, noise or not. In addition, the same weights are applied to all features, independent of their type, which could be categorical, numerical, or binary.

In summary, a k-NN model is usually a best choice if a system has to learn a sophisticated (i.e., non-linear) pattern with a small number of samples and dimensions.

KNN demonstration

This demonstration will use the automobile dataset from the UC Irvine Repository. The two required CSV data files along with the kNN.py class file may be downloaded from

```
https://github.com/amallia/kNN
```

Note   There is also a Jupyter notebook file available from this web site. This file will not be used because I provide a Python script in the following, which accomplishes the same functions as the notebook file.

The problem statement will be to predict the miles per gallon (mpg) of a car, given its displacement and horsepower. Each record in the dataset corresponds to a single car.

The kNN class file is listed in the following, which contains initialization, computation, and prediction functions. This script is named kNN.py and is available either from the listed web site or the book's companion web site. I have added comments in the script listing to indicate what functions are being performed.

```
#!/usr/bin/env python
import math
import operator
```

```python
class kNN(object):
    # Initialization
    def __init__(self, x, y, k, weighted=False):
        assert (k <= len(x)
                ), "k cannot be greater than training_set
                length"
        self.__x = x
        self.__y = y
        self.__k = k
        self.__weighted = weighted

    # Compute Euclidean distance
    @staticmethod
    def __euclidean_distance(x1, y1, x2, y2):
        return math.sqrt((x1 - x2)**2 + (y1 - y2)**2)

    # Compute the PDF
    @staticmethod
    def gaussian(dist, sigma=1):
        return 1./(math.sqrt(2.*math.pi)*sigma)*math.exp(-
        dist**2/(2*sigma**2))

    # Perform predictions
    def predict(self, test_set):
        predictions = []
        for i, j in test_set.values:
            distances = []
            for idx, (l, m) in enumerate(self.__x.values):
                dist = self.__euclidean_distance(i, j, l, m)
                distances.append((self.__y[idx], dist))
            distances.sort(key=operator.itemgetter(1))
            v = 0
            total_weight = 0
```

```
            for i in range(self.__k):
                weight = self.gaussian(distances[i][1])
                if self.__weighted:
                    v += distances[i][0]*weight
                else:
                    v += distances[i][0]
                total_weight += weight
            if self.__weighted:
                predictions.append(v/total_weight)
            else:
                predictions.append(v/self.__k)
        return predictions
```

The following script is named knnTest.py where a k-NN model is instantiated from the kNN class file. A series of predictions are made for k = 1, 3, and 20 for both non-weighted and weighted cases. The resultant errors are computed for all cases. This script is available from the book's companion web site:

```
# Import required libraries
import pandas
from kNN import kNN
from sklearn.metrics import mean_squared_error

# Read the training CSV file
training_data = pandas.read_csv("auto_train.csv")
x = training_data.iloc[:,:-1]
y = training_data.iloc[:,-1]

# Read the test CSV file
test_data = pandas.read_csv("auto_test.csv")
x_test = test_data.iloc[:,:-1]
y_test = test_data.iloc[:,-1]
```

```python
# Display the heads from each CSV file
print('Training data')
print(training_data.head())
print('Test data')
print(test_data.head())

# Compute errors for k = 1, 3, and 20 with no weighting
for k in [1, 3, 20]:
    classifier = kNN(x,y,k)
    pred_test = classifier.predict(x_test)
    test_error = mean_squared_error(y_test, pred_test)
    print('Test error with k={}: {}'.format(k, test_error *
    len(y_test)/2))

# Compute errors for k = 1, 3, and 20 with weighting
for k in [1, 3, 20]:
    classifier = kNN(x,y,k,weighted=True)
    pred_test = classifier.predict(x_test)
    test_error = mean_squared_error(y_test, pred_test)
    print('Test error with k={}: {}'.format(k, test_error *
    len(y_test)/2))
```

The script is run by entering

```
python knnTest.py
```

Figure 2-22 shows the result of running this script.

```
                              pi@raspberrypi: ~                    _  □  ×

 File  Edit  Tabs  Help
(py3cv4_1) pi@raspberrypi:~ $ python knnTest.py
Training data
   displacement  horsepower    mpg
0          307.0         130   18.0
1          350.0         165   15.0
2          318.0         150   18.0
3          304.0         150   16.0
4          302.0         140   17.0
Test data
   displacement  horsepower    mpg
0             89          71   31.9
1             86          65   34.1
2             98          80   35.7
3            121          80   27.4
4            183          77   25.4
Test error with k=1: 2868.0049999999997
Test error with k=3: 2794.729999999999
Test error with k=20: 2746.1914125
Test error with k=1: 2868.005
Test error with k=3: 2757.3065023859417
Test error with k=20: 2737.9437262401907
(py3cv4_1) pi@raspberrypi:~ $ []
```

Figure 2-22. *Results for the knnTest script*

This figure shows the first five records from each of the CSV data files. The next three test error results are for the non-weighted prediction results for k equal to 1, 3, and 20, respectively. The last three test error results are for the weighted predictions for the same k values. Reviewing the error results reveals a slight reduction in error values as k is increased and even slightly lower error values for the cases when weighting is applied.

Decision tree classifier

This will be the last data model discussed in this chapter. The decision tree classifier data model is a clever solution for common business problems. For instance, if you are a bank loan manager, you might use this model to classify customers in safe or risky categories depending upon their financial and credit histories. Classification usually is done in two steps, the first being learning and the second being prediction. The model in the learning step is developed and tuned based solely on the available training data. The model is then used to predict future outcomes using the trained data and any appropriate hyper-parameters entered based on tuning and user experience.

Decision tree algorithm

A decision tree is a flowchart-like tree structure where an internal node represents a feature or attribute, a branch represents a decision rule, and every leaf node represents an outcome. The root node is the topmost node in a decision tree. The model learns to partition on the basis of attribute values. The tree is partitioned in a recursive manner naturally called recursive partitioning. This flowchart-like structure is a reasonable analogy to how humans perform a decision-making process. Visualizing this process with a flowchart diagram will help you understand this model. Figure 2-23 shows a portion of a generic decision tree.

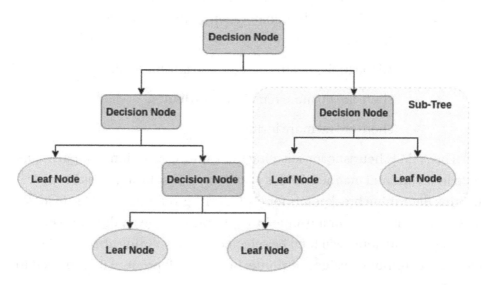

Figure 2-23. *Generic flowchart for a decision tree*

One nice characteristic of the decision tree algorithm is that the decision-making logic can readily be known. This model is known as a white box machine learning algorithm. Compare this openness to a black box which is typical for an artificial neural network (ANN) where any decision-making logic is generally unfathomable. In addition, training times for decision tree algorithms are generally much faster than ANN. The decision tree algorithm is not dependent on any particular type of training data probability distribution, which makes it a non-parametric method. Consequently, decision tree algorithms can handle high-dimensional data with good accuracy.

A decision tree algorithm follows this simple three-step process:

1. Select the best attribute using attribute selection measures (ASM) to split the records.

2. Make that attribute a decision node and break the dataset into smaller sub-sets.

3. Start tree building by repeating this process recursively for each child until *one* of the following conditions remains:

    - All the tuples belong to the same attribute value.

    - There are no more remaining attributes.

    - There are no more instances.

The ASM is heuristic for selecting the splitting criterion that partitions data in an optimal manner. ASM is also known as splitting rules because it helps determine breakpoints for tuples on a given node. ASM provides a rank to each feature or attribute by explaining the given dataset. The best scoring attribute will then be selected as the splitting attribute. In the case of a continuous-valued attribute, branch split points will also need to be defined.

The following aside provides a detailed discussion concerning information entropy, information gain, Gini index, and gain ratio. While not a prerequisite to running the decision tree demonstration, I would recommend that you take the time to read it. It will definitely improve your understanding on how this algorithm functions.

Information gain

Information gain measures how much "information" a feature gives us about a class. Any features that perfectly partitions should give maximal information. Likewise, unrelated features should provide no information. Information gain measures the reduction in entropy, where entropy is a measure of the purity or impurity present in an arbitrary collection of examples. A more formal entropy definition is

> *The average rate at which information is produced by a* stochastic *source of data.*

The measure of information entropy associated with each possible data value is computed by the negative logarithm of the probability mass function for the value.

Before jumping into the fine-grain details, it would be prudent to review some fundamental principles underlying information gain.

Split criterion

Suppose it is desired to split on the variable (x):

$$1\ 2\ 3\ 4\ 5\ 6\ 7\ 8$$

$$y\ 0\ 0\ 0\ 1\ 1\ 1\ 1\ 1$$

If we split at $x1 < 3.5$, we get an optimal split. If we split at $x < 4.5$, we make a mistake or misclassification. The idea is to position the split at such point as to make the samples "pure" or homogeneous. Of course, there is the need to measure how the split functions and that is accomplished using an ASM of information gain, gain ratio, or Gini index. All of the preceding discussion is predicated upon knowing how to measure information. Accomplishing this is all based on the concept of information entropy which was introduced by Claude Shannon in his seminal 1948 paper "A Mathematical Theory of Communication." Incidentally, Dr. Shannon is considered the "Father of Information Theory" due to his monumental contributions to this field.

Measuring information

Consider the bar shown in Figure 2-24 as an information source where regions are digitally encoded.

A	B	C	D
10	11	11	1
2 bits	3 bits	3 bits	1 bit

Figure 2-24. *Digitally encoded information source*

Larger regions in the figure are encoded with fewer bits, while smaller regions require more bits. The expected value for this information source is the sum of all the values of the product of the probability of a value and the value itself. In this example the expected value is computed as follows:

$$Expected\ Value = \frac{1}{4}*2 + \frac{1}{8}*3 + \frac{1}{8}*3 + \frac{1}{2}*1$$

Each time a region in the figure was halved in size the number of bits went up by one. The probability also decreased by 0.5 when the size was halved. The conclusion to be drawn from this figure is that the information of a random event x is proportional to the logarithm (base 2) of the reciprocal of the event's probability. In equation form, this is

$$Information(x) = log_2\left(\frac{1}{P(D=x)}\right)$$

In general, the expected information or "entropy" of a random variable is the same as the expected value with the value filled in with the information:

$$Entropy\ of\ D = \sum_x P(D=x) * Information(x)$$

$$= \sum_x P(D=x) * log_2\left(\frac{1}{P(D=x)}\right)$$

$$= -\sum_x P(D=x) * log_2(P(D=x))$$

Properties of entropy

Entropy is maximized when the constituent elements are heterogeneous (impure):

$$If\quad p_k = \frac{1}{k}$$

then,

$$Entropy = H = -K * \frac{1}{k} * log_2\left(\frac{1}{k}\right) = log_2(K)$$

Conversely, entropy is minimized when elements are homogeneous (pure):

$$\text{if } p_i = 1 \text{ or } p_i = 0$$

then,

$$Entropy = H = 0$$

With entropy defined as

$$H = -\sum_{i=1}^{K} p_k * log_2 (p_k)$$

then any change in entropy is considered as information gain and is defined as

$$\Delta H = H - \frac{m_L}{m} * H_L - \frac{m_D}{m} * H_D$$

where m is the total number of instances, with m_k instances belonging to class k, where $K = 1, \dots, k$.

Information gain example

The following example may be considered as an extension of the example shown in the Naive Bayes section. Table 2-6 has several additional features, which will be computed in the decision whether or not to play given a certain set of conditions.

Table 2-6. *Play decision*

Outlook	Temperature	Humidity	Windy	Play
Sunny	Hot	High	False	No
Sunny	Hot	High	True	No
Overcast	Hot	High	False	Yes
Rainy	Mild	High	False	Yes
Rainy	Cool	Normal	False	Yes
Rainy	Cool	Normal	True	No
Overcast	Cool	Normal	True	Yes
Sunny	Mild	High	False	No
Sunny	Cool	Normal	False	Yes
Rainy	Mild	Normal	False	Yes
Sunny	Mild	Normal	True	Yes
Overcast	Mild	High	True	Yes
Overcast	Hot	Normal	False	Yes
Rainy	Mild	High	True	No

The information value for the Play attribute is computed as follows:

$$H(Y) = -\sum_{i=1}^{K} p_k * log_2(p_k)$$

$$= -\frac{5}{14} log_2\left(\frac{5}{14}\right) - \frac{9}{14} log_2\left(\frac{9}{14}\right)$$

$$= -(0.357)*(-1.486)-(0.643)*(-0.637)$$

$$= 0.531 + 0.410$$

$$= 0.941$$

Now, consider the information gain when the Humidity attribute is selected.

$$InfoGain(Humdity) = H(Y) - \frac{m_L}{m}H_L - \frac{m_R}{m}H_R$$

where

m = number of Humidity examples

m_L = number of Humidity examples with value = Normal

m_R = number of Humidity examples with value = High

H_L = IV for Humidity examples with value = Normal

H_R = IV for Humidity examples with value = High

Substituting yields

$$InfoGain(Humdity) = H(Y) = 0.941 - \frac{7}{14}H_L - \frac{7}{14}H_R$$

$$H_L = -\frac{6}{7}log_2\left(\frac{6}{7}\right) - \frac{1}{7}log_2\left(\frac{1}{7}\right)$$

$$H_L = 0.592$$

$$H_R = -\frac{3}{7}log_2\left(\frac{6}{7}\right) - \frac{4}{7}log_2\left(\frac{4}{7}\right)$$

$$H_R = 0.985$$

$$H(Y) = 0.941 - \frac{7}{14}*0.592 - \frac{7}{14}*0.985$$

$$H(Y) = 0.152$$

Performing the preceding computations for all of the remaining features yields

Outlook = 0.247

Temperature = 0.029

Humidity = 0.152

Windy = 0.048

The initial split will be done with Outlook feature because it has the highest information gain value in accordance with the ASM process.

The optimum split for the next level is shown in Figure 2-25 with the associated selected attributes and information gain for each split.

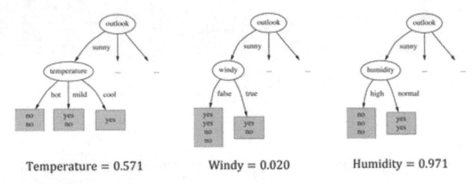

Temperature = 0.571   Windy = 0.020   Humidity = 0.971

Figure 2-25. *Next level splits with information gain values*

Figure 2-26 is the final decision tree.

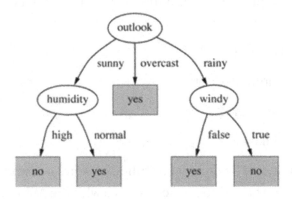

Figure 2-26. *Final decision tree diagram*

Note that not all leaves need to be pure; sometimes similar (even identical) instances have different classes. Splitting stops when data cannot be split any further.

Gini index

The decision tree algorithm CART (classification and regression tree) uses the Gini method to create split points. The equation for computing the Gini index is

$$Gini(D)=1-\sum_{k=1}^{K} p_i^2$$

where p_i is the probability that a tuple in D belongs to class C_i.

The Gini index considers a binary split for each attribute. You can compute a weighted sum of the impurity of each partition. If a binary split on attribute A partitions data D into D_1 and D_2, the Gini index of D is

$$Gini_A(D)=\frac{|D_1|}{D}Gini(D_1)+\frac{|D_2|}{D}Gini(D_2)$$

In case of a discrete-valued attribute, the sub-set that gives the minimum Gini index for that chosen is selected as a splitting attribute. In the case of continuous-valued attributes, the strategy is to select each pair of adjacent values as a possible split point and the point with smaller Gini index chosen as the splitting point.

$$\Delta Gini(A)=Gini(D)-Gini_A(D)$$

The attribute with minimum Gini index is chosen as the splitting attribute.

This index is maximized when elements are heterogeneous (impure). If

$$p_k=\frac{1}{k}$$

then

$$Gini = 1 - \sum_{k=1}^{K} \frac{1}{k^2} = 1 - \frac{1}{k}$$

Correspondingly, the index is minimized when elements are homogeneous (pure).

If

$$p_i = 1 \text{ or } p_i = 0$$

then

$$Gini = 1 - 1 - 0 = 0$$

Simple Gini index example

I will start with an arbitrary dataset shown in Table 2-7 with five features, of which feature E is the predictive one. This feature has two classes, positive or negative. There happens to be an equal number of instances in each class just to simplify the computations.

Table 2-7. *Arbitrary dataset*

Index	A	B	C	D	E
1	4.8	3.4	1.9	0.2	positive
2	5	3	1.6	1.2	positive
3	5	3.4	1.6	0.2	positive
4	5.2	3.5	1.5	0.2	positive
5	5.2	3.4	1.4	0.2	positive
6	4.7	3.2	1.6	0..2	positive
7	4.8	3.1	1.6	0.2	positive
8	5.4	3.4	1.5	0.4	positive

(continued)

118

Table 2-7. (*continued*)

Index	A	B	C	D	E
9	7	3.2	4.7	1.4	negative
10	6.4	3.2	4.7	1.5	negative
11	6.9	3.1	4.9	1.5	negative
12	5.5	2.3	4	1.3	negative
13	6.5	2.8	4.6	1.5	negative
14	5.7	2.8	4.5	1.3	negative
15	6.3	3.3	4.7	1.6	negative
16	4.9	2.4	3.3	1	negative

The first in calculating the Gini index is to choose some random values to categorize (initial split) for each feature or attribute. The values chosen for this dataset are shown in Table 2-8.

Table 2-8. *Initial split attribute values*

A	B	C	D
>= 5.0	>= 3.0	>= 4.2	>= 1.4
< 5.0	< 3.0	< 4.2	< 1.4

Computing the Gini index for attribute A:

Value >= 5

Number of instances = 12

Number of instances >=5 and positive = 5

Number of instances >= 5 and negative = 7

$$Gini_A(>=5)=1-\left(\frac{5}{12}\right)^2-\left(\frac{7}{12}\right)^2=0.486$$

Value: < 5

Number of instances = 4

Number of instances >=5 and positive = 3

Number of instances >= 5 and negative = 1

$$Gini_A(<5)=1-\left(\frac{3}{4}\right)^2-\left(\frac{1}{4}\right)^2=0.375$$

Weighting and summing yields

$$Gini_A=\frac{12}{16}*0.486+\frac{4}{16}*0.375=0.458$$

Computing in a similar manner for the remaining attributes yields

$$Gini_B=0.335$$

$$Gini_C=0.200$$

$$Gini_D=0.273$$

The initial split point when using the Gini index will always be the minimum value. The final decision tree based on the computed indices is shown in Figure 2-27.

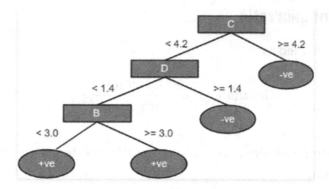

Figure 2-27. *Final decision tree for the simple Gini index example*

Gain ratio

Gain ratio is a modification of information gain that reduces its bias on highly branching features. This algorithm takes into account the number and size of branches when choosing a feature. It does this by normalizing information gain by the "intrinsic information" of a split, which is defined as the information need to determine the branch to which an instance belongs. Information gain is positively biased for an attribute with many outcomes. This means that the information gain algorithm prefers an attribute with a large number of distinct values.

Intrinsic information

The intrinsic information represents the potential information generated by splitting the dataset into K partitions:

$$IntrinsicInfo(D) = -\sum_{k=1}^{K} \frac{|D_k|}{D} * log_2\left(\frac{|D_k|}{D}\right)$$

Partitions with high intrinsic information should be similar in size. Datasets with few partitions holding the majority of tuples have inherently low intrinsic information.

Definition of gain ratio

Gain ratio is defined as

$$GainRatio(D) = \frac{Gain(D)}{IntrinsicInfo(D)}$$

The feature with the maximum gain ratio is selected as the splitting feature.

ID3 is the acronym for Iterative Dichotomiser 3 and is an algorithm invented by Ross Quinian to implement the gain ratio ASM. Ross later invented the C4.5 algorithm, which is an improvement over ID3 and is currently used in most machine learning systems using the gain ratio algorithm. It should be noted that the term *SplitInfo* is used in the C4.5 algorithm to represent *IntrinsicInfo*. Other than that ambiguity, the basic gain ratio algorithm is unchanged.

There will be no example presented for gain ratio simply because this aside is just too extensive and you likely have a pretty good understanding of the ASM process if you have read through to this ending.

Decision tree classifier demonstration with scikit-learn

This decision tree demonstration will use a classic dataset from the machine learning community called the Pima Indian Diabetes dataset. The dataset may be downloaded in CSV format from

`www.kaggle.com/uciml/pima-indians-diabetes-database#diabetes.csv`

This dataset is originally from the National Institute of Diabetes and Digestive and Kidney Diseases. The objective of this demonstration is to diagnostically predict whether or not a patient has diabetes based on certain diagnostic measurements included in the dataset. Several constraints were placed on the selection of these instances from a larger database. In particular, all patients here are females at least 21 years old of Pima Indian heritage.

The downloaded CSV file is archived and must be extracted before being used. Furthermore, you must remove the first row from the file because it contains string column header descriptions. Keeping this row in place will cause the prediction function to fail because the string contents cannot be converted to a float type. I recommend using any spreadsheet application that can load the CSV file. I happened to use Microsoft's Excel program, but any of the open source Linux applications will likely work.

I will develop the Python script in two stages while also discussing the underlying methodology regarding the decision tree classifier model. The first stage will load all the dependencies as well as the CSV file. The CSV file head information is also displayed to confirm a successful load. The second stage will be to build, train, and test the decision tree model.

The first step is to load the required libraries, which include the DecisionTreeClassifier data model from the sklearn software package. This data model uses the Gini ASM process by default, but this can be changed if another ASM process is desired.

```
# Load libraries
import pandas as pd
from sklearn.tree import DecisionTreeClassifier # Import
Decision Tree Classifier
from sklearn.model_selection import train_test_split # Import
train_test_split function
from sklearn import metrics #Import scikit-learn metrics module
for accuracy calculation
col_names = ['pregnant', 'glucose', 'bp', 'skin', 'insulin',
'bmi', 'pedigree', 'age', 'label']
```

The next step is to load the required Pima Indian Diabetes dataset using Pandas' read CSV function. Ensure the downloaded dataset is in the same current directory as the script.

```
# Load dataset
pima = pd.read_csv("diabetes.csv", header=None, names=col_
names)
pima.head()
```

Figure 2-28 shows the CSV file head portion with the first five records.

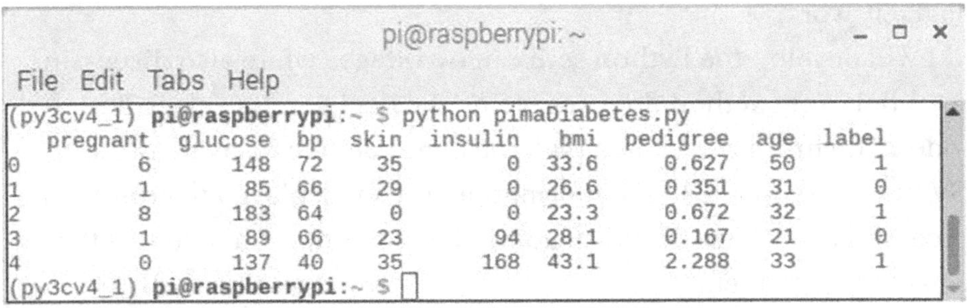

Figure 2-28. *diabetes.csv head results*

The next step is to divide the given columns into two types of variables dependent (target) and independent (feature).

```
#split dataset in features and target variable
feature_cols = ['pregnant', 'insulin', 'bmi', 'age','glucose','
bp','pedigree']
X = pima[feature_cols] # Feature variables
y = pima.label # Target variable
```

Model performance requires the dataset to be divided into a training set and a test set. The dataset can be divided by using the function `train_ test_split()`. Three parameters, namely, features, target, and test_set size, must be passed to this method.

```
# Split dataset into training set and test set
# 70% training and 30% test
X_train, X_test, y_train, y_test = train_test_split(X, y,
test_size=0.3, random_state=1)
```

The next step is to instantiate a decision tree data model from the sklearn software package. The model is named clf and is readily trained using 70% of the training dataset split from the original dataset. Finally, a series of predictions are automatically made with the remaining 30% of the dataset using the model's predict() method.

In the test data stored in X_test, the labels are regarded as sample to bc fed to the classifier in the predict() method. The sample is as given in the following data. It is invalid to feed it to the predict() method as it is string, not float. To remove it, the drop() function is used. This is the return result of X_txt.drop(0) and is what is fed to the predict () method.

```
['Pregnancies','Insulin','BMI','Age','Glucose','BloodPressure',
'DiabetesPedigreeFunction']
# Create Decision Tree classifer object
clf = DecisionTreeClassifier()
# Train Decision Tree Classifer
clf = clf.fit(X_train,y_train)
#Predict the response for test dataset
y_pred = clf.predict(X_test.drop(0))
```

The last step is to measure the overall accuracy of the prediction set. Accuracy is computed by comparing actual test set values vs. the predicted values. The metrics module from the scikit-learn package was used for this accuracy measurement.

Note that the y_test variable includes the label 'Outcome' which is string. To remove it, the drop() function is used.

```
# Model accuracy
print("Accuracy:",metrics.accuracy_score(y_test.drop(0), y_pred))
```

The final result is the following score:

Accuracy: 0.6753246753246753

The 67.5% is a reasonable accuracy score. However, it may be improved by tuning the hyper-parameters used by the decision tree algorithm, which I will demonstrate in later section.

The complete script listing is shown in the following and is named diabetesDT.py. It is available from the book's companion web site.

```
# Load libraries
import pandas as pd
from sklearn.tree import DecisionTreeClassifier
# Import Decision Tree Classifier
from sklearn.model_selection import train_test_split
# Import train_test_split function
from sklearn import metrics #Import scikit-learn metrics module
for accuracy calculation

col_names = ['pregnant', 'glucose', 'bp', 'skin', 'insulin',
'bmi', 'pedigree', 'age', 'label']
# Load dataset
pima = pd.read_csv("diabetes.csv", header=None, names=col_names)
print(pima.head())

#split dataset in features and target variable
feature_cols = ['pregnant', 'insulin', 'bmi', 'age', 'glucose',
'bp', 'pedigree']
X = pima[feature_cols] # Features
y = pima.label # Target variable
# Split dataset into training set and test set
# 70% training and 30% test
X_train, X_test, y_train, y_test = train_test_split(X, y, test_
size=0.3, random_state=1)
```

```
# Create Decision Tree classifer object
clf = DecisionTreeClassifier()
# Train Decision Tree Classifer
clf = clf.fit(X_train,y_train)

#Predict the response for test dataset
y_pred = clf.predict(X_test.drop(0))

# Model accuracy
print("Accuracy:",metrics.accuracy_score(y_test.drop(0),
y_pred))
```

Visualizing the decision tree

The scikit-learn's export_*graphviz* function can be used to display the decision tree. The pydotplus library is also needed for this display function. These libraries are installed using the following commands:

```
pip install graphviz
pip install pydotplus
sudo apt-get install python-pydot
```

The export_graphviz function converts the final decision tree classifier file into what is known as a dot file. The pydotplus application then converts this dot file to a png-formatted file, which may be displayed using the system's Image viewer application.

The following script is named diabetesDT.py and is available from the book's companion web site:

```
# Load all required libraries
import pandas as pd
from sklearn.tree import DecisionTreeClassifier
from sklearn.model_selection import train_test_split
from sklearn.tree import export_graphviz
```

```python
from sklearn.externals.six import StringIO
from sklearn import tree
import pydotplus
import collections

col_names = ['pregnant', 'glucose', 'bp', 'skin', 'insulin',
'bmi', 'pedigree', 'age', 'label']
# Load dataset
pima = pd.read_csv("diabetes.csv", header=None, names=col_names)

#split dataset in features and target variable
feature_cols = ['pregnant', 'insulin', 'bmi', 'age', 'glucose',
'bp', 'pedigree']
X = pima[feature_cols] # Features
y = pima.label # Target variable
# Split dataset into training set and test set
# 70% training and 30% test
X_train, X_test, y_train, y_test = train_test_split(X, y, test_
size=0.3, random_state=1)

# Create Decision Tree classifer object
clf = DecisionTreeClassifier()

# Train Decision Tree Classifer
clf = clf.fit(X_train,y_train)

dot_data = tree.export_graphviz(clf, out_file=None,
filled=True, rounded=True, special_characters=True, feature_
names= feature_cols, class_names=['0','1'])
graph = pydotplus.graph_from_dot_data(dot_data)

colors = ('turquoise', 'orange')
edges = collections.defaultdict(list)
```

```
for edge in graph.get_edge_list():
    edges[edge.get_source()].append(int(edge.get_
    destination()))

for edge in edges:
    edges[edge].sort()
    for i in range(2):
        dest = graph.get_node(str(edges[edge][i]))[0]
        dest.set_fillcolor(colors[i])

graph.write_png('tree.png')
```

You can generate the png tree Image by entering this command:

```
python diabetesDT.py
```

Be a bit patient because this command took about 20 seconds to complete. You will see nothing on the monitor screen other than the prompt reappearing after the script completes running. However, there will be a new Image named tree.png located in the home directory. Figure 2-29 shows this Image.

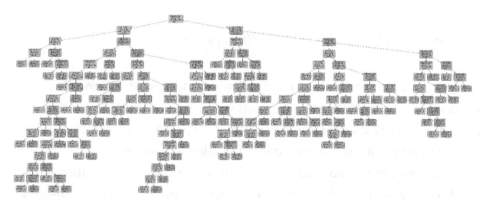

Figure 2-29. *tree.png*

I fully realize that it is impossible to read the extremely small text shown in the Image, which is why I enlarged a small portion of the Image. This portion is shown in Figure 2-30.

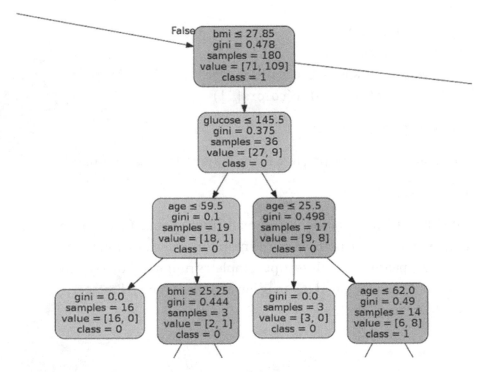

Figure 2-30. *Enlarged portion of the tree Image*

In this decision tree chart, each internal node has a decision rule that splits the data. Gini referred as Gini ratio measures the impurity of the node, which I discussed in the aside. A node is pure when all of its records belong to the same class. Such nodes are called leaf nodes.

The resultant tree created by this script is unpruned. This unpruned tree is essentially unexplainable and not easy to understand. I will discuss how to optimize it by pruning in the next section.

Optimizing a decision tree

There are three hyper-parameters available, which will allow for optimizing the performance of a decision tree classifier. These are

- criterion: optional (default="gini") or Choose attribute selection measure – This parameter allows the selection of different ASMs. Available criteria are "gini" for the Gini index and "entropy" for the information gain.

- splitter: string, optional (default="best") or Split Strategy – This parameter allows the selection of the split strategy. Available strategies are "best" to choose the best split and "random" to choose the best random split.

- max_depth: int or None, optional (default=None) or Maximum Depth of a Tree – This criterion sets the maximum depth of the tree. If None, then nodes are expanded until all the leaves contain less than min_ samples_split samples. A higher value of maximum depth will likely cause overfitting, while a lower value may cause underfitting .

In scikit-learn, the optimization of decision tree classifier is done when the classifier is instantiated. The maximum depth of the tree is used for pre-pruning. The pimaDiabetes.py script was modified to limit the tree depth to 3 and the ASM was changed to entropy. The following code changes were made to the script to accomplish this optimization:

```
# Create Decision Tree classifer object
clf = DecisionTreeClassifier(criterion="entropy", max_depth=3)
```

This script was rerun, and new accuracy score of 0.7705627705627706 was obtained. This 77% score is better than the 67.5% score obtained when no performance arguments were entered.

The diabetesDT.py was also rerun with these new performance arguments. The tree diagram was relabeled tree1.png to differentiate from the initial version. Figure 2-31 shows the new tree diagram using the optimized hyper-parameters.

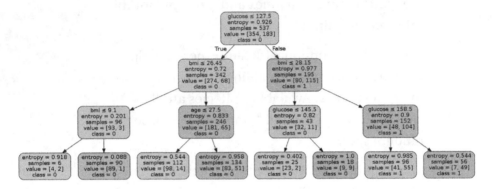

Figure 2-31.   *tree1.png*

This pruned model is much less complex and easier to understand than the previous decision tree graph.

Pros and cons for decision trees

Pros

- Decision trees are easy to interpret and visualize.

- They can easily capture non-linear patterns.

- They require less data preprocessing from the user.

- They can be used for feature engineering such as predicting missing values suitable for variable selection.

- Decision trees have no assumptions about data distribution because they are non-parametric.

Cons

- They are sensitive to noisy data. They can easily overfit due to noisy data.

- Small variations (or variance) in data can result in a different decision tree.

- Decision trees can be biased with an imbalanced dataset. It is recommended that the dataset be balanced out before creating the decision tree.

CHAPTER 3

Exploration of ML data models: Part 2

This chapter is a continuation of the discussions and demonstrations of basic ML data models that started in the previous chapter. I presented ten data models at the beginning of the previous chapter, and these were

Linear regression

Logistic regression

K-nearest neighbors classifier

Gaussian Naive Bayesian

Decision tree classifier

Principal component analysis

Linear discriminant analysis

Support vector machines

Learning vector quantization

Bagging and random forests

The first five was covered in the previous chapter, while the remaining five will be covered in this chapter. Please do not infer any relative importance to the models because of the discussion order. In each case, I specifically discuss when and how to use each model.

© Donald J. Norris 2020
D. J. Norris, *Machine Learning with the Raspberry Pi*,
https://doi.org/10.1007/978-1-4842-5174-4_3

Principal component analysis

Principal component analysis (PCA) is a powerful algorithm, which is used for linear transformations and dimensionality reduction. It is commonly used in many areas including computer vision applications and financial transactions.

The main objective in using a PCA algorithm is to reduce data dimensionality by transforming a large set of variables into a smaller one which still contains most of the information present in the large dataset. Boiled down to a few words, PCA creates small datasets which are easier to handle and facilitates data analysis and are far more compatible for use with other ML algorithms. In summary, the central idea of PCA is to reduce the number of variables in a dataset while preserving as much information as possible. PCA also performs a data compression function, which I describe in the code explanatory section.

The PCA algorithm tends to use less memory because it is computationally efficient. Additionally, PCA has good visualization functions, which help the user understand the final results.

There are six steps that should be followed when attempting to perform a PCA:

1. Standardize the data.

2. Use the standardized data to create a covariance matrix.

3. Use the resulting matrix to calculate eigenvector (principal components) and their corresponding Eigenvalues. Alternatively, the singular vector decomposition (SVD) can be applied.

4. Sort the Eigenvalues in descending order by its and choose the k Eigenvectors which explain the most variance within the data (larger Eigenvalue means the feature explains more variance).

5.   Create a new projection matrix W.

6.   Transform the original dataset X via W to obtain a
     k-dimensional sub-space Y.

I realize that there are some strange and unknown terms in the preceding process which might confuse and perhaps frighten some readers. Don't worry; they will be discussed and clarified in the following discussion and demonstration.

PCA script discussion

The first step in this demonstration is to load the dataset, which will be used. The dataset I will be using is the classic Iris dataset, which I used in the previous chapter. It is available from the following web site. The file is available with extension data. You just need to change the extension to csv.

`https://archive.ics.uci.edu/ml/datasets/Iris`

After you download the file, be sure to delete the first row, which contains the original column headers. The script will fail if you do not do this.

This Iris dataset contains measurements for 150 Iris flowers from three different species.

The three classes in the Iris dataset are

1.   Iris setosa (n = 50)

2.   Iris versicolor (n = 50)

3.   Iris virginica (n = 50)

The four features in each of the classes are

1.   Sepal length in cm

2.   Sepal width in cm

3.   Petal length in cm

4.   Petal width in cm

The following is a complete listing for a Python script named pcaDemo.py, which will accomplish a complete PCA analysis with visualizations. I also provide additional explanatory comments for those code portions as needed. This script is available from the book's companion web site:

```
# Import required libraries
import matplotlib.pyplot as plt
import numpy as np
import pandas as pd
import seaborn as sns
from sklearn import decomposition
from sklearn.preprocessing import scale
from sklearn.decomposition import PCA
from sklearn.preprocessing import StandardScaler

df = pd.read_csv('iris.csv', header=None, sep=',')
df.columns=['sepal_length', 'sepal_width', 'petal_length',
'petal_width', 'class']
df.dropna(how="all", inplace=True) # Drops empty line at EOF
# Show the first 5 records
print(df.head())

f, ax = plt.subplots(1, 4, figsize=(10,5))
vis1 = sns.distplot(df['sepal_length'],bins=10, ax= ax[0])
vis2 = sns.distplot(df['sepal_width'],bins=10, ax=ax[1])
vis3 = sns.distplot(df['petal_length'],bins=10, ax= ax[2])
vis4 = sns.distplot(df['petal_width'],bins=10, ax=ax[3])
plt.show()

# split data table into data X and class labels y
X = df.ix[:,0:4].values
y = df.ix[:,4].values
```

```python
# Standardize the data
X_std = StandardScaler().fit_transform(X)

# Compute the covariance matrix
mean_vec = np.mean(X_std, axis=0)
cov_mat = (X_std -mean_vec).T.dot(X_std - mean_vec) /
(X_std.shape[0] - 1)
print('Covariance matrix \n%s' %cov_mat)

# Compute the Eigenvectors and Eigenvalues
cov_mat = np.cov(X_std.T)
eig_vals, eig_vecs = np.linalg.eig(cov_mat)
print('Eigenvectors \n%s' %eig_vecs)
print('Eigenvalues \n%s' %eig_vals)

eig_pairs = [(np.abs(eig_vals[i]), eig_vecs[:,i]) for i in
range(len(eig_vals))]
eig_pairs.sort()
eig_pairs.reverse()
print('Eigenvalues in descending order:')
for i in eig_pairs:
    print(i[0])

# Compute the Eigenvalue ratios
tot = sum(eig_vals)
var_exp = [(i / tot)*100 for i in sorted(eig_vals,
reverse=True)]
cum_var_exp = np.cumsum(var_exp)
print('Eigenvalue ratios:%s' %cum_var_exp)

#Create the W matrix
matrix_w = np.hstack((eig_pairs[0][1].reshape(4,1),
                      eig_pairs[1][1].reshape(4,1)))
print('Matrix W:\n', matrix_w)
```

```
# Transform the X_std dataset to the sub-space Y
Y = X_std.dot(matrix_w)
features = ['sepal_length', 'sepal_width', 'petal_length',
'petal_width']

# Create a scatter plot for PC1 vs PC2
x = df.loc[:,features].values

x = StandardScaler().fit_transform(x)

pca = PCA(n_components=2)

principalComponents = pca.fit_transform(x)

principalDf = pd.DataFrame(data=principalComponents,
columns=['principal component 1','principal component 2'])
finalDf = pd.concat([principalDf, df[['class']]], axis=1)

fig = plt.figure(figsize=(8,8))
ax = fig.add_subplot(1,1,1)
ax.set_xlabel('Principal Component 1', fontsize=15)
ax.set_ylabel('Principal Component 2', fontsize=15)
ax.set_title('2 Component PCA', fontsize=20)
targets = ['setosa', 'versicolor', 'virginica']
colors = ['r', 'g', 'b']
for target, color in zip(targets, colors):
    indicesToKeep = finalDf['class'] == target
    ax.scatter(finalDf.loc[indicesToKeep, 'principal component
    1'], finalDf.loc[indicesToKeep, 'principal component 2'],
    c=color, s=50)

ax.legend(targets)
ax.grid
plt.show()
```

The following discussions expand upon what is happening in various parts of this script. I have not commented on the portions that I feel you should already be comfortable reading and understanding such as the library imports portion. In addition, I will only show the beginning and ending of the code segments to save space, unless the code is three lines or less. Do not forget to make sure the extension of the downloaded file is csv.

```
df = pd.read_csv('iris.csv', header=None, sep=',')
.
.
print(df.head())
```

A Pandas DataFrame named df is first created in this code from the CSV file located in the current directory. The column names (attributes) are then initialized, a bit of housekeeping is done, and then the head or first five records are displayed just to ensure that the DataFrame was properly created.

```
f, ax = plt.subplots(1, 4, figsize=(10,5))
.
.
plt.show()
```

This code portion creates a series of univariate plots for the first four attributes. It is always a good idea to review the original data distributions to more understand what you are dealing with. These plots are shown in the results section.

```
# split data table into data X and class labels y
X = df.ix[:,0:4].values
y = df.ix[:,4].values
```

The data needs to be split into an attribute set named *X* and class label set named *y* before standardization happens.

```
X_std = StandardScaler().fit_transform(X)
```

This code represents step 1 in the PCA process, which is to standardize the input data. If you reviewed the input dataset, you would quickly realize that the data has different scales. Standardizing the data helps maximize data variances for principal components (Eigenvectors). Without standardization a variable with a value range of 0 to 100 would have an inordinate influence when covariances were computed as compared to a variable with a 0 to 10 range. Standardization reduces any chances of inadvertent bias being introduced into the analysis. The generic standardization equation is

$$z = \frac{value - mean}{standard\ deviation}$$

In this case, all the data is transformed onto a unit scale with a mean of 0 and a variance and standard deviation of 1. Unit scale transformations are often useful to obtain maximal performance for many different ML algorithms.

```
mean_vec = np.mean(X_std, axis=0)
cov_mat = (X_std -mean_vec).T.dot(X_std - mean_vec) / (X_std.
shape[0] - 1)
print('Covariance matrix \n%s' %cov_mat)
```

Step 2 of the PCA process is to instantiate a covariance matrix. The covariance matrix is a $n \times n$ symmetric matrix (where n is the number of dimensions) that has entries for all the covariances associated with all possible pairs of the initial variables. Notice that the standardized dataset is used in this computation. Incidentally, the covariance of a standardized dataset is equivalent to the correlation matrix of that same dataset. This means the dataset correlation matrix could be used in the PCA process in lieu of the covariance matrix.

Two facts about the covariance matrix should also be helpful for your understanding:

- A positive value means two variables increase or decrease together. This is also known as correlated.

- A negative value means as one variable increases, the other decreases. This is also known as inversely correlated.

```
cov_mat = np.cov(X_std.T)
.
.
print('Eigenvalues \n%s' %eig_vals)
```

Step 3 in the PCA process is to compute the Eigenvectors and Eigenvalues related to the input dataset. These computations can be accomplished in one of three ways:

- Using the covariance matrix

- Using the correlation matrix

- Using singular value decomposition (SVD)

The covariance matrix is often used when the attribute values are similar, and the correlation matrix is used when attribute values are on different scales. However, as I explained earlier, the standardized covariance matrix is also equivalent to the correlation matrix, so basically either matrix can be used. In this code, the covariance matrix is used because the data has already been standardized and it is easier to compute the covariance matrix than the correlation matrix.

The numpy library makes it easy to compute the Eigenvectors and Eigenvalues. The `np.linalg.eig(cov_mat)` method returns these as two lists named `eig_vecs` and `eig_vals`. Eigenvectors and Eigenvalues are always paired, meaning a vector always has a value.

A key point to realize is that the `eig_vecs` are the principal components. Principal components are new variables constructed as linear combinations or mixtures of the original variables. These new variables are uncorrelated, and the majority of information held by the original variables is compressed into the first few principal components. That is why PCA is often described as a data compression algorithm. One important point to stress is that principal components don't have any real-world meaning because they are built from linear combinations of the original dataset variables. Viewing principal components from a geometric perspective yields the following:

Principal components represent data directions (i.e. vectors) that explain a maximal amount of variance.

The larger the variance carried by a vector, the larger the dispersion of the data points along it. In addition, the larger the dispersion along a vector, the more the information it carries. To simplify this concept, just think of principal components as new axes that provide the optimum angle to see and evaluate the data so that the differences between the observations are better visible.

Ranking the Eigenvectors in order of their Eigenvalues, highest to lowest, yields the principal components in order of significance.

Finally, the SVD algorithm is another computationally efficient way to compute Eigenvectors and Eigenvalues.

```
eig_pairs = [(np.abs(eig_vals[i]), eig_vecs[:,i]) for i in
.
.
for i in eig_pairs:
    print(i[0])
```

This is step 4 in the PCA process that ranks the Eigenvectors in order of their Eigenvalues, highest to lowest, which yields the principal components in order of significance. Eigenvectors with the lowest Eigenvalues contain the least amount of information concerning inherent data distributions.

```
tot = sum(eig_vals)
 .

 .

print('Eigenvalue ratios:%s' %cum_var_exp)
```

This code portion creates a list of the cumulative effect each Eigenvector contributes to the overall variance. Users should use this list to determine an optimum k value. You will shortly see in the results section that a k = 2 value accounts for over 95% of the variance in the dataset. This is a great result because the data can be easily visualized.

```
#Create the W matrix
matrix_w = np.hstack((eig_pairs[0][1].reshape(4,1),
                       eig_pairs[1][1].reshape(4,1)))
print('Matrix W:\n', matrix_w)
```

This code is step 5, which creates the **W matrix** that is needed for the final step.

```
# Transform the X_std dataset to the sub-space Y
Y = X_std.dot(matrix_w)
```

This is the sixth and final step in the PCA process where the standardized dataset is transformed into a k-dimensional sub-space named matrix Y.

```
x = df.loc[:,features].values
 .

 .

plt.show()
```

This code portion creates a scatter plot showing the data points plotted against principal components 1 and 2. This plot should provide the user an excellent way to visualize the data regarding any latent data patterns that are not observable using ordinary 2D feature scatter plots. Recall that the original dataset has four features, which have now been reduced to 2D by the PCA algorithm, allowing for this plot to be created. A plot like this is one of the key reasons to use PCA for data modeling.

PCA demonstration

First ensure that the iris.csv file is in the same directory as the script and that the first record in the csv file has been deleted as I discussed previously. The script is run by entering this command:

```
python pcaDemo.py
```

Figure 3-1 shows the univariate plots resulting from running this script.

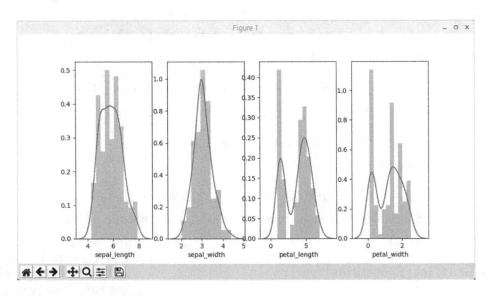

Figure 3-1. *Univariate plots*

The plots clearly indicate that the sepal values tend to more of a Gaussian distribution, while the petal values tend to more of a multi-modal distribution. These observations should be kept in mind when considering the appropriate data models to use with this dataset. Both these distributions are compatible with this PCA data model.

Figure 3-2 shows the numerical results from the script.

```
                                    pi@raspberrypi: ~                          _ □ ✗
 File  Edit  Tabs  Help
(py3cv4) pi@raspberrypi:~ $ python pcaDemo.py
    sepal_length  sepal_width  petal_length  petal_width    class
0            5.1          3.5           1.4          0.2  setosa
1            4.9          3.0           1.4          0.2  setosa
2            4.7          3.2           1.3          0.2  setosa
3            4.6          3.1           1.5          0.2  setosa
4            5.0          3.6           1.4          0.2  setosa
Covariance matrix
[[ 1.00671141 -0.11010327  0.87760486  0.82344326]
 [-0.11010327  1.00671141  0.42333836  0.350937  ]
 [ 0.87760486 -0.42333835  1.00671141  0.96921855]
 [ 0.82344326 -0.358937    0.96921855  1.00671141]]
Eigenvectors
[[ 0.52237162 -0.37231836 -0.72101681  0.26199559]
 [-0.26335492 -0.92555649  0.24203288 -0.12413481]
 [ 0.58125401 -0.02109478  0.14089226 -0.80115427]
 [ 0.56561105 -0.06541577  0.6338014   0.52354627]]
Eigenvalues
[2.93035378 0.92740362 0.14834223 0.02074601]
Eigenvalues in descending order:
2.9303537755893183
0.9274036215173417
0.14834222648816393
0.02074601399559003
Eigenvalue ratios:[ 72.77045209  95.80097536  99.48480732 100.       ]
Matrix W:
 [[ 0.52237162 -0.37231836]
 [-0.26335492 -0.92555649]
 [ 0.58125401 -0.02109478]
 [ 0.56561105 -0.06541577]]
(py3cv4) pi@raspberrypi:~ $ ▯
```

***Figure 3-2.** Numerical results*

While the interim results are useful, the key result to be closely examined is the Eigenvalue ratios list. This list shows the cumulative variance percentages associated with the four principal components or Eigenvectors. Notice that the second value in the list is 95.8%, which means the first two principal components are responsible for over 95% of the measured variance. This means that only two vectors are responsible for carrying most of the dataset information. This translates to having k = 2.

This is a great result that will allow for a very reduced matrix to be created that will still represent the majority of the information contained in the original dataset.

Table 3-1 shows the covariance matrix from the figure, which allows me to comment on several concepts that you should know.

Table 3-1. *Covariance matrix*

	Sepal length	**Sepal width**	**Petal length**	**Petal width**
Sepal length	1.00	−0.11	0.88	0.82
Sepal width	−0.11	1.00	−0.42	−0.36
Petal length	0.88	−0.42	1.00	0.97
Petal width	0.82	−0.36	0.97	1.00

The first fact to know is that each table value is also the correlation coefficient between the intersecting features. The main diagonal consists of all 1s because that is the autocorrelation coefficient or the result of computing a correlation on the same variable. The second fact is that correlation is a distributive function, meaning that the order of the variables is not a factor in the result. This results in a perfectly symmetric matrix as you can see from examining the table.

There are a few high correlation values in the table (ignoring the diagonal), which indicates that the dataset contains a good deal of redundant information. This result would also mean that a PCA would provide further insight into any hidden or latent patterns existing in the dataset, which should be of interest to the user.

Figure 3-3 is an important one for it does show the hidden patterns within this set.

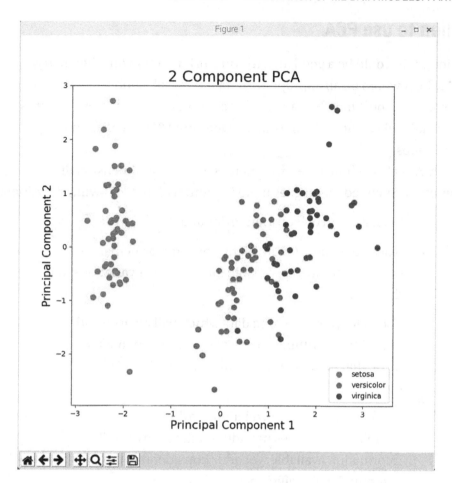

Figure 3-3. *Principal component scatter plot*

This figure is a scatter plot for the first two principal components that contribute to almost 96% of the information contained in the dataset. You should easily observe that the Setosa species is set apart quite distinctly from the other two species. The data point clusters for the two remaining species are adjoining but still distinguishable from each other. I know that observing this in a grayscale Image from the book is next to impossible, but take my word for it that the clusters do adjoin. These observations are simply not possible using the conventional 2D scatter plots as you can observe for yourself by reviewing the Iris dataset plots from Chapter 2.

149

When to use PCA

I thought it would be a good idea to add a brief section on when to use PCA. PCA would be an appropriate data model selection when there is reason to suspect that the dataset may contain hidden or latent patterns not readily observable when using conventional 2D visualization techniques.

PCA is also helpful whenever there is a need for dimensionality reduction. Such reduction goes hand in hand with the following situations:

- Visualization of high-dimensional data.

- Noise reduction. Often, higher-ordered principal components are responsible for only small variations in the data.

- Useful for preprocessing data which will be used with other ML algorithms. Those algorithms can include those that function better with smaller dimensioned datasets.

- Useful for reducing correlations within the dataset. Correlated data does not add much to the overall information available, yet adds considerably to computational inefficiency.

Linear discriminant analysis

Linear discriminant analysis (LDA) is very similar to principal component analysis (PCA), which I discussed in the previous section. One big difference is that while PCA seeks to determine those axes or principal components that maximize the variance in the data, LDA seeks those axes which maximize the separation between classes. I strongly recommend that you first read the PCA sections before reading the LDA sections because I will use terms without explanation in these sections that I first introduced and explained in the PCA sections.

LDA, like PCA, is a dimensional reduction algorithm, but it is supervised. I will shortly go into what is meant by supervised in this context. LDA projects a dataset onto a lower-dimensional space while increasing class separability. The increased class separability reduces the probability of overfitting from happening. LDA also improves computation efficiency. The ability to limit overfitting gives LDA a distinct advantage over the PCA algorithm.

Because PCA and LDA appear so similar, I have included Figure 3-4 which highlights some significant differences between these two algorithms.

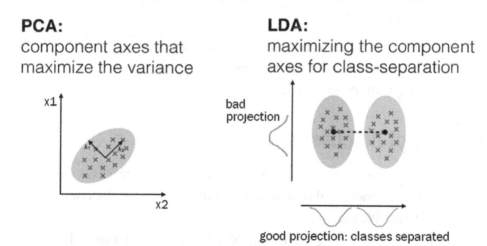

Figure 3-4. *Differences between PCA and LDA*

PCA is an "unsupervised" algorithm, since it does not use class labels and the main purpose is to compute the axes or principal components that will maximize the variance in a dataset. On the other hand, LDA is "supervised" and uses the class data in order to compute the axes or linear discriminants that maximize the separation between multiple classes.

There are five steps involved with the LDA process. These are

1. Compute d-dimensional mean vectors for different classes from the dataset, where d is the dimension of feature space.

2. Compute in-between-class and within-class scatter matrices.

3. Compute Eigenvectors and paired Eigenvalues for the scatter matrices.

4. Choose k Eigenvectors corresponding to top k Eigenvalues to form a transformation matrix of dimension d x k.

5. Transform the d-dimensional feature space X to k-dimensional feature space X_lda via the transformation matrix.

LDA script discussion

This demonstration will use the same Iris dataset used in the PCA demonstration. However, this script will automatically load the dataset as compared to the PCA script.

The following is a complete listing for a Python script named ldaTest. py, which will accomplish a complete LDA with visualizations. There is an additional feature in this script that I wish to point out. Near the script's end, I demonstrate how to perform an LDA using only the sklearn LDA module and not going through all the steps as was done in the preceding script portion.

As usual, I also provide additional explanatory comments for those code portions as needed. This script is available from the book's companion web site:

```python
#Import required libraries
import numpy as np
import pandas as pd
import matplotlib.pyplot as plt
import seaborn as sns
from sklearn.preprocessing import StandardScaler
from sklearn.discriminant_analysis import
LinearDiscriminantAnalysis

np.set_printoptions(precision=4)

#Read dataset
file_path = "https://raw.githubusercontent.com/bot13956/linear-
discriminant-analysis-iris-dataset/master/iris.data.csv"
df = pd.read_csv(file_path, header=None)
df.head()

#Encode categorical class labels
from sklearn.preprocessing import LabelEncoder
class_le = LabelEncoder()
y = class_le.fit_transform(df[4].values)

#Standardize features
stdsc = StandardScaler()
X_train_std = stdsc.fit_transform(df.iloc[:,range(0,4)].values)

# Construct within-class covariant scatter matrix S_W
S_W = np.zeros((4,4))
for i in range(3):
    S_W += np.cov(X_train_std[y==i].T)

#Construct between-class scatter matrix S_B
N=np.bincount(y) # number of samples for given class
vecs=[]
```

```python
[vecs.append(np.mean(X_train_std[y==i],axis=0)) for i in
range(3)] # class means
mean_overall = np.mean(X_train_std, axis=0) # overall mean
S_B=np.zeros((4,4))
for i in range(3):
    S_B += N[i]*(((vecs[i]-mean_overall).reshape(4,1)).
    dot(((vecs[i]-mean_overall).reshape(1,4))))

# Compute sorted eigenvalues and eigenvectors of
# inverse(S_W)dot(S_B)
eigen_vals, eigen_vecs = np.linalg.eig(np.linalg.inv(S_W).
dot(S_B))
eigen_pairs = [(np.abs(eigen_vals[i]), eigen_vecs[:,i]) for i
in range(len(eigen_vals))]
eigen_pairs = sorted(eigen_pairs,key=lambda k: k[0],
reverse=True)
print('Eigenvalues in decreasing order:\n')
for eigen_val in eigen_pairs:
    print(eigen_val[0])

# Plot the main LDA components
tot = sum(eigen_vals.real)
discr = [(i / tot) for i in sorted(eigen_vals.real,
reverse=True)]
cum_discr = np.cumsum(discr)
plt.bar(range(1, 5), discr, width=0.2,alpha=0.5, align='center'
,label='individual "discriminability"')
plt.step(range(1, 5), cum_discr, where='mid',label='cumulative
"discriminability"')
plt.ylabel('Discriminant ratio')
plt.xlabel('Linear Discriminants')
plt.ylim([-0.1, 1.1])
```

```python
plt.legend(loc='best')
plt.show()

#Project original features onto the new feature space
W=np.hstack((eigen_pairs[0][1][:, ].reshape(4,1),eigen_pairs[1]
[1][:, ].reshape(4,1))).real
X_train_lda = X_train_std.dot(W)

# List and plot transformed features in LDA sub-space
data=pd.DataFrame(X_train_lda)
data['class']=y
data.columns=["LD1","LD2","class"]
data.head()
markers = ['s', 'x','o']
sns.lmplot(x="LD1", y="LD2", data=data, markers=markers,fit_
reg=False, hue='class', legend=False)
plt.legend(loc='upper center')
plt.show()

#LDA implementation using scikit-learn
lda = LinearDiscriminantAnalysis(n_components=2)
X_train_lda = lda.fit_transform(X_train_std, y)

# List and plot the scikit-learn LDA results
data=pd.DataFrame(X_train_lda)
data['class']=y
data.columns=["LD1","LD2","class"]
data.head()
markers = ['s', 'x','o']
colors = ['r', 'b','g']
sns.lmplot(x="LD1", y="LD2", data=data, hue='class',
markers=markers,fit_reg=False,legend=False)
plt.legend(loc='upper center')
plt.show()
```

The following are explanatory discussions concerning various code segments in the preceding script which introduce new concepts not covered in the PCA sections. In addition, I will only show the beginning and ending of the code segments to save space, unless the code is three lines or less.

```
from sklearn.preprocessing import LabelEncoder
class_le = LabelEncoder()
y = class_le.fit_transform(df[4].values)
```

The class string values are converted into numeric values for easier handling in the script. The sklearn LabelEncoder module accomplishes this task.

```
S_W = np.zeros((4,4))
for i in range(3):
    S_W += np.cov(X_train_std[y==i].T)
```

A 4 x 4 matrix S_W is created that represents within-class covariances.

```
N=np.bincount(y) # number of samples for given class
.
.
mean_overall).reshape(4,1)).dot(((vecs[i]-mean_overall).
reshape(1,4))))
```

A 4 x 4 matrix S_W is created that represents between-class covariances.

```
eigen_vals, eigen_vecs = np.linalg.eig(np.linalg.inv(S_W).
dot(S_B))
.
.
for eigen_val in eigen_pairs:
    print(eigen_val[0])
```

Compute and sort Eigenvectors and Eigenvalues. The sorted Eigenvalues are also listed to the screen.

```
tot = sum(eigen_vals.real)
.

.
plt.show()
```

plots the main LDA components.

```
W=np.hstack((eigen_pairs[0][1][:, ].reshape(4,1),eigen_pairs[1]
[1][:, ].reshape(4,1))).real
X_train_lda = X_train_std.dot(W)
```

projects the original features onto the new feature space.

```
data=pd.DataFrame(X_train_lda)
.

.
plt.show()
```

plots the transformed features into LDA sub-space.

```
lda = LinearDiscriminantAnalysis(n_components=2)
X_train_lda = lda.fit_transform(X_train_std, y)
```

Implement LDA using scikit-learn.

```
data=pd.DataFrame(X_train_lda)
.

.
plt.show()
```

Plot the scikit-learn LDA results.

LDA demonstration

The script is run by entering this command:

```
python ldaTest.py
```

Figure 3-5 shows the sorted Eigenvalues resulting from running this script. You can clearly see that the top two are the only significant values, which also confirm the PCA results for the Iris dataset.

```
pi@raspberrypi: ~                                    _ □ ✕

File  Edit  Tabs  Help
(py3cv4) pi@raspberrypi:~ $ python ldaTest.py
Eigenvalues in decreasing order:

1581.3259321867627
13.600776328162288
4.982128422548999e-13
2.8373051986017588e-14
```

Figure 3-5. *Sorted Eigenvalues*

Figure 3-6 is a plot of the relative magnitudes of the linear discriminants.

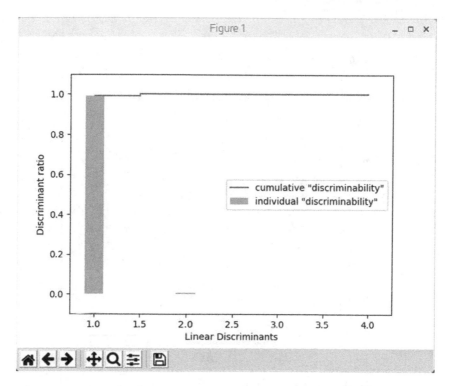

Figure 3-6. *Plot of relative magnitudes for linear discriminants*

The plot is quite skewed due to the huge value of the first linear discriminant as compared to the other three. It is over 99% greater than the second linear discriminant, which is shown as a line in the plot instead of a bar. The remaining one is too negligible to be plotted as you may discern by examining the Eigenvalues from Figure 3-5.

Figure 3-7 is a plot of the transformed Iris dataset against the first two linear discriminants.

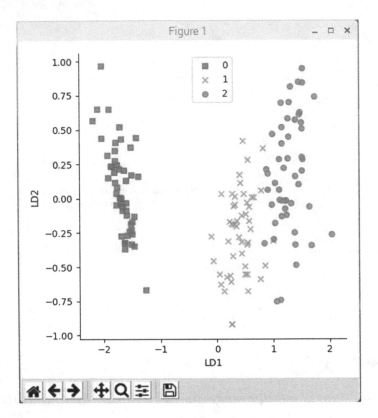

Figure 3-7. *Plot of the transformed Iris dataset*

The important takeaway from this plot is that each of the Iris classes that are now represented by numbers in this plot is distinctly separated along the linear discriminant 1 (LD1) axis. This is always an optimum result when applying the LDA algorithm. You should compare this figure with Figure 3-3 from the PCA section to see how close they are to each other. From my visual interpretation, I would say that the LDA plot shows more separation between classes than the PCA plot, but it is a close call.

Figure 3-8 is a plot of the result of using the sklearn LDA module.

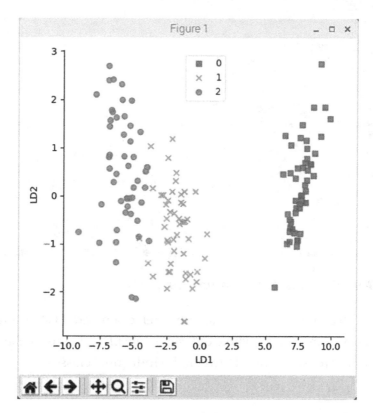

Figure 3-8. *Plot of the results from the sklearn LDA module*

You might consider using this module as a one-step process because all the interim results are not readily available. Nonetheless, the plotted results are quite acceptable and reasonable close to the results obtained by following the step-by-step process.

Comparison of PCA and LDA

I created Figure 3-9, which is a composite plot showing Figures 3-3 and 3-7 side by side to highlight the similarities and differences between the two subject algorithms.

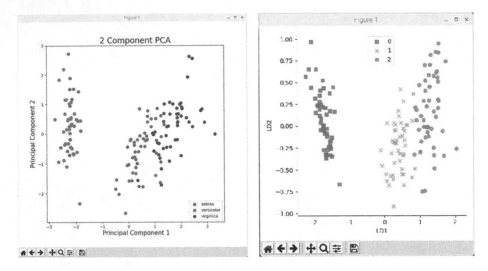

Figure 3-9. *PCA and LDA comparison plots*

Figure 3-9 confirms what has already been discussed. PCA accounts for the most variance in the whole dataset, while LDA gives us the axes that account for the most variance between the individual classes.

Support vector machines

A support vector machine (SVN) data model is focused on classification and to a lesser extent on prediction. The prime SVM objective is to determine the best or optimum boundary that can split data into at least two dimensions (2D). When dealing with more than 2D, the splitting boundary is called a separating hyperplane. The "best" hyperplane is one that creates the widest margins between support vectors. A hyperplane is also commonly referred to as a decision boundary.

I believe the best way to convey the basic concepts of a SVM is through a combination of intuitive discussion with graphics. SVMs can be described in purely mathematical terms, but the math rapidly becomes complex and obviously non-intuitive.

This initial discussion only concerns a linear SVM data model. I will cover the non-linear SVM model after part 1 of the demonstration.

I will start with a simple plot of only six data points, which are divided into two classes of three points each. Figure 3-10 shows these data points.

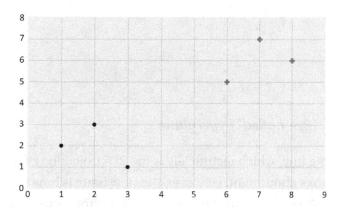

Figure 3-10. *Example data points*

If a new data point was added to the plot, it would intuitively be categorized as belonging to the class it was nearest. Of course, applying the KNN data model could accomplish that task easily. The issue with using the KNN model is that the Euclidean distance must be calculated for every single data point. This is not a problem for this tiny dataset; however, KNN does not scale up very well when dealing with large datasets, despite being fairly reliable and accurate. The SVM changes the whole viewpoint because it best fits a hyperplane to divide the dataset. Once the decision boundary is computed, any new data is automatically classified depending on its boundary side location. The decision boundary remains fixed unless the dataset is re-trained. All this means is the SVM easily scales to accommodate new data unlike the KNN model.

The natural question now arises on how is the best dividing hyperplane determined? It can be "eye-balled" as shown in Figure 3-11.

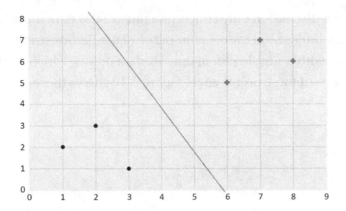

Figure 3-11. *"Eye-balled" hyperplane*

The dividing line, which technically is the 2D projection of the hyperplane, looks about right. However, the new issue is how to find the support vectors? The key to finding the support vectors is to realize that closest class data points to the decision boundary will also be part of the support vectors. Figure 3-12 shows the graphical rendering for the SVM support vectors for this example.

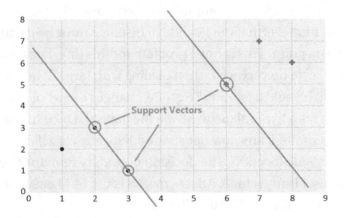

Figure 3-12. *Support vectors*

Maximally separated lines running through the support vector data points are next created. The position of the decision boundary is determined by the total width, W, as shown in Figure 3-13.

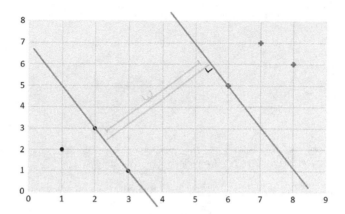

Figure 3-13. *Total width determination*

Now, simply divide W by 2 and the location of the decision boundary is now fixed. This is shown in Figure 3-14.

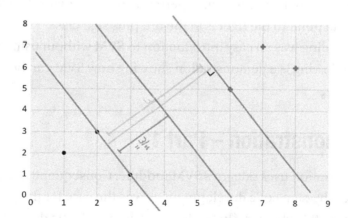

Figure 3-14. *Determine the location for the decision boundary*

Figure 3-15 is a graphical intuition for the SVM model, showing the distance to be maximized between the support vectors and the decision boundary.

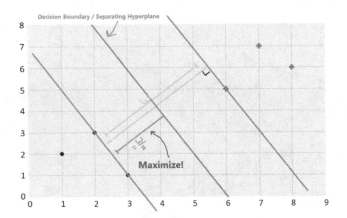

Figure 3-15. *Intuitive graph illustrating the distance to be maximized*

Looking at the figure, it can now be stated that any point to the left of the decision boundary/separating hyperplane is in the black dot class, while any data point to the right is in the red plus sign class.

The preceding was an easy introduction to SVM without using math or code. The following is a demonstration showing how SVM can be used in a beneficial way.

SVM demonstration – Part 1

This demonstration uses sklearn's SVM module. Consequently, there is no need for step-by-step code development as was the case for the previous data models in this chapter. This code uses another classic dataset titled Breast Cancer Wisconsin (Diagnostic) Data Set. It is a multivariate dataset with 30 attributes taken from 569 breast cancer needle biopsies. The attributes are cellular descriptions for both healthy and malignant cells.

Essentially, there will be two classes involved in the dataset, those patients with malignant cells and those free of them. This dataset is part of sklearn's organic dataset, and there is no need to do an explicit download. The dataset is directly imported within the script.

The ultimate objective for this SVM demonstration is to determine the probability that a test record is healthy or not given a specific set of attributes.

This script is named svmDemo1.py and is available from the book's companion web site. I have not included any additional comments because the script is short and the included comments I feel are adequate to explain the code.

```python
# Import required libraries
import pandas as pd
import numpy as np
import matplotlib.pyplot as plt
import seaborn as sns
from sklearn.model_selection import train_test_split
from sklearn.svm import SVC
from sklearn.metrics import classification_report

# Import dataset into a variable named 'cancer'
from sklearn.datasets import load_breast_cancer
cancer = load_breast_cancer()

# Load input features as a DataFrame
df_features = pd.DataFrame(cancer['data'], columns =
cancer['feature_names'])

# Add output variable 'target' into a DataFrame
df_target = pd.DataFrame(cancer['target'], columns =
['Cancer'])
```

```
# Display the first 5 records
print(df_features.head())

# Split the dataset, 70% to train, 30% to test
X_train, X_test, y_train, y_test = train_test_split(df_
features, np.ravel(df_target), test_size=0.30, random_
state=101)

# Instantiate the SVC model. SVC is the sklearn classifier
name.
model = SVC()

# Train the model using the fit method
model.fit(X_train, y_train)

# Test the model using the test dataset
predictions = model.predict(X_test)

# Display the prediction results
print(classification_report(y_test, predictions))
```

The script is run by entering this command:

```
python svmDemo1.py
```

Figure 3-16 shows the results of running the script.

```
                          pi@raspberrypi: ~                        _  □  ×
 File  Edit  Tabs  Help
(py3cv4) pi@raspberrypi:~ $ python svmDemo1.py
   mean radius   mean texture   ...   worst symmetry   worst fractal dimension
0        17.99          10.38   ...            0.4601                   0.11890
1        20.57          17.77   ...            0.2750                   0.08902
2        19.69          21.25   ...            0.3613                   0.08758
3        11.42          20.38   ...            0.6638                   0.17300
4        20.29          14.34   ...            0.2364                   0.07678

[5 rows x 30 columns]
  'precision', 'predicted', average, warn_for)
             precision    recall  f1-score   support

          0       0.00      0.00      0.00        66
          1       0.61      1.00      0.76       105

  micro avg       0.61      0.61      0.61       171
  macro avg       0.31      0.50      0.38       171
weighted avg      0.38      0.61      0.47       171

(py3cv4) pi@raspberrypi:~ $ []
```

Figure 3-16. *svmDemo1 results*

The first thing you should note is the head result, which shows portions of the first five records in the dataset. There are 30 attributes, which means this is a high-dimensional dataset that a linear hyperplane is attempting to separate. That fact alone should raise warning bells for you. It is about impossible to visualize any single plane that could effectively separate these many data points, especially where many have similar scale. This reality is borne out in the prediction results where the weighted average is 0.38. This is a dismal result that means that only 38% of the test data was correctly predicted. You could have done much better in the long run by simply flipping a coin. What can be done to improve this result? The answer is contained in the following discussion.

SVM demonstration – Part 2

There is a technique used in SVM known as the kernel "trick," which was developed to handle high-dimensional datasets, such as the breast cancer one used in this demonstration. This trick is really not a trick in the sense

169

it is "underhanded" or "devious" but is only intended to accommodate high-dimensional datasets. When data points are not linearly separable in a p-dimensional or finite space, it was proposed to map this space into a much higher-dimensional space. Customized, non-linear hyperplanes can then be constructed using the kernel trick. Every SVM kernel holds a non-linear kernel function. This function helps build a high-dimensional feature space. There are many kernels that have been developed and others currently being researched. This is an extremely active area of research.

I will use an intuitive/graphical approach in explaining the non-linear kernels as I did for the basic SVM concepts because the underlying math for this subject is far too complex and detailed for inclusion in this book.

In Figure 3-17, there are x and o data points in the left-hand side that clearly cannot be separated by a linear plane or line for the 2D case. However, if the data points are transformed by some functionØ, they can be easily separated as shown in the right-hand side of the figure.

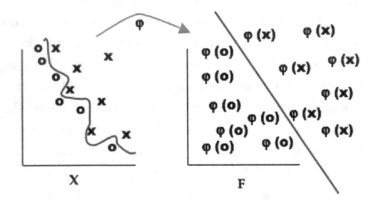

Figure 3-17. *Transformed dataset*

The main idea is to improve class linear separation by mapping the original dataset to a higher-dimensional space. In Figure 3-18, the original data points in the upper left side of the figure cannot be separated by a linear function. They can be separated after being mapped by a quadratic function as can be observed by the plot on the right-hand side.

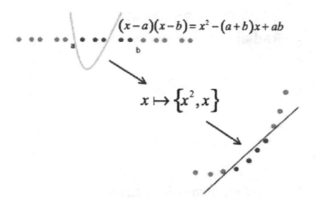

Figure 3-18. *Dataset transformed by a quadratic function*

Figure 3-19 presents another problem where the decision boundary is not readily apparent. The question is what decision function can be used to separate these data points?

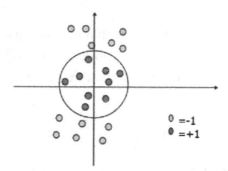

Figure 3-19. *Problematic dataset*

The answer to this problem is using polar coordinates as can be seen in Figure 3-20.

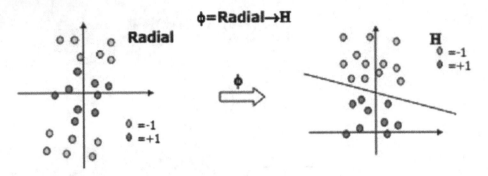

Figure 3-20. *Resolved problematic dataset*

SVM has the following kernels that solve the non-linear dataset problem:

Polynomial kernel – This kernel implements this equation

$$K(x_i, x_j) = (x_i * x_j + 1)^p$$

where p = tunable parameter. Also note that evaluating K only requires 1 addition and 1 exponentiation over the original dot product.

Radial basis function (rbf) – This kernel implements this equation

$$K(x_i, x_j) = e^{-\frac{|x_i - x_j|^2}{2*\sigma^2}}$$

The rbf is also known as the Gaussian function. Figure 3-21 shows an application of the Gaussian function to an example dataset.

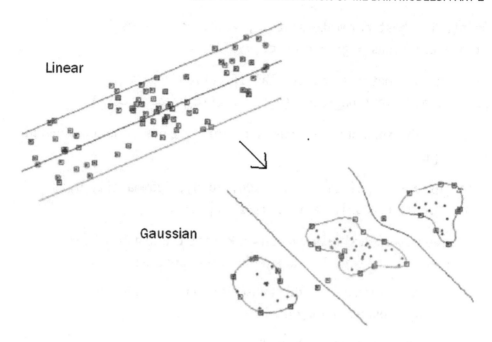

Figure 3-21. *Gaussian function application*

Sigmoid function – This is the sigmoid function, which is also used as an activation function in other data models.

The following script is named svmDemo2.py and is available from the book's companion web site. The listing only shows the additional code, which must be appended to the existing svmDemo1.py script. I have included some explanatory comments after the code.

```
# Gridsearch
param_grid = {'C':[0.1, 1, 10, 100, 1000], 'gamma':[1, 0.1,
0.01, 0.001, 0.0001], 'kernel':['rbf']}

from sklearn.model_selection import GridSearchCV
grid = GridSearchCV(SVC(), param_grid, refit=True, verbose=3)
grid.fit(X_train, y_train)
print('\n')
```

```
print('The best parameters are ', grid.best_params_)
grid_predictions = grid.predict(X_test)
```

```
from sklearn.metrics import classification_report
print(classification_report(y_test, grid_predictions))
```

These are explanatory comments regarding the new code contained in this script.

```
param_grid = {'C':[0.1, 1, 10, 100, 1000], 'gamma':[1, 0.1,
0.01, 0.001, 0.0001], 'kernel':['rbf']}
```

Three important SVM parameters of kernel, C, and gamma are set in this statement. The kernel parameter has these options:

- linear – Used when the dataset is amenable for linear hyperplane separation

- rbf – Non-linear hyperplane

- poly – Non-linear hyperplane

The C parameter is used in the training phase to specify how much data outliers are taken into account in computing support vectors. A low value for C smooths the decision surface, while a high value permits the SVM model to select more samples as support vectors.

The gamma parameter defines how far the influence of a single training example reaches, with low values meaning "far" and high values meaning "close." The gamma parameter may be interpreted as the inverse of the radius of influence of samples selected by the model as support vectors.

Selecting the appropriate parameters is mainly based on the dataset properties. In this case, the rbf is a good choice for the high-dimensional dataset. Choosing values for C and gamma is a tricky proposition. Fortunately, sklearn provides an iterative approach to selecting these parameters.

```
from sklearn.model_selection import GridSearchCV
grid = GridSearchCV(SVC(), param_grid, refit=True, verbose=3)
grid.fit(X_train, y_train)
print('\n')
print('The best parameters are ', grid.best_params_)
grid_predictions = grid.predict(X_test)
```

The GridSearchCV module generates a grid search object with cross-validation. Two tasks are being done in this code with the dataset, those being cross-validation and (hyper)parameter tuning. Cross-validation is the process of the model using one set of data and testing it using a different set. Parameter tuning is the process of selecting the values for a model's parameters that maximize the accuracy of the model. The object named grid now contains optimum values for both C and gamma parameters resulting from the iterative grid search process. The optimum parameter values are displayed, and a new set of predictions are made using the optimized parameters.

```
from sklearn.metrics import classification_report
print(classification_report(y_test, grid_predictions))
```

The accuracy of the predictions is confirmed using the classification_report module imported from sklearn's metrics library. Recall that I have used this module before in other demonstrations.

The script is run by entering this command:

```
python svmDemo2.py
```

Figure 3-22 shows the results of running the script.

```
                            pi@raspberrypi: ~                          _ □ ✕

 File  Edit  Tabs  Help
 [CV]   kernel=rbf, gamma=0.01, C=1000, score=0.6363636363636364, total=  0.1s
 [CV] kernel=rbf, gamma=0.001, C=1000 ................................
 [CV]   kernel=rbf, gamma=0.001, C=1000, score=0.8947368421052632, total=  0.1s
 [CV] kernel=rbf, gamma=0.001, C=1000 ................................
 [CV]   kernel=rbf, gamma=0.001, C=1000, score=0.9323308270676691, total=  0.1s
 [CV] kernel=rbf, gamma=0.001, C=1000 ................................
 [CV]   kernel=rbf, gamma=0.001, C=1000, score=0.9166666666666666, total=  0.1s
 [CV] kernel=rbf, gamma=0.0001, C=1000 ...............................
 [CV]   kernel=rbf, gamma=0.0001, C=1000, score=0.9097744360902256, total=  0.0s
 [CV] kernel=rbf, gamma=0.0001, C=1000 ...............................
 [CV]   kernel=rbf, gamma=0.0001, C=1000, score=0.9699248120300752, total=  0.0s
 [CV] kernel=rbf, gamma=0.0001, C=1000 ...............................
 [CV]   kernel=rbf, gamma=0.0001, C=1000, score=0.9318181818181818, total=  0.0s
 [Parallel(n_jobs=1)]: Done  75 out of  75 | elapsed:   7.2s finished


 The best parameters are  {'kernel': 'rbf', 'gamma': 0.0001, 'C': 10}
                 precision    recall  f1-score   support

             0       0.95      0.91      0.93        66
             1       0.94      0.97      0.96       105

     micro avg       0.95      0.95      0.95       171
     macro avg       0.95      0.94      0.94       171
  weighted avg       0.95      0.95      0.95       171

 (py3cv4) pi@raspberrypi:~ $ []
```

Figure 3-22. *svmDemo2 results*

The first thing you likely noticed in this figure is the scroll of interim results appearing from the top. This scroll is just a small portion of the 75 steps that were done to compute the final optimized parameters. The last line in the scroll shows that the final values are

kernel = rbf, gamma = 0.0001 and C = 1000.

Obviously, the kernel specification did not change during the iterations, but the other too certainty did. I did review this scroll and determined that the gamma value seemed to influence the final accuracy the most. It wound, being a tiny value, which meant that the radius of influence of samples selected by the model of support vectors was substantial, that is, maximum data points were included in the determination of the support vectors.

The weighted average accuracy displayed on the last line of the results is 0.95 or 95% accuracy. This is a great result and an enormous improvement over the awful 38% result from part 1 of the demonstration.

This result just proves that it is extremely important to use only an appropriate data model that "fits" the original dataset and that any tuning parameters must be optimally adjusted.

Learning vector quantization

I will begin this discussion by first crediting Dr. Jason Brownlee for his fine August 2018 blog titled "How to Implement Learning Vector Quantization from Scratch with Python" from which much of the code and key concepts in this section are based. I have used Jason's blogs in previous discussions, and I find his tutorials very clear and illuminating. I highly recommend you check out his blogs, articles, and e-books.

The learning vector quantization (LVQ) is similar to the k-NN algorithm where predictions are made by finding the closest match to an existing data pattern. The significant difference between the two is that k-NN uses the actual training patterns, while LVQ creates a library of patterns from the training data.

The library of patterns is called a codebook of vectors, and each pattern in the library is called a codebook. Codebook vectors are initialized to randomly selected values from the training dataset. Then, over a number of epochs or training cycles, they are modified to optimally summarize the training data through the use of a learning algorithm. This learning algorithm processes one training record at a time by finding the optimum match among the codebook vectors. The training record is modified so that it is "closer" to the codebook vector if they are both from the same class or moved "further away" if they are from different classes. I will shortly explain the distance metaphor to help clarify this concept of moving closer or further away from data items.

Predictions only commence after all the codebook vectors have been processed. Predictions are made using the k-NN algorithm with k = 1.

LVQ basic concepts

The first item that needs to be discussed is the dataset that will be used in all the following sections, including the demonstration. The dataset is a collection of numerical records resulting from radar "soundings" of Earth's atmosphere. Each record describes properties of the return radar signal, which might include significant measurements of the ionosphere. The purpose of the data model is to predict whether or not a particular record contains any significant ionosphere measurements.

There are 351 records in the dataset with each record containing 34 numerical data points. These points are grouped into 17 pairs for every radar return signal with numerical value range of 0 to 1 for each value. The target class has attribute values of "g" for good or "b" for bad.

The dataset is named inosphere.csv, and it can be downloaded from

`https://archive.ics.uci.edu/ml/datasets/Ionosphere`

Euclidean distance

The concept to be discussed is that of Euclidean distance. I realized I have used this term in previous discussions, and it sometimes means different things depending on the context. In this case, the ionosphere dataset is composed of rows of numbers. The Euclidean distance is defined as the square root of the sum of the squared differences between the two vectors where the vectors are constituted from the row data. The equation for the distance measurement is

$$distance = \sqrt{\sum_{i}^{N}\left(x_{1,i} - x_{2,i}\right)^2}$$

where

x_1 = first row of data

x_2 = second row of data

i = column index

N = number of columns (attributes)

The smaller the Euclidean distance, the more similar the two data records are. Conversely, the larger the distance, the more dissimilar the records are. If the distance is 0, then the records are identical.

Best matching unit

The best matching unit (BMU) is the codebook vector that is most similar to a new data record. Locating the BMU for a new record requires that the Euclidean distance be computed between the new record and every codebook vector. That is done using the distance measurement discussed previously. Once that is done, all the distances are sorted and the codebook vector associated with the least distance value is the most similar to the new record.

The preceding described process is the same way predictions are done with LVQ. The KNN algorithm with k = 1 is used to locate the most similar codebook vector to the unknown record. The associated class value of "g" or "b" is returned.

Training codebook vectors

The first step in training the codebook vectors is to initialize all the vectors with patterns constructed from random features found in the training dataset. Once initialized, the vectors must be modified to optimally summarize the training dataset. These modifications happen in an iterative fashion. At the top level, the process is repeated for a fixed number of epochs using the complete training set. Within each epoch, each training pattern is used only once to update the cookbook vectors. A BMU is detected for every training pattern and updated. Any difference between the training pattern and the BMU is computed and recorded as an error. Class values for the BMU and training pattern are then compared, and if found, matching will cause the recorded error to be added to the BMU, which brings it "closer" to the training pattern. Conversely, if the class values do not match, then the error is subtracted, which causes the BMU to be "pushed" further from the training pattern.

The learning rate (LR) parameter controls how much the BMU is adjusted. This parameter is a weighting factor that affects the change amount applied to all BMUs. For example, if the LR is 0.20 or 20%, this would mean only 20% of the detected error would be applied to the BMU. In addition, the LR itself is adjusted so that it has maximum effect during the first epoch and a lesser effect in subsequent epochs. This diminishing effect is called linear decay learning rate schedule and is also widely used for artificial neural networks.

LVQ demonstration

Before starting my customary demonstration, I thought it would be appropriate to introduce the Zero Rule algorithm. It is usually impossible to determine which data model will work best for your particular problem domain before actually trying various models. Consequentially, it is important to create a performance baseline when starting the work on your problem. A baseline performance provides a reference, which can be used as a comparison with any data models applied to the problem. Without a baseline, it is impossible to realize how well a particular model has achieved. Baselines for both classification and regression are created by the Zero Rule algorithm, which is also known as ZeroR or 0-R.

Categorical values are predicted in a classification prediction model. The Zero Rule algorithm predicts the class value that has the most observations in the training dataset. I will demonstrate how to apply the Zero Rule algorithm to the ionosphere dataset using the Waikato Environment for Knowledge Analysis (*Weka*) suite of machine learning software. The main user interface is called the *Explorer*. Weka is a Java-based application that can be run as a jar file on the RasPi. Weka may be downloaded from

```
https://sourceforge.net/projects/weka/
```

In order to use the ionosphere dataset, it must be in an arff format. The dataset titled ionosphere.arff can be downloaded from this page:

```
https://github.com/renatopp/arff-datasets/find/master
```

Before running the application, ensure that the ionosphere.arff is in the same directory as the Weka jar file. The application is then started by entering this command. Note that Weka is also available to download with the exe extension for Windows so you can use the installer for installing Weka.

```
java -jar weka.jar
```

The following seven steps should be followed to obtain the baseline results:

1. Start the Weka GUI Chooser.

2. Click the "Explorer" button to open the Weka Explorer interface.

3. Load the ionosphere dataset *ionosphere.arff* file.

4. Click the "Classify" tab to open the classification tab.

5. Select the ZeroR algorithm (it should be selected by default).

6. Select the "Cross-validation" Test options (it should be selected by default).

7. Click the "Start" button to evaluate the algorithm on the dataset.

The Weka Explorer results are shown in Figure 3-23.

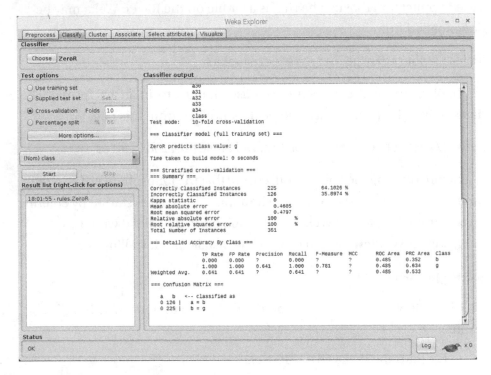

Figure 3-23. *Weka Explorer results*

The ZeroR algorithm predicts the *"g"* value for all instances as it is the majority class, and achieves an accuracy of 64.1%. For any machine learning algorithm to demonstrate that it has a better performance on this problem, it must achieve an accuracy better than this value.

The following script implements all the concepts presented in the basic concepts section. It is named lvqDemo.py and is available from the book's companion web site. I also present additional explanatory comments after the listing. Remember to make the dataset available in csv extension for being compatible with the code.

```python
# LVQ for the ionosphere dataset
from random import seed
from random import randrange
from csv import reader
from math import sqrt

# Load a CSV file
def load_csv(filename):
    dataset = list()
    with open(filename, 'r') as file:
        csv_reader = reader(file)
        for row in csv_reader:
            if not row:
                continue
            dataset.append(row)
    return dataset

# Convert string column to float
def str_column_to_float(dataset, column):
    for row in dataset:
        row[column] = float(row[column].strip())

# Convert string column to integer
def str_column_to_int(dataset, column):
    class_values = [row[column] for row in dataset]
    unique = set(class_values)
    lookup = dict()
    for i, value in enumerate(unique):
        lookup[value] = i
    for row in dataset:
        row[column] = lookup[row[column]]
    return lookup
```

```python
# Split a dataset into k folds
def cross_validation_split(dataset, n_folds):
    dataset_split = list()
    dataset_copy = list(dataset)
    fold_size = int(len(dataset) / n_folds)
    for i in range(n_folds):
        fold = list()
        while len(fold) < fold_size:
            index = randrange(len(dataset_copy))
            fold.append(dataset_copy.pop(index))
        dataset_split.append(fold)
    return dataset_split

# Calculate accuracy percentage
def accuracy_metric(actual, predicted):
    correct = 0
    for i in range(len(actual)):
        if actual[i] == predicted[i]:
            correct += 1
    return correct / float(len(actual)) * 100.0

# Evaluate an algorithm using a cross validation split
def evaluate_algorithm(dataset, algorithm, n_folds, *args):
    folds = cross_validation_split(dataset, n_folds)
    scores = list()
    for fold in folds:
        train_set = list(folds)
        train_set.remove(fold)
        train_set = sum(train_set, [])
        test_set = list()
        for row in fold:
```

```python
            row_copy = list(row)
            test_set.append(row_copy)
            row_copy[-1] = None
        predicted = algorithm(train_set, test_set, *args)
        actual = [row[-1] for row in fold]
        accuracy = accuracy_metric(actual, predicted)
        scores.append(accuracy)
    return scores

# calculate the Euclidean distance between two vectors
def euclidean_distance(row1, row2):
    distance = 0.0
    for i in range(len(row1)-1):
        distance += (row1[i] - row2[i])**2
    return sqrt(distance)

# Locate the best matching unit
def get_best_matching_unit(codebooks, test_row):
    distances = list()
    for codebook in codebooks:
        dist = euclidean_distance(codebook, test_row)
        distances.append((codebook, dist))
    distances.sort(key=lambda tup: tup[1])
    return distances[0][0]

# Make a prediction with codebook vectors
def predict(codebooks, test_row):
    bmu = get_best_matching_unit(codebooks, test_row)
    return bmu[-1]

# Create a random codebook vector
def random_codebook(train):
    n_records = len(train)
    n_features = len(train[0])
```

```
        codebook = [train[randrange(n_records)][i] for i in
        range(n_features)]
        return codebook

# Train a set of codebook vectors
def train_codebooks(train, n_codebooks, lrate, epochs):
    codebooks = [random_codebook(train) for i in range
    (n_codebooks)]
    for epoch in range(epochs):
        rate = lrate * (1.0-(epoch/float(epochs)))
        for row in train:
            bmu = get_best_matching_unit(codebooks, row)
            for i in range(len(row)-1):
                error = row[i] - bmu[i]
                if bmu[-1] == row[-1]:
                    bmu[i] += rate * error
                else:
                    bmu[i] -= rate * error
    return codebooks

# LVQ Algorithm
def learning_vector_quantization(train, test, n_codebooks,
lrate, epochs):
    codebooks = train_codebooks(train, n_codebooks, lrate,
    epochs)
    predictions = list()
    for row in test:
        output = predict(codebooks, row)
        predictions.append(output)
    return(predictions)

# Test LVQ on ionosphere dataset
seed(1)
```

```
# load and prepare data
filename = 'ionosphere.csv'
dataset = load_csv(filename)
for i in range(len(dataset[0])-1):
    str_column_to_float(dataset, i)
# convert class column to integers
str_column_to_int(dataset, len(dataset[0])-1)
# evaluate algorithm
n_folds = 5
learn_rate = 0.3
n_epochs = 50
n_codebooks = 20
scores = evaluate_algorithm(dataset, learning_vector_
quantization, n_folds, n_codebooks, learn_rate, n_epochs)
print('Scores: %s' % scores)
print('Mean Accuracy: %.3f%%' % (sum(scores)/
float(len(scores))))
```

The following are additional comments regarding the preceding code for those portions not readily understandable. In addition, I will only show three or less lines of code (except for the main portion) prior to discussing what is happening within the code portion.

```
# Split a dataset into k folds
def cross_validation_split(dataset, n_folds):
•
•
    return dataset_split
```

This method implements a n-fold cross-validation process that I have already discussed in Chapter 1. Please refer back to that chapter to refresh yourself on this process.

```
# Evaluate an algorithm using a cross validation split
def evaluate_algorithm(dataset, algorithm, n_folds, *args):
  .

  .

    return scores
```

applies the LVQ algorithm to the n-fold cross-validated dataset. This method is designed to use other algorithms if so desired.

```
# Locate the best matching unit
def get_best_matching_unit(codebooks, test_row):
  .

  .

      return distances[0][0]
```

finds the BMU for the test_row argument. This method implements the process described in the BMU section.

```
# Train a set of codebook vectors
def train_codebooks(train, n_codebooks, lrate, epochs):
  .

  .

    return codebooks
```

trains the codebook vectors. This method implements the process described in the training codebook vectors section.

```
# LVQ Algorithm
def learning_vector_quantization(train, test, n_codebooks,
lrate, epochs):
  .

  .

      return(predictions)
```

This is the actual LVQ algorithm. It is not much in the sense it just calls other methods that implement the basic LVQ concepts. The dataset is required to be preprocessed before this method is called as are the codebook vectors.

```
# Test LVQ on ionosphere dataset
seed(1)
# load and prepare data
filename = 'ionosphere.csv'
dataset = load_csv(filename)
.
.
print('Scores: %s' % scores)
print('Mean Accuracy: %.3f%%' % (sum(scores)/
float(len(scores))))
```

This is the main code portion where all the steps required to carry out an entire LVQ data model are processed. All the code that preceded this portion were function definitions that implement various steps in the LVQ process. The main body of code calls the methods in the order required to fully process the LVQ algorithm and display the final results.

The script is run by entering this command:

```
python lvqDemo.py
```

Figure 3-24 shows the results of running this script.

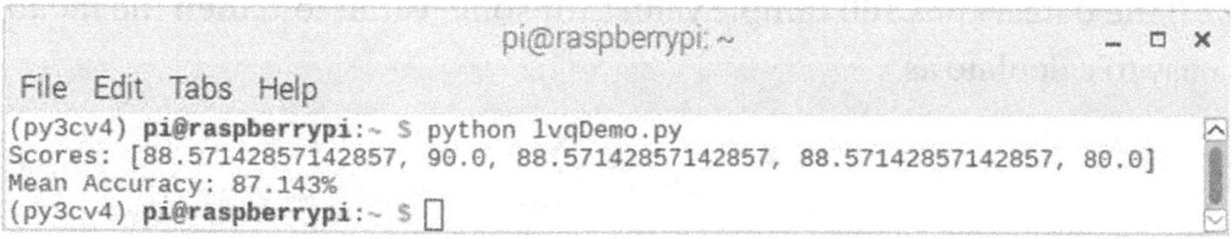

Figure 3-24. *lvqDemo results*

The figure shows that the mean accuracy for this LVQ data model is 87.1%, which is a substantial improvement beyond the Zero Rule estimate of 64.1%. This result confirms that the LVQ model is a good one to use with the ionosphere dataset and can make reasonably accurate predictions.

Bagging and random forests

I will begin this discussion by again crediting Dr. Jason Brownlee for a series of great blogs regarding bagging and random forests. These blogs are April 2016 "Bagging and Random Forest Ensemble Algorithms for Machine Learning," November 2016 "How to Implement Bagging from Scratch with Python," and November 2016 "How to Implement Random Forest from Scratch in Python." Much of the code and key concepts in this section are based on the aforementioned blogs; however, I do add my own comments and detailed explanations in those areas that warrant it, which I believe should be helpful for inexperienced readers.

Introduction to bagging and random forest

Random forest is a popular algorithm and is a type of ensemble ML algorithm called bootstrap aggregation or bagging for short. I will first discuss what is meant by the word bootstrap. It is a statistical process designed to estimate some measurement or metric from a dataset. A simple example should help clarify this concept.

If the dataset has 100 sample values for some variable x, then the mean is easy to calculate as

$$mean(x) = \frac{\sum x}{100}$$

However, there is likely to be some estimation error in this calculation, which may be improved using the bootstrap process as listed as follows:

1. Create many (e.g., 1000) random subsamples of the dataset with replacement (meaning the same value can be used multiple times).

2. Calculate the mean of each new subsample.

3. Calculate the average for all of the new means and use that as the new estimated mean for the dataset.

This process may also be extended to estimate other metrics such as standard deviation.

Bootstrap aggregation (bagging)

Bagging is an ensemble process that combines predictions collected from multiple ML algorithms into one more accurate prediction than would be possible from any single ML prediction. It is basically a synergistic prediction approach where a group of algorithms is more powerful than any single member of the group. Using bagging reduces variance for those algorithms subject to that such as classification and regression trees (CART). For example, decision trees are sensitive to the selected data used to create a tree. A particular tree trained on one data sub-set could easily provide different predicted results if it was trained on another data sub-set other than the original one. The following generic bagging process could be used to improve CART prediction accuracy:

1. Create many (e.g., 100) random subsamples of the dataset with replacement.

2. Train a CART model on each new sample.

3. Given a new dataset, calculate the average prediction from each model.

Decision trees used with a bagging process would necessarily be deep, meaning that only a few training samples would be attached at each leaf node. Such a tree would have high variance but also low bias. Please refer to my previous discussion on decision trees in Chapter 2 to refresh yourself on these terms. The key point to be mindful of is that bagging is only concerned with the number of samples and, in this case, the number of trees. This process is also quite tolerant of overfitting, and a large number of models can be run without introducing too much error, if at all. The only issues would be time to prepare the models and perform the computations.

Random forest

The random forest was developed to improve the performance of bagging with decision trees. One big issue with decision tree produced by CART is that they are greedy in the sense they choose the variable on which to split using a greedy algorithm that tries to minimize error. This makes total sense for the CART algorithm, but is a problem for the bagging process. Decision trees may often contain similar data structures, which can lead to high correlation in the subsequent predictions. Bagging performs better if predictions are made from sub-sets (sub-trees), which are relatively uncorrelated. The random forest alters the way sub-sets are learned in effort to improve the prediction accuracy. Making all the sub-sets less correlated is necessary to achieve this goal.

The random forest modification to the CART algorithm is fairly simple. In the unmodified CART algorithm, the learning portion is permitted to test all variables (features) in order to select the optimum split point. Random forest changes this procedure so that the learning portion is now limited to a random sample of variables to test. The number of variables that can be tested at each split point is also set as a parameter m to the learning algorithm. For random forest classification problem, setting m to the square root of p is recommended, where p is the number of features in the dataset.

Performance estimation and variable importance

When bootstrap samples are made, there will be data samples left out of the sub-set. These samples are known as out-of-bag (OOB) samples. An accuracy estimation for the bagged models can be made if the OOB samples are averaged. This estimated performance is often called the OOB estimate of performance. Such performance measures are a reliable test error estimate and correlate well with cross-validation estimates.

It can be calculated how much the error function drops for each additional variable at each split point as the bagged decision trees are constructed. In regression problems, this could be the drop in sum squared error, and for classification problems, this could be the Gini score.

These error drops may be averaged across all decision trees and output to provide an estimate of the importance of each input variable. The greater the error drop when the variable was selected, the greater the importance. These outputs can help identify input variable sub-sets that may be most relevant to the problem and likely candidates for removal (least relevant) from the dataset.

Bootstrap resampling demonstration

This demonstration will show how the bootstrap process functions. A factitious dataset of random numbers is first created from which various sized sub-sets are derived. Means from each of these sub-sets are then calculated, and the average of the sub-set means is then compared to the original dataset overall mean value.

The complete script for this test is named bootstrapDemo.py and is available from this book's companion web site. The script code is straightforward and requires no additional comments other than what has already been included.

```python
# Import required libraries
from random import seed
from random import random
from random import randrange

# Create a random sub-set from the dataset with replacement.
def subsample(dataset, ratio=1.0):
    sample = list()
    n_sample = round(len(dataset) * ratio)
    while len(sample) < n_sample:
        index = randrange(len(dataset))
        sample.append(dataset[index])
    return sample

 # Calculate the mean of a list of numbers.
def mean(numbers):
    return sum(numbers) / float(len(numbers))

seed(1)
# Calculate the true mean.
# The original dataset has 20 rows with a single random
# number 0 to 9 in each row.
dataset = [[randrange(10)] for i in range(20)]
print('True Mean: %.3f' % mean([row[0] for row in dataset]))

# Calculate and display the estimated means from the different
# sized sub-sets.
ratio = 0.10
for size in [1, 10, 100]:
    sample_means = list()
    for i in range(size):
        sample = subsample(dataset, ratio)
        sample_mean = mean([row[0] for row in sample])
```

```
        sample_means.append(sample_mean)
    print('Samples=%d, Estimated Mean: %.3f' % (size,
mean(sample_means)))
```

The script is run by entering the following command:

```
python bootstrapDemo.py
```

Figure 3-25 shows the result from running this script.

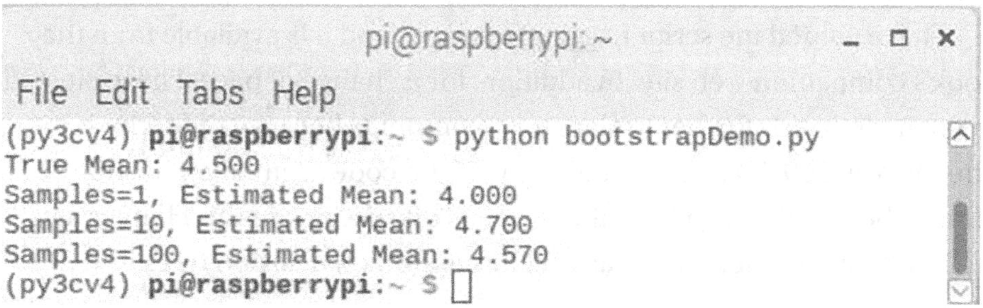

Figure 3-25. *bootstrapDemo results*

You should be able to see that the estimated mean values are starting to converge to the true mean value as the number of samples in each subset increases.

Bagging demonstration

This demonstration has the decision tree data model within the script. Bootstrap data aggregation or bagging is being applied to the model in an effort to improve the overall prediction accuracy.

The dataset being used is titled sonar-data.csv and is a collection of numerical records resulting from processed sonar "soundings" from within an ocean environment. Each record describes properties of the returns from a sonar system's chirp signals. There are 60 input variables or features, which are measurements of the return signal strength at different transmitted angles. This is a binary classification problem because the model is designed to differentiate rocks (R) from mines (M). There are 208 records in this dataset. All of the variables are continuous with a nominal range of 0 to 1. The output variable (class) is either a "M" for mine or a "R" for rock. These variables are converted into integers 1 or 0, respectively, by the script.

The dataset is named sonar.all-data.csv, and it can be downloaded from https://archive.ics.uci.edu/ml/datasets/Connectionist+ Bench+(Sonar,+Mines+vs.+Rocks). Make sure to change the extension of the downloaded file to csv.

I have named the script baggingDemo.py, and it is available from the book's companion web site. In addition, for a change of pace, I have elected to not include any further explanatory comments because the script is already over 200 lines in size and many of the code segments you should already be familiar with from the previous discussions in this chapter as well as from the extensive Chapter 2 discussion on decision trees.

```python
# Bagging Algorithm on the Sonar dataset
# Import required libraries
from random import seed
from random import randrange
from csv import reader

# Load a CSV file
def load_csv(filename):
    dataset = list()
    with open(filename, 'r') as file:
        csv_reader = reader(file)
        for row in csv_reader:
            if not row:
                continue
            dataset.append(row)
    return dataset
```

```python
# Convert string column to float
def str_column_to_float(dataset, column):
    for row in dataset:
        row[column] = float(row[column].strip())

# Convert string column to integer
def str_column_to_int(dataset, column):
    class_values = [row[column] for row in dataset]
    unique = set(class_values)
    lookup = dict()
    for i, value in enumerate(unique):
        lookup[value] = i
    for row in dataset:
        row[column] = lookup[row[column]]
    return lookup

# Split a dataset into k folds
def cross_validation_split(dataset, n_folds):
    dataset_split = list()
    dataset_copy = list(dataset)
    fold_size = int(len(dataset) / n_folds)
    for i in range(n_folds):
        fold = list()
        while len(fold) < fold_size:
            index = randrange(len(dataset_copy))
            fold.append(dataset_copy.pop(index))
        dataset_split.append(fold)
    return dataset_split

# Calculate accuracy percentage
def accuracy_metric(actual, predicted):
    correct = 0
```

```python
    for i in range(len(actual)):
        if actual[i] == predicted[i]:
            correct += 1
    return correct / float(len(actual)) * 100.0

# Evaluate an algorithm using a cross validation split
def evaluate_algorithm(dataset, algorithm, n_folds, *args):
    folds = cross_validation_split(dataset, n_folds)
    scores = list()
    for fold in folds:
        train_set = list(folds)
        train_set.remove(fold)
        train_set = sum(train_set, [])
        test_set = list()
        for row in fold:
            row_copy = list(row)
            test_set.append(row_copy)
            row_copy[-1] = None
        predicted = algorithm(train_set, test_set, *args)
        actual = [row[-1] for row in fold]
        accuracy = accuracy_metric(actual, predicted)
        scores.append(accuracy)
    return scores

# Split a dataset based on an attribute and an attribute value
def test_split(index, value, dataset):
    left, right = list(), list()
    for row in dataset:
        if row[index] < value:
            left.append(row)
        else:
            right.append(row)
    return left, right
```

```python
# Calculate the Gini index for a split dataset
def gini_index(groups, classes):
    # count all samples at split point
    n_instances = float(sum([len(group) for group in groups]))
    # sum weighted Gini index for each group
    gini = 0.0
    for group in groups:
        size = float(len(group))
        # avoid divide by zero
        if size == 0:
            continue
        score = 0.0
        # score the group based on the score for each class
        for class_val in classes:
            p = [row[-1] for row in group].count
            (class_val) / size
            score += p * p
        # weight the group score by its relative size
        gini += (1.0 - score) * (size / n_instances)
    return gini

# Select the best split point for a dataset
def get_split(dataset):
    class_values = list(set(row[-1] for row in dataset))
    b_index, b_value, b_score, b_groups = 999, 999, 999, None
    for index in range(len(dataset[0])-1):
        for row in dataset:
        # for i in range(len(dataset)):
        # row = dataset[randrange(len(dataset))]
            groups = test_split(index, row[index],
            dataset)
            gini = gini_index(groups, class_values)
```

```
                    if gini < b_score:
                            b_index, b_value, b_score, b_groups =
                            index, row[index], gini, groups
        return {'index':b_index, 'value':b_value, 'groups':b_
        groups}

# Create a terminal node value
def to_terminal(group):
        outcomes = [row[-1] for row in group]
        return max(set(outcomes), key=outcomes.count)

# Create child splits for a node or make terminal
def split(node, max_depth, min_size, depth):
        left, right = node['groups']
        del(node['groups'])
        # check for a no split
        if not left or not right:
                node['left'] = node['right'] = to_terminal(left +
                right)
                return
        # check for max depth
        if depth >= max_depth:
                node['left'], node['right'] = to_terminal(left),
                to_terminal(right)
                return
        # process left child
        if len(left) <= min_size:
                node['left'] = to_terminal(left)
        else:
                node['left'] = get_split(left)
                split(node['left'], max_depth, min_size, depth+1)
        # process right child
```

```
    if len(right) <= min_size:
        node['right'] = to_terminal(right)
    else:
        node['right'] = get_split(right)
        split(node['right'], max_depth, min_size, depth+1)

# Build a decision tree
def build_tree(train, max_depth, min_size):
    root = get_split(train)
    split(root, max_depth, min_size, 1)
    return root

# Make a prediction with a decision tree
def predict(node, row):
    if row[node['index']] < node['value']:
        if isinstance(node['left'], dict):
            return predict(node['left'], row)
        else:
            return node['left']
    else:
        if isinstance(node['right'], dict):
            return predict(node['right'], row)
        else:
            return node['right']

# Create a random subsample from the dataset with replacement
def subsample(dataset, ratio):
    sample = list()
    n_sample = round(len(dataset) * ratio)
    while len(sample) < n_sample:
        index = randrange(len(dataset))
        sample.append(dataset[index])
    return sample
```

```
# Make a prediction with a list of bagged trees
def bagging_predict(trees, row):
      predictions = [predict(tree, row) for tree in trees]
      return max(set(predictions), key=predictions.count)

# Bootstrap Aggregation Algorithm
def bagging(train, test, max_depth, min_size, sample_size, n_
trees):
      trees = list()
      for i in range(n_trees):
            sample = subsample(train, sample_size)
            tree = build_tree(sample, max_depth, min_size)
            trees.append(tree)
      predictions = [bagging_predict(trees, row) for row in test]
      return(predictions)

# Test bagging on the sonar dataset
seed(1)
# load and prepare data
filename = 'sonar.all-data.csv'
dataset = load_csv(filename)
# convert string attributes to integers
for i in range(len(dataset[0])-1):
      str_column_to_float(dataset, i)
# convert class column to integers
str_column_to_int(dataset, len(dataset[0])-1)
# evaluate algorithm
n_folds = 5
max_depth = 6
min_size = 2
sample_size = 0.50
for n_trees in [1, 5, 10, 50]:
```

```
scores = evaluate_algorithm(dataset, bagging, n_folds,
max_depth, min_size, sample_size, n_trees)
print('Trees: %d' % n_trees)
print('Scores: %s' % scores)
print('Mean Accuracy: %.3f%%' % (sum(scores)/
float(len(scores))))
```

The script is run by entering the following command:

```
python baggingDemo.py
```

Figure 3-26 shows the result from running this script.

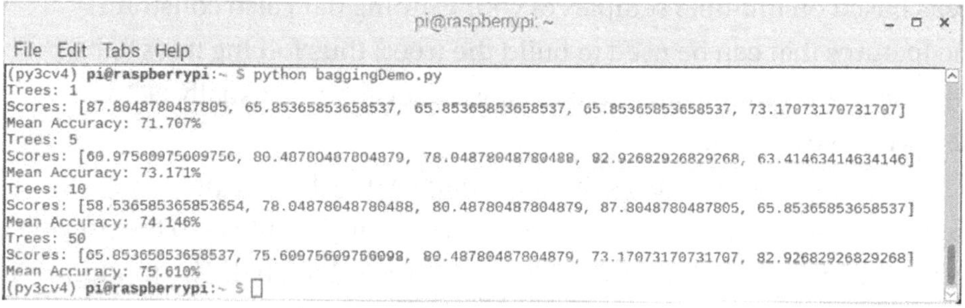

Figure 3-26. baggingDemo results

The interim accuracy score for the fivefold datasets is displayed along with the overall aggregate accuracy value. You can see that the overall accuracy value slowly increased from 71.7% with 1 tree to 75.6% with 50 trees. Not an outstanding performance, but nonetheless, a slight overall improvement was achieved using the bagging approach.

One of the difficulties in using the bagging approach is that even though deep trees are constructed, the bagged trees are similar. Thus, any predictions made using these trees will also be similar. Any high variance that was being sought among the trees based on training on different samples is also diminished. This all due to the greedy algorithm used in the decision tree split algorithm that I have previously discussed. This script tried to increase the variance by constraining the sample size used in the training process, but this met with limited success. The real answer to increasing the variance in the sub-sets is to use the random forest algorithm, which is the subject of the next demonstration.

Random forest demonstration

Decision trees often have high variance which makes any prediction results quite dependent on the training data. Building multiple models from samples of the training data in the technique called bagging can help reduce this variance, but the trees still remain highly correlated.

Random forest is a bagging extension that in addition to building trees based on multiple samples of your training data also constrains the features that can be used to build the trees, thus forcing trees to be different. This modification in building a decision tree usually yields a performance benefit.

This demonstration uses the same dataset used in the previous bagging demonstration. In fact, the script is nearly identical to the previous script except for the way the decision splits are calculated. The random forest modification causes a sample of the input attributes to be searched instead of searching for the attribute that minimizes the total cost function. This attribute sample can be chosen randomly and without replacement, meaning that each input attribute needs only to be considered once when searching for the split point that minimizes cost.

The Gini index is used to evaluate the costs in a potential split. I refer to the Gini index discussion in the decision tree section to refresh yourself on this function.

I have named the script randonForestDemo.py, and it is available from the book's companion web site. As with the preceding script, I have elected to not include any further explanatory comments because this script is already over 200 lines in size and many of the code segments are identical to the baggingDemo script.

```python
# Random Forest Algorithm on Sonar Dataset
# Import required libraries
from random import seed
from random import randrange
from csv import reader
from math import sqrt

# Load a CSV file
def load_csv(filename):
    dataset = list()
    with open(filename, 'r') as file:
        csv_reader = reader(file)
        for row in csv_reader:
            if not row:
                continue
            dataset.append(row)
    return dataset

# Convert string column to float
def str_column_to_float(dataset, column):
    for row in dataset:
        row[column] = float(row[column].strip())

# Convert string column to integer
def str_column_to_int(dataset, column):
    class_values = [row[column] for row in dataset]
    unique = set(class_values)
    lookup = dict()
    for i, value in enumerate(unique):
        lookup[value] = i
    for row in dataset:
        row[column] = lookup[row[column]]
    return lookup
```

```python
# Split a dataset into k folds
def cross_validation_split(dataset, n_folds):
    dataset_split = list()
    dataset_copy = list(dataset)
    fold_size = int(len(dataset) / n_folds)
    for i in range(n_folds):
        fold = list()
        while len(fold) < fold_size:
            index = randrange(len(dataset_copy))
            fold.append(dataset_copy.pop(index))
        dataset_split.append(fold)
    return dataset_split

# Calculate accuracy percentage
def accuracy_metric(actual, predicted):
    correct = 0
    for i in range(len(actual)):
        if actual[i] == predicted[i]:
            correct += 1
    return correct / float(len(actual)) * 100.0

# Evaluate an algorithm using a cross validation split
def evaluate_algorithm(dataset, algorithm, n_folds, *args):
    folds = cross_validation_split(dataset, n_folds)
    scores = list()
    for fold in folds:
        train_set = list(folds)
        train_set.remove(fold)
        train_set = sum(train_set, [])
        test_set = list()
        for row in fold:
```

```
                row_copy = list(row)
                test_set.append(row_copy)
                row_copy[-1] = None
            predicted = algorithm(train_set, test_set, *args)
            actual = [row[-1] for row in fold]
            accuracy = accuracy_metric(actual, predicted)
            scores.append(accuracy)
        return scores

# Split a dataset based on an attribute and an attribute value
def test_split(index, value, dataset):
    left, right = list(), list()
    for row in dataset:
        if row[index] < value:
            left.append(row)
        else:
            right.append(row)
    return left, right

# Calculate the Gini index for a split dataset
def gini_index(groups, classes):
    # count all samples at split point
    n_instances = float(sum([len(group) for group in groups]))
    # sum weighted Gini index for each group
    gini = 0.0
    for group in groups:
        size = float(len(group))
        # avoid divide by zero
        if size == 0:
            continue
        score = 0.0
```

```
            # score the group based on the score for each class
            for class_val in classes:
                    p = [row[-1] for row in group].count(class_
                    val) / size
                    score += p * p
            # weight the group score by its relative size
            gini += (1.0 - score) * (size / n_instances)
    return gini

# Select the best split point for a dataset
def get_split(dataset, n_features):
    class_values = list(set(row[-1] for row in dataset))
    b_index, b_value, b_score, b_groups = 999, 999, 999, None
    features = list()
    while len(features) < n_features:
            index = randrange(len(dataset[0])-1)
            if index not in features:
                    features.append(index)
    for index in features:
            for row in dataset:
                    groups = test_split(index, row[index],
                    dataset)
                    gini = gini_index(groups, class_values)
                    if gini < b_score:
                            b_index, b_value, b_score, b_groups =
                            index, row[index], gini, groups
    return {'index':b_index, 'value':b_value, 'groups':
    b_groups}

# Create a terminal node value
def to_terminal(group):
```

```
    outcomes = [row[-1] for row in group]
    return max(set(outcomes), key=outcomes.count)

# Create child splits for a node or make terminal
def split(node, max_depth, min_size, n_features, depth):
    left, right = node['groups']
    del(node['groups'])
    # check for a no split
    if not left or not right:
        node['left'] = node['right'] = to_terminal(left +
        right)
        return
    # check for max depth
    if depth >= max_depth:
        node['left'], node['right'] = to_terminal(left),
        to_terminal(right)
        return
    # process left child
    if len(left) <= min_size:
        node['left'] = to_terminal(left)
    else:
        node['left'] = get_split(left, n_features)
        split(node['left'], max_depth, min_size,
        n_features, depth+1)
    # process right child
    if len(right) <= min_size:
        node['right'] = to_terminal(right)
    else:
        node['right'] = get_split(right, n_features)
        split(node['right'], max_depth, min_size,
        n_features, depth+1)
```

```python
# Build a decision tree
def build_tree(train, max_depth, min_size, n_features):
    root = get_split(train, n_features)
    split(root, max_depth, min_size, n_features, 1)
    return root

# Make a prediction with a decision tree
def predict(node, row):
    if row[node['index']] < node['value']:
        if isinstance(node['left'], dict):
            return predict(node['left'], row)
        else:
            return node['left']
    else:
        if isinstance(node['right'], dict):
            return predict(node['right'], row)
        else:
            return node['right']

# Create a random subsample from the dataset with replacement
def subsample(dataset, ratio):
    sample = list()
    n_sample = round(len(dataset) * ratio)
    while len(sample) < n_sample:
        index = randrange(len(dataset))
        sample.append(dataset[index])
    return sample

# Make a prediction with a list of bagged trees
def bagging_predict(trees, row):
    predictions = [predict(tree, row) for tree in trees]
    return max(set(predictions), key=predictions.count)
```

```
# Random Forest Algorithm
def random_forest(train, test, max_depth, min_size, sample_size,
n_trees, n_features):
        trees = list()
        for i in range(n_trees):
                sample = subsample(train, sample_size)
                tree = build_tree(sample, max_depth, min_size,
                n_features)
                trees.append(tree)
        predictions = [bagging_predict(trees, row) for row in test]
        return(predictions)

# Test the random forest algorithm
seed(2)
# load and prepare data
filename = 'sonar.all-data.csv'
dataset = load_csv(filename)
# convert string attributes to integers
for i in range(0, len(dataset[0])-1):
        str_column_to_float(dataset, i)
# convert class column to integers
str_column_to_int(dataset, len(dataset[0])-1)
# evaluate algorithm
n_folds = 5
max_depth = 10
min_size = 1
sample_size = 1.0
n_features = int(sqrt(len(dataset[0])-1))
for n_trees in [1, 5, 10]:
        scores = evaluate_algorithm(dataset, random_forest,
        n_folds, max_depth, min_size, sample_size, n_trees,
        n_features)
```

```
print('Trees: %d' % n_trees)
print('Scores: %s' % scores)
print('Mean Accuracy: %.3f%%' % (sum(scores)/
float(len(scores))))
```

The script is run by entering the following command:

```
python randomForestDemo.py
```

Figure 3-27 shows the result from running this script.

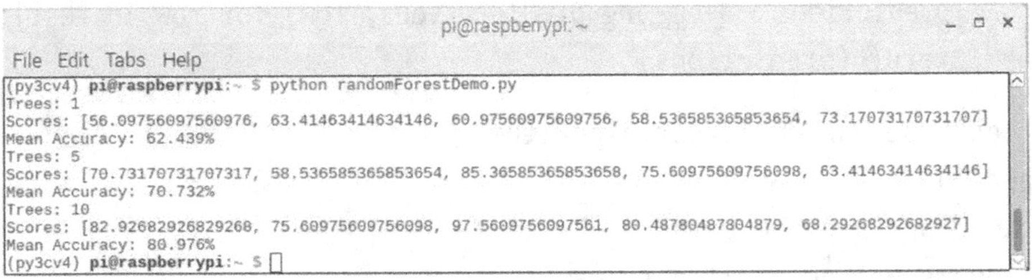

Figure 3-27. *randomForestDemo results*

A k value of 5 was used for cross-validation, giving each fold 208/5 = 41.6 or just over 40 records to be evaluated upon each iteration. Deep trees were constructed with a maximum depth of 10 and a minimum number of training rows at each node of 1. Samples of the training dataset were created with the same size as the original dataset, which is a default expectation for the random forest algorithm. The number of features considered at each split point was set to sqrt(num_features) or sqrt(60)=7.74 rounded to 7 features.

Tree suites of sizes 1, 5, and 10 were evaluated for comparison, showing the increasing accuracy as additional trees are added. The mean accuracy scores increase from 62.4% to 81.0% as the tree suite increases. The final score is over 5% improved over the bagging demonstration, which shows the random forest modification has worked as expected.

CHAPTER 4

Preparation for deep learning

This chapter will provide you with a sufficient background for the deep learning (DL) discussions that commence with the following chapters. It is important to understand some basic DL terms and concepts before trying to comprehend any actual DL algorithms. I have tried to minimize the math, but there are some unavoidable equations just because DL is essentially all math.

DL basics

The obvious start for any DL discussion must be to answer the question, "What is DL?" Like many relatively new technology areas, if you ask a dozen experts to define something, you will likely get a dozen different yet oddly similar responses. It is no different with DL. I have researched many different DL definitions and have created the following one that seems to hold the common themes among many definitions:

> *Deep Learning is a subfield of machine learning concerned with algorithms called artificial neural networks, which are inspired by the structure and function of the human brain. Learning from datasets can be supervised, semi-supervised or unsupervised.*

© Donald J. Norris 2020
D. J. Norris, *Machine Learning with the Raspberry Pi*,
https://doi.org/10.1007/978-1-4842-5174-4_4

I will introduce and discuss an artificial neural network (ANN) in the next chapter, but first I need to discuss these basics.

Machine learning from data patterns

Machine learning (ML) of which DL is a significant sub-set is generally described as the study of algorithms and data models that can perform computer-implemented tasks without being explicitly programmed to accomplish those tasks. Instead, ML relies on detecting data patterns and generating inferences regarding the data. There are four principal tasks often ascribed to ML. These tasks are

- Detection

- Classification

- Recognition

- Prediction

Most, if not all, of these tasks can be applied to a wide variety of datasets including static Images, numerical data, and real-time data streams. The last dataset mentioned includes video, audio, and even radio frequency (RF) streams. I am also absolutely positive there are other applications for ML that I have not mentioned.

I will start my basics discussion by focusing on the classification task, which I have already discussed in previous chapters. Recall that in Chapter 1 k-NN data model discussion I stated the following:

> *I described k-NN as non-parametric, which means that the model does not make any assumptions regarding the underlying data distribution. In other words, the model structure is determined from the data. Given this fact, k-NN probably should be one of your first choices for a classification study when there is little or no prior knowledge about how the data is distributed.*

You may have been a bit confused by my use of the term *non-parametric* in describing the k-NN data model. Hopefully, it will be helpful to describe what a parameterized classification algorithm is to help clarify this term. The term parameterization is defined as follows:

> *Parametrization is a mathematical process consisting of expressing the state of a system, process or model as a function of some independent quantities called parameters.*

In a ML application, the key parameters used to describe the state of a system are

- data
- scoring function
- loss function
- weights and biases

Yes, I realize the last list item has two components, but they are closely intertwined and usually considered as constituting a single parameter. I will discuss each parameter separately.

data – This is an obvious element in the process from which all ML must be based. Data has two faces, the first being the value and the second being the class label. Values can vary widely from raw pixel values in an Image to home prices in a housing dataset. Data is usually represented as a matrix in a ML domain. Such a matrix is often called a design matrix named **X** where

$$x_i = i^{th} \ element \ in \ the \ design \ matrix$$

$$y_i = i^{th} \ class \ label$$

scoring function – A function which maps input data to a predicted class label. This may be represented in a generic equation form

$$f(input \ data) = predicted \ class \ label$$

In reality, this equation simply produces a value. The class label associated with the maximum value would be the prediction for this classifier.

loss function – A function that quantifies how well predicted class labels agree with the actual class labels recorded in the dataset. The actual class labels are also known as ground truth labels in ML terminology. Low loss values are desired because that means the predictions closely agree with ground truth labels. There will be an extensive discussion later in this chapter on how to compute the loss function for minimum loss values.

weights and biases – The weight matrix W and the bias vector b are iteratively computed in order to minimize the loss function with respect to the scoring function.

Linear classifier

In this section I discuss what a linear classifier is and how it functions. The reason I have included this discussion is to present you with a framework through which you can better understand how a neural network functions. The foundational concepts for the linear classifier and the neural network are basically the same. I will also incorporate the three of the four key parameters introduced previously in this discussion. The loss function is discussed all by itself in the following section.

The dataset used for this linear classifier is named Mammals and consists of 5000 Images of three classes, namely, cat, dog, and squirrel. Each Image has a rather low resolution of 32 x 32 pixels for a total of 1024 pixels. Moreover, each pixel is a full color RGB that requires three bytes to represent the RGB color channel values, which means that there are 3072 values to be processed by the classifier. The data points representing an Image are "flattened" into a single dimension vector (1D), which is named X that has N elements, where N equals 3,072. The weighting matrix W must be shaped as 3 x 3072 because there are three classes in the dataset.

Finally, the bias vector **b** is just sized as 3 x 1. The final scoring equation using the symbols just described is

$$f(X,W,b)=W\cdot X + b$$

where **W** · **X** is the dot product between the weighting matrix and the input data vector.

Figure 4-1 is a graphical representation of the scoring function.

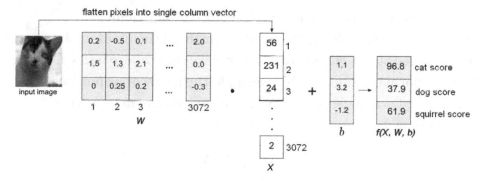

Figure 4-1. *Scoring function's graphical representation*

All the numerical values in the figure are made up, but I did make the cat class the highest value in the scoring function vector, which would make it the predicted class label.

There is common simplifying "trick" often used to reduce the number of parameters in the scoring function from three to two. This trick is to include the bias vector into the weighting matrix. Figure 4-2 shows how this is done.

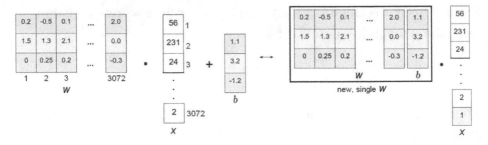

Figure 4-2. *Adding the bias vector to the weighting matrix*

The input data vector **X** has been extended by one element that always contains the value 1. The weighting matrix **W** in this example is also extended by one column which now makes its shape to be 3 x 3073. This additional column is the bias vector **b**. The new scoring function is now reduced to a single dot product multiplication as can be seen in the following equation:

$$f(X,W)=W \cdot X$$

Using this bias trick means you only have to have a single weighting matrix instead of a weighting matrix and a bias vector. This trick is only one part of preprocessing data that helps simplify the overall ML effort.

The following is an attempt to show you how to implement a linear classifier in Python. This script is most definitely "rigged" to select the first class in the labels list. This was necessary because there is no pre-trained network being used in this script. My goal was to only show how a simple linear classifier could be coded. I did not call this a demonstration, and I consider it is more in the category of pseudo-code. Again, it is just for your reference because it does use the four primary parameters I have discussed and it only is missing a call to a pre-trained network. The script is named linear_Classifier.py. I have *not* made it available on the book's companion web site because I believe this is only a pedagogical instrument for your education. Feel free to copy it from the listing if you so desire.

```python
# Import the required libraries
import numpy as np
import cv2

# Initialize class labels and set pseudo-random seed value
labels = ['dog', 'cat', 'squirrel']
np.random.seed(1)

# Randomly initialize the weighting matrix and bias vector
W = np.random.randn(3, 3072)
b = np.random.randn(3)

# Set the font used to draw the label
font = cv2.FONT_HERSHEY_SIMPLEX

# Load the image and resize it. The image is taken from the
dataset.
orig = cv2.imread('dog.png')
image = cv2.resize(orig, (32,32)).flatten()

# Compute output scores
scores = W.dot(image) + b

# Loop over the scores and labels
for (label, score) in zip(labels, scores):
    print('[INFO] {}: {:.2f}'.format(label, score))

# Get the class label for the highest scoring class
classLabel = labels[np.argmax(scores)]

# Draw the predicted label on the original image
cv2.putText(orig, classLabel, (10,30),  font, 0.9, (255,0,0), 2)

# Display image
cv2.imshow('Image', orig)
cv2.waitKey(0)
```

Run this script by entering the following command:

```
python linear_Classifier.py
```

Figure 4-3 shows the terminal window results after the command was entered.

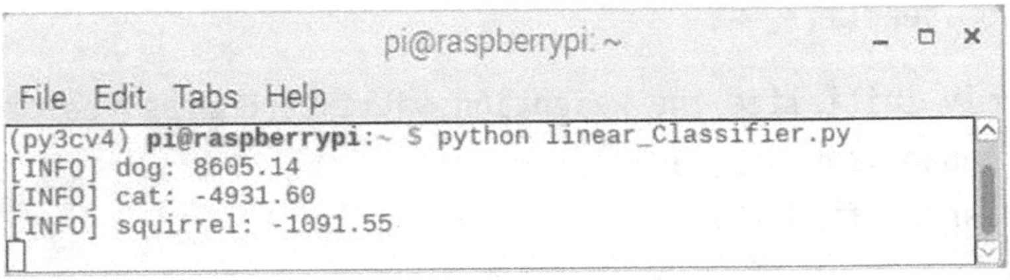

Figure 4-3. *Terminal results after running the linear_Classifier script*

You should be able to see that the dog class has the maximum value and is therefore the predicted class label.

Figure 4-4 shows the original Image with the class label superimposed on it.

Figure 4-4. *Processed Image for the linear_Classifier script*

The key takeaway from this example is to realize that the weighting matrix must be optimized in order to actually perform a real classification task. I will discuss how this is accomplished in the next chapter using a real-world problem. I am not being too concerned with the bias vector at time point because it is often used to "tune" the final network solution. It is far more important to create a working weighting matrix before worrying about the bias vector.

Loss functions

The loss function is at the heart of ML. It allows you to take your algorithm from a theoretical concept to practical implementation and transforms neural networks from abstract matrix multiplications into DL.

A loss function concept is quite simple. It is an approach to evaluate how well your algorithm models the input dataset. If predictions or classifications are in error, then the loss function will output a high number. If they are reasonable, then the number will be low. It also informs the developer how well the algorithm is improving as the network and model are being trained. The function will easily show if the training effort is converging or diverging. Convergence is good while you want to avoid divergence.

Different types of loss functions

A naive approach to a loss function might be as simple as doing the following:

$$\epsilon = abs\left(\hat{y}_i - y_i\right)$$

where

ϵ = error

$\hat{y}_i$ = predicted class label

y_i = actual class label (ground truth)

In this loss function definition, it makes no difference if predictions were too high or too low. All that matters are how incorrect they were, that is, directionally agnostic. This approach is not necessarily applied to all loss functions. A loss function will vary significantly based on the ML problem domain. In a given project, it could be much worse to guess too high rather too low, and the selected loss function must reflect that condition.

The following is a list of popular loss functions:

Mean squared error (MSE) – This is a very popular option for basic loss functions. It is easy to understand and implement and works well. The MSE is computed by taking the differences between the predictions and the ground truths, squaring them, and then averaging the sum by the size of the whole dataset. Python code for an MSE would be the following:

```
def MSE(y_Hat, y):
    sq_error = (y_Hat - y) ** 2
    sum_sq_error = np.sum(sq_error)
    mse = sum_sq_sq_error / y.size
    return mse
```

Likelihood function – The Likelihood function is also simple and is commonly used in classification problems. The function takes the predicted probability for each input data class and multiplies them. Although the output isn't human interpretable, it is useful for comparing how well models perform.

Consider the following example where a model outputs a series of probabilities associated with different dataset classes. The probabilities are shown in Table 4-1.

Table 4-1. *Probabilities for the example classification model*

Class	Ground truth (y_i)	Probability (p)	1 - p
A	0	0.4	0.6
B	1	0.6	n/a
C	1	0.9	n/a
D	0	0.1	0.9

In the case when the model outputs a False or 0 ground truth, the 1 - p probability is used in the Likelihood calculation, which is shown here:

$$0.6 * 0.6 * 0.9 * 0.9 - 0.292$$

Log loss (cross-entropy loss) – Log loss is a loss function also used frequently in classification problems. It is a modification of the Likelihood function using logarithms.

$$\epsilon = -(y * log(p) + (1-y) * log(1-p))$$

This is the same equation as for the Likelihood function, but with logarithms. However, you should recognize that when the class value is 1, the second half of the function disappears, and when the class is 0, the first half disappears. In that way, only the log of the predicted probability for the ground truth class is used in the multiplication.

The log loss function has an interesting feature in that it heavily penalizes for being *very confident* and *very wrong*. Predicting high probabilities for the wrong class makes the function "explode." Figure 4-5 illustrates what happens when the true label = 1. You can see that it skyrockets as the predicted probability for label = 0 approaches 1.

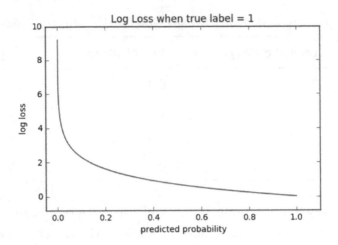

Figure 4-5. *Log loss function plot*

One final point in this discussion of loss functions is realize that they provide more than just a static representation of how a model is performing. Most ML algorithms use a loss function in the optimization process or the determination of the best parameters (weights) for the dataset.

As an example, consider the linear regression data model that I discussed in the previous chapter. In a traditional "least squares" regression, the best fit line is determined through MSE. For each set of weights that the model tries, the MSE is calculated across all input examples. The model then optimizes the MSE functions or, in other words, makes it the lowest possible through the use of an optimizer algorithm like gradient descent.

Just as there are different types of loss functions for different problems, there are different optimizers to match specific problem domains, which I discuss in the following section.

Optimizer algorithm

ML practitioners will often say that an optimizer algorithm is the heart of ML. Without a good one, ML could not exist. The most common algorithm is called gradient descent, and it comes in two flavors, linear and stochastic. I will initially discuss the linear version because it is the easiest to understand and explain. In reality, the stochastic version is the one used most often in the real world. I will explain that version after covering the linear one.

To set the stage for the gradient descent discussion, I would like you to imagine the following scenario. Suppose you were hiking in the mountains and you lost track of time and it started to get dark. You quickly realized that you had to get to lower ground before it got too dark and too cold. Let's say you also forgot to bring a flashlight or lantern so you must rely on whatever diminishing sunlight was left to reach safety and lower ground. Naturally you start hiking downhill, but with the poor light you cannot see very far ahead. This condition forces you to take small steps to avoid crashing into boulders or falling into holes or ground depressions. Essentially you are inching your way down the mountain always trying to go lower with each step and making small corrections each time you accidentally start to go uphill.

This scenario is an analogy to how gradient descent works. The peaks and valleys for gradient descent are direct consequence of how the algorithm is defined. For purposes of this discussion, consider an incredibly simple network with only two weights and no bias values. The loss function for this simple situation would be totally dependent on the two weight values. Figure 4-6 shows a hypothetical 3D plot of the loss function vs. the two independent weighting values.

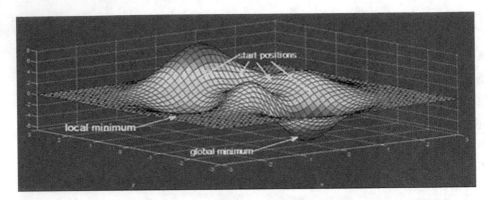

Figure 4-6. *Loss function for two weighting variables*

The peaks in this figure are maximum loss values, which are to be avoided, while the valleys are minimums which are desired for optimum network performance. I would also point out that some valleys are deeper than others in the figure. The deepest valley overall is called the global minimum and is always the most desired one for setting all the weighting values. The "not-as-deep" valleys are called local minima and while not optimal may often be "good enough." More about that a little later in the discussion.

Computing the slope of any point on the figure is the key to determining how to transverse or "walk" within the peaks and valleys. Remember from the introductory scenario, you always want to walk downhill, thus avoiding the peaks, which are the high-cost regions. Therefore, it makes sense to continually compute the instantaneous slope and proceed in the downward direction. Slopes, in an analytic sense, are computed by determining the derivative of the original equation. For this case, the original equation is the loss function, and there are two independent variables, which represent the two weights. Partial derivatives must be used in this situation because there are two independent variables involved. Also involved in finding the global minimum is the size of the step being taken. Too large a step and the minimum can easily be missed and too small can cause excessively long training times. You will shortly find out that step size and learning rate are synonymous terms.

One further point should be made at this time. The 3D figure shown earlier only relates to two weights and a loss function. In reality, there are many more weights involved in a practical neural network model than three. In the next chapter, I will be discussing a network with 100 weights. It is beyond my comprehension, and I suspect, many others, on how to conceptualize how 100 independent variables would interact with a single output function. Certainly, there is no way to visualize that interaction as I have done with only two variables. I would suggest that you simply accept the hypothesis that it mathematically makes sense to optimize 100 variables in the same way as 2 variables are handled.

Consider the case where a vertical plane intersects the plot shown in Figure 4-6 and results in a 2D plot showing the loss function vs. some range for the independent variables. What that range is immaterial for this discussion. Figure 4-7 shows a representative 2D plot with both global and local minima.

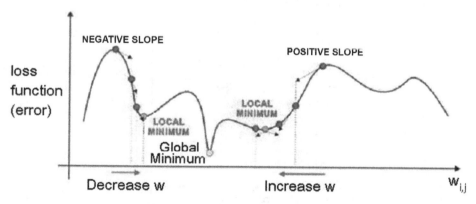

Figure 4-7. *2D plot showing global and local minima*

Deep dive into the gradient descent algorithm

An in-depth examination of the gradient descent algorithm begins with a recap of the linear regression (LR) data model that I discussed in Chapter 2. I would suggest that you review that discussion to refresh yourself regarding key points concerning that model. The generalized LR equation is

$$y = m * x + b$$

where

> m = slope of a straight line
>
> b = y-axis intercept

Note that I slightly altered the equation from the one shown in Chapter 2 by eliminating the error estimation term and changing the slope constant to m and the intercept constant to b. This was done to help conform to the figures used in this discussion.

I will start with a x-y scatter plot of some data with a flat line LR equation as shown in Figure 4-8.

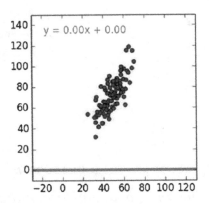

Figure 4-8. *Data scatter plot with flat line LR predictor*

The optimal LR predictor line goes through the data points in such a position to minimize the total error that would result if you were to solely use the predictor line to compute y_i for any given x_i data point. The generalized procedure for determining the optimal m and b values is to iterate through a dataset for all of those values and determine the minimum error resulting from using all of the x_i values. Some sample Python code to implement this generalized procedure is listed here:

```
# Use y = mx + b equation
# m is slope, b is y-intercept
def computeErrorForLineGivenPoints(b, m, points):
    totalError = 0
    for i in range(0, len(points)):
        totalError += (points[i].y - (m * points[i].x + b)) ** 2
    return totalError / float(len(points))
```

There would need to be a data array setup named points containing all of the original x-y points prior to calling this script. In addition, the main calling script must set the range for both the m and b variables to be tested.

The formal error function for this LR example is shown here:

$$e_{m,b} = \frac{1}{N} \sum_{i=1}^{N} \left(y_i - \left(m * x_i + b \right) \right)^2$$

The focus now is to develop an equation that optimizes this error function in terms of m and b, which will generate the minimum error. Prior to discussing this, it would be helpful to illustrate the nature of the variable interactions for this LR example. Figure 4-9 shows two perspectives on how different values for both m and b affect the error function.

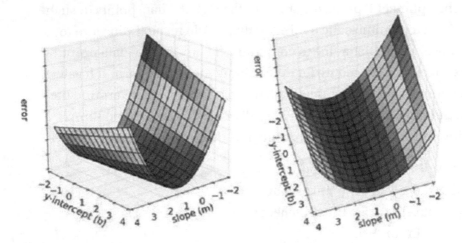

Figure 4-9. *Error plots vs. m and b variables*

You should be able to easily Image rolling a marble down from the upper slope to have it settle at some minimum point. This minimum would have a *m* and *b* value associated with the minimum $e_{m,b}$ value. Using the gradient descent search method is the equivalent of rolling the marble down the slope.

The initial step in implementing the gradient descent method is to perform two partial differentiations on the error function because there are two independent variables. This step is precisely the same step I discussed earlier with the two weight examples. The partial differentiation equations are actually simpler than the original error equation:

$$\frac{\partial}{\partial m} = \frac{2}{N}\sum_{i=N}^{N} -x_i *\left(y_i -\left(m*x_i +b\right)\right)$$

$$\frac{\partial}{\partial b} = \frac{2}{N}\sum_{i=N}^{N} -\left(y_i -\left(m*x_i +b\right)\right)$$

The search normally starts at the origin, which is $m = -1$ and $b = 0$. The -1 value simply starts rolling the marble downhill. The gradient descent algorithm is iterative, meaning that a small step is taken, the error function is then reevaluated, and another step is taken if further improvement is possible. The following Python code implements a gradient descent algorithm for the LR example:

```
def stepGradient(b_current, m_current, points, learningRate):
    b_gradient = 0
    m_gradient = 0
    N = float(len(points))
    for i in range(0, len(points)):
        b_gradient += -(2/N) * (points[i].y -
        ((m_current*points[i].x) + b_current))
        m_gradient += -(2/N) * points[i].x * (points[i].y -
        ((m_current*points[i].x) + b_current))
        new_b = b_current - (learningRate * b_gradient)
        new_m = m_current - (learningRate * m_gradient)
    return [new_b, new_m]
```

The learningRate parameter in the preceding script controls the step size. This parameter must be carefully adjusted because a too large value can easily miss the minimum, while a too small size will needlessly increase the number of iterations taken before locating the minimum.

The next series of figures will illustrate how the gradient descent algorithm converges to an optimal solution for this LR example. In each figure the plot on the left shows where the gradient descent started, and the figure on the right shows the data and the predictor line for the current m and b variables.

Figure 4-10 shows the start of the gradient search.

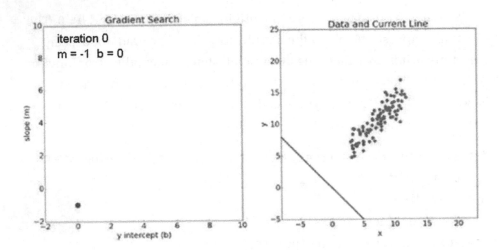

Figure 4-10. *Start of gradient search*

It is clearly obvious from this figure that the initial estimate is way off. The next iteration is shown in Figure 4-11.

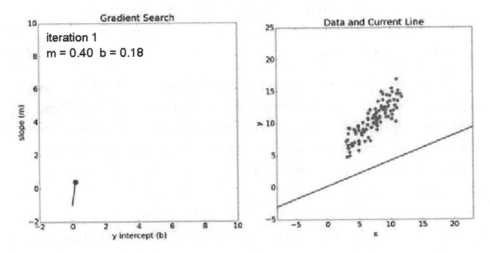

Figure 4-11. *Second iteration for gradient search*

Notice that the plot on the left-hand side of the figure now has a line, which indicates the path taken by the search algorithm from the initial starting point. The predictor line shown on the right-hand side of the figure is a big improvement over the initial plot. However, it clearly needs improvement because in no way it intercepts any of the data points.

Figure 4-12 shows the third iteration, even though the right-hand plot shows iteration 2 in the plot area. That is because the first attempt is labeled 0.

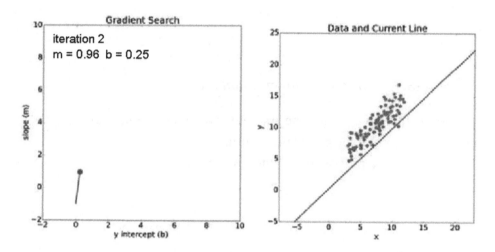

Figure 4-12. *Third iteration for gradient search*

The path taken by the search algorithm was clearly on the same path as it was for the second iteration. However, the predictor line is now barely intercepting some data points, but obviously in need of further improvement.

Jumping ahead to iteration 100 (which is actually 101 due to 0-based counting), you can see from Figure 4-13 that the predictor line visually "appears" to be a good fit.

233

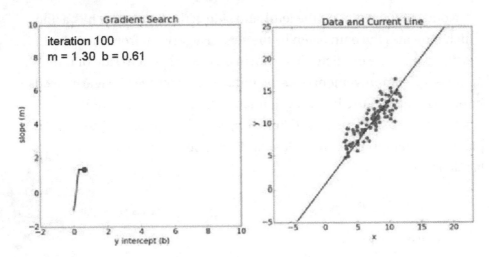

Figure 4-13. *101 iterations for gradient search*

The left-hand plot shows the gradient search path took a small jog to the right in search of the global minimum.

Figure 4-14 is a plot of error vs. iteration number.

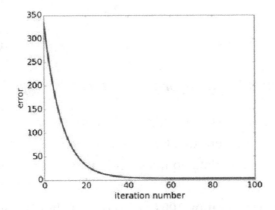

Figure 4-14. *Plot of error vs. iteration number*

It should be obvious from examining this figure that there is little to no improvement to be gained from extending the number of iteration to beyond 100. It is entirely conceivable that the global minimum was not reached; however, any marginal loss improvement is negligible. This situation is what I meant by "good enough" in my earlier discussion.

For those interested readers, the final best fit LR equation was finally determined to be

$$y = 1.3 * x + 0.61$$

Artificial neural network

The artificial neural network (ANN) has a relatively long history within the AI field. The seminal paper regarding ANNs is considered to be a 1943 paper by Warren McCulloch and Walter Pitts titled "A Logical Calculus of Ideas Immanent in Nervous Activity" in which they hypothesized a computational model for neural networks based on mathematics and algorithms they called threshold logic. This model paved the way for future neural network research to split into two approaches. One approach focused on biological processes in the brain, while the other focused on the application of neural networks to AI.

One core concept for ANNs is the neuron model, which is intended to mimic the human brain neuron to some extent. I believe it is important to first discuss a human brain neuron before proceeding to discuss the artificial variety. In this way, you should gain an understanding of why the artificial neuron was created in the manner it is in today.

A biologic diagram for a human brain neuron is depicted in Figure 4-15.

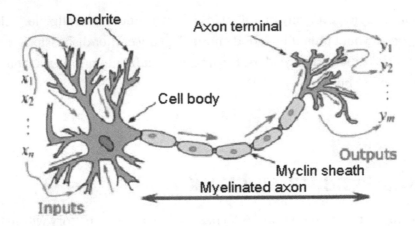

Figure 4-15. *Human brain neuron diagram*

Some of the parts of the human neuron shown in the figure are described as follows:

- Dendrites – Dendrites allow the cell body to receive signals from a large (>1000) number of neighboring neurons. Each dendrite is able to perform an electrical signal "multiplication" by that dendrite's "weight value." This multiplication is accomplished by increasing or decreasing the ratio of synaptic neurotransmitters to signal chemicals introduced into the dendrite in response to the synaptic neurotransmitter. A negative multiplication effect can be achieved by transmitting signal inhibitors (i.e., oppositely charged ions) along the dendrite body in response to the reception of synaptic neurotransmitters.

- Soma – The soma acts as a summation function. As positive and negative signals (exciting and inhibiting, respectively) arrive in the soma from the dendrites, the positive and negative ions are effectively added in summation by simple virtue of being mixed together in the solution inside the cell's body.

- Axon – The axon gets its signal from the summation behavior which occurs inside the soma. The opening to the axon essentially samples the electrical potential of the solution inside the soma. Once the soma reaches a certain potential, the axon will transmit an all-in signal pulse down its length. In this way, the axon communicates directly with other neurons.

Biological neurons fire in discrete pulses. Each time the electrical potential inside the soma reaches a preset threshold, a pulse is transmitted down the axon. This pulsing may be translated into continuous values. The rate (activations per second, etc.) at which an axon fires converts directly into the rate at which neighboring neurons get signal ions introduced into them. The faster a biological neuron fires, the faster nearby neurons accumulate electrical potential (or lose electrical potential, depending on the "weighting" of the dendrite that connects to the neuron that fired). It is this conversion that allows AI researchers to simulate biological neural networks using artificial neurons which can output distinct values, often in the range from –1 to 1.

Early AI researchers developed a relatively simple model for the brain neuron based partly on the biologic facts presented previously. Figure 4-16 shows an artificial neuron diagram with N inputs and one output.

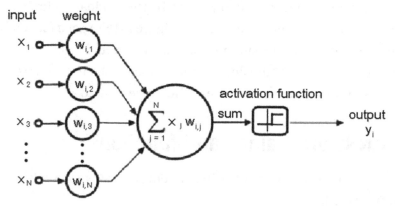

Figure 4-16. *Artificial neuron diagram*

The input branches with the weights are equivalent to the dendrites. The circle is a summing node equivalent to what happens in the soma. The box labeled activation function is equivalent to the axon, which fires when the sum of the weighted electrical signals exceeds some threshold. I believe this model is remarkably simple, yet seems to realistically capture what is occurring in a real brain neuron.

The mathematical representation of an artificial neuron is concisely shown as

$$g(x_1, x_2, x_3, \cdots x_n) = g(X) = \sum_{i=1}^{n} x_i$$

$$y = f(g(X)) = 1 \ \ if \ g(X) \geq \theta$$

$$= 0 \ \ if \ g(X) < \theta$$

The 1 and 0 outputs simply represent the state when the summed, weighted inputs exceed some threshold value, θ. Actual output value is dependent on the real summed value that is transformed by the activation function.

The activation function often used with the artificial neuron model is the sigmoid, which I introduced to you in Chapter 2. Please refer back to that discussion for a refresher and review Figure 2-16 to get a feel for how this function transforms the summed signal. You should easily realize by examining that figure that the final output signal will be in a range of 0 to 1.0 for most summed signals that are in the range of –8 to +8.

How ANNs are trained and function

It is time to explore a network of artificial neurons or ANNs as it is commonly called.

Figure 4-17 shows a generic, three-layer ANN.

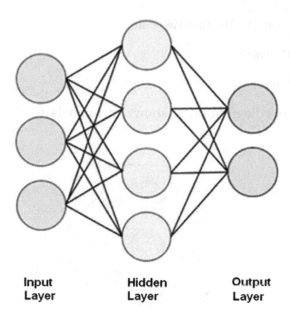

**Input
Layer**   **Hidden
Layer**   **Output
Layer**

Figure 4-17. *Three-layer ANN*

The three layers making up the ANN are

- Input – Raw data inputs are applied to this layer. These data inputs are not weighted. There is only one input layer in an ANN.

- Hidden – This refers to any layer that is either not an input or an output layer. There can be one to many hidden layers. Weights are normally associated with the interconnections between hidden layer nodes as well as the connections between the last hidden layer going to the output layer.

- Output – Processed signals appear as outputs from this layer. The number of output nodes often equals the number of classes for classification ANNs.

ANNS are often divided into two categories:

- FeedForward

- Feedback

Figure 4-18 is a diagram which shows how signals flow in each of these ANNs.

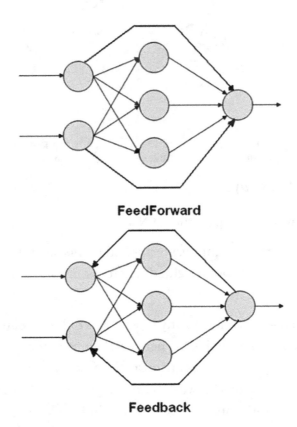

FeedForward

Feedback

Figure 4-18. *FeedForward and Feedback ANN models*

Each ANN category has its advantages and disadvantages over the other. The ANN model that is ultimately used depends on the nature of the dataset and the ANN's intended purpose. However, the feedback back model is the one always used when training an ANN. This is because the main purpose of training is to determine the weight values used for the hidden layer nodes. Determining these values is the key method on how the ANN "learns." ANN learning is done by first inputting a large dataset to the network, one record or element at a time. This input data eventually creates output data, which is then compared to the ground truth data. Any resultant errors are then used in a feedback configuration to adjust the weight values in order to reduce and minimize the errors. This individual record training cycle is normally repeated over many thousands of times in order to completely train the network. The term epoch is used to describe the process of using the entire dataset for one pass with the ANN. It is not unusual to have multiple epochs used in a training session, where the training dataset is slightly rearranged for the next epoch in order to achieve a better learning result as compared to doing only a single pass. The whole training process is called *back propagation.*

Figure 4-19 shows a three-layer ANN with the weights annotated on the nodal interconnections.

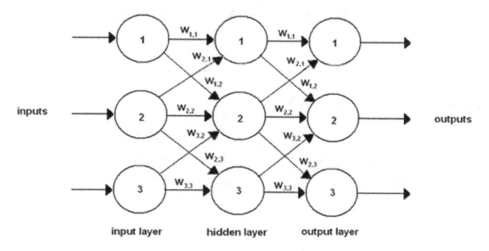

Figure 4-19. *Three-layer ANN with weights*

The weights' annotations are shown as $w_{i,j}$ where i is the source node and j is the destination node. Not all the nodes shown in the figure have interconnections because I didn't want to have too "busy" of a figure.

In reality, all nodes would be "connected" to other nodes when the learning commenced. Eventually, some weights would eventually diminish in value to where they are not used, which means the nodal connection would virtually cease to exist.

Practical ANN example

I believe it would be a useful learning exercise to show a completely "worked out" ANN example. Figure 4-20 shows a highly simplified, two-layer ANN, which I will use for this example.

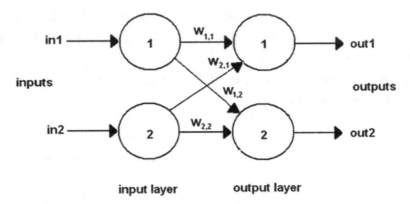

Figure 4-20.   *Two-layer ANN*

There is no need for a hidden layer in this example because I am only focusing demonstrating on the back propagation process. The initial data inputs and weights used to begin this example are shown in Table 4-2.

Table 4-2. *Initial input and weight values*

Symbol	Value
in1	0.8
in2	0.4
$w_{1,1}$	0.8
$w_{1,2}$	0.1
$w_{2,1}$	0.9
$w_{2,2}$	0.4

These values are random and do not reflect any real-world problem domain. I will describe in a later section how to preset an entire set of weights using a random number generator. One other item to note is that I will be using the sigmoid function to transform the summed values. The sigmoid equation is

$$y = \frac{1}{\left(1 + e^{-x}\right)}$$

where

$e = 2.71828 \ldots$ (Euler's number)

Plugging into the preceding equation $x = 1$ will yield $y = 0.731$. Computing *out1* requires solving the following equations:

$$sum\ of\ weighted\ inputs = x = w_{1,1} * in1 + w_{2,1} * in2$$

$$out1 = \frac{1}{\left(1 + e^{-x}\right)}$$

Substituting values from Table 4-2 yields

$$x = 0.8*0.8 + 0.9*0.4 = 1.0$$

$$out1 = \frac{1}{\left(1+e^{-1}\right)} = 0.731$$

In a similar fashion, computing *out2* requires solving these equations:

$$sum\ of\ weighted\ inputs = x = w_{1,2}*in1 + w_{2,2}*in2$$

$$out2 = \frac{1}{\left(1+e^{-x}\right)}$$

Substituting values from Table 4-2 yields

$$x = 0.1*0.8 + 0.4*0.4 = 0.24$$

$$out2 = \frac{1}{\left(1+e^{-0.24}\right)} = 0.560$$

The two ANN outputs have now been determined using a fair amount of manual computations. It should now be apparent at this point that it is simply not realistic to attempt to manually compute outputs for larger and more complex ANNs. Matrices and matrix operations will be used from now on now that I have demonstrated how tedious it is to use manual computations.

The input data for this simple example can be expressed as a vector:

$$\begin{Bmatrix} in1 \\ in2 \end{Bmatrix}$$

Likewise, the weighting matrix can be expressed as a 2 x 2 matrix:

$$\left\{ \begin{array}{cc} w_{1,1} & w_{1,2} \\ w_{2,1} & w_{2,2} \end{array} \right\}$$

Figure 4-21 shows the same manual computations being performed using matrix operation in an interactive Python session.

```
● ● ●                    ⌂ donnorris — Python — 80×61
[>>> import numpy as np
[>>> wtg = np.matrix([[0.8,0.1],[0.9,0.4]])
[>>> input = np.array([0.8, 0.4])[:,None]
[>>> X = np.dot(input.T,wtg)
[>>> X
matrix([[ 1.  ,  0.24]])
[>>> Y = 1/(1 + np.exp(-X))
[>>> Y
matrix([[ 0.73105858,  0.55971365]])
>>> 
```

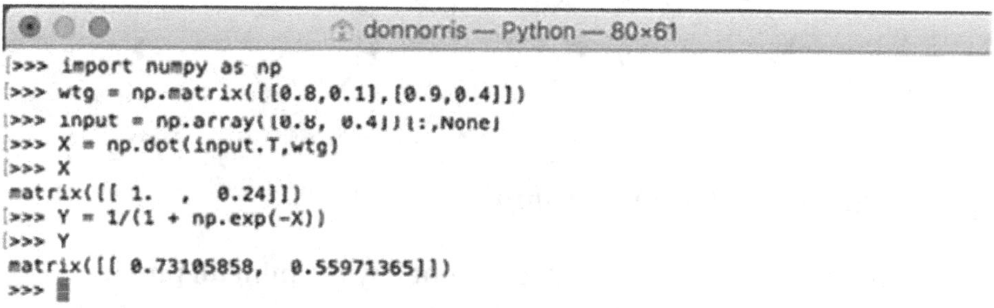

Figure 4-21. *Interactive Python session*

You can easily see that the Python session results matched the manual computations.

Complex ANN example

Figure 4-22 shows a more complex ANN example that I processed in using a Python script.

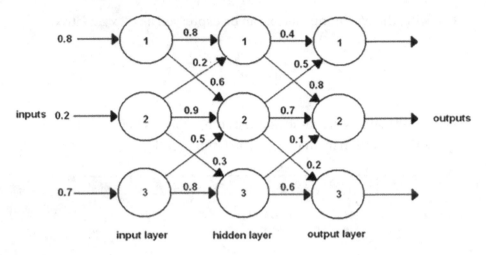

Figure 4-22. *Complex ANN example*

The input data vector does not represent any meaningful problem domain. It is just a set of random numbers because the purpose of this demonstration is to show the computing process used for a complex ANN.

The input dataset in vector format is

$$input = \begin{Bmatrix} 0.8 \\ 0.2 \\ 0.7 \end{Bmatrix}$$

The weighting matrix between the input and the hidden layers (wtg_{ih}) is

$$wtg_{ih} = \begin{Bmatrix} w_{1,1}\ w_{1,2}\ w_{1,3} \\ w_{2,1}\ w_{2,2}\ w_{2,3} \\ w_{3,1}\ w_{3,2}\ w_{3,3} \end{Bmatrix} = \begin{Bmatrix} 0.8\ 0.6\ 0.3 \\ 0.2\ 0.9\ 0.3 \\ 0.2\ 0.5\ 0.8 \end{Bmatrix}$$

The weighting matrix between the hidden and output layers (wtg_{ho}) is

$$wtg_{ho} = \begin{Bmatrix} w_{1,1}\ w_{1,2}\ w_{1,3} \\ w_{2,1}\ w_{2,2}\ w_{2,3} \\ w_{3,1}\ w_{3,2}\ w_{3,3} \end{Bmatrix} = \begin{Bmatrix} 0.4\ 0.8\ 0.4 \\ 0.5\ 0.7\ 0.2 \\ 0.9\ 0.1\ 0.6 \end{Bmatrix}$$

These matrices were assigned random numbers' elements in the range of 0 to 1.0.

The Python script used to process this ANN was named annDemo1. py and is available from the book's companion web site. The script is well commented, although I do add a little more commentary after the listing.

```python
# Import required libraries
import numpy as np

# Create the input data vector
input = np.array([0.8, 0.2, 0.7])[:,None]

# Create the wtgih matrix
wtgih = np.matrix([[0.8, 0.6, 0.3], \
                   [0.2, 0.9, 0.3], \
                   [0.2, 0.5, 0.8]])

# Create the wtgho matrix
wtgho = np.matrix([[0.4, 0.8, 0.4], \
                   [0.5, 0.7, 0.2], \
                   [0.9, 0.1, 0.6]])

# Compute the dot product of the input vector and wtgih matrix
X1 = np.dot(input.T, wtgih)
# Display the matrix
print('X1 matrix\n', X1)
print()

# Apply the activation function to the X1 matrix
out1 = 1 / (1 + np.exp(-X1))
# Display the matrix
print('out1 matrix\n', out1)
print()
```

```
# Compute the dot product of the X1 and wtgho matrices
X2 = np.dot(out1, wtgho)
# Display the matrix
print('X2 matrix\n', X2)
print()

# Apply the activation function to the X2 matrix
out2 = 1 / (1 + np.exp(-X2))
# Display the matrix
print('out2 matrix\n', out2)
```

This script takes advantage of the numpy dot product function to accomplish matrix multiplications. Also notice how easy it was to apply the activation function using the numpy exp function.

The script is run by entering the following command:

```
python annDemo1.py
```

Figure 4-23 shows the results after running the script.

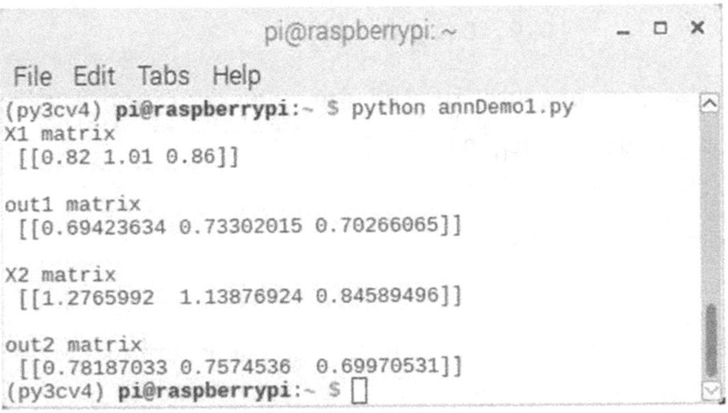

Figure 4-23. *Results for running the annDemo1 script*

The final output vector is shown as well as are all the intermediate matrices and vectors. As a side note, please do not get confused when I intermix the terms matrix and vector. I generally refer to a single row of data as a vector although you could technically label it as a 1D matrix. That label seems to me a bit too pedantic.

The final output data from this ANN is not meaningful, because the input data was not meaningful. However, the final output should be somewhat reflective of the input values. Table 4-3 compares the input and output values as well as the errors between them.

Table 4-3. *Comparison between input and output values*

Input	Output	Error
0.8	0.78187033	0.01812967
0.2	0.75745360	−0.55745360
0.7	0.69970531	0.00029469

The results are close except for the middle value in the table. This indicates that the initial weights must be modified to reduce the error. But how is this done? The answer is shown in the next section.

Modifying weight values

Consider the case where three nodes are connected as shown in Figure 4-24.

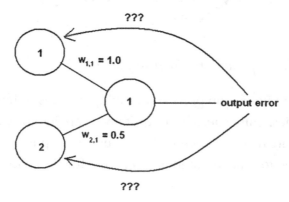

Figure 4-24. *Single error allocation setup*

There is some error in the summing node, which must be corrected by adjusting the weights between input nodes 1 and 2 and output node 1. A naive approach might be to evenly split the error between the nodes. However, that would not accurately represent the error contribution from each input node because node 1 has twice the weight as node 2. The correct solution is divide the error in direct proportion to the weights connecting the nodes. In this case, node 1 should be responsible for two-thirds of the error and node 2 for one-third.

Using the weighting matrix in this fashion is an additional feature that is not immediately apparent when first encountering an ANN. Normally, signals are propagated in a FeedForward configuration as I mentioned earlier. This modification approach uses weights with an error value to be propagated in a backward direction. This is why that error determination is called back propagation.

Now consider the case when multiple errors appear at two output nodes as shown in Figure 4-25.

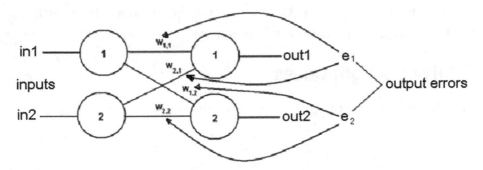

Figure 4-25. *Multiple error allocation setup*

The weight modification process for multiple nodes is the same as it is for single nodes. This is because output nodes are independent of one another. There are no direct connections between output nodes. The error amount assigned to each interconnection is the fraction based solely on the weight value on each line connected to the output node. In the case of Figure 4-25, the fractions applied to $w_{1,1}$ and $w_{2,1}$ for error e_1 are

$$\frac{w_{1,1}}{\left(w_{1,1}+w_{2,1}\right)} \text{ and } \frac{w_{2,1}}{\left(w_{1,1}+w_{2,1}\right)}$$

Similarly, the errors for e_2 are

$$\frac{w_{1,2}}{\left(w_{1,2}+w_{2,2}\right)} \text{ and } \frac{w_{2,2}}{\left(w_{1,2}+w_{2,2}\right)}$$

Thus far, the process to modify the weights based on the output errors has been simple. Errors are easily determined because the training data is readily available. There is nothing else required when training a two-layer ANN. But how is a three-layer ANN processed when there are most certainly errors in the hidden layer, yet no training data is available?

Figure 4-26 shows a three-layer, six-node ANN with two nodes per layer.

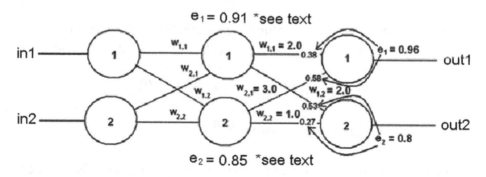

Figure 4-26. *Three-layer, six-node ANN*

This ANN has been simplified to help you focus on the few back propagation computations required. The output errors were randomly created because they are needed for the following computations. The following individual error contributions were computed using the weights shown in the figure:

For the $w_{1,1}$ line:

$$e_{1node1} * \frac{w_{1,1}}{\left(w_{1,1}+w_{2,1}\right)} = 0.96 * \frac{2}{\left(2+3\right)} = 0.96*0.4 = 0.38$$

For the $w_{2,1}$ line:

$$e_{1node2} * \frac{w_{2,1}}{\left(w_{1,1}+w_{2,1}\right)} = 0.96 * \frac{3}{\left(2+3\right)} = 0.96*0.6 = 0.58$$

For the $w_{1,2}$ line:

$$e_{2node1} * \frac{w_{1,2}}{\left(w_{1,2}+w_{2,2}\right)} = 0.8 * \frac{2}{\left(2+1\right)} = 0.8*0.66 = 0.53$$

For the $w_{2,2}$ line:

$$e_{2node2} * \frac{w_{2,2}}{\left(w_{1,2}+w_{2,2}\right)} = 0.8 * \frac{1}{\left(2+1\right)} = 0.8*0.33 = 0.27$$

The total normalized error value for each hidden node is the sum of the individual error contributions to the node and is calculated as follows:

$$e_1 = e_{1node1} + e_{2node1} = 0.38 + 0.53 = 0.91$$

$$e_2 = e_{1node2} + e_{2node2} = 0.58 + 0.27 = 0.85$$

These values are shown next to each of the hidden nodes in Figure 4-26. This error computing process may be continued to encompass all the errors for all remaining hidden layer nodes not only for the single hidden layer as shown in this example but for as many hidden layers that are in the ANN. However, there is no need to compute error values for the input layer because the error must be 0 for all input layer nodes. They simply pass the input data vector values without modifications.

You should be able to perceive that computing hidden layer error values is a tedious process and lends itself to be automated in manner to what was done with the FeedForward computations. The following matrix notation would apply if the error computations were directly translated from the manual process I just demonstrated:

$$e_{hidden} = \left\{ \begin{array}{cc} \dfrac{w_{1,1}}{\left(w_{1,1}+w_{2,1}\right)} & \dfrac{w_{1,2}}{\left(w_{1,1}+w_{2,1}\right)} \\[2ex] \dfrac{w_{2,1}}{\left(w_{2,1}+w_{2,2}\right)} & \dfrac{w_{2,2}}{\left(w_{2,1}+w_{2,2}\right)} \end{array} \right\} * \left\{ \begin{array}{c} in1 \\ in2 \end{array} \right\}$$

Unfortunately, there is no easy way to input the fractions as shown in the matrix. However, just consider that the fractions only normalize the error contribution, meaning that the contributed values will only range from 0 to 1.0. Relative error contribution can still be maintained by discarding the denominator. Removing the denominators yields

$$e_{hidden} = \left\{ \begin{array}{cc} w_{1,1} & w_{1,2} \\ w_{2,1} & w_{2,2} \end{array} \right\} * \left\{ \begin{array}{c} in1 \\ in2 \end{array} \right\}$$

This matrix formulation is identical to what was earlier demonstrated and can easily be handled with numpy functions.

Up to this point, I have only discussed how to determine individual error contributions. Now it is time to discuss how to modify the weights once the error contributions have been determined.

I will start by showing you a rather complex equation, which computes the output from a given output node for a three-layer, nine-node ANN

$$O_k = \dfrac{1}{-\sum_{j=1}^{3}\left(w_{j,k} * \dfrac{1}{\sum_{j=1}^{3}\left(w_{j,k} * x_i\right)} \right)}$$

where

$$O_k = output\ at\ kth\ node$$

$$w_{j,k} = interconnected\ weights$$

$$x_i = input\ data$$

This is a formidable equation even though it only applies to a simple three-layer, nine-node ANN. Imagine the equation that would apply for a six-input, five-layer ANN. It is extremely common to have even larger ANNs, so trying to analytically solve ANN equations is totally impractical and beyond human comprehension. Having ruled out an analytical approach, you might try a "brute-force" approach.

Consider using an extremely fast computer and trying a series of different values for each weight. Let's assume that the weight range is –1 to +1, which is entirely possible for a practical ANN. Further assume that the increment size is 0.001, which again is a reasonable assumption. This would mean that for a three-layer, nine-node ANN, there would be 18 weights to be tested with 2000 tests per connection for a grand total of 36,000 incremental tests. Let's say it took 1 second to do a test, then a total of 36,000 seconds would elapse or about 10 hours of computing time. Ten hours is long, but you could go to bed and the computer would be done in the morning. But now consider a realistic 900 node ANN, which I plan on demonstrating in the next chapter. That would require nearly one billion tests and take about 32 years to complete. I don't know about you, but waiting a generation or so for a computation to complete seems a bit too much. The practical alternative to the brute-force approach is to use the gradient descent algorithm that I have previously introduced in this chapter.

Figure 4-27 will be used as the network that I use to explain how to apply gradient descent to an ANN.

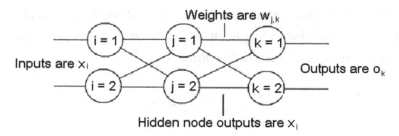

Figure 4-27. *Three-layer, six-node ANN*

There is one additional symbol e_k required beyond those shown in the figure to represent the output node error.

Output node error is expressed by

$$e_k = t_k - o_k$$

where

$t_k = ground\ truth\ value$

$o_k = output\ resulting\ from\ x_i\ input$

The total error is the sum of each node's error value. The resulting equation is

$$e_k = \sum_{i=1}^{N} (t_k - o_k)^2$$

where

$N = total\ number\ of\ nodes\ in\ ANN$

The error term is also squared for to ensure that negative errors do not cancel out positive errors as I had mentioned during the gradient descent discussion.

This error function is equivalent to the loss function. That means it must be differentiated with respect to $w_{j,k}$ to create the equation used to optimize the weights. The derivative form is

$$\frac{\partial e}{\partial w_{j,k}} = \frac{\partial}{\partial w_{j,k}} \sum_{i=1}^{N} (t_k - o_k)^2$$

This equation can be considerably simplified by taking note that the error at any given node is due solely to its input connections. This means the k_{th} node only depends on the $w_{j,k}$ weights on its input connections. Realizing this fact allows you to remove the summation from the error function because no other nodes contribute to k_{th} node's output. This simplification leads to a much simpler error function:

$$\frac{\partial e}{\partial w_{j,k}} = \frac{\partial}{\partial w_{j,k}} (t_k - o_k)^2$$

The final equation after doing the differentiation and applying the activation function is

$$\frac{\partial e}{\partial w_{j,k}} = -(t_k - o_k) * sigmoid\left(\sum_j w_{j,k} * o_j\right) * \left(1 - sigmoid\left(\sum_j w_{j,k} * o_j\right)\right) * o_j$$

The preceding equation while appearing quite complex is actually quite easy to understand if there is a physical interpretation put on it. The first part, $(t_k - o_k)$, is just the error. The summations inside of the sigmoid functions are the inputs into the k_{th} final layer node. The last term, o_j, is the output from the j_{th} node in the hidden layer.

The equation for the hidden layer gradient descent algorithm is similar to the one shown earlier. It is

$$\frac{\partial e}{\partial w_{i,j}} = -(e_j) * sigmoid\left(\sum_j w_{i,j} * o_i\right) * \left(1 - sigmoid\left(\sum_j w_{i,j} * o_i\right)\right) * o_i$$

The only remaining equation to be shown is the one which shows how to compute a new weight given the old weight and the result from the gradient descent algorithm. This equation is

$$new\ w_{j,k} = old\ w_{j,k} - \alpha * \frac{\partial e}{\partial w_{j,k}}$$

where

$$\alpha = learning\ rate$$

You should be able to see that the learning rate parameter has a strong effect how well the ANN steps through the gradient descent process.

It would be computationally efficient to express all of the preceding equations in matrix notation. The following function computes the gradient descent value for one link connecting a hidden layer node to an output node:

$$g(w_{j,k}) = \alpha * e_k * sigmoid(o_k) * (1 - sigmoid(o_k)) * o_j^T$$

where

$$o_j^T = transpose\ of\ the\ hidden\ layer\ matrix$$

The following are matrices for the three-layer, six-node ANN example:

$$\begin{bmatrix} g(w_{1,1})\ g(w_{2,1})\ g(w_{3,1}) \\ g(w_{1,2})\ g(w_{2,2})\ g(w_{3,2}) \end{bmatrix} * \begin{Bmatrix} e_1 * sigmoid_1 * (1 - sigmoid_1) \\ e_2 * sigmoid_2 * (1 - sigmoid_2) \end{Bmatrix} * \{o_1\ o_2\}$$

where

$$o_n = outputs\ from\ the\ hidden\ layer$$

At this point, I have covered all the theoretical and mathematical background necessary for you to understand a thorough example on how an ANN can learn.

Practical ANN weight modification example

I will be using a slightly changed network from the earlier model to detail how to compute modified weights. Figure 4-28 is a modified version of Figure 4-26 in which I have inserted two random values to represent outputs from the hidden layer node.

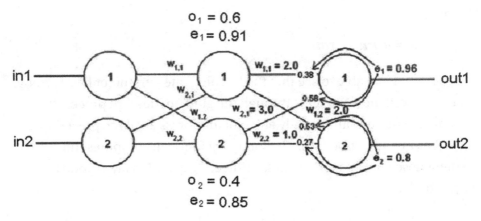

Figure 4-28. *Modified three-layer, six-node ANN*

The computation starts by updating $w_{1,1}$, which is the link connecting node 1 in the hidden layer to node 1 in the output layer. The following is the gradient descent equation for this link:

$$\frac{\partial e}{\partial w_{j,k}} = -(t_k - o_k) * sigmoid\left(\sum_j w_{j,k} * o_j\right) * \left(1 - sigmoid\left(\sum_j w_{j,k} * o_j\right)\right) * o_j$$

Substituting the values from the figure into this equation yields

$$(t_k - o_k) = e_1 = 0.96$$

$$\left(\sum_j w_{j,k} * o_j\right) = (2.0 * 0.6) + (3.0 * 0.4) = 2.4$$

$$sigmoid = \frac{1}{\left(1+e^{-2.4}\right)} = 0.9168$$

$$1 - sigmoid = 0.0832$$

$$o_1 = 0.6$$

Multiplying the preceding factors yields

$$-0.96 * 0.9168 * 0.0832 * 0.6 = -0.04394$$

If a learning rate of 0.15 is assumed, then the new weight will be

$$new\ w_{j,k} = old\ w_{j,k} - \alpha * \frac{\partial e}{\partial w_{j,k}}$$

$$new\ w_{j,k} = 2.0 - 0.15 * (-0.04394) = 2.0 + 0.0066 = 2.0066$$

The new weight is not too different from the old weight; however, you must be mindful that there will be hundreds, if not thousands, of iterations before a global minimum is reached. Small changes eventually result in large changes when accumulated over many iterations.

All the other network weights are adjusted using the same process as I just demonstrated.

Some issues with ANN learning

There are two items regarding the sigmoid activation function that you should know. I have replicated Figure 2-16 as Figure 4-29 for purpose of supporting this discussion.

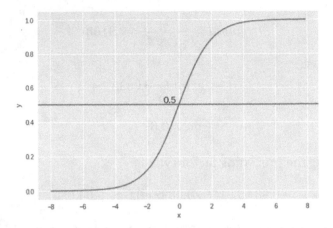

Figure 4-29. *Sigmoid function*

Examining the figure, you should be able to see that for x inputs greater than 2.5, the y output changes very little. This is because the sigmoid function asymptotically approaches 1.0 around that value. Small changes for large x inputs imply very small gradient changes happening. ANN learning becomes suppressed because the gradient descent algorithm depends upon a "reasonable" slope being present. Thus, ANN training datasets should limit x values to what might be termed a *pseudo-linear* range of approximately –3 to 3. The negative limit happens because the sigmoid function is symmetric around the y-axis and saturation occurs when x is 2.5 or less. Values of x outside the *pseudo-linear* range will cause a saturation effect for the ANN, and no effective weight updates can take place.

Another issue with the sigmoid function is that it cannot output values greater than 1.0 or less than 0. Initial weights must be selected to ensure that the function can output in its allowable range. Realistically, the output range has to be from roughly 0.01 to 0.99 because of the asymptotic nature described earlier.

Initial weight selection is important as I just described. Selecting a good initial set of ANN weights will avoid input saturation and output limit problems. The first obvious choice is to constrain weights to be within the *pseudo-linear* range I earlier specified. However, weights are more often constrained to be ±1 to be a bit more conservative.

There has been a useful rule of thumb followed by AI researchers for years to help with weight selection:

> *The weights should be initially allocated using a normal distribution set at a mean value equal to the inverse of the square root of the number of nodes in the ANN.*

If you are using a small ANN with 36 nodes, then the mean is $\dfrac{1}{\sqrt{36}}$ or 0.16667. Figure 4-30 shows a normal probability distribution with this mean and ±2 standard deviations.

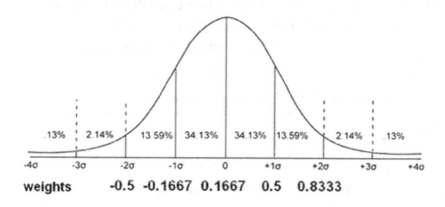

$$\text{approximate sd } (\sigma) = \frac{\text{largest value - smallest value}}{6} = \frac{1 - (1)}{6} = 0.333$$

Figure 4-30. *Normal deviation of initial weights for a 36-node ANN*

A random selection of weights in the range of approximately –0.5 to 0.833 would nicely provide an excellent starting point for learning for a 36-node ANN.

There are two final points regarding initial weight selection. The first is avoid setting all weights to the same value. ANN learning depends upon an unequal weight distribution. The second point (and hopefully obvious) is not to set all weights to 0 because that would disable the ANN.

This last section completes all my preparatory discussion regarding ANNs. It is time to take on an actual Python-based ANN.

ANN Python demonstration – Part 1

In part 1 of this demonstration, I will show you how to create an untrained ANN using Python. In part 2, I will show you how to train the ANN.

This discussion starts by describing the constituent modules of a practical ANN. Each module must have software crafted to allow it to accomplish its purpose.

The first module is the Init module, which is used to "build" the ANN structure. For this demonstration, I will be building a three-layer, nine-node ANN. This means I must have objects representing each layer, as well as inputs, outputs, and weights. Table 4-4 shows the Init module objects and references.

Table 4-4. *Init module objects and references*

Name	Description
inode	Number of nodes in the input layer
hnode	Number of nodes in the hidden layer
onode	Number of nodes in the output layer
wtgih	Weight matrix between the input and hidden layers
wtgho	Weight matrix between the hidden and output layers
w_{ij}	Individual weight matrix element
input	Vector for inputs
output	Vector for outputs
ohidden	Array for hidden layer outputs
lr	Learning rate

The following Init module code sets the number and type of nodes as well as the learning rate:

```
def __init__(self, inode, hnode, onode, lr):
    # Set local variables
    self.inode = inode
    self.hnode = hnode
    self.onode = onode
    self.lr = lr
```

This Init module code must be called with the appropriate values to structure a three-layer, nine-node ANN. These values are

- inode = 3

- hnode = 3

- onode = 3

- lr = 0.25

The next module to be discussed is one that sets up the weight matrices. I decided to use a normal distribution with a mean of 0.1667 and a standard deviation of 0.3333, as I previously discussed. Numpy contains a random number generator that nicely fulfills this requirement. The following code creates a 3 x 3 matrix named wtgih filled with random numbers with the desired statistical features:

```
self.wtgih = np.random.normal(0.1667, 0.3333, self.hnodes,
self. inodes)
```

I tested the preceding code in a Python interactive session, which is shown in Figure 4-31.

```
                                pi@raspberrypi: ~                    _  □  ×

 File  Edit  Tabs  Help
(py3cv4) pi@raspberrypi:~ $ python
Python 3.5.3 (default, Jan 19 2017, 14:11:04)
[GCC 6.3.0 20170124] on linux
Type "help", "copyright", "credits" or "license" for more information.
>>> import numpy as np
>>> wtgih = np.random.normal(0.1667, 0.3333, [3, 3])
>>> wtgih
array([[ 0.45617773, -0.35258079, -0.03437218],
       [ 1.21469934,  0.31561766,  0.13211115],
       [ 0.13550441,  0.11165721,  0.72949473]])
>>>
```

Figure 4-31. *Python interactive session for test code*

The resulting wtgih matrix is well formed with excellent initial values. The Init module can now be expanded to include the matrix generation code, where I used the rule of thumb described earlier to set the statistical parameters for the matrices.

```python
def __init__(self, inode, hnode, onode, lr):
    # Set local variables
    self.inode = inode
    self.hnode = hnode
    self.onode = onode
    self.lr = lr

    # Mean is the reciprocal of the sqrt of node sum
    mean = 1 / (pow((inode + hnode + onode), 0.5))

    # Std dev is approx 1/6 of total weight range
    # Total range = 2
    sd = 2 / 6

    # Generate both weight matrices
    # Input to hidden layer
    self.wtgih = np.random.normal(mean, sd, [hnode, inode])

    # Hidden to output layer
    self.wtgho = np.random.normal(mean, sd, [onode, hnode])
```

At this point, I will introduce a second module designed to test the Init module. This new module is named testNet, which reflects its purpose. This module takes an input vector and returns an output vector. This new module performs the following steps:

1. Converts the input data vector into a numpy array.

2. Multiplies the input array by the wtgih weight matrix.

3. Applies the sigmoid activation function.

4. Multiplies the hidden layer output by the wtgho matrix.

5. Applies the sigmoid activation function.

The listing for this new module is as follows:

```python
import numpy as np
def testNet(self, input):
    # Convert input data vector into an array
    input = np.array(input, ndmin=2).T

    # Multiply input array by wtgih matrix
    hInput = np.dot(self.wtgih, input)

    # Apply activation function
    hOutput = 1 / (1 + np.exp(-hInput))

    # Multiply hidden layer output by wtgho matrix
    oInput = np.dot(self.wtgho, hOutput)

    # Apply activation function
    oOutput = 1 / (1 + np.exp(-oInput))

    return oOutput
```

Both the Init and testNet modules were put into a Python class named ANN, which I will show you after the part 2 demonstration. However, I first need to demonstrate how a totally untrained ANN performs.

Note   You will not be able to replicate the following interactive session, at this point, because the ANN class file is not present in your home directory. You can try doing this interactive session after the class file has been created or loaded.

Figure 4-32 shows the interactive session that instantiates an ANN object named ann and then calls the testNet method. Note that the Init method is automatically called when the ann object is instantiated.

```
                              pi@raspberrypi: ~                          _ □ ✕

 File  Edit  Tabs  Help
(py3cv4) pi@raspberrypi:~ $ python
Python 3.5.3 (default, Jan 19 2017, 14:11:04)
[GCC 6.3.0 20170124] on linux
Type "help", "copyright", "credits" or "license" for more information.
>>> from ANN import ANN
>>> inode = 3
>>> hnode = 3
>>> onode = 3
>>> lr = 0.3
>>> ann = ANN(inode, hnode, onode, lr)
>>> ann.testNet([0.8, 0.5, 0.6])
array([[0.62856633],
       [0.7825606 ],
       [0.67244886]])
>>> ▯
```

Figure 4-32.   *Interactive Python session for the testNet call*

There are some serious errors present in the output, which I have detailed in Table 4-5.

Table 4-5. *Initial test errors*

Input	Output	Error	Percentage error
0.8	0.628566	−0.171434	21.4
0.5	0.782561	0.282561	56.5
0.6	0.672449	0.072449	12.1

These errors should be greatly reduced after the network is trained, which is the topic for the next demonstration.

ANN Python demonstration – Part 2

In part 2 of the demonstration, I will show you how to train the network that you created in part 1. Training will be using a third module named trainNet and is added to the ANN class file. This module functions in a similar fashion to the testNet module by computing an output dataset based on the input dataset. However, the trainNet module input dataset is a predetermined training set instead of a randomly generated dataset. What predetermined means in this context will become clearer as I go through the module development discussion.

The trainNet module computes an error dataset, which are the differences between with the ANN outputs and the input train dataset. Such behavior is called supervised learning, because the network "knows" what the correct output should be and can modify its weights to try to achieve the ground truth values contained in the input train dataset.

This next listing for trainNet module starts with some initialization code that is external to the initialization that happens within the Init module code:

```
def trainNet(self, inputT, train):
    # This module depends on values, arrays, and matrices
    # created when the init module is run
```

```
# Create the arrays from the list arguments
self.inputT = np.array(inputT, ndmin=2).T
self.train = np.arrat(train, ndmin=2).T
```

The computed errors are the differences between the training set values and the actual outputs. The error equation for the k_{th} output node as previously shown is

$$e_k = t_k - o_k$$

The matrix notation for the output errors is

$$self.eOutput = self.train - self.oOutput$$

The hidden layer error array in matrix notation for this example ANN is

$$hError = \left\{ \begin{matrix} w_{1,1} & w_{1,2} & w_{1,3} \\ w_{2,1} & w_{2,2} & w_{2,3} \\ w_{3,1} & w_{3,2} & w_{3,3} \end{matrix} \right\}^T * \left\{ \begin{matrix} e_1 \\ e_2 \\ e_3 \end{matrix} \right\}$$

The following is the Python code that generates this array:

```
self.hError = np.dot(self.wtgho.T, self.eOutput)
```

The following is the weight update equation for adjusting a link between the jth and kth layers:

$$g(w_{j,k}) = \alpha * e_k * sigmoid(o_k) * (1 - sigmoid(o_k)) * o_j^T$$

The new $g(w_{j,k})$ array must be added to the original because these are adjustments to the original. The preceding equation is easily expressed in Python code by

```
self.wtgho += self.lr*np.dot((self.eOutput*self.oOutputT*(1 -
self.oOutputT)), self.hOutputT.T)
```

The code for the weight updates between the input and hidden layers uses precisely the same format:

```
self.wtgih += self.lr*np.dot((self.hError*self.hOutputT*(1 -
self.hOutputT)), self.inputT.T)
```

The two preceding Python statements are at the heart of the gradient descent algorithm. They basically step down the complex error (loss) function contours in search of the global minimum. You should note that there is no limiting statement that will stop this search. That is the responsibility of the calling function, which I will shortly demonstrate.

The complete ANN class listing follows, which includes the trainNet module as well as the Init and testNet modules. This file is named ANN. py and is available from the book's companion web site. I have not added any additional code comments beyond what is included in the listing. I feel that all my foregoing discussions hopefully explain how this code works.

```python
# Import required libraries
import numpy as np
class ANN:

    def __init__(self, inode, hnode, onode, lr):
        # Set local variables
        self.inode = inode
        self.hnode = hnode
        self.onode = onode
        self.lr = lr

        # Mean is the reciprocal of the sqrt of total nodes
        mean = 1/(pow((inode + hnode + onode), 0.5))

        # Std dev is approx 1/6 of total range
        # Range = 2
        sd = 2/6
```

```python
    # Generate both weight matrices
    # Input to hidden layer matrix
    self.wtgih = np.random.normal(mean, sd, [hnode, inode])

    # Hidden to output layer matrix
    self.wtgho = np.random.normal(mean, sd, [onode, hnode])

def testNet(self, input):
    # Convert input data vector into numpy array
    input = np.array(input, ndmin=2).T

    # Multiply input by wtgih
    hInput = np.dot(self.wtgih, input)

    # Apply activation function
    hOutput = 1/(1 + np.exp(-hInput))

    # Multiply hidden layer output by wtgho
    oInput = np.dot(self.wtgho, hOutput)

    # Apply activation function
    oOutput = 1/(1 + np.exp(-oInput))

    return oOutput

def trainNet(self, inputT, train):
    # This module depends upon values, arrays and matrices
    # created when the init module is run

    # Create the arrays from the arguments
    self.inputT = np.array(inputT, ndmin=2).T
    self.train = np.array(train, ndmin=2).T

    # Multiply inputT array by wtgih
    self.hInputT = np.dot(self.wtgih, self.inputT)
```

```
# Apply activation function
self.hOutputT = 1/(1 + np.exp(-self.hInputT))

# Multiply hidden layer output by wtgho
self.oInputT = np.dot(self.wtgho, self.hOutputT)

# Apply activation function
self.oOutputT = 1/(1 + np.exp(-self.oInputT))

# Calculate output errors
self.eOutput = self.train - self.oOutputT

# Calculate hidden layer error array
self.hError = np.dot(self.wtgho.T, self.eOutput)

# Update weight matrix wtgho
self.wtgho += self.lr*np.dot((self.eOutput*self.
oOutputT*(1 - self.oOutputT)), self.hOutputT.T)

# Update weight matrix wtgih
self.wtgih += self.lr*np.dot((self.hError*self.
hOutputT*(1 - self.hOutputT)), self.inputT.T)
```

The following script uses the ANN class to train the same sized network I used in part 1 of the demonstration. This script is named testANN3.py and is available from the book's companion web site:

```
# Import required libraries
from ANN import ANN

# Create input data vector
inputT = [0.8, 0.5, 0.6]
# Display it
print('Input data vector')
print(inputT)
print()
```

```
# Train for 1 iteration
train = inputT
ann = ANN(3,3,3,0.3)
output = ann.testNet(inputT)
# Display output
print('After one iteration')
print(output)
print()

# Train for 499 iterations
for i in range(499):
    ann.trainNet(inputT, train)

output = ann.testNet(inputT)
# Display output
print('After 500 iterations')
print(output)
print()
```

The script is run by entering the following command:

```
python testANN3.py
```

Figure 4-33 shows the results after the script was run.

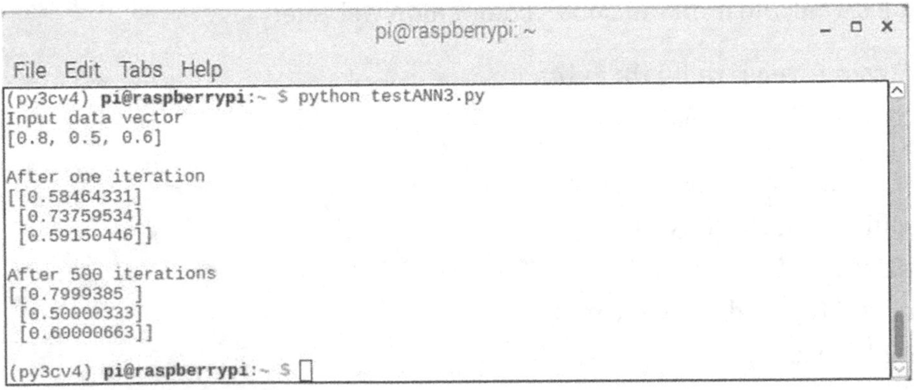

Figure 4-33. *Results after running the testANN3 script*

You can clearly see that the initial output was way off from the initial data vector, except for the third element. However, after a total of 500 iterations, the output essentially matched the input, which showed the network was fully trained for this particular input dataset vector. In case you are wondering, there is no specific reason why I chose 500 iterations as the limit other than the output results were unchanging as I tried various numbers in that region. I used a "trial-and-error" approach because it only took the RasPi a few seconds to do hundreds of iterations. This result just shows that there is no "magic" number to find regarding the number of iterations to use because each network is unique. Sometimes you just use a number which is good enough, which I have previously stated.

I was also interested in the net change in the two weight matrices from the initialized version to the fully trained version. Accordingly, I added an additional method to the ANN class, which returns the two matrices when called. This method is named getMatrices and is shown here:

```
def getMatrices(self):
    matrixList = list([self.wtgih, self.wtgho])
    return matrixList
```

The testANN3 script was then slightly modified to make two calls to the getMatrices method. The first call was after the first iteration, and the second call was after the 500th iteration. The modified testANN3.py script was renamed testANN4.py. It is available from the book's companion web site.

```
from ANN import ANN
inputT = [0.8, 0.5, 0.6]
print('Input data vector')
print(inputT)
print()

train = inputT
ann = ANN(3,3,3,0.3)
output = ann.testNet(inputT)
```

273

```
print('After one iteration')
print(output)
print()

matrixList = ann.getMatrices()
print('wtgih matrix')
print(matrixList[0])
print()
print('wtgho matrix')
print(matrixList[1])
print()

for i in range(499):
    ann.trainNet(inputT, train)

output = ann.testNet(inputT)
print('After 500 iterations')
print(output)
print()

matrixList = ann.getMatrices()
print('wtgih matrix')
print(matrixList[0])
print()
print('wtgho matrix')
print(matrixList[1])
print()
```

The script is run by entering the following command:

```
python testANN4.py
```

Figure 4-34 shows the results after the script was run.

```
                              pi@raspberrypi: ~                    _  □  ×
 File  Edit  Tabs  Help
(py3cv4) pi@raspberrypi:~ $ python testANN4.py
Input data vector
[0.8, 0.5, 0.6]

After one iteration
[[0.61899939]
 [0.68476061]
 [0.58316301]]

wtgih matrix
[[0.20764646 0.27111758 0.39396353]
 [0.00599391 0.57606642 0.32964878]
 [0.28014321 0.51896524 0.71370693]]

wtgho matrix
[[ 0.71960682 -0.42366485  0.41177852]
 [ 0.25590158  0.30174381  0.59858451]
 [-0.11056946  0.6463699   0.00654417]]

After 500 iterations
[[0.79994577]
 [0.50000026]
 [0.59999837]]

wtgih matrix
[[ 0.59664779  0.51424342  0.68571453]
 [-0.14529708  0.48150955  0.21618054]
 [ 0.39737307  0.5922339   0.80162932]]

wtgho matrix
[[ 1.10021992 -0.10030144  0.810933   ]
 [-0.1448987  -0.04058341  0.17722845]
 [-0.05075971  0.69661001  0.06890301]]

(py3cv4) pi@raspberrypi:~ $ []
```

Figure 4-34. *Results after running the testANN4 script*

There are significant differences between the beginning and final versions for the two matrices, which clearly show how the weights were changed by the gradient descent algorithm.

I was next curious to see what happened to the two matrices if the script was simply rerun. Figure 4-35 shows the rerun results.

```
                              pi@raspberrypi: ~              _ □ ×

 File  Edit  Tabs  Help
(py3cv4) pi@raspberrypi:~ $ python testANN4.py
Input data vector
[0.8, 0.5, 0.6]

After one iteration
[[0.61110985]
 [0.62448693]
 [0.62653313]]

wtgih matrix
[[-0.13535282 -0.07147734 -0.07415608]
 [ 0.10895156  0.4588935   0.03200034]
 [ 0.46201488  0.36760958  0.06870409]]

wtgho matrix
[[0.19823572 0.16275892 0.41472467]
 [0.24744928 0.6148658  0.05891661]
 [0.28599818 0.30094105 0.32945731]]

After 500 iterations
[[0.79982848]
 [0.50000652]
 [0.60003627]]

wtgih matrix
[[0.058707   0.04981005 0.07138879]
 [0.17130007 0.49786131 0.07876172]
 [0.87321271 0.62460823 0.37710247]]

wtgho matrix
[[ 0.55586367  0.59634036  0.9413429 ]
 [ 0.0193061   0.33717295 -0.27703996]
 [ 0.2095684   0.20924923  0.21661308]]

(py3cv4) pi@raspberrypi:~ $ []
```

Figure 4-35. *Results after rerunning the testANN4 script*

When comparing Figure 4-34 to Figure 4-35, it is easy to see that the starting matrices are different in each case. That is because the Init module uses a random number process to create each matrix. A more interesting feature is to observe that the final version of each matrix is different from the other for each time the script is run. I concluded that there must be no single set of optimized matrices for a particular solution and that the final set of matrices is dependent on the initialized set. From a mathematical perspective, this means there must be an infinite set of matrices that can be created to solve this particular input dataset using this particular ANN. It is my conjecture that this is one likely reason that AI researchers refer to ANNs as "black boxes" because of these non-analytical solutions.

This concludes my deep learning preparation chapter. I humbly apologize if I went a bit "overboard" with some of the topics, especially with the math, but I felt it was necessary to expose you at least once to the important underpinnings of DL. You should now be fully prepared to understand and appreciate the interesting and practical ANN demonstrations in the next chapters.

CHAPTER 5

Practical deep learning ANN demonstrations

Several practical DL demonstrations are shown in this chapter. You will be prepared to follow along with the demonstrations provided you have read the previous chapter or have acquired previous experience with DL techniques and concepts. I had two goals in mind when writing this chapter. The first was to clearly show how a complete ANN project could be accomplished to produce realistic and useful results. The second was to point out some potential pitfalls and unrealistic assumptions that are common in ANN development.

© Donald J. Norris 2020
D. J. Norris, *Machine Learning with the Raspberry Pi*,
https://doi.org/10.1007/978-1-4842-5174-4_5

Parts list

You will need a standard RasPi desktop configuration and the Pi Camera for these chapter demonstrations.

Item	Model	Quantity	Source
Raspberry Pi 3 or 4	Model B or B+ (RasPi 3) Model B (RasPi 4)	1	mcmelectronics.com adafruit.com digikey.com mouser.com farnell.com
Micro SD card	16 GB, class 10 or larger	1	amazon.com
Raspberry Pi Camera with ribbon cable	Version 2 or later	1	amazon.com
Raspberry Pi Camera holder	Any that fits a version 2 model	1	amazon.com
USB keyboard	Amazon Basic	1	amazon.com
USB mouse	Amazon Basic	1	amazon.com
HDMI monitor	Commodity	1	amazon.com

Recognizing handwritten number demonstration

This ANN project is considered a classic one within the ANN community. It is focused on recognizing handwritten numbers. However, I would first like to comment on some general project development guidelines before I delve into the specifics for this project. Following these guidelines will help you be successful in completing most projects, including small ones such as this one. The guidelines can be separated into a series of steps, which will be individually discussed after the list:

1. Write down the requirements.

2. Establish resources for personnel, hardware, and software.

3. Create a realistic schedule including milestones.

4. Start construction, development, and/or implementation.

5. Begin testing.

6. Revise development/implementation based on test results.

7. Begin production or field release.

8. Develop a maintenance plan.

Write down the requirements – It is important to write down the project requirements, even if you are the only one working on the project. Writing the requirements forces you to firmly understand what the project is supposed to accomplish when completed. This guideline becomes especially important if there are multiple team members working on the project. Committing the requirements to paper and having all the team members agree to them avoid future disagreements regarding what was to be done and how it was to be accomplished.

Establish resources for personnel, funds, hardware, and software – Knowing that all the resources required for the project are either immediately available or there is a plan to acquire them is key for any successful project completion. This step is likely optional for a single-person project with a limited requirement, but is essential for a medium to large project with a dedicated team.

Create a realistic schedule including milestones – Establishing a schedule is always a good idea, no matter what size project is being attempted. A simple note on your desk or calendar will suffice for a single-person software project, while more formal scheduling artifacts are appropriate for medium- to large-scale projects. Creating milestones is also useful, even if it is just a reminder to yourself that you are on schedule or falling behind, which is more often the case. There are often specialized project scheduling teams established for long-term, large-scale projects, which assist project managers with staying on schedule.

Start construction, development, and/or implementation – This is when the actual project work begins. For software development projects, such as described in this book, you should allocate sufficient time to work on the project without too many distractions. I know this is difficult in a family situation, but having uninterrupted time is important for efficient project completion. Formal projects are a different story because that is the *raison d'être* for their existence.

Begin testing – This step is appropriate for projects involving prototypes and/or software development. Testing hardware prototypes to determine if they meet requirements is absolutely necessary and no project can justifiably proceed without this step. Similarly, testing software to see that it meets its requirements is also a requirement. There may be formal ways of recording how well the prototype/software meets requirements depending on the nature and scale of the project.

Revise development/implementation based on test results – Altering and/or modifying the development/implementation must follow the review and acceptance of test results. Not using test results would defeat the whole purpose of testing and ultimately lead to an unsuccessful project. Sometimes, testing reveals that the initial requirements list was unrealistic or faulty in some manner. It is not unusual in a project life cycle to have requirements change somewhat due to latent discoveries or even the unfortunate event of having planned for resources unexpectedly being delayed or made unavailable. What you want to be wary of is requirements "creep," where nice to have requirements are quietly added to the list. This situation can lead to a problematic project outcome.

Begin production or field release – The project is essentially done and ready to be released for whatever purpose it was intended. Sometimes, project managers will delay the final release pending nice to have, small "tweaks." This should be avoided because if the project was developed using firm guidelines, it should be ready at the scheduled date. Appropriate documentation should also be provided at this time concerning how prospective users should interact with the project. On large projects, user training will likely have already been started or even completed by the release date.

Develop a maintenance plan – All projects, except for small individualized projects, should include a maintenance scheme. This could be a formal plan, or it could only be an update web site. It all depends on the project scope and expected project lifetime.

Only four of the preceding steps are applicable for this project. The last step is a hybrid combination of steps 4, 5, and 6 from the preceding list:

1. Write down the requirements.

2. Establish resources for personnel, hardware, and software.

3. Create a realistic schedule including milestones.

4. Start development and testing and revise development as necessary.

In real-world terms, these steps consist of the following details:
Write down the requirements:

- Create a Raspberry Pi-controlled handwritten number recognition system.

- It will use an ANN designed to accommodate the available training/validation dataset.

- It will display results on a monitor screen.

- The user will use a terminal window to interact with the system.

Establish resources for personnel, hardware, and software:

- Personnel – Self only.

- Equipment – See parts list. Internet access required to download required dataset.

Create a realistic schedule including milestones:

- Three work days to create and test the initial ANN

- One work day to test the visual recognition feature

- One work day to complete documentation

Start development and testing and revise development as necessary:

- Very much a unique experience for every developer. My approach, I suspect, differs significantly from other developer's approaches.

- I try to comment/document as I develop and will backtrack to revise the comments based on the final outcome.

Project history and preparatory details

Recognizing handwritten numbers has been an important priority for postal services worldwide. In many countries, postal codes are written on letters and packages to improve the way these items are processed in the system. Automated systems using video cameras coupled with handwritten number recognition software are used to mechanically sort letters and packages without human intervention. Of course, technologies have constantly improved to the point where most of the packages sent through a postal service are now barcoded. Nonetheless, many letters are still mailed with handwritten postal codes that still need to be handled.

ANN was created that readily recognizes handwritten numbers. The training and validation/test datasets used in this project come from two Mixed National Institute of Standards and Technology (MNIST) databases. These databases have been widely used for many years in the AI community and are widely recognized as an accepted standard for rating how well a specific ANN is for performing this task.

The MNIST databases were created from thousands of Images taken from handwritten numeric digits written by 500 people. Half of these people were US Census Bureau employees, and the other half were high school students. The original black-and-white Images were normalized to fit into a 20 x 20 pixel Image. They were further processed by using anti-aliasing to generate a 1-byte grayscale value for each pixel in the original Image.

The MNIST datasets are large, consisting of 60,000 training Images (104 MB) and 10,000 validation Images (18 MB). They are freely available in a comma-separated value format at

Training set:

```
www.pjreddie.com/media/files/mnist_train.csv
```

Test set:

```
www.pjreddie.com/media/files/mnist_test.csv
```

Both datasets will be used in this project. I would suggest that you download them and store them in a named directory that you can easily access. As mentioned previously, both datasets are in a CSV format, which makes for easy import into a Python script. Every record in both datasets has a label indicating the actual numerical digit represented by the Image. The use of the labels is critical for both training and validating the ANN. Using label datasets is termed supervised learning, and it is a fundamental concept for how ANNs can learn. The ANN used in this project cannot be trained or tested without labels being present for each record.

In this instance, there are separate datasets available for training and testing. That is not always the case. When only a single dataset is available, it must be parsed to provide training records and testing records. There is no hard or fast rule existing on how to parse a single dataset. Personally, I use an 80/20 rule where 80% of the dataset will be allotted for training and 20% for testing/validation. Other AI practitioners will likely have their own rule of thumb, but I have found that the 80/20 rule seems to work well in most instances.

Figure 5-1 shows the beginning of the first record in the training dataset. This figure is a screenshot from a hex editor running on my MacBook Pro laptop.

0	352C302C	302C302C	302C302C	302C302C	302C302C	5,0,0,0,0,0,0,0,0,0,
20	302C302C	302C302C	302C302C	302C302C	302C302C	0,0,0,0,0,0,0,0,0,0,
40	302C302C	302C302C	302C302C	302C302C	302C302C	0,0,0,0,0,0,0,0,0,0,
60	302C302C	302C302C	302C302C	302C302C	302C302C	0,0,0,0,0,0,0,0,0,0,
80	302C302C	302C302C	302C302C	302C302C	302C302C	0,0,0,0,0,0,0,0,0,0,
100	302C302C	302C302C	302C302C	302C302C	302C302C	0,0,0,0,0,0,0,0,0,0,
120	302C302C	302C302C	302C302C	302C302C	302C302C	0,0,0,0,0,0,0,0,0,0,
140	302C302C	302C302C	302C302C	302C302C	302C302C	0,0,0,0,0,0,0,0,0,0,
160	302C302C	302C302C	302C302C	302C302C	302C302C	0,0,0,0,0,0,0,0,0,0,
180	302C302C	302C302C	302C302C	302C302C	302C302C	0,0,0,0,0,0,0,0,0,0,
200	302C302C	302C302C	302C302C	302C302C	302C302C	0,0,0,0,0,0,0,0,0,0,
220	302C302C	302C302C	302C302C	302C302C	302C302C	0,0,0,0,0,0,0,0,0,0,
240	302C302C	302C302C	302C302C	302C302C	302C302C	0,0,0,0,0,0,0,0,0,0,
260	302C302C	302C302C	302C302C	302C302C	302C302C	0,0,0,0,0,0,0,0,0,0,
280	302C302C	302C302C	302C302C	302C302C	302C302C	0,0,0,0,0,0,0,0,0,0,
300	302C302C	302C332C	31382C31	382C3138	2C313236	0,0,0,3,18,18,18,126
320	2C313336	2C313735	2C32362C	3136362C	3235352C	,136,175,26,166,255,
340	3234372C	3132372C	302C302C	302C302C	302C302C	247,127,0,0,0,0,0,0,
360	302C302C	302C302C	302C302C	33302C33	362C3934	0,0,0,0,0,0,30,36,94
380	2C313534	2C313730	2C323533	2C323533	2C323533	,154,170,253,253,253
400	2C323533	2C323533	2C323235	2C313732	2C323533	,253,253,225,172,253
420	2C323432	2C313935	2C36342C	302C302C	302C302C	,242,195,64,0,0,0,0,
440	302C302C	302C302C	302C302C	302C3439	2C323338	0,0,0,0,0,0,0,49,238
460	2C323533	2C323533	2C323533	2C323533	2C323533	,253,253,253,253,253
480	2C323533	2C323533	2C323533	2C323531	2C39332C	,253,253,253,251,93,
500	38322C38	322C3536	2C33392C	302C302C	302C302C	82,82,56,39,0,0,0,0,
520	302C302C	302C302C	302C302C	302C302C	31382C32	0,0,0,0,0,0,0,0,18,2
540	31392C32	35332C32	35332C32	35332C32	35332C32	19,253,253,253,253,2
560	35332C31	39382C31	38322C32	34372C32	34312C30	53,198,182,247,241,0
580	2C302C30	2C302C30	2C302C30	2C302C30	2C302C30	,0,0,0,0,0,0,0,0,0,0
600	2C302C30	2C302C30	2C302C30	2C302C30	302C3135	,0,0,0,0,0,0,0,80,15
620	362C3130	372C3235	332C3235	332C3230	352C3131	6,107,253,253,205,11
640	2C302C34	332C3135	342C302C	302C302C	302C302C	,0,43,154,0,0,0,0,0,
660	302C302C	302C302C	302C302C	302C302C	302C302C	0,0,0,0,0,0,0,0,0,0,
680	302C302C	302C302C	31342C31	2C313534	2C323533	0,0,0,0,14,1,154,253
700	2C39302C	302C302C	302C302C	302C302C	302C302C	,90,0,0,0,0,0,0,0,0,
720	302C302C	302C302C	302C302C	302C302C	302C302C	0,0,0,0,0,0,0,0,0,0,
740	302C302C	302C302C	302C302C	302C3133	392C3235	0,0,0,0,0,0,0,139,25
760	332C3139	302C322C	302C302C	302C302C	302C302C	3,190,2,0,0,0,0,0,0,
780	302C302C	302C302C	302C302C	302C302C	302C302C	0,0,0,0,0,0,0,0,0,0,
800	302C302C	302C302C	302C302C	302C302C	31312C31	0,0,0,0,0,0,0,0,11,1
820	39302C32	35332C37	302C302C	302C302C	302C302C	90,253,70,0,0,0,0,0,

0x0 out of 0x687FF3A bytes

Figure 5-1. *A portion of the first record in the MNIST training dataset*

287

There are 784 bytes composing one Image because each Image has been rescaled from 20 x 20 to 28 x 28 pixels. Each pixel represents a grayscale pixel intensity, with values ranging from 0 to 255, where 0 is total black and 255 is total white. Every record in the database has 784 pixel values, 785 commas and 1 byte for the label value. Those values add up to 1570 bytes. When you consider that there are more than 60,000 training records, the overall dataset size is about 100 MB. Handling a dataset this size while developing a script is a chore even for the fastest processor, and the RasPi does not fall in that category. Fortunately, there are two small sub-sets for both MNIST train and test datasets, which can be used for development. These are available at

Train dataset:

https://raw.githubusercontent.com/makeyourownneuralnetwork/
makeyourownneuralnetwork/master/mnist_dataset/mnist_train_100.csv

Test dataset:

https://raw.githubusercontent.com/makeyourownneuralnetwork/
makeyourownneuralnetwork/master/mnist_dataset/mnist_test_10.csv

All the datasets described earlier are in a CSV format, where commas are used to separate individual data values. The Python language contains useful functions to input CSV data into scripts in a numerical format that can easily be used. The following code snippet opens a CSV file and "reads" the contents into a data list. A data list is an object, which efficiently stores and retrieves data for rapid access by the script.

```
dataFile = open('mnist_train_100.csv')
dataList = dataFile.readlines()
dataFile.close()
```

I entered the preceding code into an interactive Python session to reveal how this snippet works. Figure 5-2 shows the interactive session.

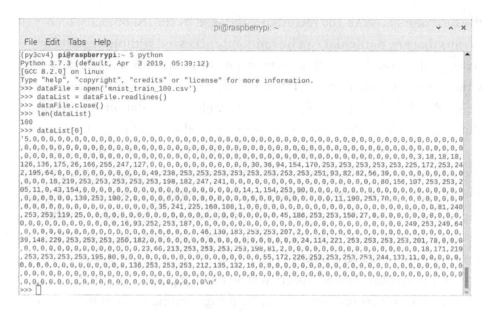

Figure 5-2. *Interactive Python session for data file operations*

You should be able to see that the data list was correctly instantiated. I also entered a length command, which returned 100. That reflected the number of elements in the data list, which is what was expected from the mnist_train_100.csv file. In addition, I displayed the contents of the first record, dataList [0], which displayed as series of 1570 integers, all separated by commas. Note that the first integer is 5, which corresponds to the record label.

You should also take note of the appearance of single quotes at the start and end of the displayed integers. This indicates that Python considers the data to be a long string. While it may appear as numbers, the Python interpreter considers it to be a string of ASCII characters. The character displayed just before the ending single quote is "\n". This is the "escaped" letter n. In ASCII terms, it represents the carriage return function, which means that a new line is to be created at this point in the record, as the ASCII characters are being interpreted. New line characters are used as delimiters for the dataset. Delimiters indicate where one record stops and

289

the next one starts. All 100 records are indexed by the list object, which means that any particular can be randomly accessed without reading or writing all the records leading up to that record. The indices are 0 based, which means the index range is 0 to 99 for all of the records. Any record can be randomly accessed using Python's array element notation. For instance, the middle or 50th element would be referenced as dataList [49].

Recall, in previous chapters, that it is important to have an awareness regarding the nature of the data you are handling, regardless of the type of mathematical operations being attempted. In this case, visually reviewing individual handwritten records could provide you with insight into the overall problem domain that simply could not be obtained by merely reviewing numerical data lists.

The Matplotlib Python library will be used to provide an Image of any selected data list record. Enter these next two commands in order to have the Matplotlib library available for import into a script:

```
sudo apt-get update
sudo apt-get install python-matplotlib
```

The following script will be used to view any record in the 100 record MNIST train dataset. The script is named viewRecord.py, and it is available from the book's companion web site:

```
# Import required libraries
import numpy as np
import matplotlib.pyplot as plt

# Create data list
dataFile = open('mnist_train_100.csv')
dataList = dataFile.readlines()
dataFile.close()
```

```
# Get the record number
print('Enter record number to be viewed: ', end = ' ')
num = input()

# Get the record
record = dataList[int(num)].split(',')

# Reshape the array for imaging
imageArray = np.asfarray(record[1:]).reshape(28,28)

# Image it as a grayscale
plt.imshow(imageArray, cmap='Greys', interpolation='None')
plt.show()
```

An object named dataList contains all 785 elements from the requested record. These are separate elements because the split method created them as such based on the comma delimiter. The dataList object must then be reshaped into a 28 x 28 numpy array in order to be Imaged. Each value in the array will now correspond to a pixel intensity as shown in the original Image. Also note that the numpy array starts with the second element, whose index equals 1. That is because the first element is the label, which you do not want to be included in the Image. Another item to note is that "Greys" is intentionally misspelled in the imshow command. I can only guess that an open source developer was not too familiar with how to correctly spell it.

The script is run by entering this command:

```
python3 viewRecord.py
```

The resulting Image for record 0 is shown in Figure 5-3.

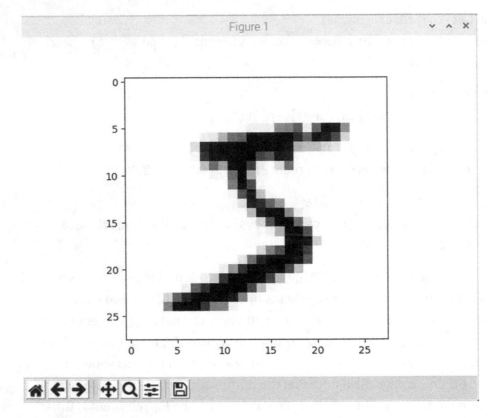

Figure 5-3. *Record 0 Image*

The figure clearly shows a rather "lazy" number 5 digit drawn. You can confirm that it is supposed to be the number 5 by examining the first element in the numerical record listing shown in Figure 5-2.

At this point, you should be comfortable in dealing with the datasets that will be used in the project. The next section shows you how to adjust or modify the datasets so that they are compatible with what a practical ANN requires as an input data source.

Adjusting the input datasets

In the preceding discussion, it was pointed out that the pixel values will range from 0 to 255. This range is significantly beyond an acceptable data value input range for an ANN. Recall, in Chapter 4, where I was discussing some issues and limitations regarding ANNs. In that section, I stated

Thus, ANN training datasets should limit x values to what might be termed a pseudo-linear range of approximately -3 to 3.

The reason was the sigmoid function's limiting action. Input data values beyond +/- 3 will saturate the function output, effectively shutting down any ANN learning function. In communication electronics terminology, this situation is often called running out of dynamic range. Fortunately, it is easy to adjust the input data values to an acceptable range of 0.01 to 1.00 without any loss in ANN accuracy. The Python statement to make this adjustment is

```
adjustedRecord = (np.asfarray(record[1:])/255.0 * 0.99) + 0.01
```

I added this statement to the interactive Python session I ran earlier. Figure 5-4 shows the revised results along with the interactive session.

```
File  Edit  Tabs  Help
pi@raspberrypi:~ $ python3
Python 3.7.3 (default, Apr  3 2019, 05:39:12)
[GCC 8.2.0] on linux
Type "help", "copyright", "credits" or "license" for more information.
>>> import numpy as np
>>> dataFile = open('mnist_train_100.csv')
>>> dataList = dataFile.readlines()
>>> dataFile.close()
>>> record = dataList[0].split(',')
>>> adjustedRecord = (np.asfarray(record[1:]) / 255.0 * 0.99) + 0.01
>>> print(adjustedRecord)
[0.01        0.01        0.01        0.01        0.01        0.01
 0.01        0.01        0.01        0.01        0.01        0.01
 0.01        0.01        0.01        0.01        0.01        0.01
 0.01        0.01        0.01        0.01        0.01        0.01
 0.01        0.01        0.01        0.01        0.01        0.01
 0.01        0.01        0.01        0.01        0.01        0.01
 0.01        0.01        0.01        0.01        0.01        0.01
 0.01        0.01        0.01        0.01        0.01        0.01
 0.01        0.01        0.01        0.01        0.01        0.01
 0.01        0.01        0.01        0.01        0.01        0.01
 0.01        0.01        0.01        0.01        0.01        0.01
 0.01        0.01        0.01        0.01        0.01        0.01
 0.01        0.01        0.01        0.01        0.01        0.01
 0.01        0.01        0.01        0.01        0.01        0.01
 0.01        0.01        0.01        0.01        0.01        0.01
 0.01        0.01        0.01        0.01        0.01        0.01
 0.01        0.01        0.01        0.01        0.01        0.01
 0.01        0.01        0.01        0.01        0.01        0.01
 0.01        0.01        0.01        0.01        0.01        0.01
 0.01        0.01        0.01        0.01        0.01        0.01
 0.01        0.01        0.01        0.01        0.01        0.01
 0.01        0.01        0.01        0.01        0.01        0.01
 0.01        0.01        0.01        0.01        0.01        0.01
 0.01        0.01        0.01        0.01        0.01        0.01
 0.01        0.01        0.01        0.01        0.01        0.01
 0.01        0.01        0.02164706  0.07988235  0.07988235  0.07988235
 0.49917647  0.538       0.68941176  0.11094118  0.65447059  1.
 0.96894118  0.50305882  0.01        0.01        0.01        0.01
 0.01        0.01        0.01        0.01        0.01        0.01
 0.01        0.01        0.12647059  0.14976471  0.37494118  0.60788235
 0.67        0.99223529  0.99223529  0.99223529  0.99223529  0.99223529
 0.88352941  0.67776471  0.99223529  0.94952941  0.76705882  0.25847059
 0.01        0.01        0.01        0.01        0.01        0.01
 0.01        0.01        0.01        0.01        0.01        0.20023529
 0.934       0.99223529  0.99223529  0.99223529  0.99223529  0.99223529
 0.99223529  0.99223529  0.99223529  0.98447059  0.37105882  0.32835294
 0.32835294  0.22741176  0.16141176  0.01        0.01        0.01
 0.01        0.01        0.01        0.01        0.01        0.01
 0.01        0.01        0.01        0.07988235  0.86023529  0.99223529
 0.99223529  0.99223529  0.99223529  0.99223529  0.77870588  0.71658824
```

Figure 5-4. *Revised interactive Python session for data file operations*

I added the record adjustment statement to script in order to set an acceptable value range for the input data values. But what about the output data values? I address that question next.

Interpreting ANN output data values

I have mentioned in previous chapters that ANNs do one of two things. They either predict or classify. The ANN to be used in this project is a classification type because its purpose is to accept a digitized handwritten number and classify it into one of ten classes, namely, the digits 0 to 9. I have just showed how the input data values will now all be adjusted to stay within the range of 0.01 to 1.00. This can only mean that all ANN outputs must also stay within that range. There is no multiplicative or gain function existing in an ordinary ANN, which will produce output values greater than the maximum input values. Therefore, the outputs will range from 0.0 to 1.0. Notice that I lowered the output lower range limit to 0.0 from the input lower range limit of 0.01. This is because it is entirely possible to have absolutely no input to a given output node. In reality, there will always be some noise present on the output of all nodes in the output layer. You will see levels like $5 \times 10\text{-}9$, which for all practical purposes is 0.

The answer to the question is not on how the output levels can or should be adjusted, but on how to interpret the levels that ultimately are generated. In an ideal handwritten number recognition ANN, when record

0 from the training set is presented to the ANN, the output would be as shown in the following data vector:

$$\begin{Bmatrix} 0.0 \\ 0.0 \\ 0.0 \\ 0.0 \\ 0.0 \\ 1.0 \\ 0.0 \\ 0.0 \\ 0.0 \\ 0.0 \end{Bmatrix}$$

In reality, you might see a vector like

$$\begin{Bmatrix} 0.178 \\ 0.052 \\ 0.027 \\ 0.035 \\ 0.042 \\ 0.686 \\ 0.109 \\ 0.063 \\ 0.051 \\ 0.018 \end{Bmatrix}$$

There are nine out of ten numbers near 0 and one much higher than the rest. It is not unreasonable to consider that the high value is the probability that the ANN "believes" the input Image is that of a 5. There is no formal mathematical logic, which can be applied to prove that this ANN has produced a true probability, but most practitioners accept my interpretation of the results. Note that in other ANN structures there are layers that can be added, which will generate true probabilities, but not in this simplified ANN. Sometimes, there may be another class or two with a higher number, but less than the maximum value. Such a situation indicates that the ANN is having a difficult time in classifying the input and "believes" the input data pattern may be somewhat associated with other classes. In such cases, only more training can alleviate this situation. Just remember it is practically impossible to train an ANN which will make perfect predictions or classifications. This is also true when considering a human expert. There is no one who can 100% correctly classify any handwritten number presented to him or her.

The next step in this project development is to create an ANN structure, which is paramount to have a successful outcome.

Creating an ANN that does handwritten number recognition

The first decision to be made is to determine the basic ANN structure to be used. I decided that a three-layer ANN would be the simplest and still an effective design. Three-layer ANNs are not to be underestimated just because there is only one hidden layer. Additional hidden layers can always be added if it is found that the three-layer design is under-performing. The ANN structure used in this demonstration uses the multi-layer perceptron model. This is because the basic elemental artificial neural, which is used as a computing element, was named the perceptron in 1958 by Frank Rosenblatt of the Cornell Aeronautical Laboratory.

The next step in creating an ANN structure is to determine the number of nodes in each layer. In this application, setting the number of nodes for the input and output layer nodes is easy. The input layer must have 784 nodes to represent the input from each pixel value. The output layer must have ten nodes to represent each class that may be recognized. The hidden layer is the remaining one which must have a node number set.

Determining the number of nodes to be assigned to the hidden layer is more difficult than setting the node numbers for either the input or output nodes. I have done a good amount of research regarding how to set the hidden layer node amount. There are a variety of "rules of thumb" to determine this number. The following are among the most common:

- Use the mean of the number of input layer nodes (N_i) and output layer nodes (N_o).

- Use the square root of N_i times N_o.

- The number of hidden layer nodes (N_h) should be between the size of N_i and N_o.

- N_h should be two-thirds the size of N_i plus N_o.

- N_h should be less than twice the size of N_i.

It soon became clear to me that setting N_h is kind of a trial-and-error experiment. There are two terms that I wish to discuss at this time, which are appropriate when considering how many hidden layer nodes to instantiate. The first is underfitting which can happen when too few nodes are created. The symptoms for underfitting is that the ANN cannot be trained and/or the error rate is unacceptably high. The other term is overfitting, where there is a surplus of nodes. In this case, symptoms include the situation when training never converges because of the extra nodes and accuracy diminishes because the ANN is overly sensitive to noise and artifacts. When overfitting occurs, the ANN has so much information that the input dataset is insufficient to train all the nodes in the hidden layer; in addition, the length of training time can dramatically increase to the point where it never stops or converges as previously stated. The optimal goal in setting an appropriate number of hidden layer nodes is to avoid both under-fitting and overfitting.

Based on the preceding discussion and my experiments, I arrived at the following conclusion regarding setting the number of hidden layer nodes:

The number of hidden layer nodes in a three-layer ANN should be set at the square of the number of output nodes, but should not exceed the mean of the input and output layer nodes.

This guideline is a mashup of several rules of thumb that I earlier cited. I have also noted anecdotally that there seems to be a squaring relationship that often occurs in designing ANN structures. This relationship was present when the mean was calculated for setting weights and when the error function slope was computed. Squaring the 10 output node number means that 100 hidden layer nodes should be set. This value seems proper given the large size of the input layer and the relatively small size of the output layer. If the ANN performs poorly, the 100 number can always be modified.

It is time to show you the initial training script now that the ANN structure has been determined.

Initial ANN training script demonstration

The following data implements a short script that set ups an ANN and trains it using the abbreviated 100 record MNIST train dataset. It does not yet test the ANN for accuracy. That will come after this script is discussed. This script is named trainANN.py, and it uses the ANN class that was developed in Chapter 4. Please reread that chapter regarding this class because it is a key part of this script. This script is available from the book's companion web site:

```
# Import required libraries
import numpy as np
import matplotlib.pyplot as plt
from ANN import ANN
```

```
# Setup the ANN configuration
inode =784
hnode =100
onode =10

# Set the learning rate
lr = 0.2

# Instantiate an ANN object named ann
ann = ANN(inode, hnode, onode, lr)

# Create the training list data
dataFile = open('mnist_train_100.csv')
dataList = dataFile.readlines()
dataFile.close()

# Train the ANN using all the records in the list
for record in dataList:
        recordx = record.split(',')
        inputT = (np.asfarray(recordx[1:])/255.0*0.99) + 0.01
        train = np.zeros(onode) + 0.01
        train[int(recordx[0])] =0.99
        # Training begins here
        ann.trainNet(inputT, train)
```

There are several prerequisites that must be set prior to running the preceding script. The file ANN.py must be in the same directory as the script, and the mnist_train_100.csv dataset must also be in the same directory. Simply enter this command to run the script:

```
python trainANN.py
```

There are no results shown if the script ran without any errors because the intention was just to train the ANN. You should correct any errors before proceeding with the next portion of this demonstration.

ANN test script demonstration

The trained ANN completed in the previous section must now be tested in order to assess how well it performs in classifying handwritten numbers. The test dataset to be used is the small 10 record set downloaded from the same web site where the 100 record training dataset was downloaded. A modified version of the trainANN script will be used for this test. I renamed the modified trainANN script to testANN_short.py to reflect both its new purpose and to differentiate it from a follow-on version which will employ the full-sized train and test datasets.

This script is available from the book's companion web site:

```
# Import required libraries
import numpy as np
import matplotlib.pyplot as plt
from ANN import ANN

# Setup the ANN configuration
inode =784
hnode =100
onode =10

# Set the learning rate
lr = 0.2

# Instantiate an ANN object named ann
ann = ANN(inode, hnode, onode, lr)

# Create the training list data
dataFile = open('mnist_train_100.csv')
dataList = dataFile.readlines()
dataFile.close()
# Create the test list data
testDataFile = open('mnist_test_10.csv')
```

```
testDataList = testDataFile.readlines()
testDataFile.close()

# Train the ANN using all the records in the list
for record in dataList:
        recordx = record.split(',')
        inputT = (np.asfarray(recordx[1:])/255.0*0.99) + 0.01
        train = np.zeros(onode) + 0.01
        train[int(recordx[0])] =0.99
        # Training begins here
        ann.trainNet(inputT, train)

# Iterate through all 10 test records and display output
# data vectors
for record in testDataList:
        recordz = record.split(',')
        # Determine record's label
        labelz = int(recordz[0])
        # Adjust record values for ANN
        inputz = (np.asfarray(recordz[1:])/255.0*0.99)+0.01
        outputz = ann.testNet(inputz)
        print('output for label = ', labelz)
        print(outputz)
```

As in the preceding script, ensure that the file ANN.py, mnist_train_100.csv, and mnist_test_10.csv datasets are in the same directory as the script. Enter this command to run the script:

```
python testANN.py
```

Figure 5-5 shows the complete results after running the script. I made a composite figure from two screenshots in order to capture all the results.

```
pi@raspberrypi:~ $ python3 testANN.py
output for label =  7                    output for label =  1
[[0.3651228 ]                            [[0.01754469]
 [0.00908035]                             [0.8873932 ]
 [0.05115461]                             [0.06721963]
 [0.28202892]                             [0.15823746]
 [0.0324156 ]                             [0.0361807 ]
 [0.03686317]                             [0.10288544]
 [0.01013092]                             [0.03116356]
 [0.49527917]                             [0.02676047]
 [0.13856681]                             [0.12148664]
 [0.15943197]]                            [0.0344749 ]]
output for label =  2                    output for label =  4
[[0.41738211]                            [[0.06766221]
 [0.15342856]                             [0.02159815]
 [0.04579331]                             [0.02242331]
 [0.16457149]                             [0.12256782]
 [0.01250789]                             [0.32884644]
 [0.0215661 ]                             [0.01839584]
 [0.08606825]                             [0.04119256]
 [0.02326149]                             [0.41215928]
 [0.07590292]                             [0.10913643]
 [0.05716249]]                            [0.06757988]]
output for label =  1                    output for label =  9
[[0.02084893]                            [[0.01337863]
 [0.8809285 ]                             [0.28607229]
 [0.04154846]                             [0.02521336]
 [0.25483219]                             [0.22281996]
 [0.02951309]                             [0.35917428]
 [0.07935856]                             [0.01121576]
 [0.03937777]                             [0.14492311]
 [0.0283552 ]                             [0.09799644]
 [0.10949139]                             [0.35744773]
 [0.06083629]]                            [0.01852624]]
output for label =  0                    output for label =  5
[[0.87920702]                            [[0.06807495]
 [0.00282297]                             [0.24051637]
 [0.00923521]                             [0.03031659]
 [0.03017904]                             [0.02104054]
 [0.06414061]                             [0.1697321 ]
 [0.01042678]                             [0.01571563]
 [0.15713118]                             [0.04008098]
 [0.1110997 ]                             [0.04968168]
 [0.04230118]                             [0.0829022 ]
 [0.0171685 ]]                            [0.00850344]]
output for label =  4                    output for label =  9
[[0.06765975]                            [[0.05668552]
 [0.08560741]                             [0.08174132]
 [0.05740208]                             [0.03795929]
 [0.09532876]                             [0.02819786]
 [0.60686901]                             [0.38267175]
 [0.0216582 ]                             [0.02059329]
 [0.04648322]                             [0.01748166]
 [0.26071802]                             [0.52653503]
 [0.27898538]                             [0.1466567 ]
 [0.03982088]]                            [0.05140844]]
```

Figure 5-5. *testANN script results*

The 60% match rate displayed in Table 5-1 is barely satisfactory; however, it is not surprising considering that the ANN was only trained with 100 records out of a potential 60,000 that are available for training. I also like to delve into the details when confronted with an apparently large error result. Consequently, I modified the viewResults script to examine the four records, which were not correctly identified. I collected and combined their Images into Figure 5-6 in order to identify any common attributes, which might have led to the misidentifications.

Table 5-1. *The results of the ANN test run*

Label	7	2	1	0	4	1	4	9	5	9
Index	7	3	1	0	4	1	4	8	1	4
Match	x		x	x	x	x	x			

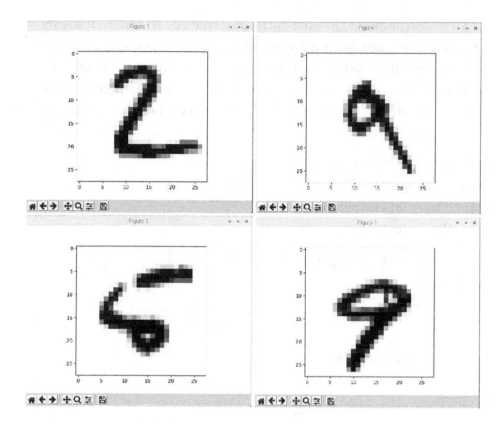

Figure 5-6. *Misidentified handwritten numeric digits*

You can immediately see that the ANN has trouble with the number 9. Two of the four Images are that number. The number 5, which is the one on the lower left-hand side, is so badly written, that no one (machine or human) could recognize it, so the ANN is excused. That leaves the number 2 Image on the upper left-hand side. That is clearly written and should have been properly identified. The only solution to these problems, with the possible exception of the number 5 digit, is to further train the ANN. Given the results of this early experiment, I would fully expect that a fully trained ANN would easily score above 90% in accuracy.

I was also interested in what the results would be if I ran the testANN script multiple times, but not displaying the output data vectors, but only the match results, which is an accuracy metric. Accordingly, I modified the testANN_short script to accommodate these changes and renamed it testANN_metrics.py. This script is available from the book's companion web site:

```python
# Import required libraries
import numpy as np
import matplotlib.pyplot as plt
from ANN import ANN

# Setup the ANN configuration
inode =784
hnode =100
onode =10

# Set the learning rate
lr = 0.2

# Instantiate an ANN object named ann
ann = ANN(inode, hnode, onode, lr)

# Create the training list data
dataFile = open('mnist_train_100.csv')
dataList = dataFile.readlines()
dataFile.close()

# Create the test list data
testDataFile = open('mnist_test_10.csv')
testDataList = testDataFile.readlines()
testDataFile.close()
```

```
# Train the ANN using all the records in the list
for record in dataList:
        recordx = record.split(',')
        inputT = (np.asfarray(recordx[1:])/255.0*0.99) + 0.01
        train = np.zeros(onode) + 0.01
        train[int(recordx[0])] =0.99
        # Training begins here
        ann.trainNet(inputT, train)

# Iterate through all 10 test records and display output
# data vectors
match = 0
no_match = 0
for record in testDataList:
        recordz = record.split(',')
        # Determine record's label
        labelz = int(recordz[0])
        # Adjust record values for ANN
        inputz = (np.asfarray(recordz[1:])/255.0*0.99)+0.01
        outputz = ann.testNet(inputz)
        max_value = np.argmax(outputz)
        if max_value == labelz:
                match = match + 1
        else:
                no_match = no_match + 1
        success = float(match) / float(match + no_match)
print('success rate = {0}'.format(success))
```

The script is run by entering this command:

```
python3 testANN_metrics.py
```

Figure 5-7 shows the results after I ran the script ten consecutive times.

```
pi@raspberrypi: ~                                    ⌄  ∧  ✕

File  Edit  Tabs  Help

pi@raspberrypi:~ $ python3 testANN_metrics.py
success rate = 0.4
pi@raspberrypi:~ $ python3 testANN_metrics.py
success rate = 0.6
pi@raspberrypi:~ $ python3 testANN_metrics.py
success rate = 0.6
pi@raspberrypi:~ $ python3 testANN_metrics.py
success rate = 0.5
pi@raspberrypi:~ $ python3 testANN_metrics.py
success rate = 0.5
pi@raspberrypi:~ $ python3 testANN_metrics.py
success rate = 0.5
pi@raspberrypi:~ $ python3 testANN_metrics.py
success rate = 0.5
pi@raspberrypi:~ $ python3 testANN_metrics.py
success rate = 0.6
pi@raspberrypi:~ $ python3 testANN_metrics.py
success rate = 0.4
pi@raspberrypi:~ $ python3 testANN_metrics.py
success rate = 0.6
pi@raspberrypi:~ $ []
```

Figure 5-7. *Results for ten consecutive runs of script testANN_metrics*

You should be able to see that the success rate ranged between 0.4 and 0.6. I averaged all ten values and determined the average success rate was equal to 0.52. This is a rather poor result, but again as I explained earlier, the ANN was poorly trained using only 100 out of 60,000 plus available records. Incidentally, those readers with Python skills might have wondered why I didn't include a loop for ten consecutive script runs or epochs. I didn't because the ANN must be reinitialized for each run or else the same trained ANN would be used for each pass, yielding the same success rate. Rewriting the script to accommodate a reinitialized ANN was certainly doable, but I didn't want to commit the time to do so when it was much simpler to just manually rerun the script ten times.

You might question why the results for each epoch were different? The answer is that the initially weighting matrices are generated using a random normal distribution. Therefore, some of the matrices were slightly better suited to produce more accurate results than others. These initial distribution variations will disappear when the ANN is trained using the full 60,000 training record set which is next in the demonstration schedule.

ANN test script demonstration using the full training dataset

You only have to make one slight change to the testANN_metrics script to use the full training set. Change the following statement from

```
dataFile = open('mnist_train_100.csv')
```

to

```
dataFile = open('mnist_train.csv')
```

I have not included a new script listing because the modifications are minor and easily done. You can then rerun the testANN_metrics script with the ten test records; however, it will take much longer to finish executing because there are over 60,000 training records to be processed. Expect to wait up to 10 minutes depending on the RasPi processor speed. I ran the newly modified script and found that it only took 6 minutes and 3 seconds to finish. This was a pleasant surprise and showed me just how powerful the A-72 ARM, Quad Core, 1.5 GHz processor is in the RasPi 4.

The result showed a 0.9 success rate, which I actually expected, since one of the ten Images I considered is undecipherable.

The next step in this demonstration series is to run the script with the full 10,000 record test dataset. Again, this is easily accomplished by modifying one statement as follows

```
testDataFile = open('mnist_test_10.csv')
```

to

```
testDataFile = open('mnist_test.csv')
```

Again, I have not included a new script listing because the modifications are minor and easily done to the existing script. You can then rerun the testANN_metrics script with the 10,000 test records; however, it will take even longer to finish executing than above because there are 10,000 test records to process in addition to training with the 60,000 records. Fortunately, it is much quicker to test the ANN per record than it is to train it per record.

I reran the newly modified script and found that it only took 6 minutes and 15 seconds to finish. The result showed a 0.9458 success rate, which I expected based on all the previous discussions regarding a fully trained ANN. This success rate value is generally considered a good ANN result.

The learning rate can also have a significant impact on the ANN accuracy. I again modified the testANN_metrics script to test the learning rate impact on accuracy. The modification consisted of creating a loop that modified the learning rate from 0.1 to 0.6 while recalculating the success rate. I also believe learning rate values beyond 0.6 is not realistic to set in any practical ANN. This time, the modifications were of sufficient magnitude that I believed it was appropriate to include a full script listing. I also renamed the script testANN_metrics_lr.py to indicate the learning rate variations. This listing is available from the book's companion web site:

```
# Import required libraries
import numpy as np
from ANN import ANN

# Setup the ANN configuration
inode =784
hnode =100
onode =10

# Set the initial learning rate
lr = 0.1
```

```
# Create the training list data
dataFile = open('mnist_train.csv')
dataList = dataFile.readlines()
dataFile.close()

#  Create the test list data
testDataFile = open('mnist_test.csv')
testDataList = testDataFile.readlines()
testDataFile.close()

# Loop to iterate learning rates from 0.1 to 0.6 in 0.1 steps
for i in range(6):
    # Instantiate an ANN object named ann
    ann = ANN(inode, hnode, onode, lr)

    # Train the ANN using all the records in the list
    for record in dataList:
        recordx = record.split(',')
        inputT = (np.asfarray(recordx[1:])/255.0*0.99) + 0.01
        train = np.zeros(onode) + 0.01
        train[int(recordx[0])] =0.99
        # Training begins here
        ann.trainNet(inputT, train)

    # Iterate through all the test records
    match = 0
    no_match = 0
    for record in testDataList:
        recordz = record.split(',')
        # Determine record's label
        labelz = int(recordz[0])
        # Adjust record values for ANN
```

```
        inputz = (np.asfarray(recordz[1:])/255.0*0.99)+0.01
        outputz = ann.testNet(inputz)
        max_value = np.argmax(outputz)
        if max_value == labelz:
                match = match + 1
        else:
                no_match = no_match + 1
        success = float(match) / float(match + no_match)

    # Display the learning rate and success rate
    print('lr = {0} success rate = {1}'.format(lr,success))
    lr = lr + 0.1
```

Be forewarned that this script takes almost an hour to run through completely. It is run by entering this command:

```
python3 testANN_metrics_lr.py
```

Figure 5-8 shows the results after I ran the script.

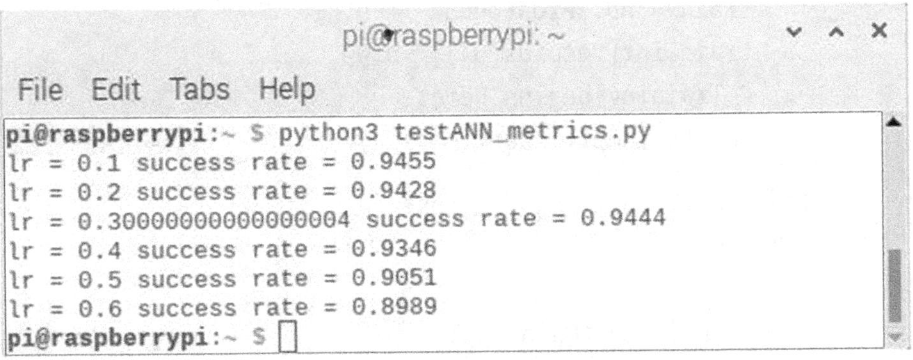

Figure 5-8. *Results after running the testANN_metrics_lr script*

You should be able to see that the success rate ranged down from 0.9456 to 0.8989 for learning rates that range up from 0.1 to 0.6, respectively. The ANN accuracy decreases substantially as the learning rate increases. This is because the global minimum is not being reached because the gradient descent algorithm steps are increasing in magnitude. If you are confused by the proceeding, I would suggest that you reread the appropriate sections in Chapter 4 to refresh yourself on how learning rate and the gradient descent algorithm are related. I would suggest that the 0.2 learning rate that I selected for the initial test run was optimal because the success rate of 0.9458 was higher than any recorded in this run. However, the actual success rate differences are miniscule and likely related to random variation. In any case, a learning rate of 0.1 or 0.2 would be ideal for this ANN.

You will now have a well-performing ANN if you replicated the demonstrations to this point. Any ANN with an accuracy of approximately 95% is generally considered high performing. I would recommend to continue experimenting with this ANN such as changing the number of hidden nodes to see what effect it has on the network performance.

The next series of demonstrations expands on this ANN by incorporating a Pi Camera to enable real-time number recognition.

Recognizing your own handwritten numbers

It is a natural extension of the previous demonstrations to experiment with your own handwritten number recognition instead of relying on stored examples. This feature can easily be implemented using a Pi Camera, which is a video camera especially designed to work seamlessly with a RasPi. The Pi Camera interface has been incorporated into all recent versions of the Raspbian Linux distributions. All that is need is to activate it, which I will shortly discuss. But first, you need to see how to install the hardware.

Installing the Pi Camera

I will be discussing how to install version 2 of the Pi Camera on a RasPi 4. These instructions are also applicable for RasPi 2 and 3 versions. Figure 5-9 shows a Pi Camera, version 2, that will be used in the next few demonstrations.

Figure 5-9. *Pi Camera, version 2*

The camera's specifications are impressive given its compact size and low cost. I have summarized the key specifications as follows:

- 8 megapixel native resolution, high quality Sony IMX219 Image sensor

- Maximum still photograph resolution of 3280 x 2464 pixels

- Capture video at 1080p30, 720p60, and 640x480p90 resolutions

- All software supported within the latest version of the Raspbian Operating System

- Optical size of 1/4"

- Wide angle lens with a range of 4 inches to infinity

The camera comes with a short flex ribbon cable that is plugged into the Camera Serial Interface (CSI) socket that is located directly behind the RJ45 socket on the RasPi. Figure 5-10 shows where the CSI socket is located on a RasPi.

Figure 5-10. *CSI socket location*

Note, there is another similar socket located on the RasPi 2, 3, and 4 models. That one is the Display Serial Interface (DSI) socket. You might accidentally plug in the camera cable into that socket, but it shouldn't do any damage. The camera would simply not work.

To plug in the camera cable into the CSI socket, you must carefully pull directly up on two black plastic tabs on each side of a slim plastic bar. Be very careful because the plastic bar is flimsy and could easily be broken by the excessive use of force. The plastic bar will become loose, yet still stay attached to the socket when it is lifted.

Next, carefully insert the flex cable into the socket with the exposed, silver-colored finger contacts facing away from the RJ45 connector. The blue backing on the ribbon cable should now face the RJ45 connector. Ensure the cable is firmly seated at the bottom of the socket and the cable is perpendicular to the board and not slanted. Next, gently push down on the black plastic tabs to lock the cable in place. Just use a firm, but gentle pressure to lock down the cable.

Please note that it is possible, if not probable, that the cable can become dislodged when the RasPi is moved or relocated. If this happens, the OS will start reporting strange errors that it wasn't able to load certain drivers or that you should enable the camera. I always check to see that the camera cable is inserted properly before chasing down those errors. Figure 5-11 shows a properly inserted camera cable.

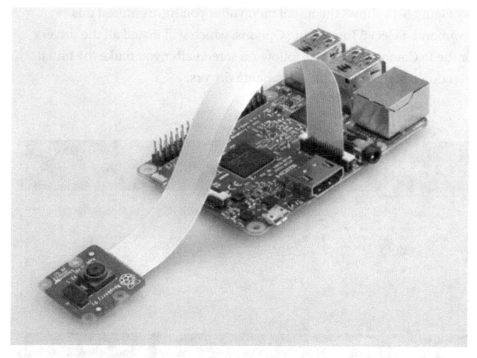

Figure 5-11. *Properly inserted camera cable*

You will next need to install some additional software packages in order to use the camera with the demonstrations.

Installing the Pi Camera software

The first action to be taken is to enable the camera within the Raspbian OS. This is done using the raspi-config utility. This utility is started by entering the following command:

```
sudo raspi-config
```

Figure 5-12 shows the initial menu after you have entered this command. Select 5 Interfacing Options, which will install all the drivers for the Pi Camera. There is a follow-on screen after you make the initial selection where you enable the camera drivers.

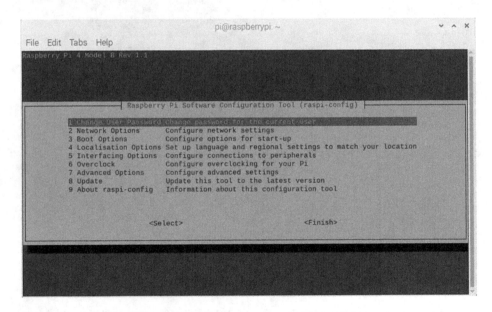

Figure 5-12. *raspi-config menu screen*

Once the camera has been enabled, you will need to install some additional software. Enter the following command to install the Python picamera library:

```
sudo apt-get update
sudo apt-get install python-picamera
```

318

You need to install the Pillow package, which contains the Python Imaging Library (PIL). Enter this next command:

```
sudo apt-get install python-pillow
```

That's all the software that needs to be installed in order to start the demonstrations.

Handwritten number recognition demonstration

The first action you should try is to test the Pi Camera installation. Enter this command:

```
raspistill -t 5000
```

You should see a full-height, color video displayed on your monitor for 5 seconds at whatever the camera was pointing at. The width will not quite expand to the monitor width because of the aspect ratio; however, if you see a live Image, you can be assured that the Pi Camera is operating correctly. If no Image was displayed, I would recheck the camera cable connections to ensure that they are proper and correct. In my experience, at least 95% of hardware issues are related to electrical connections.

If you passed this first check, you will be ready for the initial demonstration for handwritten number recognition using a Pi Camera.

You will need to make a target to Image. I would suggest using 3 x 5 white card stock to write on and a fine tip black "Sharpie" marker. The marker on white card stock will provide a good contrast for imaging the number. Using a pen or pencil on paper is not recommended because there will not be sufficient contrast to define an Image consistent with the Images used to train the ANN. Remember, the ANN cannot perform correctly if it is presented with Images it was not trained to recognize. Figure 5-13 shows my target handwritten number.

Figure 5-13. *Target handwritten number*

This figure was imaged using the following command:

```
raspistill -o zerobw.jpg
```

The Image will need to be preprocessed before it is in form suitable for inputting into the ANN for number recognition. This preprocessing will be part of a modified testANN script that I used to process this Image. I renamed the modified script testANN_Image.py, and it is available from the book's companion web site.

```
# Import required libraries
import numpy as np
import matplotlib.pyplot as plt
from ANN import ANN
import PIL
from PIL import Image

# Setup the ANN configuration
inode = 784
```

```
hnode = 100
onode = 10

# Set the learning rate
lr = 0.1

# Instantiate an ANN object named ann
ann = ANN(inode, hnode, onode, lr)

# Create the training list data
dataFile = open('mnist_train.csv')
dataList = dataFile.readlines()
dataFile.close()

# Train the ANN using all the records in the list
for record in dataList:
      recordx = record.split(',')
      inputT = (np.asfarray(recordx[1:])/255.0*0.99) + 0.01
      train = np.zeros(onode) + 0.01
      train[int(recordx[0])] = 0.99
      # Training begins here
      ann.trainNet(inputT, train)

# Create the test list data from an image
img = Image.open('zerobw.jpg')
img = img.resize((28,28), PIL.Image.ANTIALIAS)

# Read pixels into list
pixels = list(img.getdata())

# Convert into single values from tuples
pixels = [i[0] for i in pixels]

# Save to a temp file named test.csv with comma delimiters
imgTmp = np.array(pixels)
imgTmp.tofile('test.csv', sep=',')
```

```
# Open the temp file and read into list
testDataFile = open('test.csv')
testDataList = testDataFile.readlines()
testDataFile.close()

# Iterate through all list elements
for record in testDataList:
        recordx = record.split(',')
        # Adjust record values for ANN
        input = (np.asfarray(recordx[0:])/255.0*0.99)+0.01
        output = ann.testNet(input)

# Display output data vector
print(output)
```

The following comments apply to the modifications incorporated into the script to preprocess the Image acquired using the Pi Camera.

```
import PIL
from PIL import Image
```

The Python Imaging Library (PIL) and its sub-library Image are required to process the acquired Image with Python.

```
img = Image.open('zerobw.jpg')
img = img.resize((28,28), PIL.Image.ANTIALIAS)
```

The first command loads the file, which is hard-coded into the script. The loaded Image is then resized into a 28 x 28 pixel sized Image. The ANTIALIAS argument ensures that no artifacts are created during the downsizing operation.

```
pixels = list(img.getdata())
```

This command converts the 784 pixel values into a list named pixels.

```
imgTmp = np.array(pixels)
imgTmp.tofile('test.csv', sep=',')
```

These commands convert the list into an array named imgTmp. This array is then converted into a comma-delimited array, which is subsequently stored into a file named test.csv.

I ran this script by entering this command:

```
python3 testANN_image.py
```

The script took over 6 minutes to run, which was expected because all 60,000 records are being used to train the ANN. The results are shown in Figure 5-14.

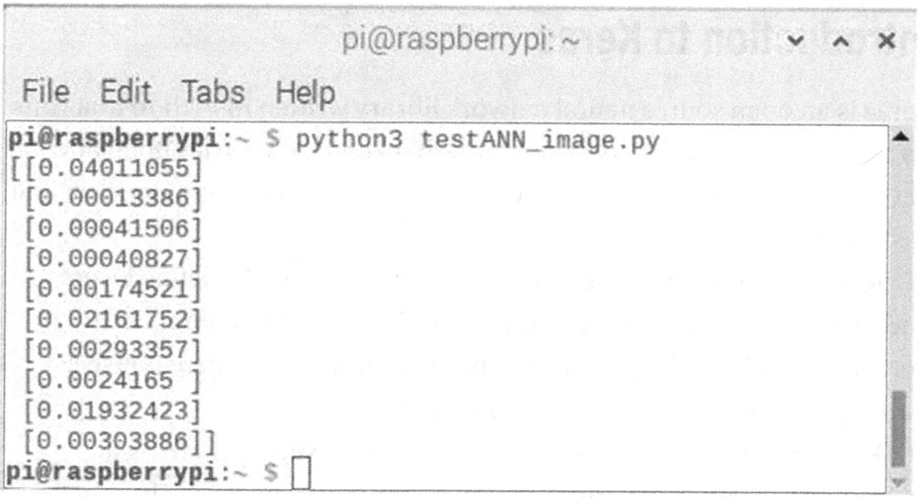

Figure 5-14. *Results for running the testANN_image script*

The results clearly showed that the 0th index had the highest value, which meant the ANN classified the input Image as a 0, which was the correct result.

This last demonstration took a considerable amount of effort in order to show you that a RasPi-controlled camera coupled with a well-trained ANN can recognize a handwritten number.

Handwritten number recognition using Keras

There are a number of techniques available to recognize handwritten numbers beyond the relatively simple approach I just demonstrated. It is entirely possible to achieve an accuracy rating beyond 95% by using a Keras ANN. But now, I have to explain what Keras is and how it can be used for this application.

Introduction to Keras

Keras is an open source neural network library written in Python that runs on top of Theano, CNTK, or TensorFlow backends. It was designed and developed by François Chollet, a Google engineer, to be modular, fast, and easy to use.

Keras is a high-level API that is used to make models, define layers, and/or set up multiple input-output models. Keras also compiles the network model with both loss and optimizer functions. There is also a training process available with a fit function.

Keras doesn't handle low-level API functions such as making a computational graph, creating tensors, or other variables because those functions are relegated to the back-end engine, that is, TensorFlow, CNTK, or Theano.

In Keras, neural layers, cost functions, optimizers, initialization schemes, activation functions, and regularization schemes are stand-alone modules that may be combined to create new models. New modules are simple to add, as are new classes and functions. All models are defined in regular Python code and do not require the use of separate model configuration files.

As mentioned earlier, Keras does not do low-level operations, such as tensor products and convolutions. Instead, it relies on a back-end engine for that. Although Keras supports multiple back-end engines, its primary (and default) backend is TensorFlow, and its primary corporate supporter is Google. The Keras API comes packaged in TensorFlow as `tf.keras`, which became the primary TensorFlow API as of the beginning of 2019.

Installing Keras

Keras should be installed in a Python virtual environment, preferably the same one that supports OpenCV. The following commands will install the latest versions of TensorFlow and Keras. The most current version at the time of this writing for the TensorFlow backend is 2.0, and the latest version for Keras is 2.2.4.

Instantiate the virtual environment and enter this command to install TensorFlow:

```
pip install tensorflow
```

Next, enter this command to install Keras:

```
pip install keras
```

Note that the TensorFlow version installed using the pip package manager is 1.13 and not 2.0. This was because at the time of this writing version 2.0 was still being classified as beta and apparently the folks in charge of the pip repository did not want to make a beta version available. In any case, this TensorFlow version worked quite well in all the book demonstrations.

Next, ensure that the following Python dependencies are installed in the virtual environment:

> numpy

> scipy

> Matplotlib

At this point, a relatively simple multi-layer perceptron (MLP) model can be created using Keras.

Downloading the dataset and creating a model

The first step in this section is to show you how to download the full MNIST dataset. The Keras deep learning library provides a convenience method for loading the MNIST dataset. The following statement loads both the full-sized training and test datasets:

```
(X_train, y_train), (X_test, y_test) = mnist.load_data()
```

I will be presenting the Python script in sections with commentary following the code listings.

```
# Import required Keras libraries
from keras.datasets import mnist
from keras.models import Sequential
from keras.layers import Dense
from keras.utils import np_utils
import numpy as np
```

This code imports Keras modules that will be used to build the ANN as well as the MNIST dataset. Numpy is also imported.

```
# Set a random seed
seed = 42
np.random.seed(seed)
```

Initialize a random number generator, which ensures ANN results are reproducible.

```
# Load the MNIST dataset into training and test datasets.
(X_train, y_train), (X_test, y_test) = mnist.load_data()
```

loads the training and test datasets.

```
# Flatten the 28 x 28 image into a 784 element input data
vector
num_pixels = X_train.shape[1] * X_train.shape[2]
X_train = X_train.reshape(X_train.shape[0], num_pixels).
astype('float32')
X_test = X_test.reshape(X_test.shape[0], num_pixels).
astype('float32')
```

This code portion converts the 3D datasets into 1D data vectors. The use of 4-byte data float values helps reduce memory usage.

```
# Normalize data input values from 0 - 255 to 0 -1.0.
X_train = X_train / 255.0
X_test = X_test / 255.0
```

This code is just another way to adjust the pixel intensities which range from 0 to 255 to the 0 to 1.0 needed for the ANN.

```
# One hot encoding of the categorical outputs
y_train = np_utils.to_categorical(y_train)
y_test = np_utils.to_categorical(y_test)
num_classes = y_test[1]
```

One hot encoding is the representation of categorical variables as binary vectors. It should always be used to encode ANN outputs that have categories or classes as outputs, even in the case where the outputs are numbers, which is true for this case.

This encoding first requires that the categorical values be mapped to integer values. Then, each integer value is represented as a binary vector, that is, all zero values except the index of the integer, which is marked with a 1.

The following example should help clarify this concept:

Assume that there is a sequence of labels with the values "red" and "green."

Assign "red" an integer value of 0 and "green" an integer value of 1. It is called integer encoding as long as these numbers are assigned to these labels. Consistency is important so that the encoding can later be inverted and labels be restored from integer values.

Next, create a binary vector to represent each integer value. The vector will have a length of 2 for the 2 possible integer values. The "red" label, encoded as a 0, will be represented with a binary vector [1, 0] where the 0th index is marked with a value of 1. In turn, the "green" label encoded as a 1 will be represented with a binary vector [0, 1] where the index 1 is equal to 1.

Thus, if the sequence was

"red," "red," "green"

it would be represented by the following integer encoding

0, 0, 1

and a one hot encoding of

[1, 0]

[1, 0]

[0, 1]

One question that beginners often asked is why bother with one hot encoding? The answer is that machine learning algorithms cannot work with categorical data directly. The categories must be converted into numbers. This is true for both input and output variables that are categorical.

328

Sometimes, integer encoding can be directly applied and rescaled as needed. This may work for problems where there is a natural ordinal relationship between the categories and in turn the integer values, such as labels for temperature "cold," "warm," and "hot." Problems arise when there is no ordinal relationship, and allowing the representation to exist would likely be problematic for ANN learning to happen. Consider how labels such as "dog" and "cat" could be handled.

```python
# Baseline model definition
def baseline_model():
    # Create model
    model = Sequential()
    model.add(Dense(num_pixels, input_dim=num_pixels, kernel
    initializer='normal', activation='relu'))
    model.add(Dense(num_classes, kernel_initializer='normal',
    activation='softmax'))
    # Compile model
    model.compile(loss='categorical_crossentropy',
    optimizer='adam', metrics=['accuracy'])
    return model
```

This is the code portion that defines an ANN and compiles it. The ANN definition is in the form of a method, which allows to be called as needed to further refine the model. There is one hidden layer in the definition, which uses a "relu" activation function. ReLU is short for rectified linear unit and is the most commonly used activation function in deep learning models. This function returns 0 if it receives any negative inputs. For positive inputs it returns values according to the following equation:

$$f(x) = \max(0,x) = \max(0,x)$$

Graphically, the function is as plotted in Figure 5-15.

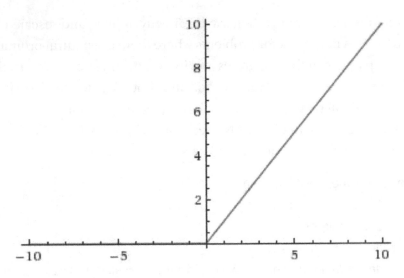

Figure 5-15. *ReLU plot*

It is surprising that such a simple function (and one composed of two linear pieces) will allow a model to account for non-linearities and interactions so well. But the ReLU function works great in most applications, and it is very widely used as a result.

The final layer uses a "softmax" activation function. The softmax function, also known as softargmax or normalized exponential function, is a function that takes as input a vector of K real numbers and normalizes it into a probability distribution consisting of K probabilities. That is, prior to applying softmax, some vector components could be negative or greater than one and might not sum to 1; but after applying softmax, each component will be in the *interval* 0 to 1 and all the components will add up to 1, so that they can be interpreted as probabilities. Furthermore, the larger input components will correspond to larger probabilities. The softmax function is thus commonly used as an activation function in ANNs to map the non-normalized output of a network to a probability distribution over all the predicted output classes.

The last statement in this code portion compiles the model. Compilation is needed before training the model. The model is configured during compilation according to three arguments:

- A loss function – This is the objective that the model will try to minimize. It can be the string identifier of an existing loss function (such as categorical_ crossentropy or mse), or it can be an objective function.

- An optimizer – This could be the string identifier of an existing optimizer (such as adam, rmsprop, or adagrad) or an instance of the Optimizer class.

- A list of metrics – For any classification problem, this argument would be set to metrics=['accuracy']. A metric could be the string identifier of an existing metric or a custom metric function.

```
# Run the demo
model = baseline_model()
model.fit(X_train, y_train, validation_data=(X_test,
y_test), epochs=10, batch_size=200, verbose=2)
# Final evaluation
scores = model.evaluate(X_test, y_test, verbose=0)
print('Baseline error: %.2f%%'%(100-scores[1]*100))
```

The last code portion is the driver code, which tests the new ANN with the MNIST dataset. A model named model is first instantiated and then trained using the Keras fit function. A scores tuple is then generated by calling the Keras evaluate method. The testing continues for 10 epochs with the final statement showing the ultimate ANN accuracy.

The complete script with commentary is shown in the following data. I named the script kerasTest.py, and it is available from the book's companion web site.

```
# Import required libraries
import numpy as np
from keras.datasets import mnist
from keras.models import Sequential
from keras.layers import Dense
from keras.utils import np_utils

# Random seeding
seed = 42
np.random.seed(seed)

# Load MNIST data
(X_train, y_train), (X_test, y_test) = mnist.load_data()

# Flatten the 28 x 28 image
num_pixels = X_train.shape[1] * X_train.shape[2]
X_train = X_train.reshape(X_train.shape[0], num_pixels).
astype('float32')
X_test = X_test.reshape(X_test.shape[0], num_pixels).
astype('float32')

# Normalize inputs from 0-255 to 0-1
X_train = X_train / 255.0
X_test = X_test / 255.0

# One hot encoding
y_train = np_utils.to_categorical(y_train)
y_test = np_utils.to_categorical(y_test)
num_classes = y_test.shape[1]
```

```python
# Define baseline model
def baseline_model():
    # Create model
    model = Sequential()
    model.add(Dense(num_pixels, input_dim=num_pixels, kernel_
    initializer='normal', activation='relu'))
    model.add(Dense(num_classes, kernel_initializer='normal',
    activation='softmax'))
    # Compile model
    model.compile(loss='categorical_crossentropy',
    optimizer='adam', metrics=['accuracy'])
    return model

# Run the demo
model = baseline_model()
model.fit(X_train, y_train, validation_data=(X_test, y_test),
epochs=10, batch_size=200, verbose=2)

# Final evaluation
scores = model.evaluate(X_test, y_test, verbose=0)
print('Baseline error: %.2f%%'%(100-scores[1]*100))
```

The script should be run in the virtual environment using the following command:

```
python kerasTest.py
```

The script does take some time to complete because it not only trains the model using the full 60,000 MNIST training dataset, it repeats the 10,000 test record tests ten times or 10 epochs. The final results are shown in Figure 5-16.

```
                              pi@raspberrypi: ~                     ✓  ∧  ✕

 File  Edit  Tabs  Help
Train on 60000 samples, validate on 10000 samples
Epoch 1/10
 - 34s - loss: 0.2778 - acc: 0.9210 - val_loss: 0.1418 - val_acc: 0.9580
Epoch 2/10
 - 34s - loss: 0.1095 - acc: 0.9685 - val_loss: 0.0941 - val_acc: 0.9710
Epoch 3/10
 - 33s - loss: 0.0716 - acc: 0.9788 - val_loss: 0.0791 - val_acc: 0.9763
Epoch 4/10
 - 33s - loss: 0.0496 - acc: 0.9859 - val_loss: 0.0677 - val_acc: 0.9801
Epoch 5/10
 - 33s - loss: 0.0359 - acc: 0.9896 - val_loss: 0.0648 - val_acc: 0.9796
Epoch 6/10
 - 34s - loss: 0.0262 - acc: 0.9930 - val_loss: 0.0594 - val_acc: 0.9814
Epoch 7/10
 - 33s - loss: 0.0192 - acc: 0.9955 - val_loss: 0.0646 - val_acc: 0.9806
Epoch 8/10
 - 33s - loss: 0.0153 - acc: 0.9962 - val_loss: 0.0575 - val_acc: 0.9812
Epoch 9/10
 - 33s - loss: 0.0104 - acc: 0.9980 - val_loss: 0.0572 - val_acc: 0.9825
Epoch 10/10
 - 34s - loss: 0.0074 - acc: 0.9988 - val_loss: 0.0638 - val_acc: 0.9804
Baseline error: 1.96%
(py3cv4) pi@raspberrypi:~ $ []
```

Figure 5-16. *Final results after running the kerasTest script*

This remarkable simple network implemented using Keras and running in the TensorFlow 2 backend achieved an excellent accuracy slightly above 98%. This is three percentage points higher than my earlier MLP model. However, believe it or not, it is even possible to achieve slightly higher accuracy using a more advanced algorithm, which I will discuss in the next chapter.

CHAPTER 6

CNN demonstrations

Several practical DL demonstrations are shown in this chapter. You will
be prepared to follow along with the demonstrations provided you have
read the previous chapter or have acquired previous experience with
DL techniques and concepts. I had two goals in mind when writing this
chapter. The first was to clearly show how a complete ANN project could
be accomplished to produce realistic and useful results. The second was
to point out some potential pitfalls and unrealistic assumptions that are
common in ANN development.

Parts list

You will need a standard RasPi desktop configuration for the chapter
demonstrations.

Item	Model	Quantity	Source
Raspberry Pi 4	Model B (RasPi 4 with 2 or 4 GB RAM)	1	mcmelectronics.com adafruit.com digikey.com mouser.com farnell.com
Micro SD card	16 GB, class 10 or larger	1	amazon.com

(*continued*)

© Donald J. Norris 2020
D. J. Norris, *Machine Learning with the Raspberry Pi*,
https://doi.org/10.1007/978-1-4842-5174-4_6

Item	Model	Quantity	Source
USB keyboard	Amazon Basic	1	amazon.com
USB mouse	Amazon Basic	1	amazon.com
HDMI monitor	Commodity	1	amazon.com

Note   A minimum of 2 GB RAM is required to enable the RasPi 4 to compile and train the CNN models used in the chapter demonstrations. RasPis with only 1 GB of RAM will not be successful in the demonstrations.

Introduction to the CNN model

CNN is short for convolutional neural network. In the previous chapter, I used a multi-layer perceptron (MLP) model, which is based on longstanding, conventional model using the classic artificial neuron known as the perceptron. The MLP model is fully connected in the sense that every neuron is connected, at least initially, to every other neuron in a given network layer. That is not true for a CNN model, which is considered a sparsely connected network.

CNNs are similar to regular neural networks discussed in the previous chapter because they are made up of neurons that have weights and biases, which are modified based on learning. Each CNN neuron receives some inputs, performs a dot product, and optionally follows with a non-linearity. The whole CNN still expresses a scoring function using raw Image pixels on one input end to class scores at the output end. CNNs still have a loss function and employ the softmax function on the last, fully connected layer. Basically, all the techniques and concepts discussed for the regular neural networks apply to CNNs.

So what are the significant changes between regular neural networks and CNNs? The CNN architecture makes the explicit assumption that the inputs are Images. This basic assumption permits certain optimizations to be applied to the network, which allows for the encoding of certain properties into the architecture. These optimizations make the forward propagation function more efficient to implement and vastly reduce the amount of parameters in the network.

Recall from the previous chapter that regular neural networks receive an input as a single input data vector and transform it through a series of *hidden layers*. Each hidden layer is made up of a set of neurons, where each neuron is fully connected to all neurons in the previous layer and where neurons in a single layer function are completely independently and do not share any connections. The last fully connected layer is called the output layer, and the classification settings it generates represent the class scores.

Regular neural networks do not scale well to full-sized Images. In the popular CIFAR-10 dataset, Images are of size 32 x 32 x 3 (32 wide, 32 high, 3 color channels), so a single fully connected neuron in a first hidden layer of a regular neural network would have 3072 (32 X 32 X 3) weights. Although this amount of weights is manageable, it still clearly hints that a full-sized Image would require an enormous amount of weights. For example, an Image of a more common size of say 400 x 300 x 3 would require 360,000 weights. In addition, there would likely be several hidden layers involved, so it is apparent that the computational complexity rapidly becomes an exponential explosion. It should be clear that a regular neural network with full connectivity is not a good approach to use with decent sized Images. Dealing with a super abundance of parameters would likely lead to overfitting and consequent poor performance by the network.

A CNN design takes advantage of the fact that its input consists of only Images and therefore the architecture can be designed in an optimal way. In particular, unlike a regular neural network, the layers of a CNN have neurons arranged in three dimensions of **width**, **height**, and **depth**. Note that the word *depth* here refers only to the third dimension of the activation volume. In a CNN design, the neurons in a succeeding layer will only be connected to a small region of the preceding layer.

At this point, I need to discuss the convolution operation. Figure 6-1 shows the Image volume along with a smaller Image volume that is 5 x 5 x 3 in dimension. The smaller volume is called a filter.

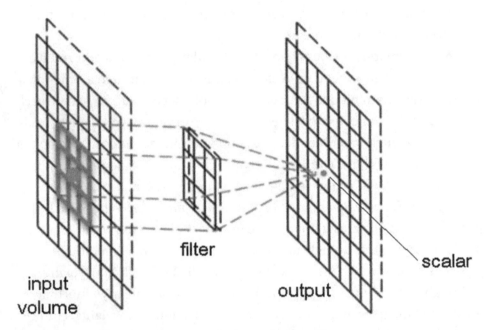

Figure 6-1. *Image volume with convolution filter*

In a convolution operation, a small filter block is "slid" over the larger Image volume in steps, while a dot product is done between the filter and the Image volume that is covered at each step. Computing a dot product for each step results in a scalar value being created. The sum total of all the step-by-step convolution operations results in a 1D Image as depicted by the output layer shown on the right-hand side of the figure. Applying actual dimensions should help clarify the operation. Let's assume the input Image volume is 32 x 32 x 3. This means it has a height and width of 32 pixels and a depth of 3. The 3 in this case refers to three color layers representing the RGB or red, green, and blue values comprising the input Image volume. Now if the filter is, say, 5 x 5 x 3, then it can only be "slid" over the input volume in 28 steps both horizontally and vertically. This means the output "Image" must be 28 x 28 x 1 because that is the only way 5 x 5 x 3 filter can be uniquely stepped through the original Image volume.

However, the convolution operation for a typical CNN is not quite over. Please think of the filter used in the convolution operation as a feature extractor, which was the original intent of the CNN creator, Yann LeCun. I will shortly discuss Professor LeCun's contributions in the next section. It is therefore reasonable to reapplying a different filter and repeating the convolution operation results in an effort to extract a different feature. That is precisely what is being conveyed in Figure 6-2, where five additional features are being applied to the original Image volume. This ultimately results in a final processed block that is 28 x 28 x 6 in size. The processed output block is now referred to as feature or activation maps.

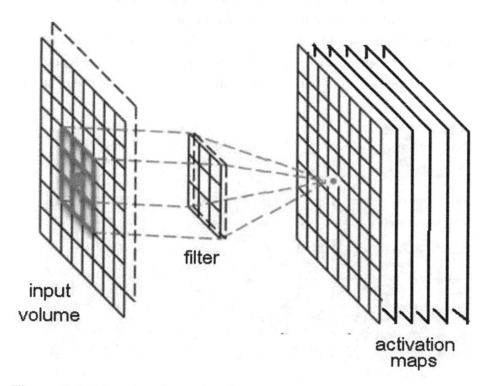

Figure 6-2. *Creating the activation maps*

Multiple convolution layers are used in a typical CNN. Figure 6-3 shows the results of stacking convolutional layers. Notice that activation functions are also used immediately after each convolution layer.

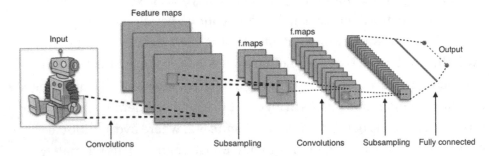

Figure 6-3. *Typical CNN architecture*

CNN learning "happens" when the randomized filters are applied to the Image volumes through all the convolution layers.

The next figure should help you understand how the convolution layers and features are related. Figure 6-4 shows an input Image volume being applied to a series of three convolutional layers and one "output-like" layer.

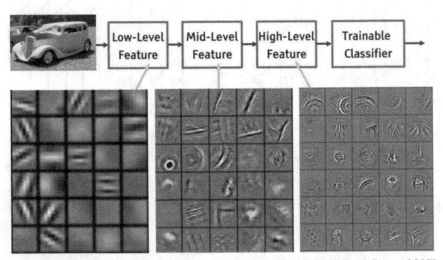

Feature visualization of convolutional net trained on ImageNet from [Zeiler & Fergus 2013]

Figure 6-4. *CNN example with convolutional features exposed*

340

Closely examine the filter outputs in the first layer, which are 5 x 5 x 3 filters. Through back propagation, they have tuned themselves to become colored blobs of Image pieces and edges. As the data flows through additional convolution layers, the filters are performing dot product operations to the output of previous convolution operations. Traditional CNN architectures use linear filters to do the convolution and extract features out of Images. The early layers try to extract primitive features like lines, edges, and corners, while the later layers build on early layers and extract higher-level features like eyes, ears, nose, and so on. These are called latent features.

There can be variations in each Image feature, such as many different variations in eyes alone. A linear filter designed to detect eyes might try to draw straight lines to extract these features. Thus, a conventional CNN implicitly makes the assumption that the latent concepts are linearly separable. But a straight line may not always fit. The separation of the various types of eye features and non-eye features may not be a straight line but something more non-linear. In that case, using a non-linear function would likely serve as a better feature extractor.

Closely examine the Images in the figure associated with the high-level feature convolutional layer and try to imagine them as being representative of the outputs from a grid of 28 x 28 neurons. In a particular feature map, each neuron is connected to only a small portion of the input Image volume. Additionally, all the neurons in a given feature map have the same connection weights. This sharing of weights is called parameter sharing.

Neurons in a CNN also have local connectivity because they are only connected to a sub-set of the input Image, unlike a conventional ANN where all the neurons are fully connected. Local connectivity reduces the number of parameters in the whole system and makes for greater computational efficiency.

History and evolution of the CNN

CNNs have been in existence since 1994 when the first one was created by Dr. Yann LeCun, who is considered by many to be one of the pioneering researchers in the DL field. He named it network LeNet-5, which reflected changes from previous networks he created starting in 1988.

The LeNet-5 architecture was revolutionary because it capitalized on a fundamental insight that Image features are typically distributed across the entire Image and convolution operations with learnable parameters are an effective way to extract similar features at multiple locations using few parameters. It is helpful to remember that existing computers at the time had no graphics processing units (GPU) to assist with training and desktop processor speeds were quite slow in comparison to modern-day processors. Therefore, anything that could be done reduce the number of parameters and associated computation was a significant advantage. The CNN approach was contrasted to the existing approach where each pixel of an input Image was separately processed as an input to a large multi-layer neural network. LeCun explained that those pixels should not be used in the first layer, because Images are highly spatially correlated, and using individual pixels of the Image as separate input features would not take advantage of these correlations.

The LeNet-5 model features may be summarized as follows:

- Convolutional neural network uses a sequence of three layers, convolution, pooling, and non-linearity. This feature remains true to this day regarding CNNs.

- Use the convolution operation to extract spatial features.

- Subsample using spatial averages of the activation maps.

- Non-linearity activation functions in in the form of tanh or sigmoids.

- Use a full connection multi-layer perceptron network (MLP) as final classifier with a softmax classifier.

- Use sparse connection matrices between layers to maximize computational efficiency.

Figure 6-5 shows the LeNet-5 architecture.

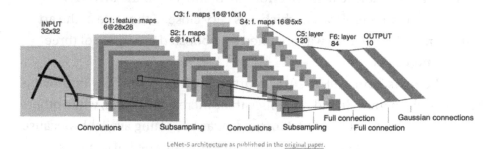

LeNet-5 architecture as published in the original paper.

Figure 6-5. *LeNet-5 architecture*

LeNet-5 is a simple network by today's standards. It only has seven layers, of which there are three convolutional layers (C1, C3, and C5), two subsampling (pooling) layers (S2 and S4), and one fully connected layer (F6), that are followed by the output layer. The convolutional layers use 5 x 5 convolutions with stride 1. Subsampling layers consist of 2 x 2 average pooling layers. The tanh activation function is used throughout the network. The LeNet-5 uses two architectural choices for the network that are not in common use in modern DL networks.

The first choice is that the individual convolutional kernels in layer C3 do not use all of the features produced by layer S2. A key reason for that choice is to make the network more computationally efficient. Another reason was to make convolutional kernels learn different patterns. This makes perfect sense if different kernels receive different inputs, they will learn different patterns.

The second choice was to have ten Euclidean Radial Basis Function neurons in the output layer, which compute the L2 distance between an input vector of dimension 84 and **manually predefined weights vectors** of the same dimension. The number 84 comes from the fact that the weights represent a 7 x 12 binary mask, one for each handwritten digit. This design forces the network to transform the input Image into an internal representation that makes the outputs of layer F6 as close as possible to hand-coded weights of the ten neurons of the output layer.

LeNet-5 was able to achieve error rate below 1% on the MNIST handwritten number dataset, which was very close to the state of the art at the time, which in turn was obtained by a boosted ensemble of three LeNet-4 networks.

In the years from 1998 to 2010, neural networks were slowly improving. Most people in the field did not notice their increasing power, while other researchers slowly progressed. More data was becoming available because of the rise of smartphones and relatively inexpensive digital cameras. Computing power was on the rise; CPUs were becoming faster, and GPUs became less expensive and readily available. Both of these trends made neural network research progress at a slow rate. The increase in computing power along with available data made the tasks that neural networks could handle more interesting.

In 2010 Ciresan et al. published one of the first implementations of a GPU neural network designed to work with the handwritten number recognition problem. This implementation used both forward and backward propagation and ran on an early NVIDIA GTX 280 GPU using up to nine layers in a neural network.

In 2012, Alex Krizhevsky created AlexNet, which was a scaled up version of the LeNet CNN. AlexNet is used to learn about more complex objects than is possible with LeNet. The AlexNet paper included the following contributions:

- Use of rectified linear units (ReLU) as non-linearities.

- Use of the dropout technique to selectively ignore single neurons during training. This technique avoids overfitting of the model.

- Overlapping max pooling, avoiding the averaging effects of average pooling.

- Use of GPUs (NVIDIA GTX580) to reduce training time.

At the time of the AlexNet paper, GPUs offered a much larger number of cores than CPUs and permitted faster training time. All this led to use larger datasets and Images. The AlexNet network success clearly showed the vision community that CNNs were the "stars" of DL. Useful and practical problems could now be tackled using the much improved computing hardware.

In 2013, Yann LeCun, who was working at the NYU DL lab, introduced the OverFeat framework, which was a way to achieve object recognition, localization, and detection using CNNs. Overfeat was a derivative of AlexNet. LeCun also proposed to use learning bounding boxes in object recognition, which are now the accepted way to identify objects in an Image.

In 2014, a team from Oxford University introduced VGG networks. This CNN implementation used small 3 × 3 filters in each convolutional layers and also combined them as a sequence of convolutions. At first, this seemed to be contrary to the principles that LeCun espoused for LeNet, where large convolution filter sizes were used to capture similar features in an Image. Thus, the larger filter sizes of LeNet and AlexNet started to shrink, perhaps coming too close to the infamous 1 × 1 convolutions that LeNet wanted to avoid. However, the great insight that the VGG network provided was that multiple 3 × 3 convolution in sequence can emulate the effect of larger receptive fields, for example, 5 × 5 or even 7 × 7 convolution filters. These concepts have been used in more recent network architectures as Inception and ResNet. VGG networks use multiple 3 × 3 convolutional layers to represent complex features. Notice blocks 3, 4, and 5 of VGG-E where 256 × 256 and 512 × 512, 3 × 3 filters are used multiple times in sequence to extract more complex features and the combination of such features. One disadvantage of VGG networks is that training is computationally expensive. This can be mitigated somewhat by splitting larger networks into smaller ones and adding layers one by one.

Network in Network (NiN) had the simple insight of using 1 × 1 convolutions to provide more combinational power to the features of convolutional layers. The NiN architecture, as shown in Figure 6-6, used spatial MLP layers after each convolution in order to better combine features before another layer.

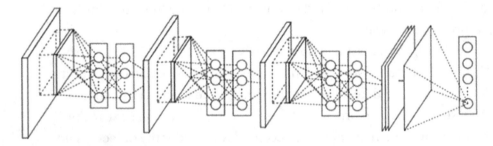

Figure 6-6. *NiN architecture*

Again, one can believe the 1 × 1 convolutions are against the original principles of LeNet, but they instead help combine convolutional features in a more optimal manner, which is not possible by simply stacking additional convolutional layers. This is different from using raw pixels as input to the next layer. Here 1 × 1 convolutions are used to spatially combine features across feature maps after convolution, so they effectively use very few parameters, with shared pixels across all of the features.

The power of MLP can greatly increase the effectiveness of individual convolutional features by combining them into more complex groups. This idea will be later used in most recent architectures as ResNet and Inception and their derivatives.

NiN also used an average pooling layer as part of the last classifier, another practice that has become commonplace. This was done to average the response of the network to multiple the input Image before classification.

In the Fall of 2014, Christian Szegedy from Google began a project aimed at reducing the computational burden of deep neural networks. He and his team created GoogLeNet, the first model using the Inception architecture. During that timeframe, DL models were becoming highly useful in categorizing the content of Images and video frames. Google became very interested in efficient and large deployments of DL architectures to their server farms. Christian considered a lot of ways to reduce the computational burden of deep neural networks while still obtaining state-of-art performance. The main objective was to maintain or reduce computational costs while achieving improved performance. He and his team came up with the Inception module, which is shown in Figure 6-7 block diagram.

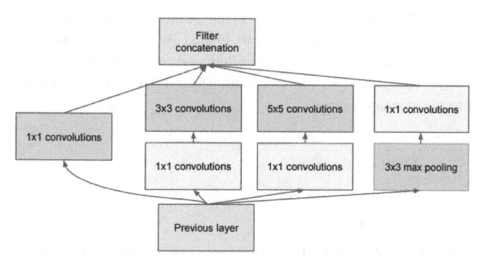

Figure 6-7. *GoogLeNet block diagram*

The diagram appears at first glance to be basically the parallel combination of 1×1, 3×3, and 5×5 convolutional filters. But the great insight of the Inception module was the use of 1×1 convolutional blocks (NiN) to reduce the number of features before the expensive parallel blocks. This is commonly referred to as "bottleneck," which is explained in the following data.

Reducing the bottleneck in the Inception model is done by reducing the number of features to be processed. Inference times would be minimized by reducing the number of features; however, the issue was not to lose too much data quality.

For example, say that there are 256 features being applied to a convolution layer and 256 features being passed out. If the Inception layer is only performing 3 x 3 convolutions, there will still need to be about 589,000 multiply and accumulate operations required. That is the result from this calculation:

$$256 * 256 * 3 * 3 = 589,824$$

Instead of doing this, it is decided to reduce the number of features that will have to be convolved, say to 64. In this case, first perform 256 -> 64 1×1 convolutions and then 64 convolutions on all Inception branches, and then use again a 1×1 convolution from 64 -> 256 features back again. The operations are now

- $256 \times 64 \times 1 \times 1 = 16,384$

- $64 \times 64 \times 3 \times 3 = 36,864$

- $64 \times 256 \times 1 \times 1 = 16,384$

    Total = 69,632

This is a total of about 70,000 operations vs. the almost 600,000 that were required using the full feature set. Although there are significantly less operations involved, there is no loss in processing accuracy because the input features are correlated, and thus redundancy can be removed by combining them appropriately with the 1 × 1 convolutions. The reason for the success is that after convolution with a smaller number of features, they can be expanded again into a meaningful combination for the next layer.

In February 2015, the Google team introduced batch-normalized Inception V2. With batch normalization, the mean and standard deviation of all feature maps are computed and then the output of a layer is normalized with these values. This action "whitens" the data and makes all the neural maps have responses in the same range with zero mean. This action promotes training as the next layer does not have to learn offsets in the input data and can focus on how to best combine features.

In December 2015, the team released version 3 of the Inception modules. The following list details the ideas and concepts contained in that version:

- Maximize information flow into the network by carefully constructing networks that balance depth and width. Before each pooling, increase the feature maps.

- When depth is increased, the number of features or width of the layer is also increased systematically.

- Use width increase at each layer to increase the combination of features before the next layer.

- Use only 3 × 3 convolution when possible, given that filter of 5 × 5 and 7 × 7 can be decomposed with multiple 3 × 3.

- Filters can also be decomposed by flattened convolutions into more complex modules.

- Inception modules can also decrease the size of the data by providing pooling while performing the Inception computation. This is basically identical to performing a convolution with strides in parallel with a simple pooling layer.

At approximately the same time as Inception V3 was being introduced, K. He et al. introduced a rather revolutionary CNN they named ResNet. Their simple idea was to connect the outputs of two successive convolutional layers and also to bypass the input to the next layer. Figure 6-8 shows the flow diagram that illusrates the ResNet idea.

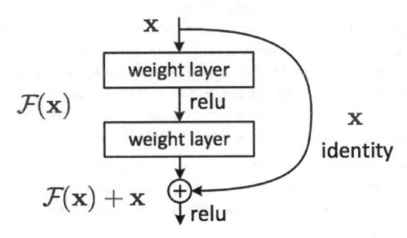

Figure 6-8. *ResNet core concept flow diagram*

One question that would naturally come to mind is why would bypassing convolutional layers improve performance? The answer lies in the nature of deep networks, which are simply networks containing many layers. Since the introduction of AlexNet, which had five convolutional layers, CNNs have generally become deeper. For instance, Inception V1 started with 19 layers and eventually had 22 layers. However, network performance does not always improve simply by stacking more and more layers. This is due to the vanishing gradient problem. As the gradient is back propagated to earlier layers, repeated multiplications start to make the gradient infinitely smaller. As a result, as the network becomes deeper, its performance gets saturated or even starts degrading rapidly.

The core concept of ResNet is to introduce a so-called identity shortcut connection that skips one or more layers, as was shown in Figure 6-8. The ResNet authors argued that stacking layers shouldn't degrade the network performance, because simply stacking identity mappings (a layer that doesn't do anything) upon the current network and the resulting architecture would perform the same. This indicates that the deeper model should not produce a training error higher than shallower counterparts.

This is similar to older ideas like this one. But here they bypass two layers and are applied to large scales. Bypassing two layers is the key intuition, because bypassing a single layer did not provide much improvement. But a two-layer bypass can be considered as a small classifier or a Network in Network.

ResNet is also the first time that a network of several hundred to one thousand layers was trained. ResNet also is starting to use the bottleneck reduction scheme created with the Inception V2 network. Figure 6-9 shows the flow diagram with a bottleneck scheme embedded as well as the identity bypass.

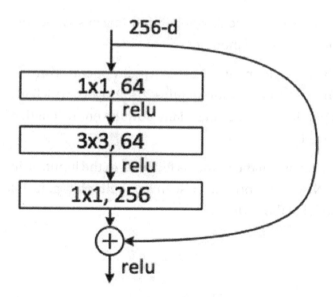

Figure 6-9. *ResNet core concept flow diagram with bottleneck elimination*

The number of features at each layer is reduced by first using a 1 × 1 convolution with a smaller output (usually one-quarter of the input), then a 3 × 3 layer, and then again a 1 × 1 convolution to a larger number of features. As in the case of Inception modules, this scheme allows the computation to be kept low while still providing a rich combination of features.

ResNet uses a fairly simple initial layer at the input (stem), a 7 × 7 conv layer, followed with a pool of 2. ResNet also uses a pooling layer plus softmax as final classifier.

Here are some additional insights about the ResNet architecture:

- ResNet can be seen as both parallel and serial modules by just thinking of the input as going to many modules in parallel, while the output of each modules connects in series.

- ResNet can also be thought as multiple ensembles of parallel or serial modules.

- It has been found that ResNet usually operates on blocks of relatively low depth ~20–30 layers, which act in parallel, rather than serially flow the entire length of the network.

- ResNet, when the output is fed back to the input, as in RNN, the network can be seen as a better bio-plausible model of the cortex.

In February 2016, Christian and his team at Google introduced Inception V4 to the community. This Inception module after the stem is similar to Inception V3. Figure 6-10 shows the initial V4 architecture.

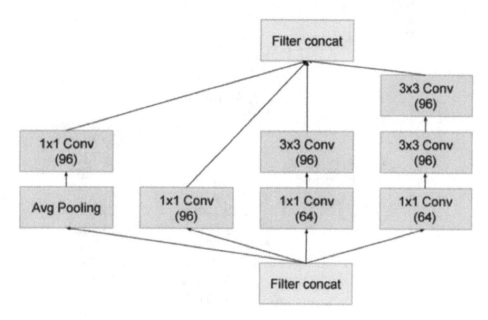

Figure 6-10. *Initial Inception V4 architecture*

However, they also combined the Inception V4 module with the ResNet module. This is shown in Figure 6-11.

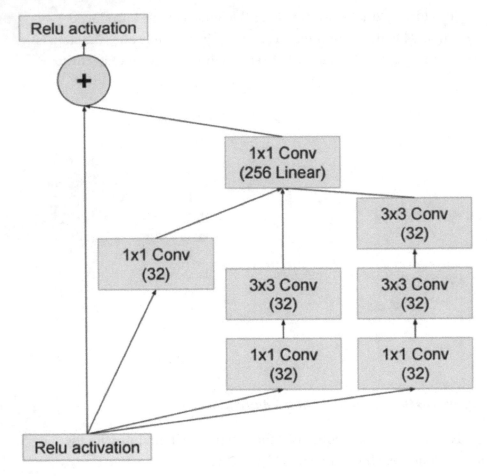

Figure 6-11. *Inception V4 architecture with ResNet*

The team renamed this module Inception-ResNet V1 to indicate that it was a substantial transformation from the original Inception design protocol. It was determined that this new module had roughly the same computational cost of Inception V3 but trained much faster. Unfortunately, it reached a slightly worse final accuracy than the Inception V3 module.

In 2016, SqueezeNet was released by researchers at the University of California, Berkeley and Stanford University. The authors' goal in designing SqueezeNet was to create a smaller neural network with fewer parameters that can more easily fit into limited computer memory and could be easily transmitted over a computer network.

This original version of SqueezeNet was implemented on top of the Caffe DL software framework. Shortly thereafter, the open source research community ported SqueezeNet to a number of other deep learning frameworks including Chainer, Apache MXNet, and Keras. In 2017, several commercial companies demonstrated SqueezeNet running on low-power processing platforms such as smartphones and FPGAs.

As of 2018, SqueezeNet ships "natively" as part of the source code of a number of deep learning frameworks such as PyTorch, Apache MXNet, and Apple_CoreML. In addition, third-party developers have created implementations of SqueezeNet that are compatible with the TensorFlow framework.

Xception improves on the Inception module with a simple and elegant architecture that is as effective as ResNet and Inception V4. Figure 6-12 shows the Xception module architecture.

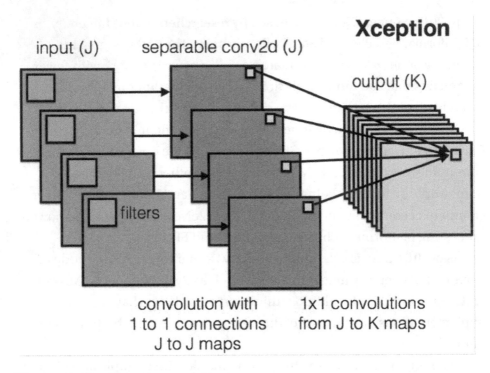

Figure 6-12. *Xception architecture*

The Xception architecture has 36 convolutional stages, which is close in similarity to a ResNet-34. Figure 6-13 shows the Xception data flow diagram.

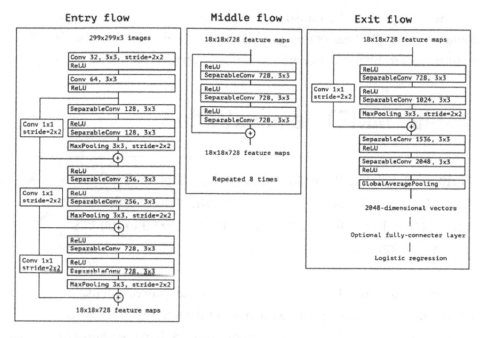

Figure 6-13. *Xception data flow diagram*

The Xception code is as simple as ResNet and is more comprehensible than Inception V4.

Xception has been implemented in Torch7 and Keras with TensorFlow.

The last CNN model I will mention in this evolution discussion is FractalNet, which uses a recursive architecture. The authors Larsson et al. state in their introductory paper:

> *We introduce a design strategy for neural network macro-architecture based on self-similarity. Repeated application of a simple expansion rule generates deep networks whose structural layouts are precisely truncated fractals. These networks contain interacting subpaths of different lengths, but do not include any pass-through or residual connections; every internal signal is transformed by a filter and nonlinearity before being seen by subsequent layers.*

The excerpt from their abstract seems to indicate a rather radical departure from the ResNet design philosophy. I believe the verdict is still pending regarding the performance of this deep layered CNN design.

Fashion MNIST demonstration

Note   You will use the exact same configuration on the RasPi that was in effect when the last demonstration in Chapter 5 was run. Keras with the TensorFlow backend is required to run this demonstration's script.

This demonstration, like the one at the end of Chapter 5, will use a MNIST dataset, but it will not be the handwritten number set. Instead it is a dataset consisting of clothing Images. And just like the handwritten number dataset, there will be ten classes, but in this new dataset, each class will be different clothing article. The dataset Images will all be 28 x 28 in size to make them "drop in" compatible with the handwritten number dataset. Additionally, there are approximately 60,000 training Images and 10,000 testing Images. This new dataset is named fashion_ mnist, and it is instantly available using the Keras import dataset library.

The following snippet of code shows how this new dataset will be loaded:

```
from keras.datasets import fashion_mnist
(train_images, train_labels),(test_images, test_labels) =
fashion_mnist.load_data()
```

You may notice that I used different names for the training and test datasets in this demonstration than were used in the handwritten number demonstration. I mention this because you would get into trouble if you simply tried to cut and paste between the two scripts.

As mentioned previously, all the Images are 28 x 28 arrays, with pixel integer intensity values ranging between 0 and 255. The Image labels are also an array of integers, ranging from 0 to 9. These integers correspond to the class of clothing the Image represents. Table 6-1 shows the integer to clothing descriptions.

Table 6-1. *Integer to clothing description relationships*

Label	Class
0	T-shirt/top
1	Trouser
2	Pullover
3	Dress
4	Coat
5	Sandal
6	Shirt
7	Sneaker
8	Bag
9	Ankle boot

Using integers to represent string descriptions is required when configuring a CNN. String variables and network computations are inherently incompatible.

Each Image in a given class is mapped to a single label. Since the class names are not included with the dataset, these labels must be stored to be used later when Images are plotted. The following statement stores the labels:

```
class_names = ['T-shirt/top', 'Trouser', 'Pullover', 'Dress',
'Coat', 'Sandal', 'Shirt', 'Sneaker', 'Bag', 'Ankle boot']
```

It is always prudent to inspect and/or sample the data to be used in order to be knowledgeable about it and become aware of any potential issues or problems. To achieve this goal, I would suggest running the following short script named reviewData.py. This script is available from the book's companion web site:

```
from keras.datasets import fashion_mnist

(train_images, train_labels),(test_images, test_labels) =
fashion_mnist.load_data()

print('Number of training records and size of each training
record: ', train_images.shape)
print()
print('Number of training labels: ', len(train_labels))
print()
print('Training label: ', train_labels)
print()
print('Number of test records and size of each test record:',
test_images.shape)
print()
print('Number of test labels: ', len(test_labels))
print()
```

The script is run by entering this next command:

```
python reviewData.py
```

Figure 6-14 shows the results after running the script.

```
                              pi@raspberrypi: ~                        ∨  ∧  ✕

 File  Edit  Tabs  Help
Number of training records and size of each training record:  (60000, 28, 28)

Number of training labels:  60000

Training label:  [9 0 0 ... 3 0 5]

Number of test records and size of each test record: (10000, 28, 28)

Number of test labels:  10000

(py3cv4) pi@raspberrypi:~ $ ▯
```

Figure 6-14. *reviewData script results*

In examining the figure, you should see that the datasets are the same and shape as the datasets used in the earlier handwritten number recognition demonstration. In addition, the first three and the last three of the 60,000 training label values are displayed. This confirms that the training_labels dataset was properly loaded.

Additionally, it is always useful and informative to Image a sample of the input dataset as was the case with the handwritten number recognition project. For this task, I started a Python interactive session to Image a sample. The following code, when entered into an interactive Python session, will Image the first training dataset Image. You should initiate this session immediately after you have run the reviewData script to ensure that the fashion_mnist datasets have been downloaded and are available for access.

```
import matplotlib.pyplot as plt
plt.figure()
plt.imshow(train_images[0])
plt.colorbar()
plt.grid(False)
plt.show()
```

Figure 6-15 shows the object Imaged in the first training record with a color bar inserted to reflect the associated pixel intensities present in the Image.

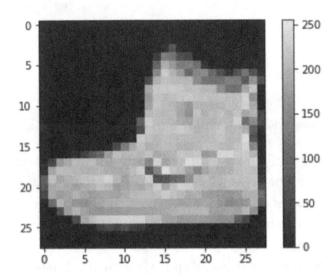

Figure 6-15. *First training record Image*

Note that this Image is of an ankle length boot, which corresponds to the integer "9" class reference shown in the reviewData script results for the class label print-out. This check is just another way to confirm the consistency of the input datasets.

```
# Model definition
def cnn_model():
    # create model
    model = Sequential()
    model.add(Conv2D(32, (5, 5), input_shape=(1, 28, 28),
    activation='relu'))
    model.add(MaxPooling2D(pool_size=(2, 2)))
    model.add(Dropout(0.2))
    model.add(Flatten())
```

```
model.add(Dense(128, activation='relu'))
model.add(Dense(numClass, activation='softmax'))
# Compile model
model.compile(loss='categorical_crossentropy',
optimizer='adam', metrics=['accuracy'])
return model
```

This is the code portion that defines the CNN and then compiles it. This model is considerably different than the MLP model used in the last demonstration in Chapter 5. For starters, it has six layers ordered as follows:

1. Convolutional layer

2. Pooling layer

3. Dropout layer

4. Flatten layer

5. Full connection layer

6. Output layer

Each layer contributes a sequential operation to the CNN resulting in the transformation from an input Image to classification output.

In the Keras demonstration in Chapter 5, I briefly mentioned the Adam optimizer in the discussion regarding the compile function. I will expand upon the use of an optimizer because it is important to understand its function and assumptions it uses. An optimizer for a CNN is a function that controls how the network learns. In a non-Keras network such as the MLP in Chapter 5, the learning rate (lr) controlled the gradient step size. A small lr means small steps are taken in trying to locate the global minimum of the cost function. This meant that a very small step size could take the gradient descent algorithm literally hours to eventually settle in on the global minimum. An optimizer takes a different approach and uses a dynamic technique to set the step size in order to minimize the total time to locate the global minimum.

The Adam optimizer computes individual adaptive learning rates for different parameters from estimates of first and second moments of the gradients. The Adam authors describe it as combining the advantages of two other extensions of stochastic gradient descent. Specifically:

- Adaptive Gradient Algorithm (AdaGrad) that maintains a per-parameter learning rate that improves performance on problems with sparse gradients.

- Root Mean Square Propagation (RMSProp) that also maintains per-parameter learning rates that are adapted based on the average of recent magnitudes of the gradients for the weight (e.g., how quickly it is changing). This means the algorithm does well on online and non-stationary problems (e.g., noisy).

The Adam algorithm realizes the benefits of both AdaGrad and RMSProp algorithms. Instead of adapting the parameter learning rates based on the average first moment (the mean) as in RMSProp, Adam also makes use of the average of the second moment of the gradients (the uncentered variance). Specifically, the algorithm calculates an exponential moving average of the gradient and the squared gradient. The parameters, beta1 and beta2, control the decay rates of these moving averages.

Adam is a popular algorithm in the field of deep learning because it achieves good results, fast. Empirical results have demonstrated that Adam works well in practice and compares favorably to other stochastic optimization methods. In the original paper, Adam demonstrated that its convergence meets the expectations of the paper's theoretical analysis. Adam has been applied to the logistic regression algorithm on the MNIST handwritten number recognition and IMDB sentiment analysis datasets. The authors have concluded that Adam can efficiently solve practical DL problems.

```
# Run the demo and evaluate it
from keras.layers import Conv2D
model = cnn_model()
model.fit(train_images, train_labels, validation_data=(test_
images, test_labels), epochs=10, batch_size=200, verbose=2)

# Final evaluation
scores = model.evaluate(test_images, test_labels, verbose=0)
print(scores[1])
```

The last code portion is the driver code, which tests the new CNN with the fashion_mnist dataset. A model object named model is first instantiated and then trained using the Keras fit function. A scores tuple is then generated by calling the Keras evaluate method. The testing continues for 10 epochs with the final statement showing the ultimate CNN error rate.

The complete script is named kerasFashionTest.py and is listed in the following with comments. It is available from the book's companion web site.

```
import numpy as np
from keras.datasets import fashion_mnist
from keras.models import Sequential
from keras.layers import Dense
from keras.layers import Dropout
from keras.layers import Flatten
from keras.layers.convolutional import Conv2D
from keras.layers.convolutional import MaxPooling2D
from keras.utils import np_utils
from keras import backend as K
K.set_image_dim_ordering('th')

# Set a random seed
seed = 42
np.random.seed(seed)
```

```python
# Load the datasets
(train_images, train_labels),(test_images, test_labels) =
fashion_mnist.load_data()

# Flatten all of the 28 x 28 images into 784 element numpy
input
# data vectors.
pixelNum = train_images.shape[1] * train_images.shape[2]
train_images = train_images.reshape(train_images.
shape[0],1,28,28).astype('float32')
test_images = test_images.reshape(test_images.
shape[0],1,28,28).astype('float32')

# Normalize inputs from 0-255 to 0-1
train_images = train_images / 255.0
test_images = test_images / 255.0

# One hot encoding
train_labels = np_utils.to_categorical(train_labels)
test_labels = np_utils.to_categorical(test_labels)
numClass = test_labels.shape[1]

# Model definition
def cnn_model():
    # create model
    model = Sequential()
    model.add(Conv2D(32, (5, 5), input_shape=(1, 28, 28),
    activation='relu'))
    model.add(MaxPooling2D(pool_size=(2, 2)))
    model.add(Dropout(0.2))
    model.add(Flatten())
    model.add(Dense(128, activation='relu'))
    model.add(Dense(numClass, activation='softmax'))
```

```
    # Compile model
    model.compile(loss='categorical_crossentropy',
    optimizer='adam', metrics=['accuracy'])
    return model

# Run the demo and evaluate it
model = cnn_model()
model.fit(train_images, train_labels, validation_data=(test_
images, test_labels), epochs=10, batch_size=200, verbose=2)

# Final evaluation
scores = model.evaluate(test_images, test_labels, verbose=0)
print(scores[1])
```

The script should be run in the virtual environment using the following command:

```
python kerasFashionTest.py
```

The script takes about 30 minutes to run to completion because it trains the model using the full 60,000 fashion_mnist training dataset and then tests the model with the 10,000 fashion_mnist test dataset for ten times or 10 epochs. The final results are shown in Figure 6-16.

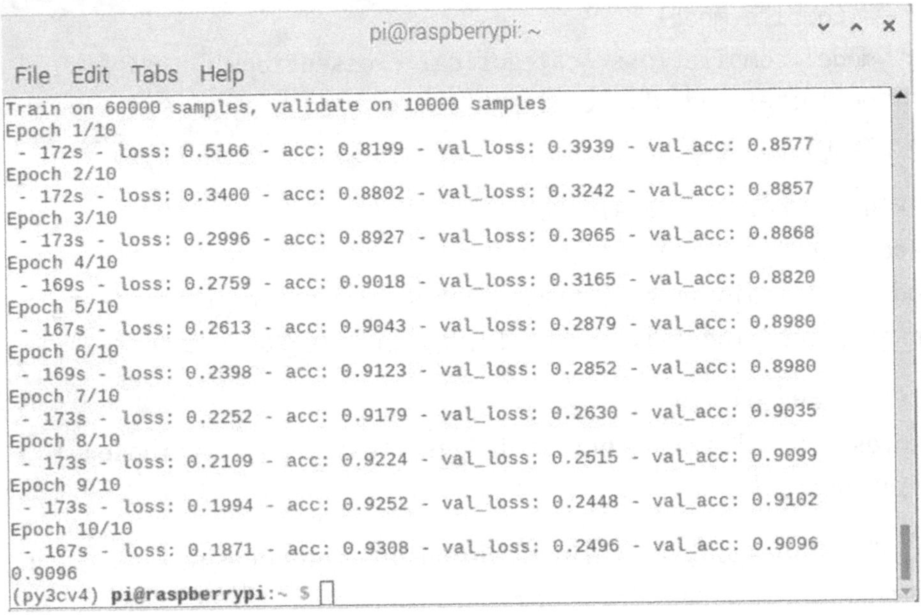

Figure 6-16. *Final results after running the kerasFashionTest script*

The final accuracy was 90.96%, which is considered to be a good score for a CNN – not quite excellent, which would need scores around 98% to 99%, but still quite accurate. To obtain the ultimate in CNN accuracy, one must match the CNN design to the dataset being processed. How to do this is much more of an art than it is a science. There are many CNN design strategies existing, which you hopefully have gleaned from reading the CNN evolution discussion earlier in this chapter. Which one to use with any given dataset must necessarily lie with a practitioner's judgment and experience. I cannot provide any guidance in this area because I have simply not acquired sufficient experience with using the many CNN designs that currently are available as well as the multitude of current datasets. The number of combinations is enormous. My only suggestion is to try new strategies on a dataset and see what develops.

With the thought of trying a new design, I will now present a variation of the previous demonstration using a somewhat more complex CNN model and see what happens.

More complex Fashion MNIST demonstration

I will show you a more complex CNN model in this demonstration as compared to the previous one. Everything else in the script remains the same. The purpose of this demonstration is to determine what effect a new CNN model will have on the overall accuracy of dataset classifications.

The following code defines the model used in this demonstration:

```
def complex_model():
    # Create model
    model = Sequential()
    model.add(Conv2D(30, (5, 5), input_shape=(1, 28, 28),
    activation='relu'))
    model.add(MaxPooling2D(pool_size=(2, 2)))
    model.add(Conv2D(15, (3, 3), activation='relu'))
    model.add(MaxPooling2D(pool_size=(2, 2)))
    model.add(Dropout(0.2))
    model.add(Flatten())
    model.add(Dense(128, activation='relu'))
    model.add(Dense(50, activation='relu'))
    model.add(Dense(numClass, activation='softmax'))
```

This model uses nine layers as compared to the six layers used in the previous demonstration. The kerasFashionTest script was used with these layers added to its model definition:

- One convolution layer

- One pooling layer

- One full connection layer

The newly modified script was renamed kerasComplexFashionTest.py and is available from the book's companion web site.

```python
import numpy as np
from keras.datasets import fashion_mnist
from keras.models import Sequential
from keras.layers import Dense
from keras.layers import Dropout
from keras.layers import Flatten
from keras.layers.convolutional import Conv2D
from keras.layers.convolutional import MaxPooling2D
from keras.utils import np_utils
from keras import backend as K
K.set_image_dim_ordering('th')

# Set a random seed
seed = 42
np.random.seed(seed)

# Load the datasets
(train_images, train_labels),(test_images, test_labels) =
fashion_mnist.load_data()

# Flatten all of the 28 x 28 images into 784 element numpy
input
# data vectors.
pixelNum = train_images.shape[1] * train_images.shape[2]
train_images = train_images.reshape(train_images.
shape[0],1,28,28).astype('float32')
test_images = test_images.reshape(test_images.
shape[0],1,28,28).astype('float32')

# Normalize inputs from 0-255 to 0-1
train_images = train_images / 255.0
test_images = test_images / 255.0
```

```
# One hot encoding
train_labels = np_utils.to_categorical(train_labels)
test_labels = np_utils.to_categorical(test_labels)
numClass = test_labels.shape[1]

# Complex model definition
def complex_model():
    # Create model
    model = Sequential()
    model.add(Conv2D(30, (5, 5), input_shape=(1, 28, 28),
    activation='relu'))
    model.add(MaxPooling2D(pool_size=(2, 2)))
    model.add(Conv2D(15, (3, 3), activation='relu'))
    model.add(MaxPooling2D(pool_size=(2, 2)))
    model.add(Dropout(0.2))
    model.add(Flatten())
    model.add(Dense(128, activation='relu'))
    model.add(Dense(50, activation='relu'))
    model.add(Dense(numClass, activation='softmax'))
    # Compile model
    model.compile(loss='categorical_crossentropy',
    optimizer='adam', metrics=['accuracy'])
    return model

# Run the demo and evaluate it
model = complex_model()
model.fit(train_images, train_labels, validation_data=(test_
images, test_labels), epochs=10, batch_size=200, verbose=2)

# Final evaluation
scores = model.evaluate(test_images, test_labels, verbose=0)
print(scores[1])
```

The script should be run in the virtual environment using the following command:

python kerasComplexFashionTest.py

This script took about 27 minutes to run to completion, which is slightly less than the previous demonstration. The final results are shown in Figure 6-17.

```
pi@raspberrypi: ~                                          ⌄ ∧ ✕
File  Edit  Tabs  Help
Train on 60000 samples, validate on 10000 samples
Epoch 1/10
 - 163s - loss: 0.7239 - acc: 0.7373 - val_loss: 0.4746 - val_acc: 0.8300
Epoch 2/10
 - 163s - loss: 0.4575 - acc: 0.8343 - val_loss: 0.4148 - val_acc: 0.8484
Epoch 3/10
 - 163s - loss: 0.3930 - acc: 0.8581 - val_loss: 0.3636 - val_acc: 0.8702
Epoch 4/10
 - 163s - loss: 0.3611 - acc: 0.8696 - val_loss: 0.3503 - val_acc: 0.8720
Epoch 5/10
 - 162s - loss: 0.3398 - acc: 0.8768 - val_loss: 0.3335 - val_acc: 0.8770
Epoch 6/10
 - 162s - loss: 0.3214 - acc: 0.8823 - val_loss: 0.3080 - val_acc: 0.8907
Epoch 7/10
 - 162s - loss: 0.3088 - acc: 0.8864 - val_loss: 0.3020 - val_acc: 0.8894
Epoch 8/10
 - 162s - loss: 0.2924 - acc: 0.8920 - val_loss: 0.2917 - val_acc: 0.8945
Epoch 9/10
 - 162s - loss: 0.2854 - acc: 0.8947 - val_loss: 0.3047 - val_acc: 0.8863
Epoch 10/10
 - 162s - loss: 0.2776 - acc: 0.8981 - val_loss: 0.2823 - val_acc: 0.8965
0.8965
(py3cv4) pi@raspberrypi:~ $ □
```

Figure 6-17. *Final results after running the kerasComplexFashionTest script*

The final accuracy was 89.65%, which is slightly less than the previous demonstration's score of 90.96%. This result at first might seem a bit strange considering that a more complex CNN model was used in this demonstration. However, such results are common with CNN projects. It is likely impossible to predict how a particular CNN model will perform on any given dataset. The only reasonable conclusion to draw from this result is that a model must first be used on a dataset to determine its performance. In this case, the simpler CNN model was the better performer. That's not always the case, but you will never know unless the model is tested.

VGG Fashion MNIST demonstration

A VGG CNN model will be used in this demonstration in order to show you another way to test the fashion_mnist datasets. I will first give credit to Adrian Rosebrock for his February 2019 blog titled "Fashion MNIST with Keras and Deep Learning" from which I drew much inspiration and the model I used in this demonstration. I will admit to slightly changing the model code to fit my preprocessing statements as well as the way the model was compiled.

In this demonstration, the model definition was put into a class and separately stored in a file named VGG.py. The class listing is shown in the following, and it is available from this book's companion web site.

```
# Import the required libraries
from keras.models import Sequential
from keras.layers.normalization import BatchNormalization
from keras.layers.convolutional import Conv2D
from keras.layers.convolutional import MaxPooling2D
from keras.layers.core import Activation
from keras.layers.core import Flatten
from keras.layers.core import Dropout
from keras.layers.core import Dense
from keras import backend as K

class VGG:
    @staticmethod
    def build(width, height, depth, classes):
```

```
# Initialize the model along with the input shape to
# be "channels last" and the channels dimension itself
model = Sequential()
inputShape = (height, width, depth)
chanDim = -1

# If we are using "channels first", update the input
# shape and channels dimension
if K.image_data_format() == "channels_first":
    inputShape = (depth, height, width)
    chanDim = 1

# First CONV => RELU => CONV => RELU => POOL layer
model.add(Conv2D(32, (3, 3), padding="same",
    input_shape=inputShape))
model.add(Activation("relu"))
model.add(BatchNormalization(axis=chanDim))
model.add(Conv2D(32, (3, 3), padding="same"))
model.add(Activation("relu"))
model.add(BatchNormalization(axis=chanDim))
model.add(MaxPooling2D(pool_size=(2, 2)))
model.add(Dropout(0.25))

# Second CONV => RELU => CONV => RELU => POOL layer
model.add(Conv2D(64, (3, 3), padding="same"))
model.add(Activation("relu"))
model.add(BatchNormalization(axis=chanDim))
model.add(Conv2D(64, (3, 3), padding="same"))
model.add(Activation("relu"))
model.add(BatchNormalization(axis=chanDim))
model.add(MaxPooling2D(pool_size=(2, 2)))
model.add(Dropout(0.25))
```

```python
# First (and only) set of FC => RELU layers
model.add(Flatten())
model.add(Dense(512))
model.add(Activation("relu"))
model.add(BatchNormalization())
model.add(Dropout(0.5))

# Softmax classifier
model.add(Dense(classes))
model.add(Activation("softmax"))

    # Compile model
model.compile(loss='categorical_crossentropy',
optimizer='adam', metrics=['accuracy'])

# Return the constructed network architecture
return model
```

The main script is listed in the following and is named kerasVGGTest.
py, and it too is available from the book's companion web site.

```python
import numpy as np
from VGG import VGG
from keras.datasets import fashion_mnist
from keras.utils import np_utils
from keras import backend as K
K.set_image_dim_ordering('th')

# Set a random seed
seed = 42
np.random.seed(seed)

# Load the datasets
(train_images, train_labels),(test_images, test_labels) =
fashion_mnist.load_data()
```

```
# Flatten all of the 28 x 28 images into 784 element numpy
input
# data vectors.
pixelNum = train_images.shape[1] * train_images.shape[2]
train_images = train_images.reshape(train_images.
shape[0],1,28,28).astype('float32')
test_images = test_images.reshape(test_images.
shape[0],1,28,28).astype('float32')

# Normalize inputs from 0-255 to 0-1
train_images = train_images / 255.0
test_images = test_images / 255.0

# One hot encoding
train_labels = np_utils.to_categorical(train_labels)
test_labels = np_utils.to_categorical(test_labels)
numClass = test_labels.shape[1]

# Run the demo and evaluate it
vgg = VGG()
model = vgg.build(28, 28, 1, numClass)
train_images = train_images.reshape(60000, 28, 28, 1)
test_images = test_images.reshape(10000, 28, 28, 1)
model.fit(train_images, train_labels, validation_data=(test_
images, test_labels), epochs=10, batch_size=100, verbose=2)

# Final evaluation
scores = model.evaluate(test_images, test_labels, verbose=0)
print(scores[1])
```

You should be aware that running this script with 10 epochs will take a long time, roughly 3 hours. This is mainly due to the nature of the model. A long duration training time for the VGG CNN was mentioned in the CNN evolution discussion.

Please ensure that the class file VGG.py is in the same directory as this script prior to running it. This script should be run in the virtual environment using the following command:

```
python kerasVGGTest.py
```

This script took about 3 hours to run to completion. The final results are shown in Figure 6-18.

```
                                    pi@raspberrypi: ~                          ∨  ∧  ✕
 File  Edit  Tabs  Help
Train on 60000 samples, validate on 10000 samples
Epoch 1/10
 - 1734s - loss: 0.4620 - acc: 0.8422 - val_loss: 0.2890 - val_acc: 0.8986
Epoch 2/10
 - 1771s - loss: 0.2928 - acc: 0.8932 - val_loss: 0.2633 - val_acc: 0.9067
Epoch 3/10
 - 1790s - loss: 0.2544 - acc: 0.9063 - val_loss: 0.2317 - val_acc: 0.9153
Epoch 4/10
 - 1766s - loss: 0.2318 - acc: 0.9158 - val_loss: 0.2566 - val_acc: 0.9033
Epoch 5/10
 - 1748s - loss: 0.2163 - acc: 0.9213 - val_loss: 0.2396 - val_acc: 0.9150
Epoch 6/10
 - 1761s - loss: 0.1987 - acc: 0.9277 - val_loss: 0.2231 - val_acc: 0.9187
Epoch 7/10
 - 1764s - loss: 0.1883 - acc: 0.9314 - val_loss: 0.2061 - val_acc: 0.9245
Epoch 8/10
^[ - 1794s - loss: 0.1778 - acc: 0.9347 - val_loss: 0.2198 - val_acc: 0.9213
Epoch 9/10
 - 1762s - loss: 0.1685 - acc: 0.9378 - val_loss: 0.2140 - val_acc: 0.9248
Epoch 10/10
 - 1801s - loss: 0.1596 - acc: 0.9417 - val_loss: 0.1908 - val_acc: 0.9313
0.9313
(py3cv4) pi@raspberrypi:~ $ []
```

Figure 6-18. Final results after running the kerasVGGTest script

The final accuracy score was 93.13%, which is a very good score. This score is more than two points higher than the simple CNN score of 90.96%. A gain of 2 points in CNN performance is significant when you consider there is only about a 10-point spread in ratings for high-performance CNNs.

Jason's Fashion MNIST demonstration

This last CNN demonstration using the Fashion MNIST dataset comes from a May 2019 blog written by Dr. Jason Brownlee titled "How to Develop a Deep CNN for Fashion MNIST Clothing Classification." I choose to use Jason's script because it is highly modular and well performing and provides some informative plots concerning on how well it functions. The CNN model used in the script is similar to the ones used in previous chapter demonstrations, and its performance is also on par with them.

You will need to install some additional Python libraries in order to run this script. Enter the following commands to install these libraries:

```
pip install matplotlib
pip install pandas
pip install sklearn
```

The complete script listing, which I named jasonTest.py, is shown in the following and is available from the book's companion web site. I have also added some explanatory comments after the listing.

```
# Model with double the filters for the fashion mnist dataset
from numpy import mean
from numpy import std
from matplotlib import pyplot
from sklearn.model_selection import KFold
from keras.datasets import fashion_mnist
from keras.utils import to_categorical
from keras.models import Sequential
from keras.layers import Conv2D
from keras.layers import MaxPooling2D
from keras.layers import Dense
from keras.layers import Flatten
from keras.optimizers import SGD
```

```python
# Load train and test dataset
def load_dataset():
    # load dataset
    (trainX, trainY), (testX, testY) = fashion_mnist.load_data()
    # reshape dataset to have a single channel
    trainX = trainX.reshape((trainX.shape[0], 28, 28, 1))
    testX = testX.reshape((testX.shape[0], 28, 28, 1))
    # one hot encode target values
    trainY = to_categorical(trainY)
    testY = to_categorical(testY)
    return trainX, trainY, testX, testY

# Scale pixels
def prep_pixels(train, test):
    # convert from integers to floats
    train_norm = train.astype('float32')
    test_norm = test.astype('float32')
    # normalize to range 0-1
    train_norm = train_norm / 255.0
    test_norm = test_norm / 255.0
    # return normalized images
    return train_norm, test_norm

# Define cnn model
def define_model():
    model = Sequential()
    model.add(Conv2D(64, (3, 3), padding='same',
    activation='relu', kernel_initializer='he_uniform',
    input_shape=(28, 28, 1)))
    model.add(MaxPooling2D((2, 2)))
    model.add(Flatten())
    model.add(Dense(100, activation='relu', kernel_
    initializer='he_uniform'))
```

```python
    model.add(Dense(10, activation='softmax'))
    # compile model
    opt = SGD(lr=0.01, momentum=0.9)
    model.compile(optimizer=opt, loss='categorical_
    crossentropy', metrics=['accuracy'])
    return model

# Evaluate a model using k-fold cross-validation
def evaluate_model(dataX, dataY, n_folds=5):
    scores, histories = list(), list()
    # prepare cross validation
    kfold = KFold(n_folds, shuffle=True, random_state=1)
    # enumerate splits
    for train_ix, test_ix in kfold.split(dataX):
        # define model
        model = define_model()
        # select rows for train and test
        trainX, trainY, testX, testY = dataX[train_ix],
        dataY[train_ix], dataX[test_ix], dataY[test_ix]
        # fit model
        history = model.fit(trainX, trainY, epochs=10,
        batch_size=32, validation_data=(testX, testY),
        verbose=0)
        # evaluate model
        _, acc = model.evaluate(testX, testY, verbose=0)
        print('> %.3f' % (acc * 100.0))
        # append scores
        scores.append(acc)
        histories.append(history)
    return scores, histories

# Plot diagnostic learning curves
def summarize_diagnostics(histories):
```

```python
    for i in range(len(histories)):
        # plot loss
        pyplot.subplot(211)
        pyplot.title('Cross Entropy Loss')
        pyplot.plot(histories[i].history['loss'], color='blue',
        label='train')
        pyplot.plot(histories[i].history['val_loss'],
        color='orange', label='test')
        # plot accuracy
        pyplot.subplot(212)
        pyplot.title('Classification Accuracy')
        pyplot.plot(histories[i].history['acc'], color='blue',
        label='train')
        pyplot.plot(histories[i].history['val_acc'],
        color='orange', label='test')
    pyplot.show()

# summarize model performance
def summarize_performance(scores):
    # print summary
    print('Accuracy: mean=%.3f std=%.3f, n=%d' %
    (mean(scores)*100, std(scores)*100, len(scores)))
    # box and whisker plots of results
    pyplot.boxplot(scores)
    pyplot.show()

# Run the test harness for evaluating a model
def run_test_harness():
    # load dataset
    trainX, trainY, testX, testY = load_dataset()
    # prepare pixel data
    trainX, testX = prep_pixels(trainX, testX)
```

```
    # evaluate model
    scores, histories = evaluate_model(trainX, trainY)
    # learning curves
    summarize_diagnostics(histories)
    # summarize estimated performance
    summarize_performance(scores)

# Entry point, run the test harness
run_test_harness()
```

This script uses k-fold cross-validation as part of the model evaluations. In this case, k equals 5. I would refer you back to Chapter 1 where I discussed k-fold cross-validation if you need a refresher on this concept. Jason's use of k-fold cross-validation essentially causes 5 epochs to be performed, which you will see in the results screen. In addition, the individual result of each epoch is stored in a list named histories. This list is then used when the performance plots are generated.

Jason also uses a test harness structure to schedule how all the modules are invoked. I personally like this style and would recommend it to anyone desiring to create modular software that is understandable and maintainable. One of the nice features of writing software in a modular manner is that it is relatively easy to decouple the modules such that they are independent of one and another. Therefore, any changes that you make to a particular module will not affect other modules. This programming style is an excellent example of the software design principle, *high cohesion, loose coupling*. This principle means that software should be written so that modules do one or two things well (*high cohesion*) and not depend "too much" on other modules (*loose coupling*). Software written using this principle in mind tends to be more understandable, less fragile to change, and easily maintained.

This script should be run in the virtual environment using the following command:

```
python jasonTest.py
```

This script took about 3.5 hours to run to completion. The final results are shown in Figure 6-19.

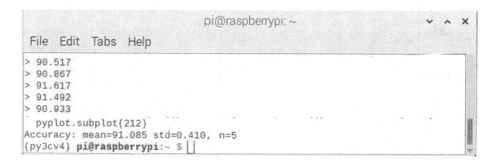

Figure 6-19. *Final results after running the jasonTest script*

The final accuracy score was 91.09%, which was the mean of the 5 epoch scores. Notice that the standard deviation was 0.41%, which provides some insight into the accuracy variance. I should point out that the results screen was after I had removed many superfluous Keras warnings.

Figure 6-20 is a box and whisker plot that summarizes the distribution of the accuracy scores.

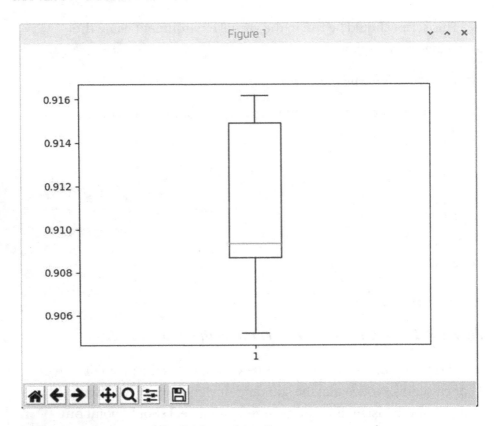

Figure 6-20. *Box and whisker plot of accuracy scores'*
distribution

You should be able to see from the vertical scale that the scores are tightly grouped with a "whisker" range of approximately 0.905 to 0.916 and a mean of 0.919. The bulk of the accuracy values lie above the mean, which you can see from the box position.

Figure 6-21 contains plots for the cross-entropy loss and classification accuracy.

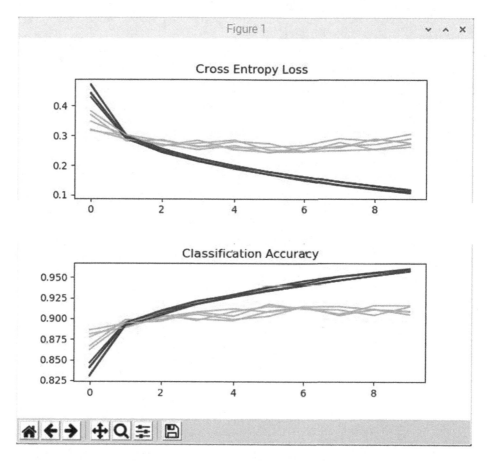

Figure 6-21. *Cross-entropy loss and classification accuracy plots*

These plots are known as learning curves because they show how the model converges as the training process progresses. The darker colored plot lines are for the training dataset, and the lighter colored plot lines are for the test dataset. Overall, these plots indicate the model generally achieves a good fit with the train and test learning curves converging. There may be some small degree of overfitting because of the separation between the two sets of plot lines.

385

## CHAPTER 7

Predictions using ANNs and CNNs

In the previous chapters, I have repeatedly demonstrated how ANNs and CNNs can classify a variety of objects including handwritten numbers and clothing articles. In this chapter I will explore how ANNs and CNNs can predict an outcome. I have noticed repeatedly that DL practitioners often conflate classification and prediction. This is understandable because these tasks are closely intertwined. For instance, when presented with an unknown Image, a CNN will attempt to identify it as belonging to one of the classes it has been trained to recognize. This is clearly a classification process. However, if just view this process from a wider perspective, you could say the CNN has been tasked to predict what the Image represents. I choose to take the narrower view and restrict my interpretation of prediction, at least as far as it concerns ANNs and CNNs to the following definition:

> *Prediction refers to the output of a DL algorithm after it has been trained on a dataset and when new data is applied to forecast the Likelihood of a particular outcome.*

The word prediction can also be misleading. In some cases, it does mean that a future outcome is being predicted, such as when you're using DL to determine the next best action to take in a marketing campaign. In other cases, the prediction has to do with whether or not a transaction that has already occurred was a fraud. In that case, the transaction has already

© Donald J. Norris 2020
D. J. Norris, *Machine Learning with the Raspberry Pi*,
https://doi.org/10.1007/978-1-4842-5174-4_7

happened and the algorithm is making an educated guess about whether or not it was legitimate. My initial demonstration is very straightforward and the ANN will make a binary choice when presented with a set of facts. The choice is whether or not the applied record is part of a class or is not. This last statement will become quite clear when I next present the demonstration.

Pima Indian Diabetes demonstration

The Pima Indian Diabetes project is another one of the classic problems that DL students always study. It is an excellent case study on how an ANN can make predictions based on an applied record when that ANN has been thoroughly trained on an historical dataset.

Background for the Pima Indian Diabetes study

Diabetes mellitus is a group of metabolic disorders where the blood sugar levels are higher than normal for prolonged periods of time. Diabetes is caused either due to the insufficient production of insulin in the body or due to improper response of the body's cells to insulin. The former cause of diabetes is also called type 1 DM or insulin-dependent diabetes mellitus, and the latter is known as type 2 DM or non-insulin-dependent DM. Gestational diabetes is a third type of diabetes where women not suffering from DM develop high sugar levels during pregnancy. Diabetes is especially hard on women as it can affect both the mother and their unborn children during pregnancy. Women with diabetes have a higher Likelihood at having a heart attack, miscarriages, or babies born with birth defects

The diabetes data containing information about Pima Indian females, near Phoenix, Arizona, has been under continuous study since 1965 due to the high incidence rate of diabetes in Pima females. The dataset was originally published by the National Institute of Diabetes and Digestive and Kidney Diseases, consisting of diagnostic measurements pertaining to females of age greater than 20. It contains information of 768 females, of which 268 females were diagnosed with diabetes. Information available includes eight variables which are detailed in Table 7-1. The response variable in the dataset is a binary classifier, Outcome, that indicates if the person was diagnosed with diabetes or not.

Table 7-1. *Eight factors in the Pima Indian Diabetes Study*

Variable name	Data type	Variable description
Pregnancies	integer	Number of times pregnant
Glucose	integer	Plasma glucose concentration at 2 hours in an oral glucose tolerance test
BloodPressure	integer	Diastolic blood pressure
SkinThickness	integer	Triceps skin-fold thickness
Insulin	integer	2-hour serum insulin (μU/ml)
BMI	numeric	Body mass index
DiabetesPedigreeFunction	numeric	Synthesis of the history of diabetes mellitus in relatives, generic relationship of those relatives to the subject
Outcome	integer	Occurrence of diabetes

Preparing the data

The first thing you will need to do is download the dataset. This dataset is available from several web sites. I used the following one:

www.kaggle.com/kumargh/pimaindiansdiabetescsv

This download was in an archive format. After extracting it, I renamed the file diabetes.csv just to keep it short and memorable.

The next thing you should do is inspect the data and see if it appears proper and nothing strange or unusual is visible. I used the Microsoft Excel application to do my initial inspection because this dataset was in the CSV format, which is nicely handled by Excel. Figure 7-1 shows the first 40 of 768 rows from the dataset.

	A	B	C	D	E	F	G	H	I
1	Pregnancies	Glucose	BloodPressui	SkinThicknes	Insulin	BMI	DiabetesPed	Age	Outcome
2	6	148	72	35	0	33.6	0.627	50	1
3	1	85	66	29	0	26.6	0.351	31	0
4	8	183	64	0	0	23.3	0.672	32	1
5	1	89	66	23	94	28.1	0.167	21	0
6	0	137	40	35	168	43.1	2.288	33	1
7	5	116	74	0	0	25.6	0.201	30	0
8	3	78	50	32	88	31	0.248	26	1
9	10	115	0	0	0	35.3	0.134	29	0
10	2	197	70	45	543	30.5	0.158	53	1
11	8	125	96	0	0	0	0.232	54	1
12	4	110	92	0	0	37.6	0.191	30	0
13	10	168	74	0	0	38	0.537	34	1
14	10	139	80	0	0	27.1	1.441	57	0
15	1	189	60	23	846	30.1	0.398	59	1
16	5	166	72	19	175	25.8	0.587	51	1
17	7	100	0	0	0	30	0.484	32	1
18	0	118	84	47	230	45.8	0.551	31	1
19	7	107	74	0	0	29.6	0.254	31	1
20	1	103	30	38	83	43.3	0.183	33	0
21	1	115	70	30	96	34.6	0.529	32	1
22	3	126	88	41	235	39.3	0.704	27	0
23	8	99	84	0	0	35.4	0.388	50	0
24	7	196	90	0	0	39.8	0.451	41	1
25	9	119	80	35	0	29	0.263	29	1
26	11	143	94	33	146	36.6	0.254	51	1
27	10	125	70	26	115	31.1	0.205	41	1
28	7	147	76	0	0	39.4	0.257	43	1
29	1	97	66	15	140	23.2	0.487	22	0
30	13	145	82	19	110	22.2	0.245	57	0
31	5	117	92	0	0	34.1	0.337	38	0
32	5	109	75	26	0	36	0.546	60	0
33	3	158	76	36	245	31.6	0.851	28	1
34	3	88	58	11	54	24.8	0.267	22	0
35	6	92	92	0	0	19.9	0.188	28	0
36	10	122	78	31	0	27.6	0.512	45	0
37	4	103	60	33	192	24	0.966	33	0
38	11	138	76	0	0	33.2	0.42	35	0
39	9	102	76	37	0	32.9	0.665	46	1
40	2	90	68	42	0	38.2	0.503	27	1
41	4	111	72	47	207	37.1	1.39	56	1

Figure 7-1. *First 40 rows from the diabetes.csv dataset*

What immediately stood out to me was the inordinate amount of zeros present both in the SkinThickness and Insulin columns. There should not be any zeros in these columns because a living patient can neither have zero skin thickness nor zero insulin levels. This prompted me to do a bit of research, and I determined that the original researchers who built this dataset simply inserted zeros for empty or null readings. This practice is totally unacceptable and may corrupt a dataset to the point where it could easily generate false or misleading results when processed by an ANN. So, what could I do about it?

Further research on my part leads to the following process, which "corrected" for the missing values in a reasonable manner and also illustrated a nice way to visualize the data. I like to give credit to Paul Mooney and his blog "Predict Diabetes from Medical Records" for providing useful insights into solving this issue. Paul used a Python notebook format for his computations. I changed and modified his interactive commands into conventional Python scripts for this discussion.

Please ensure you are in a Python virtual environment prior to beginning this session. You will then need to ensure that the Seaborn, Matplotlib, and Pandas libraries are installed prior to running the script. Enter the following commands to install these libraries if you are unsure they are present:

```
pip install seaborn
pip install matplotlib
pip install pandas
```

The following script loads the diabetes.csv dataset and then does a series of data checks, summaries, and histogram plots. I named this script diabetesTest.py, and it is available from the book' companion web site. I also included some explanatory comments after the script to help clarify what is happening within it.

```python
# Import required libraries
import matplotlib.pyplot as plt
import seaborn as sns
import pandas as pd
# Load the CSV dataset
dataset = pd.read_csv('diabetes.csv')
dataset.head(10)

# Define a histogram plot method
def plotHistogram(values, label, feature, title):
    sns.set_style("whitegrid")
    plotOne = sns.FacetGrid(values, hue=label, aspect=2)
    plotOne.map(sns.distplot, feature, kde=False)
    plotOne.set(xlim=(0, values[feature].max()))
    plotOne.add_legend()
    plotOne.set_axis_labels(feature, 'Proportion')
    plotOne.fig.suptitle(title)
    plt.show()

# Plot the Insulin histogram
plotHistogram(dataset, 'Outcome', 'Insulin', 'Insulin vs
Diagnosis (Blue = Healthy; Orange = Diabetes)')

# Plot the SkinThickness histogram
plotHistogram(dataset, 'Outcome', 'SkinThickness',
'SkinThickness vs Diagnosis (Blue = Healthy; Orange =
Diabetes)')

# Summary of the number of 0's present in the dataset by
feature
dataset2 = dataset.iloc[:, :-1]
print("Num of Rows, Num of Columns: ", dataset2.shape)
print("\nColumn Name          Num of Null Values\n")
print((dataset[:] == 0).sum())
```

```
# Percentage summary of the number of 0's in the dataset
print("Num of Rows, Num of Columns: ", dataset2.shape)
print("\nColumn Name          %Null Values\n")
print(((dataset2[:] == 0).sum()) / 768 * 100)

# Create a heat map
g = sns.heatmap(dataset.corr(), cmap="BrBG", annot=False)
plt.show()

# Display the feature correlation values
corr1 = dataset.corr()
print(corr1[:])
```

Explanatory comments:

dataset = pd.read_csv('diabetes.csv') – Reads the CSV dataset into the script using the Pandas read_csv method.

dataset.head(10) – Displays the first ten records in the dataset.

def plotHistogram(values, label, feature, title) – Defines a method which will plot the histogram of the dataset feature provided in the arguments list. This method uses the Seaborn library, which I discussed in Chapter 2. Two histograms are then plotted after this definition, one for Insulin and the other for SkinThickness. Each of those features had a significant amount of 0s present.

dataset2 = dataset.iloc[:, :-1] – Is the start of the code segment which displayed the actual amount of 0s present for each dataset feature. The only features that should have any 0s are Outcome and Pregnancies.

```
print("Num of Rows, Num of Columns: ",
dataset2.shape)
```
– Is the start of the code segment which displayed the percentages of 0s present for each dataset feature.

```
g = sns.heatmap(dataset.corr(), cmap="BrBG",
annot=False)
```
– Generates a heatmap for the dataset's correlation map. A heatmap is a way of representing the data in a 2D form. Data values are represented as colors in the graph. The goal of the heatmap is to provide a colored visual summary of information.

```
corr1 = dataset.corr()
```
– Creates a table of correlation values between the dataset feature variables. This statistic will be of considerable interest after the values in the dataset have been adjusted.

This script should be run in the virtual environment with the diabetes.csv dataset in the same directory as this script. Enter the following command to run the script:

```
python diabetesTest.py
```

This script runs immediately and produces a series of results. The final screen results are shown in Figure 7-2.

```
                                                    pi@raspberrypi: ~                        ⌄  ᴧ  ✕
 File  Edit  Tabs  Help
(py3cv4) pi@raspberrypi:~ $ python diabetesTest.py
   Pregnancies  Glucose  BloodPressure  SkinThickness  Insulin   BMI  DiabetesPedigreeFunction  Age  Outcome
0            6      148             72             35        0  33.6                     0.627   50        1
1            1       85             66             29        0  26.6                     0.351   31        0
2            8      183             64              0        0  23.3                     0.672   32        1
3            1       89             66             23       94  28.1                     0.167   21        0
4            0      137             40             35      168  43.1                     2.288   33        1
5            5      116             74              0        0  25.6                     0.201   30        0
6            3       78             50             32       88  31.0                     0.248   26        1
7           10      115              0              0        0  35.3                     0.134   29        0
8            2      197             70             45      543  30.5                     0.158   53        1
9            8      125             96              0        0   0.0                     0.232   54        1
Num of Rows, Num of Columns:  (768, 8)

Column Name          Num of Null Values

Pregnancies               111
Glucose                     5
BloodPressure              35
SkinThickness             227
Insulin                   374
BMI                        11
DiabetesPedigreeFunction    0
Age                         0
Outcome                   500
dtype: int64
Num of Rows, Num of Columns:  (768, 8)

Column Name          %Null Values

Pregnancies          14.453125
Glucose               0.651042
BloodPressure         4.557292
SkinThickness        29.557292
Insulin              48.697917
BMI                   1.432292
DiabetesPedigreeFunction  0.000000
Age                   0.000000
dtype: float64
                       Pregnancies   Glucose  BloodPressure  SkinThickness   Insulin       BMI  DiabetesPedigreeFunction       Age   Outcome
Pregnancies               1.000000  0.129459       0.141282      -0.081672 -0.073535  0.017683                 -0.033523  0.544341  0.221898
Glucose                   0.129459  1.000000       0.152590       0.057328  0.331357  0.221071                 -0.137337  0.263514  0.466581
BloodPressure             0.141282  0.152590       1.000000       0.207371  0.088933  0.281805                  0.041265  0.239528  0.065068
SkinThickness            -0.081672  0.057328       0.207371       1.000000  0.436783  0.392573                  0.183928 -0.113970  0.074752
Insulin                  -0.073535  0.331357       0.088933       0.436783  1.000000  0.197859                  0.185071 -0.042163  0.130548
BMI                       0.017683  0.221071       0.281805       0.392573  0.197859  1.000000                  0.140647  0.036242  0.292695
DiabetesPedigreeFunction -0.033523  0.137337       0.041265       0.183928  0.185071  0.140647                  1.000000  0.033561  0.173844
Age                       0.544341  0.263514       0.239528      -0.113970 -0.042163  0.036242                  0.033561  1.000000  0.238356
Outcome                   0.221898  0.466581       0.065068       0.074752  0.130548  0.292695                  0.173844  0.238356  1.000000
(py3cv4) pi@raspberrypi:~ $ ▯
```

Figure 7-2.   *Final results after running the diabetesTest script*

The first table in the figure lists the nulls (0s) for each feature. There is clearly an unacceptable amount of 0s in both the SkinThickness and Insulin feature columns. Almost 50% of the Insulin data points are missing, which you can easily see from looking at the next table in the figure. There will be an inadvertent bias introduced into any ANN, which uses this dataset because of these missing values. How it will affect the overall ANN prediction performance is uncertain, but it will be an issue nonetheless.

The last table in the figure shows the correlation values between the feature variables. Usually, I would like to see low values between the variables except for those features which are naturally related such as age and pregnancies. You should also note that this table is a symmetric matrix around the identity diagonal. The identity diagonal (all 1s) results because the correlation value for a variable with itself must always equal to 1.

The symmetric matrix results because the correlation function is commutative (order of variables does not matter). The key value I will be looking for is how the current correlation value of 0.436783 between SkinThickness and Insulin changes after the data is modified to get rid of the 0s.

Figure 7-3 is the histogram showing the relationship between insulin levels and the proportion of healthy to sick patients.

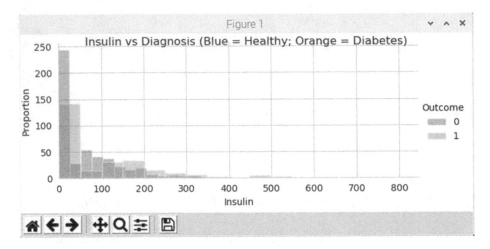

Figure 7-3. *Histogram for insulin levels and proportion of healthy to sick patients*

There seems to be a strong clustering of unhealthy patients below the 40 level which doesn't make sense because it is unlikely that any living patient would have such low levels. Additionally, having a strong spike of heathy patients with insulin levels at 20 or below is simply not realistic. They too could not live will such low levels. Clearly the excess 0 problem is skewing the data and causing the ANN to make erroneous predictions.

Figure 7-4 is the histogram showing the relationship between skin thickness measurements and the proportion of healthy to sick patients.

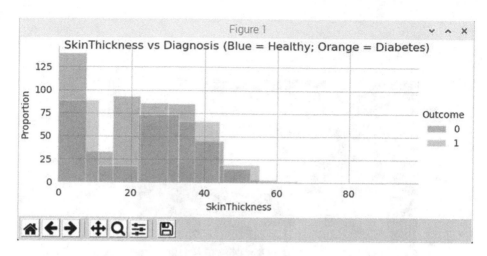

Figure 7-4. *Histogram for skin thickness measurements and proportion of healthy to sick patients*

In this figure, just like the previous figure, there are abnormal spikes in the skin thickness measurements for both healthy and sick patients near the 0 skin thickness measurement. It is simply not possible to have 0 skin thickness. The excess 0 problem is solely causing this anomaly.

Figure 7-5 shows the heatmap for the correlation matrix between all the dataset feature variables.

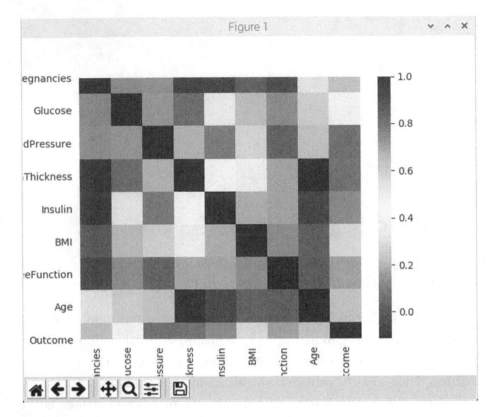

Figure 7-5. *Correlation heatmap for dataset feature variables*

What you should look for in this figure are the white blocks, which indicate correlation values at or above 0.4. Most correlation values for this dataset are relatively low except for

- Glucose and Outcome

- Age and Pregnancies

- Insulin and SkinThickness

The first two in the list make perfect sense. Glucose (sugar levels in the blood) are definitely correlated with diabetes and hence the Outcome. Age and Pregnancies are naturally correlated because women have fewer pregnancies as they age, or if they are young, they haven't had the time to sustain many pregnancies. The last one in the list is the suspect one, which is an artificially high correlation value due to the excess-zero problem.

It is now time to fix the excess 0's problem. The question naturally becomes how to do this without causing too much disruption to the dataset? The answer most statisticians would cite is to impute the missing data. Imputing data is a tricky process because it can insert additional bias into the dataset. The process of imputing data can take on several forms depending on the nature of the data. If the data is from a time series, then missing data can easily be replaced by interpolating between the data surrounding the missing values. Unfortunately, the diabetes dataset is not time sensitive, so this option is out.

Another way to impute is to simply eliminate those records with missing data. This is called listwise imputation. Unfortunately, using listwise imputation would cause nearly 50% of existing dataset records to disappear. This would wreak havoc on the ANN learning process so that option is out. One of the remaining impute options is to use all the existing feature data to determine a value to replace the missing data. There are imputation processes called hot card, cold card, mean, and median value, which use this approach. Without going into the details, I decided to use median value as the option to replace the missing data values.

The following script is a revision of the previous script where I have imputed the dataset to remove all 0s from the feature variables. The dataset has also been split into two dataset, one for training and the other for testing. The script is named revisedDiabetesTest.py and is available from the book's companion web site. I have also provided some explanatory comments after the listing.

```
# Import required libraries
import numpy as np
import matplotlib.pyplot as plt
import seaborn as sns
```

```
import pandas as pd
from sklearn.model_selection import train_test_split
from sklearn.impute import SimpleImputer

# Load the dataset
data = pd.read_csv('diabetes.csv')
X = data.iloc[:, :-1]
y = data.iloc[:, -1]

# Split the dataset into 80% training and 20% testing sets
X_train, X_test, y_train, y_test = train_test_split(X, y, test_
size=0.2, random_state=1)

# Impute the missing values using feature median values
imputer = SimpleImputer(missing_values=0, strategy='median')
X_train2 = imputer.fit_transform(X_train)
X_test2 = imputer.transform(X_test)

# Convert the numpy array into a Dataframe
X_train3 = pd.DataFrame(X_train2)

# Display the first 10 records
print(X_train3.head(10))

def plotHistogram(values, label, feature, title):
    sns.set_style("whitegrid")
    plotOne = sns.FacetGrid(values, hue=label, aspect=2)
    plotOne.map(sns.distplot, feature, kde=False)
    plotOne.set(xlim=(0, values[feature].max()))
    plotOne.add_legend()
    plotOne.set_axis_labels(feature, 'Proportion')
    plotOne.fig.suptitle(title)
    plt.show()
```

```
# Plot the heathy patient histograms for insulin and skin
# thickness
plotHistogram(X_train3,None,4,'Insulin vs Diagnosis')
plotHistogram(X_train3,None,3,'SkinThickness vs Diagnosis')

# Check to see if any 0's remain
data2 = X_train2
print("Num of Rows, Num of Columns: ", data2.shape)
print("\nColumn Name         Num of Null Values\n")
print((data2[:] == 0).sum())

print("Num of Rows, Num of Columns: ", data2.shape)
print("\nColumn Name         %Null Values\n")
print(((data2[:] == 0).sum()) / 614 * 100)

# Display the correlation matrix
corr1 = X_train3.corr()
print(corr1)
```

Explanatory comments:

> X_train, X_test, y_train, y_test = train_
> test_split(X, y, test_size=0.2, random_
> state=1) – Splits the input dataset into two, one 80%
> of the input for training purposes and the other 20%
> for testing purposes

> X_train3 = pd.DataFrame(X_train2) – Converts
> the training dataset from a numpy array into a
> Pandas DataFrame so it is compatible with the
> Pandas cross-correlation function

Again, this script should be run in the virtual environment with the diabetes.csv dataset in the same directory as this script. Enter the following command to run the script:

```
python revisedDiabetesTest.py
```

401

This script runs immediately and produces a series of results. The final screen results are shown in Figure 7-6.

```
                              pi@raspberrypi: ~                          ⌄  ⌃  ✕

 File  Edit  Tabs  Help
(py3cv4) pi@raspberrypi:~ $ python revisedDiabetesTest.py
        0      1     2     3      4     5      6     7
0    9.0  145.0  80.0  46.0  130.0  37.9  0.637  40.0
1   10.0  129.0  62.0  36.0  125.0  41.2  0.441  38.0
2    7.0  102.0  74.0  40.0  105.0  37.2  0.204  45.0
3    8.0  120.0  78.0  29.0  125.0  25.0  0.409  64.0
4    2.0  120.0  76.0  37.0  105.0  39.7  0.215  29.0
5    4.0   94.0  72.0  29.0  125.0  32.0  0.256  25.0
6    1.0  189.0  60.0  23.0  846.0  30.1  0.398  59.0
7    3.0  158.0  70.0  30.0  328.0  35.5  0.344  35.0
8    4.0   95.0  64.0  39.0  105.0  44.6  0.366  22.0
9    1.0   92.0  62.0  25.0   41.0  19.5  0.482  25.0
Num of Rows, Num of Columns:  (614, 8)

Column Name         Num of Null Values

0
Num of Rows, Num of Columns:  (614, 8)

Column Name          %Null Values

0.0
          0         1         2         3         4         5         6         7
0  1.000000  0.145744  0.268856  0.119665  0.034196  0.085739 -0.001278  0.510301
1  0.145744  1.000000  0.198667  0.186303  0.428870  0.214237  0.144361  0.262496
2  0.268856  0.198667  1.000000  0.147580  0.055370  0.259920 -0.026191  0.329781
3  0.119665  0.186303  0.147580  1.000000  0.168746  0.508620  0.087195  0.129815
4  0.034196  0.428870  0.055370  0.168746  1.000000  0.201882  0.194708  0.101887
5  0.085739  0.214237  0.259920  0.508620  0.201882  1.000000  0.139795  0.023083
6 -0.001278  0.144361 -0.026191  0.087195  0.194708  0.139795  1.000000  0.050760
7  0.510301  0.262496  0.329781  0.129815  0.101887  0.023083  0.050760  1.000000
(py3cv4) pi@raspberrypi:~ $ ▯
```

Figure 7-6. *Final results after running the revisedDiabetesTest script*

You can immediately see that all 0 values in the first ten training set records have been replaced with other values. This is true for all of the feature variables, but not the Outcome column, which is required for supervised learning.

The 0 summary code displays now that there are no 0s remaining in the dataset.

Figure 7-7 is the revised histogram showing the insulin distribution for healthy patients. There is no longer any insulin values at or near 0. The distribution peak is centered around 130, which seems reasonable to me, but again, I am not an MD.

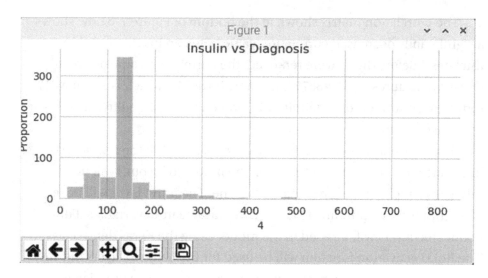

Figure 7-7. *Insulin histogram for healthy patients*

Figure 7-8 is the revised histogram showing the skin thickness distribution for healthy patients. As was the case for the insulin plot, this plot shows no values whatsoever below 8. The peak appears to center on a value of 29, which I presume is a reasonable number.

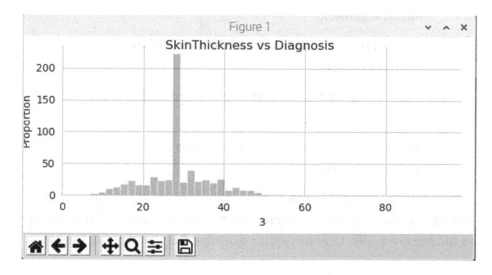

Figure 7-8. *Skin thickness histogram for healthy patients*

The correlation matrix shown at the bottom of Figure 7-6 now shows a significantly decreased correlation value between insulin and skin thickness. Before the 0s were removed, the correlation value between these two features was 0.436783. It is now 0.168746, which is about a 61% reduction. The 0 removal definitely improved the data quality, at least with these two features.

It is time to discuss the Keras ANN model now that the dataset has been "cleaned up" into a better state. The model to be built will be a relatively simple three-layer, sequential one. The input layer will have eight inputs corresponding to the eight dataset feature variables. Fully connected layers will be used in the model using the Keras dense class. The ReLU activation function will be used for the first two layers because it has been found to be a best performance function. The third layer, which is the output, will use the sigmoid function for activation because the output must be between 0 and 1. Recall this is a prediction model and the output is binary with only either a 0 or 1 value. In summary the model assumptions are

- Expects rows of data with eight variables (the *input_dim=8* argument).

- The first hidden layer has 12 nodes and uses the ReLU activation function.

- The second hidden layer has eight nodes and uses the ReLU activation function.

- The output layer has one node and uses the sigmoid activation function.

Note that the first hidden layer is actually performing two functions. It is acting as an input layer in accepting eight variables, and it is also acting as a hidden layer with 12 nodes with associated ReLU activation functions.

The following script is named kerasDiabetesTest.py, and it is available from the book's companion web site. Explanatory comments follow the listing.

```python
# Import required libraries
import numpy as np
import pandas as pd
from sklearn.model_selection import train_test_split
from sklearn.impute import SimpleImputer
from keras.models import Sequential
from keras.layers import Dense

# Load the dataset
data = pd.read_csv('diabetes.csv')
X = data.iloc[:, :-1]
y = data.iloc[:, -1]

# Split the dataset into 80% training and 20% testing sets
X_train, X_test, y_train, y_test = train_test_split(X, y,
test_size=0.2, random_state=1)

# Impute the missing values using feature median values
imputer = SimpleImputer(missing_values=0,strategy='median')
X_train2 = imputer.fit_transform(X_train)
X_test2 = imputer.transform(X_test)

# Convert the numpy array into a Dataframe
X_train3 = pd.DataFrame(X_train2)

# Define the Keras model
model = Sequential()
model.add(Dense(12, input_dim=8, activation='relu'))
model.add(Dense(8, activation='relu'))
model.add(Dense(1, activation='sigmoid'))
```

```
# Compile the keras model
model.compile(loss='binary_crossentropy', optimizer='adam',
metrics=['accuracy'])
# fit the keras model on the dataset
model.fit(X_train2, y_train, epochs=150, batch_size=10)

# Evaluate the keras model
_, accuracy = model.evaluate(X_test2, y_test)
print('Accuracy: %.2f' % (accuracy*100))
```

The first part of the script is the same as the first part of the revisedDiabetesTest.py script with the exception of some added and deleted imports. The model definition is in line in lieu of a separate definition as was the case for the CNN scripts. This was done because it is a very simple and concise model. The compile process is almost the same as it was for the CNN models, except for the loss function, which is binary_ crossentropy instead of categorical_crossentropy, which is required for multiple classes. This model will train and test very quickly, which allows for many epochs to be run in an effort to improve the accuracy. In this case, there are 150 epochs set. The overall accuracy is done using the Keras evaluate method as it was done for the CNN models.

This script should be run in the virtual environment with the diabetes. csv dataset in the same directory as this script. Enter the following command to run the script:

```
python kerasDiabetesTest.py
```

This script runs immediately and produces a series of results. The final screen results are shown in Figure 7-9.

```
                                    pi@raspberrypi: ~                          v  ^  x
 File  Edit  Tabs  Help
 Epoch 1/150
 614/614 [==============================] - 1s 2ms/step - loss: 2.2769 - acc: 0.5863
 Epoch 2/150
 614/614 [==============================] - 0s 352us/step - loss: 1.3094 - acc: 0.5489
 Epoch 3/150
 614/614 [==============================] - 0s 357us/step - loss: 0.9869 - acc: 0.5603
 Epoch 4/150
 614/614 [==============================] - 0s 356us/step - loss: 0.8838 - acc: 0.5749
 Epoch 5/150
 614/614 [==============================] - 0s 354us/step - loss: 0.8322 - acc: 0.5896
 Epoch 6/150
 614/614 [==============================] - 0s 355us/step - loss: 0.8022 - acc: 0.5896
 Epoch 7/150
 614/614 [==============================] - 0s 355us/step - loss: 0.7744 - acc: 0.6026
 Epoch 8/150
 614/614 [==============================] - 0s 354us/step - loss: 0.7451 - acc: 0.6205
 Epoch 9/150
 614/614 [==============================] - 0s 354us/step - loss: 0.7300 - acc: 0.6140
 Epoch 10/150
 614/614 [==============================] - 0s 352us/step - loss: 0.7117 - acc: 0.6384
                                          .
                                          .
                                          .
 Epoch 140/150
 614/614 [==============================] - 0s 351us/step - loss: 0.5207 - acc: 0.7410
 Epoch 141/150
 614/614 [==============================] - 0s 354us/step - loss: 0.5169 - acc: 0.7476
 Epoch 142/150
 614/614 [==============================] - 0s 442us/step - loss: 0.5189 - acc: 0.7329
 Epoch 143/150
 614/614 [==============================] - 0s 351us/step - loss: 0.5114 - acc: 0.7476
 Epoch 144/150
 614/614 [==============================] - 0s 353us/step - loss: 0.5301 - acc: 0.7231
 Epoch 145/150
 614/614 [==============================] - 0s 351us/step - loss: 0.5172 - acc: 0.7378
 Epoch 146/150
 614/614 [==============================] - 0s 352us/step - loss: 0.5232 - acc: 0.7410
 Epoch 147/150
 614/614 [==============================] - 0s 352us/step - loss: 0.5228 - acc: 0.7394
 Epoch 148/150
 614/614 [==============================] - 0s 352us/step - loss: 0.5193 - acc: 0.7459
 Epoch 149/150
 614/614 [==============================] - 0s 352us/step - loss: 0.5203 - acc: 0.7427
 Epoch 150/150
 614/614 [==============================] - 0s 354us/step - loss: 0.5162 - acc: 0.7459
 154/154 [==============================] - 0s 733us/step
 Accuracy: 70.78
 (py3cv4) pi@raspberrypi:~ $
```

Figure 7-9. *Final results after running the kerasDiabetesTest script*

This figure is a composite showing the beginning and ending epoch results. The final, overall accuracy score was 70.78%. This would normally be considered an OK, but not great score. However, I did some research on others who have run this project with similar models and found that this result was in line with the majority of other results. It appears that the Pima Indian Diabetes Study predictions are approximately successful (or accurate) around 70% of the time. I believe that this level of accuracy would not be an acceptable level if used in actual clinical trials, but is perfectly acceptable in this learning and experimentation environment.

Using the scikit-learn library with Keras

The Python scikit-learn library uses the scipy stack for efficient numerical computations. It is a fully featured library for general ML library that provides many utilities which are useful in the developing models. These utilities include

- Model evaluation using resampling methods such as k-fold cross-validation

- Efficient evaluation of model hyper-parameters

The Keras library is a convenient wrapper for DL models used for classification or regression estimations with the scikit-learn library.

The following demonstration uses the KerasClassifier wrapper for a classification neural network created in Keras and is used with the scikit-learn library. I will also be using the same modified Pima Indian Diabetes dataset that is used in the last demonstration.

This demonstration script is very similar to the previous one in that it uses the same Keras ANN model. The significant difference is that in this script the model is used by the KerasClassifier instead of having the modified dataset directly applied to the model via the Keras fit function. I will explain how the KerasClassifier works after the script listing because it is important for you to see how it is invoked.

The following script is named kerasScikitDiabetesTest.py to indicate that it now uses the scikit-learn classifier in lieu of the normal Keras fit function. It is available from the book's companion web site.

```
# Load required libraries

from keras.models import Sequential
from keras.layers import Dense
from keras.wrappers.scikit_learn import KerasClassifier
from sklearn.model_selection import StratifiedKFold
```

```python
from sklearn.model_selection import cross_val_score
from sklearn.model_selection import train_test_split
from sklearn.impute import SimpleImputer
import pandas as pd

# Function to create model, required for the KerasClassifier
def create_model():
    # create model
    model = Sequential()
    model.add(Dense(12, input_dim=8, activation='relu'))
    model.add(Dense(8, activation='relu'))
    model.add(Dense(1, activation='sigmoid'))
    model.compile(loss='binary_crossentropy', optimizer='adam',
    metrics=['accuracy'])

    return model

# fix random seed for reproducibility
seed = 42

# Load the dataset
data = pd.read_csv('diabetes.csv')
X = data.iloc[:, :-1]
y = data.iloc[:, -1]

# Split the dataset into 80% training and 20% testing sets
X_train, X_test, y_train, y_test = train_test_split(X, y, test_
size=0.2, random_state=1)

# Impute the missing values using feature median values
imputer = SimpleImputer(missing_values=0,strategy='median')
X_train2 = imputer.fit_transform(X_train)
X_test2 = imputer.transform(X_test)
```

```
# Convert the numpy array into a Dataframe
X_train3 = pd.DataFrame(X_train2)
# create model
model = KerasClassifier(build_fn=create_model, epochs=150,
batch_size=10, verbose=0)
# evaluate using 10-fold cross validation
kfold = StratifiedKFold(n_splits=10, shuffle=True, random_
state=seed)

# Evaluate using cross_val_score function
results = cross_val_score(model, X_train2, y_train, cv=kfold)
print(results.mean())
```

This script should be run in the virtual environment with the diabetes. csv dataset in the same directory as this script. Enter the following command to run the script:

```
python kerasScikitDiabetesTest.py
```

This script runs immediately and produces a single result. The final screen result is shown in Figure 7-10.

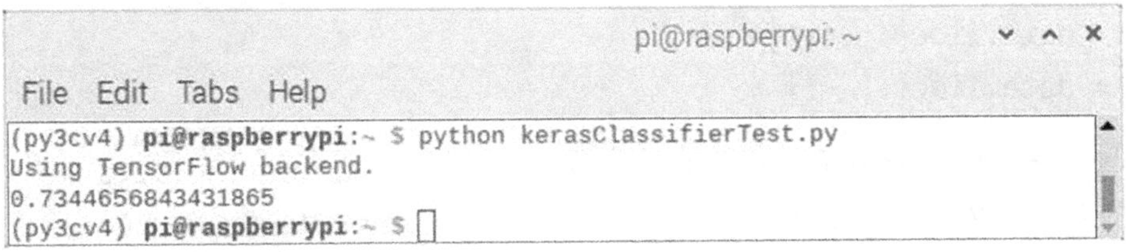

Figure 7-10. *Final result after running the kerasScikitDiabetesTest script*

The accuracy value displayed in the figure is 73.45%. This value was based on only using the training dataset, which is 80% of the original dataset. Consequently, I reran the script with the split changed to 99% for the training set, which meant it was almost the size of the unsplit dataset.

The result was an accuracy was 73.40%, which is a statistically insignificant difference from the first run.

The KerasClassifier and KerasRegressor classes in Keras take an argument named build_fn which is the model's function name. In the preceding script, a method named create_model() that creates a MLP for this case. This function is passed to the KerasClassifier class by the build_fn argument. There are additional arguments of nb_epoch=150 and batch_size=10 that are automatically used by the fit() function, which is called internally by the KerasClassifier class.

In this example, the scikit-learn StratifiedKFold function is then used to perform a tenfold stratified cross-validation. This is a resampling technique that provides a robust estimate of the accuracy for the defined model with the applied dataset.

The scikit-learn function cross_val_score is used to evaluate the model using a cross-validation scheme and display the results.

Grid search with Keras and scikit-learn

In this follow-on demonstration, a grid search is used to evaluate different configurations for the ANN model. The configuration that produces the best estimated performance is reported.

The **create_model()** function is defined with two arguments, optimizer and Init, both of which have default values. Varying these argument values allows for the evaluation of the effect of using different optimization algorithms and weight initialization schemes on the network model.

After model creation, there is a definition of parameter arrays used in the grid search. The search is intended to test

- Optimizers for searching different weight values

- Initializers for preparing the network weights using different schemes

- Epochs for training the model for a different number of exposures to the training dataset

- Batches for varying the number of samples before a weight update

The preceding options are stored in a dictionary and then passed to the configuration of the GridSearchCV scikit-learn class. This class evaluates a version of the ANN model for each combination of parameters (2 x 3 x 3 x 3 for the combinations of optimizers, initializations, epochs, and batches). Each combination is then evaluated using the default threefold stratified cross-validation.

There are a lot of models, and it all takes a considerable amount of computation time as you will find out if you replicate this demonstration using a RasPi. The estimation duration for this RasPi setup is about 2 hours, which is reasonable considering the relatively small network and the small dataset (less than 800 records instances and 9 features and attributes).

After the script has finished, the performance and combination of configurations for the best model are displayed, followed by the performance for all of the combinations of parameters.

The following script is named kerasScikitGridSearchDiabetesTest. py to indicate that it uses the scikit-learn grid search algorithm to help determine the optimal configuration for the ANN model. This script is available from the book's companion web site:

```
# Import required libraries
import numpy as np
import pandas as pd
from keras.models import Sequential
from keras.layers import Dense
from sklearn.model_selection import train_test_split
from sklearn.impute import SimpleImputer
```

```python
from keras.wrappers.scikit_learn import KerasClassifier
from sklearn.model_selection import GridSearchCV
from sklearn.model_selection import cross_val_score

# Function to create model, required for KerasClassifier
def create_model(optimizer='rmsprop', init='glorot_uniform'):
    # create model
    model = Sequential()
    model.add(Dense(12, input_dim=8, kernel_initializer=init,
    activation='relu'))
    model.add(Dense(8, kernel_initializer=init,
    activation='relu'))
    model.add(Dense(1, kernel_initializer=init,
    activation='sigmoid'))
    # Compile model
    model.compile(loss='binary_crossentropy',
    optimizer=optimizer, metrics=['accuracy'])
    return model

# Random seed for reproducibility
seed = 42
np.random.seed(seed)

# Load the dataset
data = pd.read_csv('diabetes.csv')
X = data.iloc[:, :-1]
y = data.iloc[:, -1]

# Split the dataset into 80% training and 20% testing sets
X_train, X_test, y_train, y_test = train_test_split(X, y,
test_size=0.2, random_state=1)
```

```python
# Impute the missing values using feature median values
imputer = SimpleImputer(missing_values=0,strategy='median')
X_train2 = imputer.fit_transform(X_train)
X_test2 = imputer.transform(X_test)

# Convert the numpy array into a Dataframe
X_train3 = pd.DataFrame(X_train2)

# Create model
model = KerasClassifier(build_fn=create_model, verbose=0)

# Grid search epochs, batch size and optimizer
optimizers = ['rmsprop', 'adam']
init = ['glorot_uniform', 'normal', 'uniform']
epochs = [50, 100, 150]
batches = [5, 10, 20]
param_grid = dict(optimizer=optimizers, epochs=epochs,
batch_size=batches, init=init)
grid = GridSearchCV(estimator=model, param_grid=param_grid)
grid_result = grid.fit(X_train2, y_train)

# Summarize results
print("Best: %f using %s" % (grid_result.best_score_,
grid_result.best_params_))
means = grid_result.cv_results_['mean_test_score']
stds = grid_result.cv_results_['std_test_score']
params = grid_result.cv_results_['params']
for mean, stdev, param in zip(means, stds, params):
    print("%f (%f) with: %r" % (mean, stdev, param))
```

This script should be run in the virtual environment with the diabetes.
csv dataset in the same directory as this script. Enter the following
command to run the script:

```
python kerasScikitGridSearchDiabetesTest.py
```

This script takes about 2 hours to complete because of the many sets of epochs being run. The final screen results are shown in Figure 7-11, which is a composite that I made showing the beginning and ending set of epoch interim results.

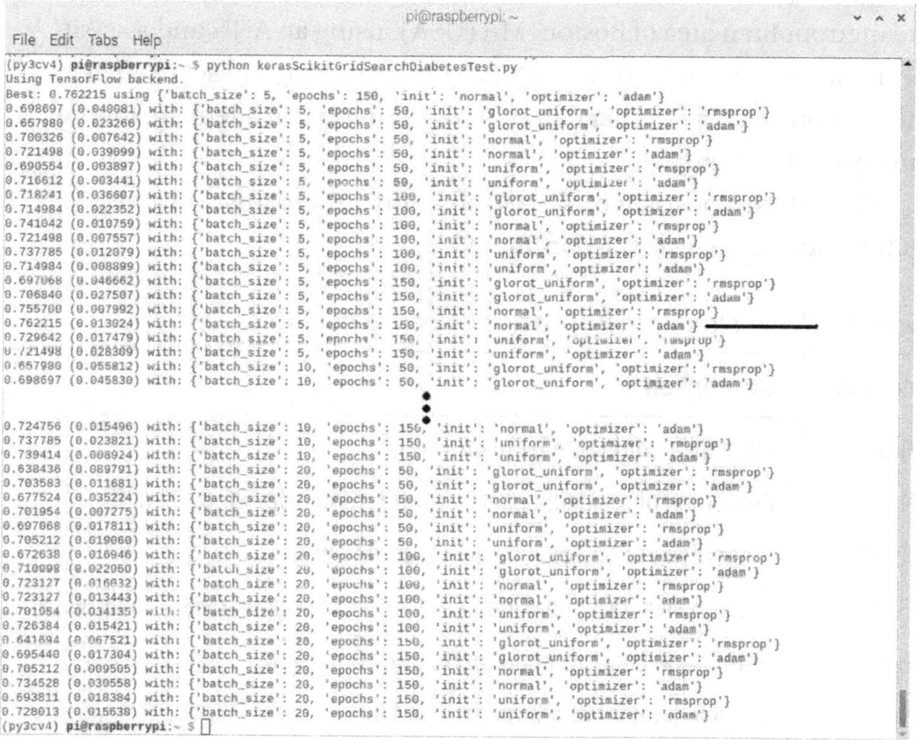

Figure 7-11. *Final results after running the kerasScikitGridSearch DiabetesTest script*

The highest accuracy achieved for all the sets of epochs run was 76.22%. Note that I drew line pointing to the optimal set in the figure. This set was configured for 150 epochs, a batch size of 5, a normal distribution, and the Adam optimizer.

Housing price regression predictor demonstration

Modern online property companies offer valuations of houses using ML techniques. This demonstration will predict the prices of houses in the metropolitan area of Boston, MA (USA), using an ANN and a scikit-learn multiple linear regression (MLR) function. The dataset used in this demonstration is rather dated (1978), but it is still adequate for the purposes of this project.

The dataset consisted of 13 variables and 507 records. The dataset feature variables are detailed in Table 7-2.

Table 7-2. *Boston housing dataset feature variables*

Columns	Description
CRIM	Per capita crime rate by town
ZN	Proportion of residential land zoned for lots over 25,000 sq. ft.
INDUS	Proportion of non-retail business acres per town
CHAS	Charles River dummy variable (= 1 if tract bounds river; 0 otherwise)
NOX	Nitric oxide concentration (parts per 10 million)
RM	Average number of rooms per dwelling
AGE	Proportion of owner-occupied units built prior to 1940
DIS	Weighted distances to five Boston employment centers
RAD	Index of accessibility to radial highways
TAX	Full-value property tax rate per $10,000
PTRATIO	Pupil-teacher ratio by town
LSTAT	Percentage of lower status of the population
MEDV	Median value of owner-occupied homes in $1000s

The price of the house indicated by the variable MEDV is the *target variable,* and the remaining features are the *feature variables* on which the value of a house will be predicted.

Preprocessing the data

It is always good practice to become familiar with the dataset to be used in a project. The obvious first step is to download the dataset. Fortunately, this dataset is readily available using the scikit-learn repository. The following statements will download the dataset into a script:

```
from sklearn.datasets import load_boston
boston_dataset = load_boston()
```

I next created a small script to investigate the dataset characteristics including the keys and first few records. I named this script inspectBoston. py, and it is available from the book's companion web site.

```
# Load the required libraries
import pandas as pd
from sklearn.datasets import load_boston

# Load the Boston housing dataset
boston_dataset = load_boston()

# Display the dataset keys
print(boston_dataset.keys())

# Display the first five records
boston = pd.DataFrame(boston_dataset.data, columns=boston_
dataset.feature_names)
print(boston.head())

# Display the extensive dataset description key
print(boston_dataset.DESCR)
```

417

Run this script by using this command:

```
python inspectBoston.py
```

Figure 7-12 shows the result of running this script session.

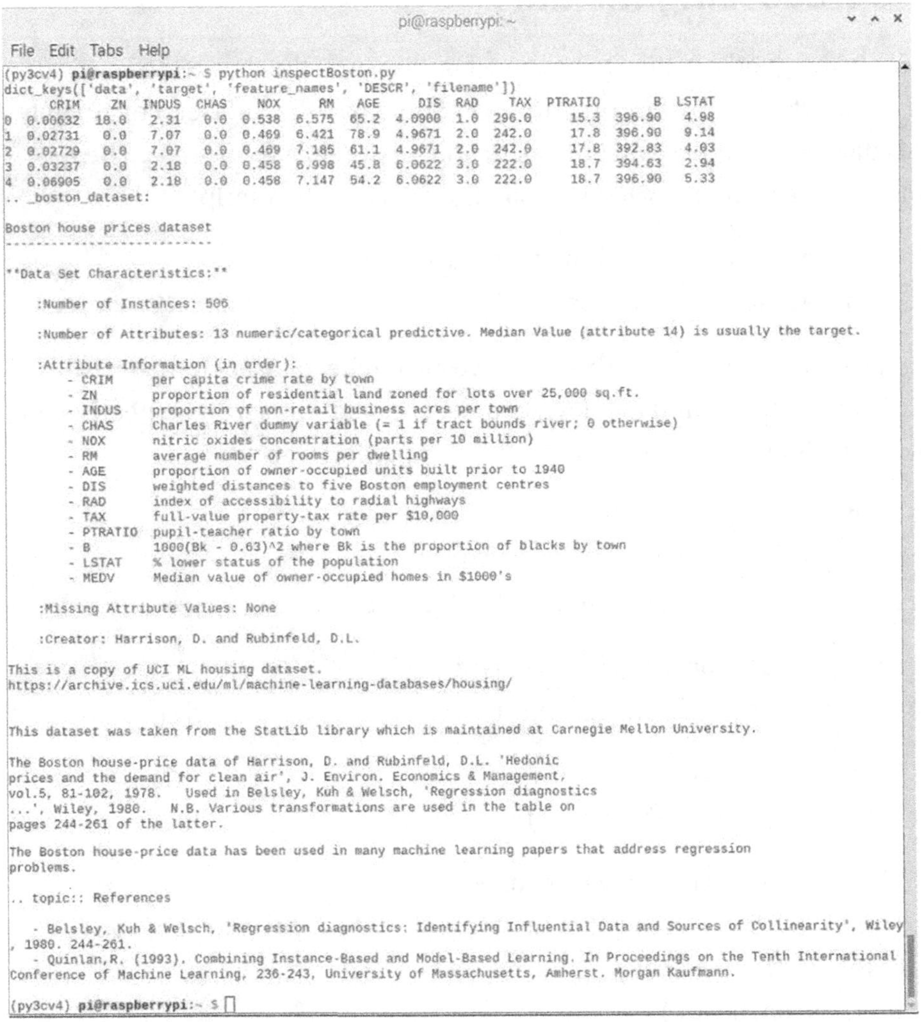

```
(py3cv4) pi@raspberrypi:~ $ python inspectBoston.py
dict_keys(['data', 'target', 'feature_names', 'DESCR', 'filename'])
      CRIM    ZN  INDUS  CHAS    NOX     RM   AGE     DIS  RAD    TAX  PTRATIO       B  LSTAT
0  0.00632  18.0   2.31   0.0  0.538  6.575  65.2  4.0900  1.0  296.0     15.3  396.90   4.98
1  0.02731   0.0   7.07   0.0  0.469  6.421  78.9  4.9671  2.0  242.0     17.8  396.90   9.14
2  0.02729   0.0   7.07   0.0  0.469  7.185  61.1  4.9671  2.0  242.0     17.8  392.83   4.03
3  0.03237   0.0   2.18   0.0  0.458  6.998  45.8  6.0622  3.0  222.0     18.7  394.63   2.94
4  0.06905   0.0   2.18   0.0  0.458  7.147  54.2  6.0622  3.0  222.0     18.7  396.90   5.33
.. _boston_dataset:

Boston house prices dataset
---------------------------

**Data Set Characteristics:**

    :Number of Instances: 506

    :Number of Attributes: 13 numeric/categorical predictive. Median Value (attribute 14) is usually the target.

    :Attribute Information (in order):
        - CRIM     per capita crime rate by town
        - ZN       proportion of residential land zoned for lots over 25,000 sq.ft.
        - INDUS    proportion of non-retail business acres per town
        - CHAS     Charles River dummy variable (= 1 if tract bounds river; 0 otherwise)
        - NOX      nitric oxides concentration (parts per 10 million)
        - RM       average number of rooms per dwelling
        - AGE      proportion of owner-occupied units built prior to 1940
        - DIS      weighted distances to five Boston employment centres
        - RAD      index of accessibility to radial highways
        - TAX      full-value property-tax rate per $10,000
        - PTRATIO  pupil-teacher ratio by town
        - B        1000(Bk - 0.63)^2 where Bk is the proportion of blacks by town
        - LSTAT    % lower status of the population
        - MEDV     Median value of owner-occupied homes in $1000's

    :Missing Attribute Values: None

    :Creator: Harrison, D. and Rubinfeld, D.L.

This is a copy of UCI ML housing dataset.
https://archive.ics.uci.edu/ml/machine-learning-databases/housing/


This dataset was taken from the StatLib library which is maintained at Carnegie Mellon University.

The Boston house-price data of Harrison, D. and Rubinfeld, D.L. 'Hedonic
prices and the demand for clean air', J. Environ. Economics & Management,
vol.5, 81-102, 1978.   Used in Belsley, Kuh & Welsch, 'Regression diagnostics
...', Wiley, 1980.   N.B. Various transformations are used in the table on
pages 244-261 of the latter.

The Boston house-price data has been used in many machine learning papers that address regression
problems.

.. topic:: References

   - Belsley, Kuh & Welsch, 'Regression diagnostics: Identifying Influential Data and Sources of Collinearity', Wiley
, 1980. 244-261.
   - Quinlan,R. (1993). Combining Instance-Based and Model-Based Learning. In Proceedings on the Tenth International
Conference of Machine Learning, 236-243, University of Massachusetts, Amherst. Morgan Kaufmann.

(py3cv4) pi@raspberrypi:~ $
```

Figure 7-12. *Results after running the inspectBoston script*

The DESCR portion of the dataset keys is extensive and provides an unusual and comprehensive historical review for this useful dataset. I wish other ML datasets would include such informative data.

Reviewing the initial five records reveals that the target variable MEDV is missing from the DataFrame. This is easily remedied by adding this line of code:

```
boston['MEDV'] = boston_dataset.target
```

One quick dataset check that is easy to implement and quite useful is to check for any missing or 0 values in the dataset. This can be done using the isnull() method along with a summing operation. The statement to do this is

```
boston.isnull().sum()
```

I incorporated this null check along with the MEDV correction into a revised inspectBoston script. This revised script, which is now named inspectBostonRev.py, does not display the extensive description as shown in the original script. This script is available from the book's companion web site:

```
# Load the required libraries
import pandas as pd
from sklearn.datasets import load_boston

# Load the Boston housing dataset
boston_dataset = load_boston()

# Display the dataset keys
print(boston_dataset.keys())

# Create the boston Dataframe
boston = pd.DataFrame(boston_dataset.data, columns=boston_
dataset.feature_names)
```

```
# Add the target variable to the Dataframe
boston['MEDV'] = boston_dataset.target

# Display the first five records
print(boston.head())

# Check for null values in the dataset
print(boston.isnull().sum())
```

Run this script by using this command:

```
python inspectBostonRev.py
```

Figure 7-13 shows the result of running this script session.

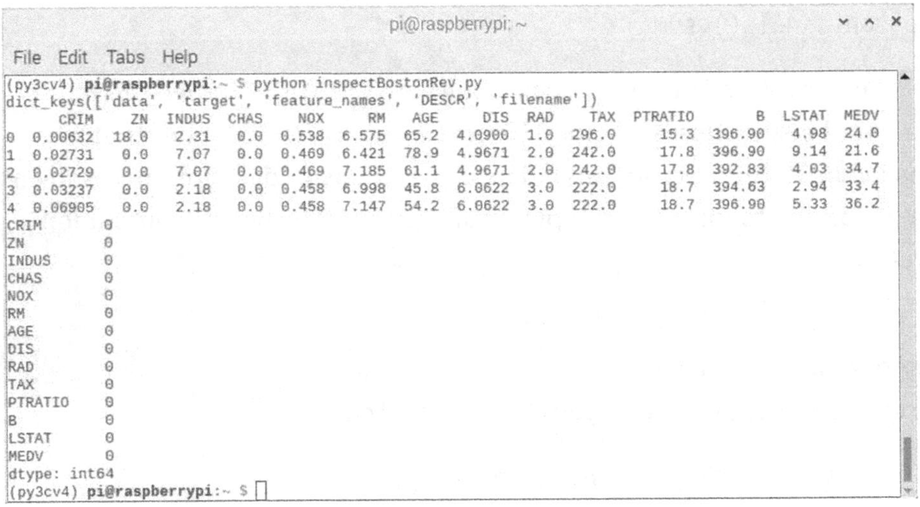


```
(py3cv4) pi@raspberrypi:~ $ python inspectBostonRev.py
dict_keys(['data', 'target', 'feature_names', 'DESCR', 'filename'])
      CRIM    ZN  INDUS  CHAS    NOX     RM   AGE     DIS  RAD    TAX  PTRATIO       B  LSTAT  MEDV
0  0.00632  18.0   2.31   0.0  0.538  6.575  65.2  4.0900  1.0  296.0     15.3  396.90   4.98  24.0
1  0.02731   0.0   7.07   0.0  0.469  6.421  78.9  4.9671  2.0  242.0     17.8  396.90   9.14  21.6
2  0.02729   0.0   7.07   0.0  0.469  7.185  61.1  4.9671  2.0  242.0     17.8  392.83   4.03  34.7
3  0.03237   0.0   2.18   0.0  0.458  6.998  45.8  6.0622  3.0  222.0     18.7  394.63   2.94  33.4
4  0.06905   0.0   2.18   0.0  0.458  7.147  54.2  6.0622  3.0  222.0     18.7  396.90   5.33  36.2
CRIM       0
ZN         0
INDUS      0
CHAS       0
NOX        0
RM         0
AGE        0
DIS        0
RAD        0
TAX        0
PTRATIO    0
B          0
LSTAT      0
MEDV       0
dtype: int64
(py3cv4) pi@raspberrypi:~ $
```

***Figure 7-13.** Results after running the inspectBoston script*

The results display shows that the MEDV target variable has been successfully added to the DataFrame and that there are no null or 0 values present in the dataset. Based on all of the preceding checks, I would say that this dataset was ready to be applied to a model.

The baseline model

A MLP Keras model will first be created and then used with a scikit-learn wrapper regression function to evaluate the Boston housing dataset. This action is almost identical to what happened in the first chapter demonstration where the scikit-learn wrapper function was a classifier instead of a regression package. This method of using Keras models with scikit-learn wrapper functions is quite powerful because it allows for the use of easy-to-build Keras models with the impressive evaluation capabilities built in with the scikit-learn library.

The baseline model is a simple structure with a single fully connected hidden layer with the same number of nodes as the input feature variables (13). The network also uses the efficient ReLU activation functions. However, no activation function is used on the output layer because this network is designed to predict numerical values and does not need any transformations applied.

The Adam optimizer is used and a mean squared error (MSE) loss function is the target function to be optimized. The MSE will also be the same metric used to evaluate the network performance. This is a desirable metric because it can be directly understood in the context of the problem, which is a house price in thousands of dollars squared.

The Keras wrapper object used with the scikit-learn library is named KerasRegressor. This is instantiated using the same argument types as used with the KerasClassifier object. A reference to the model is required along with several parameters (number of epochs and batch size) that are eventually passed to the fit() function, which does the training.

A random number is also used in the script to help generate consist and reproducible results when the script is repeatedly run.

The model is eventually evaluated using a tenfold cross-validation process as I have previously discussed in this and previous chapters. The final metrics are the MSE including the average and standard deviation across all tenfolds for the cross-validation evaluation.

The dataset must be normalized prior to applying it to the model and evaluation framework. This is because it contains values of widely varying magnitude, which you should realize by now is not a good thing for an ANN to attempt to handle. A normalized dataset is also commonly referred to as a standardized dataset. In this case the scikit-learn `StandardScaler` function is used to normalize (standardize) the data during the model evaluation within each fold of the cross-validation process.

The following script incorporates all the items discussed earlier. It is named kerasRegressionTest.py and is available from the book's companion web site.

```python
# Import required libraries
import pandas as pd
from keras.models import Sequential
from keras.layers import Dense
from keras.wrappers.scikit_learn import KerasRegressor
from sklearn.model_selection import cross_val_score
from sklearn.model_selection import KFold
from sklearn.preprocessing import StandardScaler
from sklearn.pipeline import Pipeline
from sklearn.datasets import load_boston

# Load the Boston housing dataset
boston_dataset = load_boston()

# Create the boston Dataframe
dataframe = pd.DataFrame(boston_dataset.data, columns=boston_
dataset.feature_names)

#  Add the target variable to the dataframe
dataframe['MEDV'] = boston_dataset.target

# Setup the boston dataframe
boston = dataframe.values
```

```
# Split into input (X) and output (y) variables
X = boston[:,0:13]
y = boston[:,13]

# Define the base model
def baseline_model():
    # Create model
    model = Sequential()
    model.add(Dense(13, input_dim=13,  kernel_
    initializer='normal', activation='relu'))
    model.add(Dense(1, kernel_initializer='normal'))
    # Compile model
    model.compile(loss='mean_squared_error', optimizer='adam')
    return model

# Random seed for reproducibility
seed = 42

# Create a regression object
estimator = KerasRegressor(build_fn=baseline_model, epochs=100,
batch_size=5, verbose=0)

# Evaluate model with standardized dataset

estimators = []
estimators.append(('standardize', StandardScaler()))
estimators.append(('mlp', KerasRegressor(build_fn=baseline_
model, epochs=50, batch_size=5, verbose=0)))
pipeline = Pipeline(estimators)
kfold = KFold(n_splits=10, random_state=seed)
results = cross_val_score(pipeline, X, y, cv=kfold)
print("Standardized: %.2f (%.2f) MSE" % (results.mean(),
results.std()))
```

Run this script by using this command:

```
python kerasRegressionTest.py
```

Figure 7-14 shows the result of running this script session.

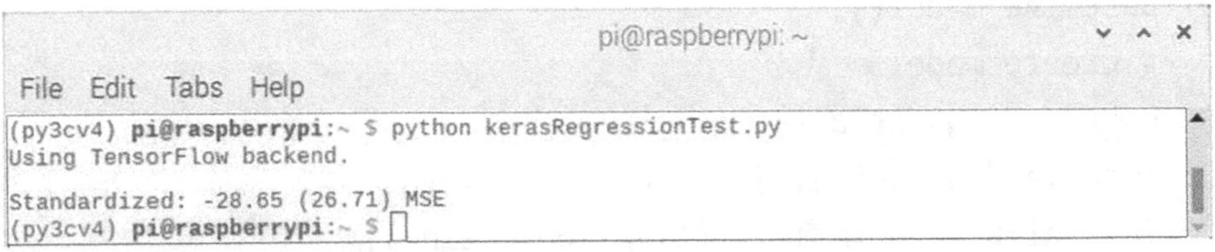

Figure 7-14. *Results after running the kerasRegressionTest script*

The resulting MSE was 28.65, which is not a bad result. For those readers that have some difficulty in working with a statistical measure such as MSE, I will offer a somewhat naive interpretation but perhaps a bit intuitive. I did the following brief set of calculations:

> Mean of all the MEDV values = 22.49 (That's 1978 house prices in the Boston area)
>
> Square root of MSE = 5.35
>
> Ratio of square root of MSE to mean = 0.238
>
> 1 - above value = 0.762 or "accuracy" = 76.2%

Now, before statisticians start yelling at me, I only present the preceding calculations to provide a somewhat meaningful interpretation of the MSE metric. Clearly an MSE approaching 0 is ideal, but as you can see from this approach, the model is reasonably accurate. In fact, I did some additional research regarding the results of other folks who have used this same dataset and similar networks. I found that the reported accuracies were in the range of 75 to 80%, so this demonstration was right where it should have been.

Improved baseline model

One of the great features of the preceding script is that changes can be made in the baseline model not affecting any other parts of the script. That inherent feature is another subtle example of *high cohesion, loose coupling* that I mentioned earlier. Another layer will be added to the model in an effort to improve its performance. This "deeper" model "may" allow the model to extract and combine higher ordered features embedded in the data, which in turn will allow for better predictive results. The code for this model is

```
# define the model
def larger_model():
    # create model
    model = Sequential()
    model.add(Dense(13, input_dim=13, kernel_
    initializer='normal', activation='relu'))
    model.add(Dense(6, kernel_initializer='normal',
    activation='relu'))
    model.add(Dense(1, kernel_initializer='normal'))
    # Compile model
    model.compile(loss='mean_squared_error', optimizer='adam')
    return model
```

The modified script was renamed to kerasDeeperRegressionTest.py and is listed in the following. It is available from the book's companion web site.

```
# Import required libraries
import pandas as pd
from keras.models import Sequential
from keras.layers import Dense
from keras.wrappers.scikit_learn import KerasRegressor
```

```
from sklearn.model_selection import cross_val_score
from sklearn.model_selection import KFold
from sklearn.preprocessing import StandardScaler
from sklearn.pipeline import Pipeline
from sklearn.datasets import load_boston

# Load the Boston housing dataset
boston_dataset = load_boston()

# Create the boston Dataframe
dataframe = pd.DataFrame(boston_dataset.data, columns=boston_
dataset.feature_names)

#  Add the target variable to the dataframe
dataframe['MEDV'] = boston_dataset.target

# Setup the boston dataframe
boston = dataframe.values

# Split into input (X) and output (y) variables
X = boston[:,0:13]
y = boston[:,13]

# Define the model
def larger_model():
    # create model
    model = Sequential()
    model.add(Dense(13, input_dim=13, kernel_
    initializer='normal', activation='relu'))
    model.add(Dense(6, kernel_initializer='normal',
    activation='relu'))
    model.add(Dense(1, kernel_initializer='normal'))
    # Compile model
    model.compile(loss='mean_squared_error', optimizer='adam')
    return model
```

```python
# Random seed for reproducibility
seed = 42

# Create a regression object
estimator = KerasRegressor(build_fn=larger_model, epochs=100,
batch_size=5, verbose=0)

# Evaluate model with standardized dataset
estimators = []
estimators.append(('standardize', StandardScaler()))
estimators.append(('mlp', KerasRegressor(build_fn=larger_model,
epochs=50, batch_size=5, verbose=0)))
pipeline = Pipeline(estimators)
kfold = KFold(n_splits=10, random_state=seed)
results = cross_val_score(pipeline, X, y, cv=kfold)
print("Standardized: %.2f (%.2f) MSE" % (results.mean(),
results.std()))
```

Run this script by using this command:

```
python kerasDeeperRegressionTest.py
```

Figure 7-15 shows the result of running this script.

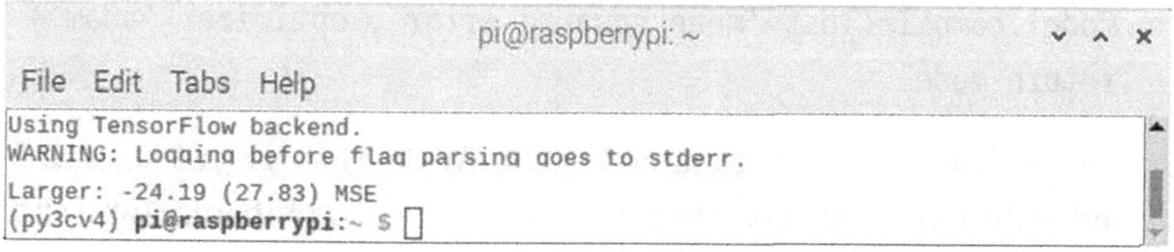

Figure 7-15. *Results after running the kerasDeeperRegressionTest script*

The result from using a deeper model is an MSE equals to 24.19, which is moderately less than the previous result of 28.65. This shows that the new model is better with predictions than the shallower model. I also repeated my naive calculations and came up with an accuracy of 78.13%. This is almost two points higher than the previous script results. The deeper model is definitely a better performer.

Another improved baseline model

Going deeper is not the only way to improve a model. Going wider can also improve a model by increasing the number of nodes in the hidden layer and hopefully increasing the network's ability to extract latent features. The code for this model is

```
# Define the wider model
def wider_model():
    # create model
    model = Sequential()
    model.add(Dense(20, input_dim=13, kernel_
    initializer='normal', activation='relu'))
    model.add(Dense(1, kernel_initializer='normal'))
    # Compile model
    model.compile(loss='mean_squared_error', optimizer='adam')
    return model
```

The modified script was renamed to kerasWiderRegressionTest.py and is listed in the following. It is available from the book's companion web site.

```
# Import required libraries
import pandas as pd
from keras.models import Sequential
from keras.layers import Dense
from keras.wrappers.scikit_learn import KerasRegressor
```

```
from sklearn.model_selection import cross_val_score
from sklearn.model_selection import KFold
from sklearn.preprocessing import StandardScaler
from sklearn.pipeline import Pipeline
from sklearn.datasets import load_boston

# Load the Boston housing dataset
boston_dataset = load_boston()

# Create the boston Dataframe
dataframe = pd.DataFrame(boston_dataset.data, columns=boston_
dataset.feature_names)

#  Add the target variable to the dataframe
dataframe['MEDV'] = boston_dataset.target

# Setup the boston dataframe
boston = dataframe.values

# Split into input (X) and output (y) variables
X = boston[:,0:13]
y = boston[:,13]

# Define the wider model
def wider_model():
    # create model
    model = Sequential()
    model.add(Dense(20, input_dim=13, kernel_
    initializer='normal', activation='relu'))
    model.add(Dense(1, kernel_initializer='normal'))
    # Compile model
    model.compile(loss='mean_squared_error', optimizer='adam')
    return model
```

429

```
# Random seed for reproducibility
seed = 42

# Create a regression object
estimator = KerasRegressor(build_fn=wider_model, epochs=100,
batch_size=5, verbose=0)

# Evaluate model with standardized dataset
estimators = []
estimators.append(('standardize', StandardScaler()))
estimators.append(('mlp', KerasRegressor(build_fn=wider_model,
epochs=50, batch_size=5, verbose=0)))
pipeline = Pipeline(estimators)
kfold = KFold(n_splits=10, random_state=seed)
results = cross_val_score(pipeline, X, y, cv=kfold)
print("Wider: %.2f (%.2f) MSE" % (results.mean(), results.
std()))
```

Run this script by using this command:

```
python kerasWiderRegressionTest.py
```

Figure 7-16 shows the result of running this script.

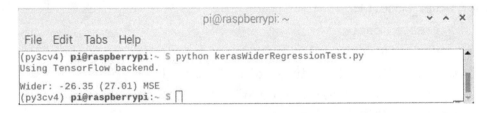

Figure 7-16. *Results after running the kerasWiderRegressionTest script*

The result from using a wider model is an MSE equals to 26.35, which is a disappointing result because it is moderately higher than the deeper model result of 24.19. This wider result is still less than the original, unmodified version 28.65. The naive accuracy calculation is 77.17%, which is about halfway between the original and deeper model accuracies.

I believe that experimenting with different node numbers will likely change the outcome to the better. The 20 node value used in this demonstration was just a reasoned guess. You can easily double that and see what happens; however, be careful of either over- or underfitting the model.

One more suggestion I have for curious readers is to try a model that incorporates both a deeper and wider architecture. That very well may be the sweet spot for this project.

Predictions using CNNs

Making a prediction using a CNN at first glance (pardon the pun) might seem like a strange task. CNNs are predicated on using Images as input data sources, and the question that naturally arises is what is a "predicted" Image? The answer lies in the intended use of the Images. CNNs are neural networks just like their ANN counterparts. They are only designed to process numerical arrays and matrices, nothing more. How users interpret CNN outputs are entirely up to the users.

In recent years, CNNs have been used in cellular microscopy applications for cancer and other diseases. The prediction in such case is whether or not a patient has a certain diagnosis based on the analysis of microscopic cell Images. This type of analysis is also widely used for radioscopic (x-ray) examinations, where CNNs have been applied to large-scale Images in an effort to assist with patient diagnosis. Medical predictions have enormous consequences, and CNN analysis is only one tool of many that doctors use to assist in their diagnostic efforts. The subject of CNN medical analysis is quite complicated, and I decided to devote the entire next chapter to it.

Another area where CNN predictions are commonly used is with time series analysis, and this one is fortunately not nearly as complicated as the medical diagnosis one. I have included a series of relatively simple demonstrations to illustrate how to use a CNN with a time series. However, I will first answer the obvious question, what is a time series? A time series is just a series of data point indexed in time order. Most commonly, a time series is a numerical sequence sampled at successive equally spaced data points in time. It is only a sequence of discrete, time-related data points. Examples of time series are ocean tide heights, sunspot activity, and the daily closing value of the Dow Jones Industrial Average. The common attribute shared by all-time series is that they are all historical. That is where the CNN comes in. A CNN uses the historical record to predict the next data point. In reality, this is not a big problem if the time series is logical and well ordered. If I presented you with the following time series

5, 10, 15, 20, 25, 30, 35, 40, 45, 50, 55, ?

and asked you to predict the next number in the series, I don't think anyone of my bright readers would have a problem doing that. But, if I presented you with the following sequence

86.6, 50, 0, –50, –86.6, –100, –86.6, –50, 0, 50, 86.6, ?

some of you may have a bit of difficulty in arriving at an answer (hint: cosine times 100). Although some readers could have instantly noticed the repetitive pattern in the sequence, a CNN would have had no issue in detecting the pattern. In the preceding case, plotting the data points would have allowed you to instantly recognize the sinusoidal pattern.

But if the time series were truly random, how would the next data point be determined? That is where a CNN would help us – one area where there has been a vast amount of resources applied in the prediction of stock market indices. The time series involved with such indices is vastly complicated depending on many conflicting factors such as financial stability, global status, societal emotions, future uncertainties, and so on.

Nonetheless, many brilliant data scientists have been tackling this problem and applying some of the most innovative and complex DL techniques including vastly complex CNNs. Obviously, the stakes in developing a strong predictor would be hugely rewarding. I suspect if someone has already developed a strong algorithm, it has been kept secret and likely would remain so.

The following demonstrations are vastly underwhelming and are meant to be as such. They are only designed to show how to apply a CNN to a variety of time series. These are basic concepts that you can use to build more complex and realistic predictors.

Univariate time series CNN model

A univariate time series is a series of data points sampled in a timed sequence, where the intervals between samples are equal. The CNN model goal is to use this 1D array of values to predict the next data point in the sequence. The time series or dataset as I will now refer to it must first be preprocessed a bit to make compatible with a CNN model. I will discuss how to build the CNN model after the dataset preprocessing section.

Preprocessing the dataset

Keep in mind that the CNN must learn a function that maps an historical numerical sequence as an input to a single numerical output. This means the time series must be transformed into multiple examples that the CNN can learn from.

Suppose the following time series is provided as the input:

> 50, 100, 150, 200, 250, 300, 350, 400, 450, 500, 550,
> 600, 650

Break up the preceding sequence into a series of input/output sample patterns as shown in Table 7-3.

433

Table 7-3. *Time series to sample distribution*

X	y
50, 100, 150	200
100, 150, 200	250
150, 200, 250	300
200, 250, 300	350
250, 300, 350	400
300, 350, 400	450
350, 400, 450	500
400, 450, 500	550
450, 500, 550	600
500, 550, 600	650

The following script parses a time series into a dataset suitable for use with a CNN. This script is named splitTimeSeries.py and is available from the book's companion web site:

```
# Import required library
from numpy import array

# Split a univariate time series into samples
def split_sequence(sequence, n_steps):
    X, y = list(), list()
    for i in range(len(sequence)):
        # find the end of this pattern
        end_ix = i + n_steps
        # check if we are beyond the sequence
        if end_ix > len(sequence)-1:
            break
```

```
    # gather input and output parts of the pattern
    seq_x, seq_y = sequence[i:end_ix], sequence[end_ix]
    X.append(seq_x)
    y.append(seq_y)
  return array(X), array(y)

# Define input time series
raw_seq = [50, 100, 150, 200, 250, 300, 350, 400, 450, 500,
550, 600, 650]

# Choose a number of time steps
n_steps = 3

# Split into samples
X, y = split_sequence(raw_seq, n_steps)

# Display the data
for i in range(len(X)):
    print(X[i], y[i])
```

Run this script by using this command:

```
python splitTimeSeries.py
```

Figure 7-17 shows the result of running this script.

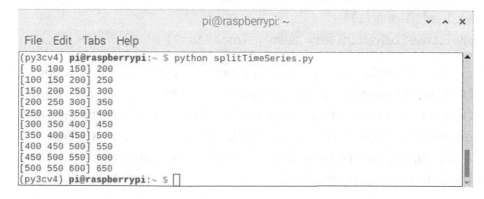

Figure 7-17. *Results after running the splitTimeSeries script*

You can see from the figure that the script has created ten learning examples for the CNN. This should be enough to train a CNN model to effectively predict a data point. The next step in this demonstration is to create a CNN model.

Create a CNN model

The CNN model must have a 1D input/convolutional layer to match the 1D applied dataset. A pooling layer follows the first layer, which will subsample the convolutional layer output in an effort to extract the salient features. The pooling layer then feeds a fully connected layer, which interprets the features extracted by the convolutional layer. Another fully connected layer follows to help with further feature definition, and finally the output layer reduces the feature maps to a 1D vector.

The code for this model is

```
# Define 1-D CNN model
model = Sequential()
model.add(Conv1D(filters=64, kernel_size=2, activation='relu',
input_shape=(n_steps, n_features)))
model.add(MaxPooling1D(pool_size=2))
model.add(Flatten())
model.add(Dense(50, activation='relu'))
model.add(Dense(1))
model.compile(optimizer='adam', loss='mse')
```

The convolution layer has two arguments, which specify the number of time steps (intervals) and the number of features to expect. The number of features for a univariate problem is one. The time steps will be the same number used to split up the 1D time series, which is three for this case.

The input dataset has multiple records, each with a shape dimension of [samples, timesteps, features].

The `split_sequence` function provides the X vector with the shape of [samples, timesteps], which means the dataset must be reshaped to add an additional element to cover the number of features. The following code snippet does precisely that reshaping:

```
n_features = 1
X = X.reshape(X.shape[0], X.shape[1], n_features))
```

The model needs to be trained, and that is done using the conventional Keras fit function. Because this is a simple model and the dataset is tiny as compared to others I have demonstrated, the training will be extremely brief for a single epoch. This means a large number of epochs can be used to try to obtain a maximum performance model. In this case, that number is 1000. The following code invokes the fit function for the model:

```
model.fit(X, y, epochs=1000, verbose=0)
```

Finally, the Keras predict function will be used to predict the next value in the input sequence. For instance, if the input sequence is {150, 200, 250], then the predicted value should be [300]. The code for the prediction is

```
# Demonstrate prediction
x_input = array([150, 200, 250])
x_input = x_input.reshape((1, n_steps, n_features))
yhat = model.predict(x_input, verbose=0)
```

The complete script incorporating all of the code snippets discussed earlier is named univariateTimeSeriesTest.py and is listed in the following. It is available from the book's companion web site.

```
# Import required libraries
from numpy import array
from keras.models import Sequential
from keras.layers import Dense
from keras.layers import Flatten
```

```python
from keras.layers.convolutional import Conv1D
from keras.layers.convolutional import MaxPooling1D

# Split a univariate sequence into samples
def split_sequence(sequence, n_steps):
    X, y = list(), list()
    for i in range(len(sequence)):
        # find the end of this pattern
        end_ix = i + n_steps
        # check if we are beyond the sequence
        if end_ix > len(sequence)-1:
            break
        # gather input and output parts of the pattern
        seq_x, seq_y = sequence[i:end_ix], sequence[end_ix]
        X.append(seq_x)
        y.append(seq_y)
    return array(X), array(y)

# Define input sequence
raw_seq = [50, 100, 150, 200, 250, 300, 350, 400, 450, 500,
550, 600, 650]

# Choose a number of time steps
n_steps = 3

# Split into samples
X, y = split_sequence(raw_seq, n_steps)

# Reshape from [samples, timesteps] into [samples, timesteps,
features]
n_features = 1
X = X.reshape((X.shape[0], X.shape[1], n_features))
```

```
# Define 1-D CNN model
model = Sequential()
model.add(Conv1D(filters=64, kernel_size=2, activation='relu',
input_shape=(n_steps, n_features)))
model.add(MaxPooling1D(pool_size=2))
model.add(Flatten())
model.add(Dense(50, activation='relu'))
model.add(Dense(1))
model.compile(optimizer='adam', loss='mse')

# Fit the model
model.fit(X, y, epochs=1000, verbose=0)

# Demonstrate prediction
x_input = array([150, 200, 250])
x_input = x_input.reshape((1, n_steps, n_features))
yhat = model.predict(x_input, verbose=0)
print(yhat)
```

Run this script by using this command:

```
python univariateTimeSeriesTest.py
```

Figure 7-18 shows the result of running this script.

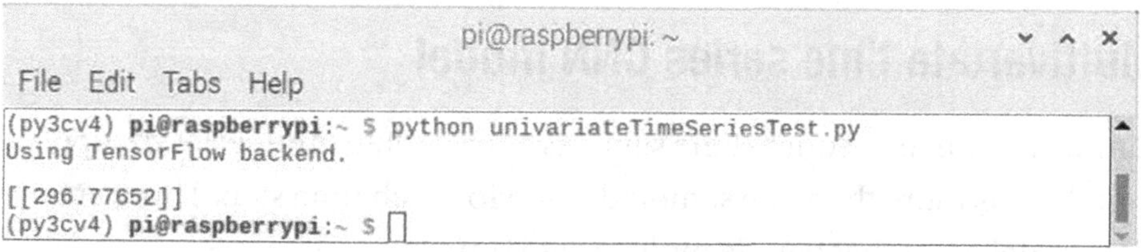

Figure 7-18. *Results after running the univariateTimeSeriesTest script*

The predicted value displayed is 296.78, not quite 300 as was expected, but still fairly close. There is a degree of randomness in the algorithm, and I tried running it a few more times. The following list shows the results of ten retries:

286.68

276.35

279.15

299.96

279.66

299.86

300.07

281.75

294.20

300.09

You can see from the list that the expected value (rounded) was displayed four out of ten times. The mean of the ten values was 289.78, the standard deviation was 10.03, and range was from 276.35 to 300.09. I would rate this CNN predictor as good with those performance statistics.

Multivariate time series CNN model

A multivariate time series is the same as a univariate time series except that there is more than one sampled value for each time step. There are two model types that handle multivariate time series data:

- Multiple input series
- Multiple parallel series

Each model type will be discussed separately.

Multiple input series

I will start by explaining that multiple input series has parallel input time series, which is not to be confused with the other model type. This will be clear in a moment. This parallel time series has had its values sampled at the sample time step. For example, consider the following sets of raw time series values:

> [50, 100, 150, 200, 250, 300, 350, 400, 450, 500, 550, 600, 650]

> [50, 75, 100, 125, 150, 175, 200, 225, 250, 275, 300, 325, 350]

The output sequence will be the sum of each sampled value pair for the entire length of each series. In code the aforementioned would be expressed as

```
from numpy import array
in_seq1 = array([50, 100, 150, 200, 250, 300, 350, 400, 450,
500, 550, 600, 650])
in_seq2 = array([50,   75, 100, 125, 150, 175, 200, 225, 250,
275, 300, 325, 350])
out_seq = array([in_seq1[i] + in_seq2[i] for i in range(in_
seq1))])
```

These arrays must be reshaped as was done in the previous demonstration. The columns must also be stacked horizontally for processing. The code segment to do all that is

```
# Convert to [rows, columns] structure
in_seq1 = in_seq1.reshape((len(in_seq1), 1))
in_seq2 = in_seq2.reshape((len(in_seq2), 1))
out_seq = out_seq.reshape((len(out_seq), 1))

# Horizontally stack columns
dataset = hstack((in_seq1, in_seq2, out_seq))
```

Preprocessing the dataset

The complete script to preprocess the datasets described earlier is
named shapeMultivariateTimeSeries.py and is listed in the following. It is
available from the book's companion web site.

```
# Multivariate data preparation
from numpy import array
from numpy import hstack

# Define input sequences
in_seq1 = array([50, 100, 150, 200, 250, 300, 350, 400, 450,
500, 550, 600, 650])
in_seq2 = array([50,  75, 100, 125, 150, 175, 200, 225, 250,
275, 300, 325, 350])
out_seq = array([in_seq1[i]+in_seq2[i] for i in range(len(in_
seq1))])

# Convert to [rows, columns] structure
in_seq1 = in_seq1.reshape((len(in_seq1), 1))
in_seq2 = in_seq2.reshape((len(in_seq2), 1))
out_seq = out_seq.reshape((len(out_seq), 1))
# Horizontally stack columns
dataset = hstack((in_seq1, in_seq2, out_seq))

# Display the datasets
print(dataset)
```

Run this script by using this command:

```
python shapeMultivariateTimeSeries.py
```

Figure 7-19 shows the result of running this script.

```
                              pi@raspberrypi: ~              ⌄  ∧  ✕

 File  Edit  Tabs  Help
(py3cv4) pi@raspberrypi:~ $ python shapeMultivariateTimeSeries.py
[[  50   50  100]
 [ 100   75  175]
 [ 150  100  250]
 [ 200  125  325]
 [ 250  150  400]
 [ 300  175  475]
 [ 350  200  550]
 [ 400  225  625]
 [ 450  250  700]
 [ 500  275  775]
 [ 550  300  850]
 [ 600  325  925]
 [ 650  350 1000]]
(py3cv4) pi@raspberrypi:~ $ []
```

Figure 7-19. *Results after running the shapeMultivariateTimeSeries*
script

The results screen shows the dataset with one row per time step and
columns for the two inputs and summed output for each of the elements in
the parallel time series.

This reshaped raw data vectors now must be split into input/output
samples as was done with the univariate time series. A 1D CNN model
needs sufficient inputs to learn a mapping from an input sequence to an
output value. The data needs to be split into samples maintaining the
order of observations across the two input sequences.

If three input time steps are chosen, then the first sample would look
as follows:

Input:

> 50, 50

> 100, 75

> 150, 100

Output:

> 250

The first three time steps of each parallel series are provided as input to the model, and the model associates this with the value in the output series at the third time step, in this case, 250.

It is apparent that some data will be discarded when transforming the time series into input/output samples to train the model. Choosing the number of input time steps will have a large effect on how much of the training data is eventually used. A function named *split_sequences* will take the dataset that was previously shaped and return the needed input/output samples. The following code implements the *split_sequences function*:

```
# split a multivariate sequence into samples
def split_sequences(sequences, n_steps):
    X, y = list(), list()
    for i in range(len(sequences)):
        # find the end of this pattern
        end_ix = i + n_steps
        # check if we are beyond the dataset
        if end_ix > len(sequences):
            break
        # gather input and output parts of the pattern
        seq_x, seq_y = sequences[i:end_ix, :-1], sequences[end_
        ix-1, -1]
        X.append(seq_x)
        y.append(seq_y)
    return array(X), array(y)
```

The following code tests all the previous code snippets and functions. I named this script splitMultivariateTimeSeries.py. It is available from the book's companion web site.

```python
# Import required libraries
from numpy import array
from numpy import hstack

# Split a multivariate sequence into samples
def split_sequences(sequences, n_steps):
    X, y = list(), list()
    for i in range(len(sequences)):
        # find the end of this pattern
        end_ix = i + n_steps
        # check if we are beyond the dataset
        if end_ix > len(sequences):
            break
        # gather input and output parts of the pattern
        seq_x, seq_y = sequences[i:end_ix, :-1], sequences[end_
        ix-1, -1]
        X.append(seq_x)
        y.append(seq_y)
    return array(X), array(y)

# Define input sequences
in_seq1 = array([50, 100, 150, 200, 250, 300, 350, 400, 450,
500, 550, 600, 650])
in_seq2 = array([50,  75, 100, 125, 150, 175, 200, 225, 250,
275, 300, 325, 350])
out_seq = array([in_seq1[i]+in_seq2[i] for i in range(len(in_
seq1))])

# Convert to [rows, columns] structure
in_seq1 = in_seq1.reshape((len(in_seq1), 1))
in_seq2 = in_seq2.reshape((len(in_seq2), 1))
out_seq = out_seq.reshape((len(out_seq), 1))
```

```
# Horizontally stack columns
dataset = hstack((in_seq1, in_seq2, out_seq))

# Choose a number of time steps
n_steps = 3

# Convert into input/output samples
X, y = split_sequences(dataset, n_steps)
print(X.shape, y.shape)

# Display the data
for i in range(len(X)):
    print(X[i], y[i])
```

Run this script by using this command:

```
python splitMultivariateTimeSeries.py
```

Figure 7-20 shows the result of running this script.

```
                                    pi@raspberrypi: ~                    ∨  ∧  ✕

 File  Edit  Tabs  Help
(py3cv4) pi@raspberrypi:~ $ python splitMultivariateTimeSeries.py
(11, 3, 2) (11,)
[[ 50  50]
 [100  75]
 [150 100]] 250
[[100  75]
 [150 100]
 [200 125]] 325
[[150 100]
 [200 125]
 [250 150]] 400
[[200 125]
 [250 150]
 [300 175]] 475
[[250 150]
 [300 175]
 [350 200]] 550
[[300 175]
 [350 200]
 [400 225]] 625
[[350 200]
 [400 225]
 [450 250]] 700
[[400 225]
 [450 250]
 [500 275]] 775
[[450 250]
 [500 275]
 [550 300]] 850
[[500 275]
 [550 300]
 [600 325]] 925
[[550 300]
 [600 325]
 [650 350]] 1000
(py3cv4) pi@raspberrypi:~ $ []
```

Figure 7-20. *Results after running the splitMultivariateTimeSeries script*

Running the script first displays the shape of the *X* and *y* components. You can see that the *X* component has a 3D structure. The first dimension is the number of samples, in this case 11. The second dimension is the number of time steps per sample, in this case 3, and the last dimension specifies the number of parallel time series or the number of variables, in this case 2, for the two parallel series. The dataset as shown in the rest of the figure is the exact 3D structure expected by a 1D CNN for input.

447

The model used for this demonstration is exactly the same one used for the univariate demonstration. The discussion I used for that model applies to this situation.

The Keras predict function will be used to predict the next value in the output series, provided the input values are

200, 125

300, 175

400, 225

The predicted value should be 625. The code for the prediction is

```
# Demonstrate prediction
x_input = array([[200, 125], [300, 175], [400, 225]])
x_input = x_input.reshape((1, n_steps, n_features))
yhat = model.predict(x_input, verbose=0)
```

The complete script incorporating all of the code snippets discussed earlier is named multivariateTimeSeriesTest.py and is listed in the following. It is available from the book's companion web site.

```
# Import required libraries
from numpy import array
from numpy import hstack
from keras.models import Sequential
from keras.layers import Dense
from keras.layers import Flatten
from keras.layers.convolutional import Conv1D
from keras.layers.convolutional import MaxPooling1D

# Split a multivariate sequence into samples
def split_sequences(sequences, n_steps):
    X, y = list(), list()
    for i in range(len(sequences)):
```

```
        # Find the end of this pattern
        end_ix = i + n_steps
        # Check if we are beyond the dataset
        if end_ix > len(sequences):
            break
        # Gather input and output parts of the pattern
        seq_x, seq_y = sequences[i:end_ix, :-1], sequences[end_
        ix-1, -1]
        X.append(seq_x)
        y.append(seq_y)
    return array(X), array(y)

# Define input sequence
in_seq1 = array([50, 100, 150, 200, 250, 300, 350, 400, 450,
500, 550, 600, 650])
in_seq2 = array([50,  75, 100, 125, 150, 175, 200, 225, 250,
275, 300, 325, 350])
out_seq = array([in_seq1[i]+in_seq2[i] for i in range(len(in_
seq1))])

# Convert to [rows, columns] structure
in_seq1 = in_seq1.reshape((len(in_seq1), 1))
in_seq2 = in_seq2.reshape((len(in_seq2), 1))
out_seq = out_seq.reshape((len(out_seq), 1))

# Horizontally stack columns
dataset = hstack((in_seq1, in_seq2, out_seq))

# Choose a number of time steps
n_steps = 3

# Convert into input/output samples
X, y = split_sequences(dataset, n_steps)
```

```
# The dataset knows the number of features, e.g. 2
n_features = X.shape[2]

# Define model
model = Sequential()
model.add(Conv1D(filters=64, kernel_size=2, activation='relu',
input_shape=(n_steps, n_features)))
model.add(MaxPooling1D(pool_size=2))
model.add(Flatten())
model.add(Dense(50, activation='relu'))
model.add(Dense(1))
model.compile(optimizer='adam', loss='mse')

# Fit model
model.fit(X, y, epochs=1000, verbose=0)

# Demonstrate prediction
x_input = array([[200, 125], [300, 175], [400, 225]])
x_input = x_input.reshape((1, n_steps, n_features))
yhat = model.predict(x_input, verbose=0)

# Display the prediction
print(yhat)
```

Run this script by using this command:

```
python multivariateTimeSeriesTest.py
```

Figure 7-21 shows the result of running this script.

```
                              pi@raspberrypi: ~                        ∨  ∧  ✕

 File  Edit  Tabs  Help
(py3cv4) pi@raspberrypi:~ $ python multivariateTimeSeriesTest.py
Usina TensorFlow backend.
[[616.74]]
(py3cv4) pi@raspberrypi:~ $ ▯
```

Figure 7-21. *Results after running the multivariateTimeSeriesTest script*

The predicted value displayed is 616.74.78, not quite 625 as was expected, but still reasonably close. There is a degree of randomness in the algorithm, and I tried running it a few more times. The following list shows the results of ten retries:

586.93

610.88

606.86

593.37

612.66

604.88

597.40

577.46

605.50

605.94

The mean of the ten values was 600.19, the standard deviation was 11.28, and range was from 577.46 to 612.66. I would rate this CNN predictor as fair to good with those performance statistics.

CHAPTER 8

Predictions using CNNs and MLPs for medical research

In the previous chapter, I introduced you to how both ANNs and CNNs are used to make predictions. The predictions discussed were strictly related to numerical datasets and did not directly involve any input Images. In this chapter, I will discuss how to use Images with CNNs to make medical diagnosis predictions. Currently, this area of research is extremely important, and many AI researchers are pursuing viable lines of research to advance the subject matter. In truth, I added one more data-oriented MLP demonstration at the chapter's end to hopefully show you that data-only projects are still relevant in this area.

Much of this chapter's content has been inspired from Adrian Rosebrock's February 2019 blog titled "Breast Cancer Classification with Keras and Deep Learning." As Adrian points out in his blog, most of his readers "know someone who has had cancer at some point." I am sure that statement is true for most of the readers of this book. Hopefully, this chapter's content will provide some measure of hope to potential cancer patients that real progress is being made in the early detection of some types of cancer using AI, ML, and DL.

© Donald J. Norris 2020
D. J. Norris, *Machine Learning with the Raspberry Pi*,
https://doi.org/10.1007/978-1-4842-5174-4_8

Parts list

You will need a standard RasPi desktop configuration for the chapter demonstrations.

Item	Model	Quantity	Source
Raspberry Pi 4	Model B (RasPi 4 with 2 or 4 GB RAM)	1	mcmelectronics.com adafruit.com digikey.com mouser.com farnell.com
Micro SD card	32 GB, class 10 or larger	1	amazon.com
USB keyboard	Amazon Basic	1	amazon.com
USB mouse	Amazon Basic	1	amazon.com
HDMI monitor	Commodity	1	amazon.com

Note   A minimum of 2 GB RAM is required to enable the RasPi 4 to compile and train the CNN models used in the chapter demonstrations. RasPis with only 1 GB of RAM will not be successful in the demonstrations.

The use of a 32 GB micro SD card is required because the combined memory requirements for OpenCV, Keras, TensorFlow, dataset used in the demonstrations, and the latest Raspbian OS in a virtual Python environment exceed 16 GB.

Downloading the breast cancer histology Image dataset

Histology, also known as microscopic anatomy or microanatomy is the branch of biology which studies the microscopic anatomy of biological tissues. Specifically, the histology referenced in this problem domain are the microscopic Images taken from patients with and without malignant breast cancer cells.

The dataset used in this demonstration is for invasive ductal carcinoma (IDC). This dataset is available for download at

www.kaggle.com/paultimothymooney/breast-histopathology-images

It is a very large download (1.6 GB) and will need to be unarchived twice to gain access to the raw Images. The final extracted dataset size exceeds 2.4 GB.

The following are the context and content descriptions from the dataset download web site:

Context:

Invasive ductal carcinoma (IDC) is the most common subtype of all breast cancers. To assign an aggressiveness grade to a whole mount sample, pathologists typically focus on the regions which contain the IDC. As a result, one of the common preprocessing steps for automatic aggressiveness grading is to delineate the exact regions of IDC inside of a whole mount slide.

Content:

The original dataset consisted of 162 whole mount slide Images of Breast Cancer (BCa) specimens scanned at 40x. From that, 277,524 patches of size 50 x 50 were extracted (198,738 IDC negative and 78,786 IDC positive). Each patch's filename is of the format u_xX_yY_classC.png. For example, 10253_idx5_x1351_y1101_class0.png, where u is the patient ID (10253_idx5), X is the x-coordinate of where this patch was cropped from, Y is the y-coordinate of where this patch was cropped from, and C indicates the class where 0 is non-IDC and 1 is IDC.

In summary, from the preceding descriptions there are

- 277,524 Image patches of 50×50 pixels each

- 78,786 positive examples (i.e., indicating breast cancer detected in the patch)

- 198,738 negative examples (i.e., no breast cancer detected)

From my examination of a sample of the patch coordinates, I have inferred that the original whole mount slide Image size in pixels must be 1600 x 1600. This means that a maximum of 1024 patches could be extracted from any given slide, provided there were no overlapping patches taken. This means the whole dataset has a potential for a maximum of the number of patient's time 1024, assuming each patient has cancer and cancer-free patches. I will shortly show you that there are 837 patients in this study, which means there is a potential maximum of 857,088 patch Images. In actuality, there are 277,524 Images in the dataset, which means that only 32% of the potential patches were sampled. While this statistic might be meaningful to statisticians regarding the overall "quality" of any prediction, I will choose to ignore it for purposes of this demonstration.

There is, however, an obvious imbalance in the Image types in the dataset. There are twice as many negative class Images as positive class Images. This is something that will be handled when the data is preprocessed.

Figure 8-1 shows a tiny fraction of both positive and negative Images from the dataset.

Positive   Negative

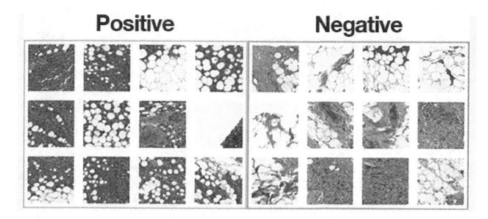

Figure 8-1. *Representative sample of dataset Images*

There are 837 sub-directories present under the main directory named IDC_regular_ps50_idc5. You will next need to rename this directory to dataset to make it compatible with the configuration script I will shortly discuss. You can either use the cp command or use the File Manager utility to make this change. I almost always use the File Manager because of its convenience.

Figure 8-2 is the result of running the tree command, where you can see a small portion of the 837 sub-directories.

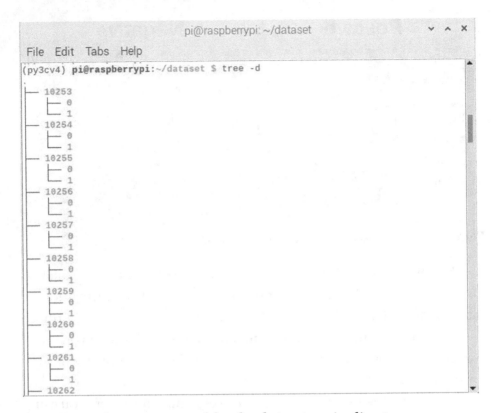

Figure 8-2. `tree` *command for the dataset main directory*

Each sub-directory contains both positive and negative Images for a given patient, whose numerical id is the name of the sub-directory. In each sub-directory, there are two more sub-directories named 0 and 1. The 0 directory contains Images, which do have any cancer cells detected. The 1 directory has Images containing detected cancer cells.

The ultimate goal of this demonstration is to train a CNN model to distinguish between positive and negative Image classes, thus predicting if a given patient has or does not have IDC.

Preparing the project environment

The first step before trying any project script is to set up a Python virtual environment. I have used this environment type in previous demonstrations and will continue to use for this chapter's demonstrations. Refer back to Chapter 1 regarding how to create a virtual environment if you need a refresher.

There are five dependencies that must be installed to support the scripts used in this chapter. You have likely installed most, if not all, if you have been replicating the previous chapter demonstrations. In any case, all you need to do is enter the following commands to ensure that the required dependencies are installed:

```
pip install numpy opencv-contrib-python
pip install pillow
pip install tensorflow keras
pip install imutils
pip install scikit-learn matplotlib
```

You will have problems when using the imutils package if you have not installed OpenCV. While OpenCV functions are not directly called by any of the chapter scripts, imutils does have some embedded dependencies with this package. Refer back to Chapter 2 if you need guidance on installing OpenCV.

You will be ready to tackle the first script once the virtual environment is set up.

Configuration script

The following script set ups the appropriate directory paths and defines the amount of data to be used for training and validation. This script is named config_IDC.py and is available from the book's companion web site:

```python
# Import the required library
import os

# Initialize the path to the input image directory.
ORIG_INPUT_DATASET = "dataset"

# Initialize the base path to the directory that contain the
# images remaining after the training and testing splits.
BASE_PATH = "datasets/idc"

# Define the training, validation, and testing directory paths.
TRAIN_PATH = os.path.sep.join([BASE_PATH, "training"])
VAL_PATH = os.path.sep.join([BASE_PATH, "validation"])
TEST_PATH = os.path.sep.join([BASE_PATH, "testing"])

# Define the data split that will be used for training.
TRAIN_SPLIT = 0.8

# Define the data split that will be used for validation.
VAL_SPLIT = 0.1

# Display to user that configuration is complete.
print('[INFO]: Configuration complete')
```

This configuration script will be run when the next script to be discussed is run.

The next step in the demonstration is to build the dataset.

Building the dataset

Building the dataset consists, in part, of splitting up the original dataset into three smaller datasets as shown in Figure 8-3 diagram.

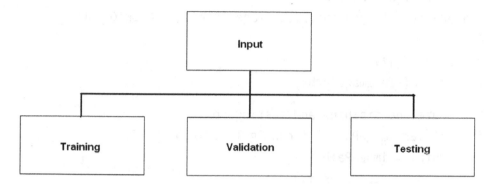

Figure 8-3. *Dataset splits*

One of the first items you should realize is that the original dataset is a little over 5.8 GB in size. This is clearly too large for even a 4 GB RasPi 4, which I am using to run this demonstration. In order to avoid this issue, the Keras ImageDataGenerator class will be used to create smaller batches from the split datasets, which will eliminate the requirement to load the whole original dataset in RAM. However, the original dataset must first be split and reorganized.

This script is named build_IDC_dataset.py and will be used to organize the original dataset. The script uses configuration constants which are set up when the config_IDC script is run at the start of this script. This script is available from the book's companion web site. Some explanatory comments follow the listing.

```
# Import the required libraries
from config_IDC import config_IDC
from imutils import paths
import random
```

461

```
import shutil
import os

# Grab the paths to all input images in the original input
# directory and shuffle them.
imagePaths = list(paths.list_images(config_IDC.ORIG_INPUT_
DATASET))
random.seed(42)
random.shuffle(imagePaths)

# Compute the training and testing split.
i = int(len(imagePaths) * config_IDC.TRAIN_SPLIT)
trainPaths = imagePaths[:i]
testPaths = imagePaths[i:]

# Use part of the training data for validation.
i = int(len(trainPaths) * config.VAL_SPLIT)
valPaths = trainPaths[:i]
trainPaths = trainPaths[i:]

# Define the datasets that are built.
datasets = [
    ("training", trainPaths, config.TRAIN_PATH),
    ("validation", valPaths, config.VAL_PATH),
    ("testing", testPaths, config.TEST_PATH)
]

# Loop over the datasets.
for (dType, imagePaths, baseOutput) in datasets:
    # Show which data split created
    print("[INFO] building '{}' split".format(dType))

    # If the base output directory does not exist,
    # create it.
```

```
if not os.path.exists(baseOutput):
    print("[INFO] 'creating {}' directory".format(baseOutput))
    os.makedirs(baseOutput)

# Loop over the input image paths.
for inputPath in imagePaths:
    # Extract the filename of the input image and extract
    # the class label ("0" for "negative" and "1" for
    # "positive").
    filename = inputPath.split(os.path.sep)[-1]
    label = filename[-5:-4]

    # Build the path to the label directory.
    labelPath = os.path.sep.join([baseOutput, label])

    # If the label output directory does not exist, create
    # it.
    if not os.path.exists(labelPath):
        print("[INFO] 'creating {}' directory".
        format(labelPath))
        os.makedirs(labelPath)

    # Construct the path to the destination image and then
    # copy the image itself.
    p = os.path.sep.join([labelPath, filename])
    shutil.copy2(inputPath, p)
```

Explanatory comments:

Configuration settings and paths are collected after the config_IDC script is run at the start of this script. The Python random library is used to randomly shuffle the paths. The shutil library is used to copy Images and the os library is used for joining paths and making directories.

Next, all the dataset imagePaths are shuffled to improve the randomness for better final results. The index of the training/testing split is then computed and trainPaths and testPaths are constructed by slicing the imagePaths. The trainPaths are further split to reserve a portion for use for validation.

A list named datasets is then defined. Inside this list are three tuples, each with the information required to organize all of the imagePaths into training, validation, and testing data.

Iteration over all the datasets is then started. The following steps occur in the loop:

- A base output directory is created (one time only).

- A nested loop over all input Images in the current split happens where

  - The filename is extracted from the input path and the class label is extracted from the filename.

  - A labelPath is constructed as well as creating a label output directory (one time only).

  - Each file is copied into its destination directory.

Running the build dataset script

The build_IDC_datascript is run by entering the following command:

```
python build_IDC_dataset.py
```

Figure 8-4 shows the results of running the script.

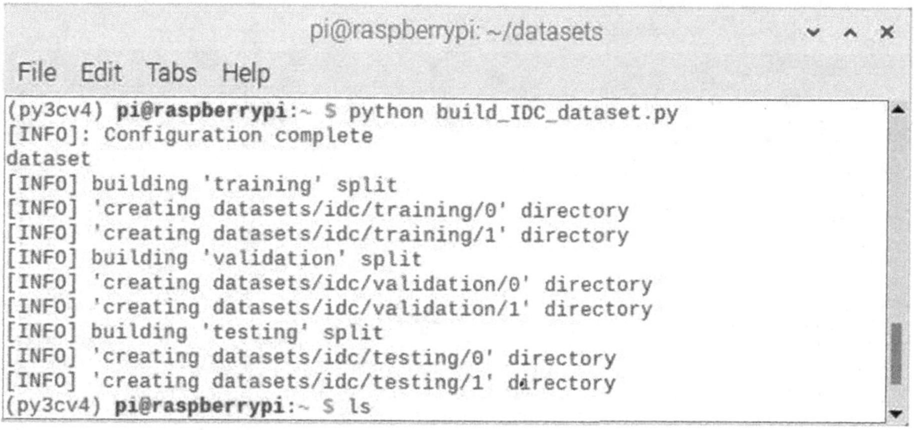

```
                         pi@raspberrypi: ~/datasets              ⌄  ∧  ✕

  File  Edit  Tabs  Help
  (py3cv4) pi@raspberrypi:~ $ python build_IDC_dataset.py
  [INFO]: Configuration complete
  dataset
  [INFO] building 'training' split
  [INFO] 'creating datasets/idc/training/0' directory
  [INFO] 'creating datasets/idc/training/1' directory
  [INFO] building 'validation' split
  [INFO] 'creating datasets/idc/validation/0' directory
  [INFO] 'creating datasets/idc/validation/1' directory
  [INFO] building 'testing' split
  [INFO] 'creating datasets/idc/testing/0' directory
  [INFO] 'creating datasets/idc/testing/1' directory
  (py3cv4) pi@raspberrypi:~ $ ls
```

Figure 8-4. *Results after running the build_IDC_dataset script*

I next ran the tree command on the newly built datasets directory to
confirm that the required datasets were constructed as desired. Figure 8-5
shows the results of running the tree command.

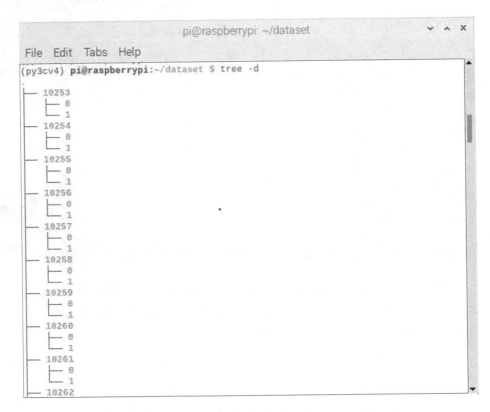

Figure 8-5.   *tree command applied to the datasets directory*

It is now time to discuss the CNN model once the datasets have been set.

The CNN model

The model used in this demonstration is based mainly on a VGGNet style model, which I discussed in the previous chapter. There are multiple stacked convolutional layers, which use 3 x 3 filters, typical for the VGG model. However, this VGG model uses depthwise separable convolutional layers rather than the standard convolutional layers. Without going into any details, I will simply say that depthwise separable convolution is a process that is more computationally efficient as compared to conventional convolution.

This CNN model is named CancerNet, which seems appropriate given its role in predicting whether or not a patient has that disease based on the patient's histologic study. Figure 8-6 diagrams the CancerNet structure.

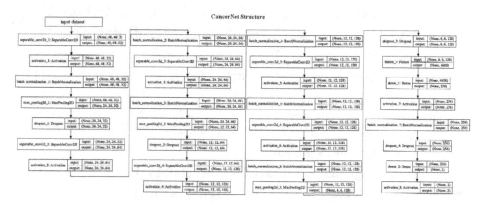

Figure 8-6. *CancerNet structure*

It should be obvious from this figure that this CNN network is complex with many layers. This CNN is truly a classic representation of a deep network. There are 31 layers shown in the figure, which you can confirm by counting the layers added to the model in the following class definition.

The following class definition file is named cancernet.py and is available from the book's companion web site:

```
# Import the required libraries
from keras.models import Sequential
from keras.layers.normalization import BatchNormalization
from keras.layers.convolutional import SeparableConv2D
from keras.layers.convolutional import MaxPooling2D
from keras.layers.core import Activation
from keras.layers.core import Flatten
```

```python
from keras.layers.core import Dropout
from keras.layers.core import Dense
from keras import backend as K

class CancerNet:
    @staticmethod
    def build(width, height, depth, classes):
        # Initialize the model along with the input shape to
        # be "channels last" and the channels dimension itself
        model = Sequential()
        inputShape = (height, width, depth)
        chanDim = -1

        # If using "channels first", update the input shape
        # and channels dimension.
        if K.image_data_format() == "channels_first":
            inputShape = (depth, height, width)
            chanDim = 1

        # CONV => RELU => POOL
        model.add(SeparableConv2D(32, (3, 3), padding="same",
            input_shape=inputShape))
        model.add(Activation("relu"))
        model.add(BatchNormalization(axis=chanDim))
        model.add(MaxPooling2D(pool_size=(2, 2)))
        model.add(Dropout(0.25))

        # (CONV => RELU => POOL) * 2
        model.add(SeparableConv2D(64, (3, 3), padding="same"))
        model.add(Activation("relu"))
        model.add(BatchNormalization(axis=chanDim))
        model.add(SeparableConv2D(64, (3, 3), padding="same"))
        model.add(Activation("relu"))
        model.add(BatchNormalization(axis=chanDim))
```

```
model.add(MaxPooling2D(pool_size=(2, 2)))
model.add(Dropout(0.25))

# (CONV => RELU => POOL) * 3
model.add(SeparableConv2D(128, (3, 3), padding="same"))
model.add(Activation("relu"))
model.add(BatchNormalization(axis=chanDim))
model.add(SeparableConv2D(128, (3, 3), padding="same"))
model.add(Activation("relu"))
model.add(BatchNormalization(axis=chanDim))
model.add(SeparableConv2D(128, (3, 3), padding="same"))
model.add(Activation("relu"))
model.add(BatchNormalization(axis=chanDim))
model.add(MaxPooling2D(pool_size=(2, 2)))
model.add(Dropout(0.25))

# First (and only) set of FC => RELU layers
model.add(Flatten())
model.add(Dense(256))
model.add(Activation("relu"))
model.add(BatchNormalization())
model.add(Dropout(0.5))

# Softmax classifier
model.add(Dense(classes))
model.add(Activation("softmax"))

# Return the constructed network architecture
return model
```

This model is structured as sequential, which means layers are added in a serial fashion. Most of the layer types used in this model were used in Chapter 7 CNN model except for the SeparableConv2D layer, which implements the depthwise separable convolution mentioned earlier.

Three DEPTHWISE_CONV => RELU => POOL blocks are defined in the model with increased stacking and filters applied. BatchNormalization and Dropout layers have also been added.

FC => RELU layers and softmax classifier finish the network. The output of the softmax classifier will create prediction percentages for each predicted class.

The model is structured as a callable method, which means the instantiated model will be returned to the training script.

Training and testing script

The training script is the key piece, which finally ties all the whole project together. This script is named train_IDC_model.py, and it not only trains the model but it also tests it for prediction accuracy. This script is available from the book's companion web site. Explanatory comments follow the listing.

```
# Set the matplotlib backend so figures can be saved in the
# background
import matplotlib
matplotlib.use("Agg")

# Import the required libraries
from keras.preprocessing.image import ImageDataGenerator
from keras.callbacks import LearningRateScheduler
from keras.optimizers import Adagrad
from keras.utils import np_utils
from sklearn.metrics import classification_report
from sklearn.metrics import confusion_matrix
from cancernet import CancerNet
import config_IDC as config
from imutils import paths
import matplotlib.pyplot as plt
```

```
import numpy as np
import argparse
import os

# Construct the argument parser and parse the arguments.
ap = argparse.ArgumentParser()
ap.add_argument("-p", "--plot", type=str, default="plot.png",
    help="path to output loss/accuracy plot")
args = vars(ap.parse_args())

# Initialize the number of epochs, initial learning rate, and
# batch size.
NUM_EPOCHS = 40
INIT_LR = 1e-2
BS = 32

# Determine the total number of image paths in training,
# validation, and testing directories.
trainPaths = list(paths.list_images(config.TRAIN_PATH))
totalTrain = len(trainPaths)
totalVal = len(list(paths.list_images(config.VAL_PATH)))
totalTest = len(list(paths.list_images(config.TEST_PATH)))

# Account for skew in the labeled data
trainLabels = [int(p.split(os.path.sep)[-2]) for p in
trainPaths]
trainLabels = np_utils.to_categorical(trainLabels)
classTotals = trainLabels.sum(axis=0)
classWeight = classTotals.max() / classTotals

# Initialize the training data augmentation object
trainAug = ImageDataGenerator(
    rescale=1 / 255.0,
    rotation_range=20,
```

```
    zoom_range=0.05,
    width_shift_range=0.1,
    height_shift_range=0.1,
    shear_range=0.05,
    horizontal_flip=True,
    vertical_flip=True,
    fill_mode="nearest")

# Initialize the validation (and testing) data augmentation
# object.
valAug = ImageDataGenerator(rescale=1 / 255.0)

# Initialize the training generator.
trainGen = trainAug.flow_from_directory(
    config.TRAIN_PATH,
    class_mode="categorical",
    target_size=(48, 48),
    color_mode="rgb",
    shuffle=True,
    batch_size=BS)

# Initialize the validation generator.
valGen = valAug.flow_from_directory(
    config.VAL_PATH,
    class_mode="categorical",
    target_size=(48, 48),
    color_mode="rgb",
    shuffle=False,
    batch_size=BS)

# Initialize the testing generator.
testGen = valAug.flow_from_directory(
    config.TEST_PATH,
    class_mode="categorical",
```

```python
    target_size=(48, 48),
    color_mode="rgb",
    shuffle=False,
    batch_size=BS)

# Initialize the CancerNet model and compile it.
model = CancerNet.build(width=48, height=48, depth=3,
    classes=2)
opt = Adagrad(lr=INIT_LR, decay=INIT_LR / NUM_EPOCHS)
model.compile(loss="binary_crossentropy", optimizer=opt,
    metrics=["accuracy"])

# Fit the model.
H = model.fit_generator(
    trainGen,
    steps_per_epoch=totalTrain // BS,
    validation_data=valGen,
    validation_steps=totalVal // BS,
    class_weight=classWeight,
    epochs=NUM_EPOCHS)

# Reset the testing generator and then use the trained model to
# make predictions on the data.
print("[INFO] evaluating network...")
testGen.reset()
predIdxs = model.predict_generator(testGen,
    steps=(totalTest // BS) + 1)

# For each image in the testing set find the index of the
# label with corresponding largest predicted probability.
predIdxs = np.argmax(predIdxs, axis=1)
```

```python
# Show a nicely formatted classification report.
print(classification_report(testGen.classes, predIdxs,
    target_names=testGen.class_indices.keys()))

# Compute the confusion matrix and use it to derive the raw
# accuracy, sensitivity, and specificity.
cm = confusion_matrix(testGen.classes, predIdxs)
total = sum(sum(cm))
acc = (cm[0, 0] + cm[1, 1]) / total
sensitivity = cm[0, 0] / (cm[0, 0] + cm[0, 1])
specificity = cm[1, 1] / (cm[1, 0] + cm[1, 1])

# Show the confusion matrix, accuracy, sensitivity, and
# specificity.
print(cm)
print("acc: {:.4f}".format(acc))
print("sensitivity: {:.4f}".format(sensitivity))
print("specificity: {:.4f}".format(specificity))

# Plot the training loss and accuracy.
N = NUM_EPOCHS
plt.style.use("ggplot")
plt.figure()
plt.plot(np.arange(0, N), H.history["loss"], label="train_
loss")
plt.plot(np.arange(0, N), H.history["val_loss"], label="val_
loss")
plt.plot(np.arange(0, N), H.history["acc"], label="train_acc")
plt.plot(np.arange(0, N), H.history["val_acc"], label="val_
acc")
plt.title("Training Loss and Accuracy on Dataset")
plt.xlabel("Epoch #")
```

```
plt.ylabel("Loss/Accuracy")
plt.legend(loc="lower left")
plt.savefig(args["plot"])
```

Explanatory comments follow:

The following libraries are used by this script with brief explanations for each:

1. Matplotlib – This is the scientific plotting package that is the de facto standard for Python. This library is set to use the "Agg" backend to enable saving training plots to disk.

2. Keras – Use the Keras ImageDataGenerator, LearningRateScheduler, Adagrad optimizer, and np_utils.

3. sklearn – Use the scikit-learn implementations of a classification_report and a confusion_matrix.

4. config_IDC – Use this script config to grab the paths to the three data splits.

5. cancernet – Class definition for CancerNet required for training and evaluation.

6. imutils – Using the paths module to grab paths to each of the Images.

7. numpy – Required for numerical processing with Python.

8. argparse – Used to parse the command-line arguments.

9. os – Used for access to OS level commands.

475

There is one optional command-line argument that can be used with this script and that is --plot. When this argument is provided in a terminal at runtime, the script will use that name to save the plot to disk. If you don't specify a command-line argument with the plot filename, a default name of plot.png will be used.

The number of training epochs, initial learning rate, and batch size are defined after the parser code.

After these definitions, the total number of Image paths in the training, validation, and testing directories is determined.

A `classWeight` parameter is then computed for the training data to account for class imbalance/skew. Class imbalance happens when there is a disproportionate share of data elements among training datasets. This was the case in this project as I noted at the beginning of the chapter. There are over twice as many benign sample Images as there are malignant sample Images. Class imbalance can cause two problems with a model:

- Never get optimized results for the class which is unbalanced because the model is never sufficiently trained.

- Validation becomes difficult because of misrepresentation across the classes where one or more classes are severely under-represented.

The `classWeight` parameter is used by the Keras fit function to help correct for the datasets unbalance. I am unsure how that is implemented within the function.

The next code portion deals with data augmentation, which is a form of regularization. Regularization is important for nearly all DL experiments to assist with model generalization. This function perturbs the training dataset, slightly modifying its content, before passing it into the network for training. This approach partially reduces the need to gather additional training data.

The data augmentation object, `trainAug`, is first initialized. Random rotations, shifts, shears, and flips are then applied to the training dataset as it is being applied. Image pixel intensities are also rescaled to the range 0 to 1 by the `trainAug` object.

Next, the training, validation, and testing generators are initialized. Each generator provides batches of Images on demand, as is specified by the `batch_size` parameter.

The model is then initialized with the Adagrad optimizer. Recall that I mentioned some of the various optimizers that are available with Keras in the previous chapter. The Adagrad optimizer is an algorithm for gradient-based optimization that adapts the learning rate (lr) to the parameters, performing smaller updates (i.e., low lr) for parameters associated with frequently occurring features and larger updates (i.e., high lr) for parameters associated with infrequent features. For this reason, it is well suited for dealing with sparse data, which is the situation with this training dataset, at least for one class. The Adagrad optimizer uses both an initial lr and a decay lr in its operations.

The model is then compiled using the `binary_crossentropy` loss function because there are only two data classes.

The Keras fit_generator method starts the training process. By using this method, the training Image data can reside on disk and be applied in batches rather than having the whole dataset in RAM throughout training. This approach is the only way a RasPi system could possibly handle such a large training dataset.

Predictions are made on all of the testing data once the training has completed. A generator object is again used in the prediction process.

The highest prediction indices for each sample are collected and a classification_report is then displayed.

A confusion matrix is then generated. This matrix displays model accuracy, sensitivity, and specificity.

Finally, training history plots consisting of training/validation loss and training/validation accuracy are generated. These are temporal plots to allow for the detection of over-/underfitting.

Running the training and testing script

Note   This script is extremely computationally intensive. I determined that it takes 2.7 hours to complete only 1 epoch using a RasPi 4 system. If you elect to do the 40 epochs, as was done with the original blog, then expect to wait approximately 108 hours until it completes. That's 4.5 days! The alternative is to reduce the number of epochs to something more manageable such as 8, which still means you will have to wait about 21 hours to complete. I have estimated that the loss in accuracy is only in the order of 0.5% to 1.0% maximum, which I believe is an acceptable trade-off to save a wait of almost 4 days. Running this demonstration has convinced me of the usefulness of GPU-enabled processing.

I ran the train_IDC_model script on a RasPi 4 system (with 4 GB) using the default configuration values except for setting the number of epochs to 8. I am not confident that this script with the training set could even run on a standard RasPi 3 system.

The script is run by entering the following command:

```
python train_IDC_model.py
```

Figure 8-7 shows the result when the script started running.

```
File  Edit  Tabs  Help

[INFO]: Configuration complete
Found 199818 images belonging to 2 classes.
Found 22201 images belonging to 2 classes.
Found 55505 images belonging to 2 classes.
Epoch 1/8
   1/6244 [..............................] - ETA: 12:04:4
   2/6244 [..............................] - ETA: 7:20:31
   3/6244 [..............................] - ETA: 5:48:43
   4/6244 [..............................] - ETA: 5:03:39
   5/6244 [..............................] - ETA: 4:34:51
   6/6244 [..............................] - ETA: 4:15:35
   7/6244 [..............................] - ETA: 4:01:44
   8/6244 [..............................] - ETA: 3:51:07
   9/6244 [..............................] - ETA: 3:44:36
  10/6244 [..............................] - ETA: 3:38:13
  11/6244 [..............................] - ETA: 3:33:11
  12/6244 [..............................] - ETA: 3:28:33
 - loss: 0.9435 - acc: 0.7526
```

Figure 8-7. *Start of running the script*

21.5 hours later, the script finished with the final results shown in Figure 8-8.

```
                        pi@raspberrypi: ~                      ∨  ∧  ✕
File  Edit  Tabs  Help
[INFO] evaluating network...
              precision    recall  f1-score   support

           0       0.91      0.88      0.89     39843
           1       0.72      0.78      0.75     15662

    accuracy                          0.85     55505
   macro avg       0.81      0.83      0.82     55505
weighted avg       0.86      0.85      0.85     55505

[[35055  4788]
 [ 3455 12207]]
acc: 0.8515
sensitivity: 0.8798
specificity: 0.7794
(py3cv4) pi@raspberrypi:~ $
```

Figure 8-8. *Results after running the train_IDC_model script*

479

The confusion matrix (error matrix) displayed in the figure is replicated in Table 8-1. Please refer back to Chapter 1 discussion on the confusion matrix if you need a refresher.

Table 8-1. *CNN confusion matrix*

	Predicted	
Actual	0	1
0	35055 (TN)	4788 (FP)
1	3455 (FN)	12207 (TP)

where

0 = no cancer cells detected (negatives)

1 = cancer cells detected (positives)

See the following data for TN, FN, TP, and FP definitions.

Figure 8-9 contains temporal plots for training loss and accuracy. These plots are simply the interim results after each epoch has completed.

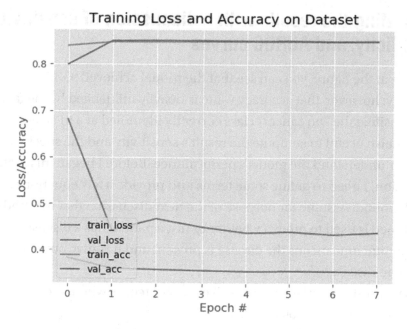

Figure 8-9. *Temporal plots for training loss and accuracy*

There are several items to be aware of in these plots. First and foremost, the accuracy plots for both training and validation converge after the first epoch is completed and stay together for all the remaining epochs. This indicates that there is little to none over-/underfitting with the CNN model. The model appears to be an excellent fit with this dataset. The next item to notice is that the accuracy plots appear horizontal after the second epoch has completed, which confirms my assumption that 8 epochs were more than enough to produce reliable results. Also looking at the loss plots shows they have stabilized around values that only slightly vary with more epochs confirming the stability of the final results.

Evaluating the results with a discussion of sensitivity, specificity, and AUROC curves

Looking at the figure, you can see that the model achieved 85.15% accuracy; however, that accuracy value is heavily influenced by the fact that classified the "no cancer" class correctly identified at a 91% rate.

It is also useful to compute the result's sensitivity and the specificity to better understand the model's performance. Before I began this metric discussion, I need to define some terms and provide a few equations as a background. Assume for purpose of the next discussion that the model mentioned is used to predict whether or not a patient has a disease. Positive outcome means the disease is present and negative outcome means no disease.

True positive (TP) – A true positive is an outcome where the model correctly predicts the positive class.

True negative (TN) – A true negative is an outcome where the model correctly predicts the negative class.

False positive (FP) – A false positive is an outcome where the model incorrectly predicts the positive class.

False negative (FN)) – A false negative is an outcome where the model incorrectly predicts the negative class.

True positive rate (TPR)/sensitivity/recall equation:

$$TPR = \frac{TP}{TP + FN}$$

Specificity equation:

$$Specificity = \frac{TN}{TN + FP}$$

False positive rate (FPR) equation:

$$FPR = 1 - Specificity$$

$$= \frac{FP}{TN + FP}$$

False negative rate (FNR) equation:

$$FNR = \frac{FN}{TP + FN}$$

In the demonstration model, the sensitivity measured the proportion of the TP that was also predicted as positive at an 87.98% rate. Conversely, specificity measures the TN rate at 77.94%. It is important to be careful regarding false negatives. You definitely don't want to classify someone as "cancer-free" when they are in fact "cancer positive."

A FPR is also important because you don't want to mistakenly classify patients as "cancer positive" and then subject them to extensive and likely painful treatment when they don't really need it.

There is a balance between sensitivity and specificity that any AI practitioner must be mindful of especially when it comes to DL and healthcare/health treatment.

What is sensitivity?

Sensitivity is a measure of the proportion of actual positive cases that are predicted as positive (TP). Another name for sensitivity is recall, which implies that there will be another proportion of actual positive cases, which would be predicted incorrectly as negative and could be termed as FN. This is also represented in the form of a FNR. The sum of sensitivity and false negative rate (FNR) will always be 1. This concept may be easier to understand when a model is used to predict whether a person is suffering from a disease. Sensitivity is a measure of the proportion of people suffering from a disease who are predicted correctly as the ones suffering from a disease. In other words, the person who is unhealthy actually is predicted as unhealthy.

Ideally, the model should seek to have low FNs as it might prove to be life-threatening.

A higher value of sensitivity would mean higher value of TPs and lower value of FNs. The lower value of sensitivity would mean lower value of TPs and higher value of FNs. For healthcare and financial reasons, models with high sensitivity are desired.

What is specificity?

Specificity is defined as the proportion of actual negatives, which were predicted as negative (TN). This implies that there will be another proportion of actual negative, which are predicted as positive and could be termed as FP. This proportion is also called a FPR. The sum of specificity and FPR is always 1. This concept may be easier to understand when a model is used to predict whether a person is suffering from a disease. Specificity is a measure of the proportion of people not suffering from a disease who are predicted correctly as the ones who are not suffering from a disease. In other words, specificity is when a person who is healthy actually is predicted as healthy.

A higher value of specificity would mean higher value of TN and lower FPR. The lower value of specificity would mean lower value of TN and higher value of FP.

What are the differences between sensitivity and specificity and how are they used?

Sensitivity measure is used to determine the proportion of actual positive cases, which were predicted correctly. Specificity measure is used to determine the proportion of actual negative cases, which were predicted correctly.

Sensitivity and specificity measures can be used to plot area under curve-receiver operating characteristic (AUC-ROC) curves. A AUC-ROC (also called AUROC) curve is a graphical plot that illustrates the diagnostic ability of a binary classifier system as its discrimination threshold is varied. ROC is a probability curve and AUC represents degree or measure of class separability. It tells how much model is capable of distinguishing between classes. The higher the AUC value, the better the model is at predicting 0s as 0s and 1s as 1s. By analogy, the higher the AUC value, the better the model is at distinguishing between patients with disease and those with no disease.

An AUROC curve is created by plotting the true positive rate (TPR) on the y-axis against the false positive rate (FPR) on the x-axis at various threshold settings. The FPR is also known as the fall-out or probability of false alarm and can be calculated as $1 - TPR$. The AUROC curve is thus the sensitivity as a function of fall-out. Figure 8-10 shows a generic AUROC curve.

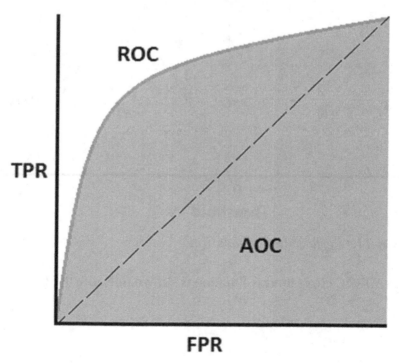

Figure 8-10. *Generic AUROC curve*

An excellent model has AUC near to 1.0 which means it has good measure of separating class predictions. A poor model has AUC close to 0 which means it has worst measure of separability. In fact, it is predicting 0s as 1s and 1s as 0s. This condition is called reciprocating the classes. When AUC is 0.5, it means that model does not separate the classes at all.

The next series of figure should help to clarify how an AUROC curve can be useful in interpreting a model's performance.

As stated previously, the ROC is a probability curve, so I will be using probability distribution plots for this discussion. Assume the right-hand curve in a figure is for the positive class or patients with a disease. Correspondingly, the left-hand curve is for healthy patients. Figure 8-11 shows a situation where the two classes are perfectly separated and the AUC is 1.0. The model is able to completely distinguish between positive and negative class samples.

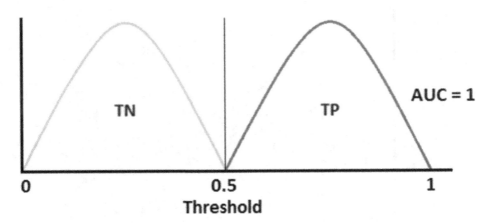

Figure 8-11. *Perfect class separation*

The AUROC curve for this situation is shown in Figure 8-12.

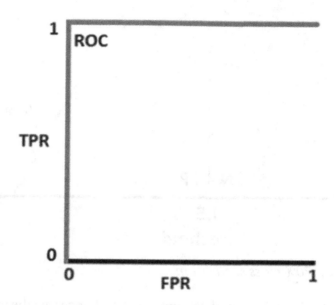

Figure 8-12. *AUROC curve for AUC = 1.0*

Now, let the situation change a little and assume that the probability distributions have a little overlap. This introduces the opportunity to have what statisticians call type 1 and type 2 errors to occur. A type 1 error is a FP or, for this situation, predicting a patient has a disease when it is not present. Similarly, a type 2 error is a FN or predicting a patient has no disease when it is present. Figure 8-13 shows the distributions with an AUC equal to 0.7.

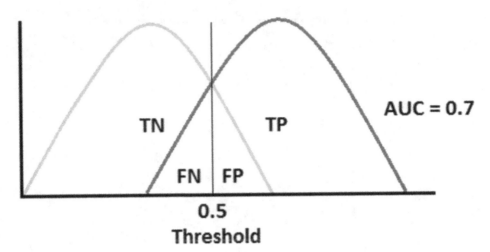

Figure 8-13. *70% class separation*

With an AUC of 0.7 means that there is a 70% chance that the model will be able to successfully distinguish between the positive and negative classes. The AUROC curve for this situation is shown in Figure 8-14.

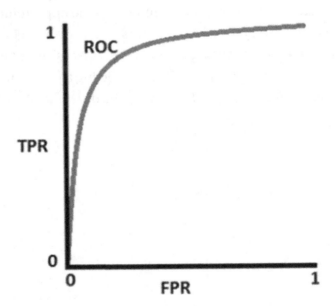

Figure 8-14. *AUROC curve for AUC = 0.7*

Now, make the situation substantially worse by letting the AUC equal to 0.5. With this AUC, the model cannot discriminate between the classes. Figure 8-15 shows the overlapping probability distribution curves, which proves why the model is ineffectual.

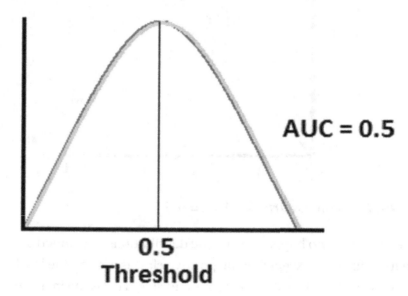

Figure 8-15. *50% class separation*

The AUROC curve for this situation is shown in Figure 8-16.

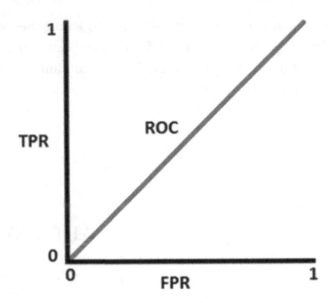

Figure 8-16. *AUROC curve for AUC = 0.5*

The final scenario happens when the distributions are flipped as shown in Figure 8-11 except that the positive class is now on the left-hand side and the negative class on the right-hand side. This is the inversion case I previously mentioned, and the AUROC curve for this case is shown in Figure 8-17.

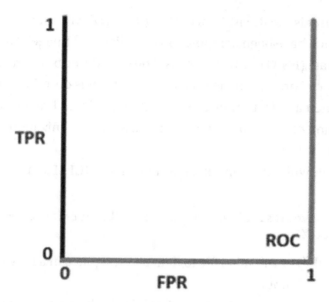

Figure 8-17. *AUROC curve for AUC = 0.0*

Inversion is an extreme case that never should happen in any practical model. It was only shown to complete the background discussion.

I will be showing you an actual AUROC curve in the next demonstration.

Using a MLP model for breast cancer prediction

This demonstration uses the results from the histologic studies done on breast cancer samples from 699 patients to predict the presence or absence of cancer based on the recorded features. This demonstration differs significantly from the first demonstration in the chapter that used a CNN model. In this case, the results from the pathologist's biopsy exams are used instead of directly processing the raw Images as was done in the first demonstration. This model is a MLP application rather than a CNN application.

The dataset is the Breast Cancer Wisconsin (Diagnostic) Data Set Features which have been computed from a digitized Image of a fine-needle aspirate (FNA) of a breast mass. The data describe characteristics of the cell nuclei present in the Image. This dataset is described in detail by K. P. Bennett and O. L. Mangasarian: "Robust Linear Programming Discrimination of Two Linearly Inseparable Sets," Optimization Methods and Software 1, 1992.

You can download the input dataset from the UCI Machine Learning Repository.

```
https://archive.ics.uci.edu/ml/datasets/Breast+Cancer+Wisconsin+
%28Diagnostic%29
```

Rename the downloaded file to data.csv and place in a new sub-directory named input.

You will now need to replace 16 '?' entries in the seventh column with a 1. I know that this may bias the dataset a bit, but the script cannot run without the character being replaced with a number. The number I selected is by far the most common one present in the column. I used the MS Excel program for the changes, but you can use the LibreOffice Calc application that should already be installed on the RasPi system.

The following script is named bcMLP.py, and it is available from the book's companion web site. No further explanatory comments are necessary because I have previously presented identical or nearly identical code to you in previous scripts.

```
# Import required libraries libraries
import pandas as pd
import numpy as np
import matplotlib.pyplot as plt
import seaborn as sns
from sklearn.preprocessing import LabelEncoder
from sklearn.model_selection import train_test_split
from sklearn.preprocessing import StandardScaler
```

```python
from sklearn.metrics import confusion_matrix
from sklearn.metrics import roc_curve, auc
from sklearn.ensemble import RandomForestClassifier
import keras
from keras.models import Sequential
from keras.layers import Dense, Dropout

# Load data
data = pd.read_csv('input/data.csv')
#del data['Unnamed: 32']
X = data.iloc[:, 1:9].values
y = data.iloc[:, 10].values

# Encoding categorical data
labelencoder_X_1 = LabelEncoder()
y = labelencoder_X_1.fit_transform(y)

# Split the dataset into Training and Test sets
X_train, X_test, y_train, y_test = train_test_split(X, y,
test_size = 0.1, random_state = 0)

#Feature Scaling
sc = StandardScaler()
X_train = sc.fit_transform(X_train)
X_test = sc.transform(X_test)

# Initialise the ANN
classifier = Sequential()

# Add the input layer and the first hidden layer
classifier.add(Dense(output_dim=16, init='uniform',
activation='relu', input_dim=8))

# Add dropout to prevent overfitting
classifier.add(Dropout(p=0.1))
```

```python
# Add the second hidden layer
classifier.add(Dense(output_dim=16, init='uniform',
activation='relu'))

# Add dropout to prevent overfitting
classifier.add(Dropout(p=0.1))

# Add the output layer
classifier.add(Dense(output_dim=1, init='uniform',
activation='sigmoid'))

# Compile the ANN
classifier.compile(optimizer='adam', loss='binary_
crossentropy', metrics=['accuracy'])

# Fit the ANN to the Training set
# The batch size and number of epochs have been set using trial
# and error.
classifier.fit(X_train, y_train, batch_size=100, nb_epoch=150)

# Predict the Test set results
y_pred = classifier.predict(X_test)
y_pred = (y_pred > 0.5) # Converts continuous to binary

#  Create confusion matrix object
cm = confusion_matrix(y_test, y_pred)

# Display accuracy
print('Accuracy is {}%'.format((((cm[0][0] + cm[1][1])/70)*100))

# Display the confusion matrix
print('\nConfusion Matrix\n',cm)

# Generate and display a Seaborn heatmap
sns.heatmap(cm, annot=True)
plt.savefig('bcHeatmap.png')
plt.show()
```

494

```python
# Instantiate a random forest classifier
rf_clf = RandomForestClassifier(n_estimators=100)
rf_clf.fit(X_train, y_train)

# Compute the probability distributions
probas = rf_clf.predict_proba(X_test)# plot
plt.figure(dpi=150)
plt.hist(probas, bins=20)
plt.title('Classification Probabilities')
plt.xlabel('Probability')
plt.ylabel('# of Instances')
plt.xlim([0.5, 1.0])
plt.legend('01')
plt.show()

# Compute the false and true positive rates
fpr, tpr, thresholds = roc_curve(y_test, probas[:,0],
pos_label=0)

# Compute the area under the curve
roc_auc = auc(fpr, tpr)

# Plot the AUROC curve
plt.figure(dpi=150)
plt.plot(fpr, tpr, lw=1, color='green', label=f'AUC =
{roc_auc:.3f}')
plt.title('ROC Curve for RF classifier')
plt.xlabel('False Positive Rate')
plt.ylabel('True Positive Rate (Recall)')
plt.xlim([-0.05, 1.05])
plt.ylim([-0.05, 1.05])
plt.legend()
plt.show()
```

Running the MLP script

The script is run by entering the following command:

```
python bcMLP.py
```

Figure 8-18 shows the results after running the script.

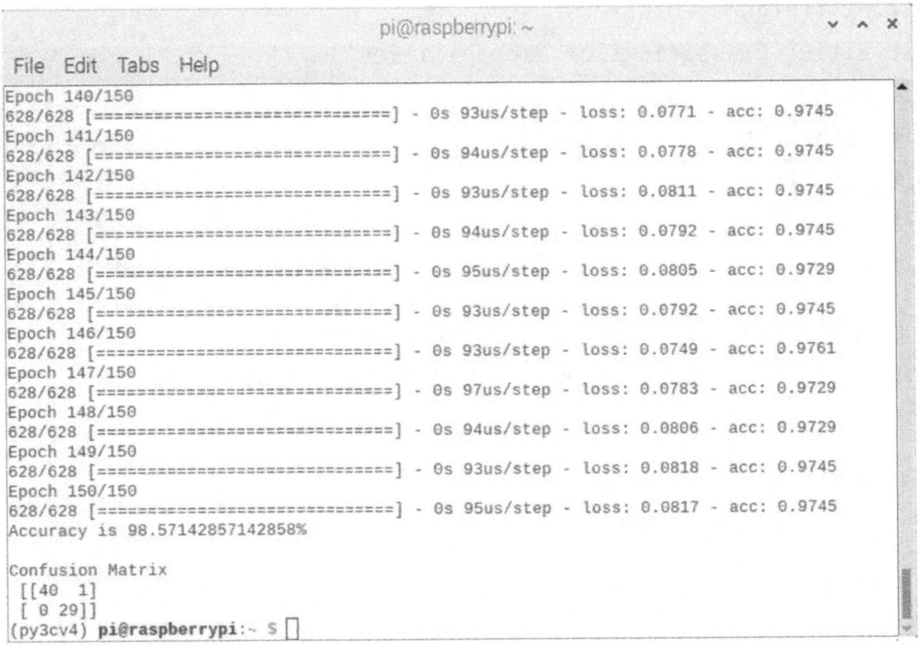

Figure 8-18. *Results after running the bcMLP script*

The confusion matrix displayed in the figure is replicated in Table 8-2.

Table 8-2. *MLP confusion matrix*

	Predicted	
Actual	0	1
0	40	1
1	0	29

where

0 = no cancer detected (negatives)

1 = cancer detected (positives)

You can clearly see from the table that the model was 100% accurate in predicting when cancer was not present (0 false positives) and was 98.57% accurate in predicting when it was (1 false negative). This last metric is precisely the same accuracy value displayed after the script was run. Of course, the real-life consequences of reporting a patient cancer-free while cancer is still present can be devastating to a patient. So even a 1.43% error rate, while exceedingly low, must be viewed with caution due to the enormous consequences involved with patient safety.

Incidentally, while most readers will have figured it out, I will explicitly state the sum total of 70 shown in the confusion matrix results from having a 10% split for the test dataset size. Since there are 699 patients in the original dataset, the test dataset size was rounded to 70.

Figure 8-19 is a heatmap which provides another way to visualize the confusion matrix results.

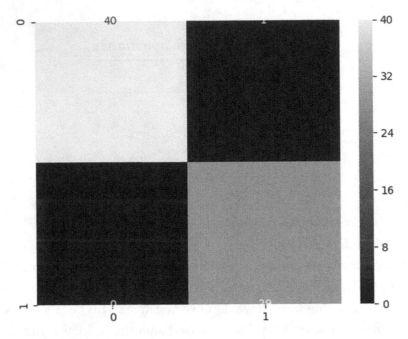

Figure 8-19. *Heatmap*

For print book readers, I highly recommend looking at the color Image version of Figure 8-19 contained in the PDF with all of the book's color figures.

Probability distributions must first be created in order to generate an AUROC plot. Because probability distributions are not readily available from the MLP model is the reason why I instantiated a random forest classifier object named `rf_clf`. While the underlying models are different, the final AUROC plot should be almost identical because of the nature of the dataset. Figure 8-20 is a bar chart of the probability distributions for both the positive (1) and negative (0) classes.

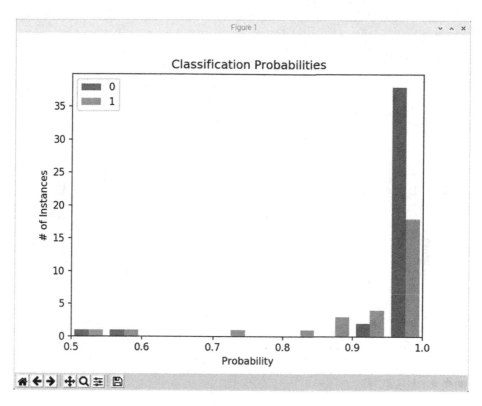

Figure 8-20. *Dataset class probability distributions*

You can clearly see that both class distributions are highly skewed to the right, which will force the AUROC plot to be similar to Figure 8-12. This is precisely what happened when the plot was generated as you can see in Figure 8-21.

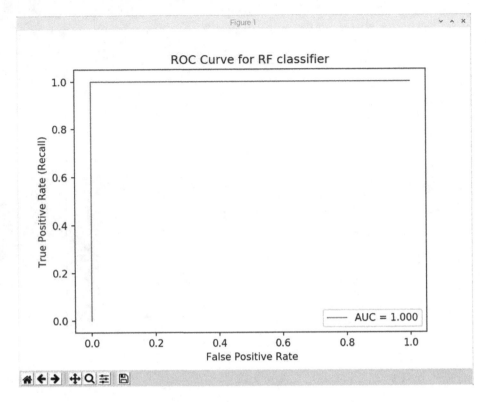

Figure 8-21. *AUROC plot for random forest model breast cancer dataset*

Your immediate takeaway when viewing a plot like this is that the classifier model is an excellent performer for that particular dataset. That conclusion is backed up by other performance measures used to quantify the model.

CHAPTER 9

Reinforcement learning

Most readers have probably heard of AI learning to play computer games on their own, a very popular example being DeepMind. The DeepMind team was in the international news in 2016 when their AlphaGo program defeated the South Korean Go world champion. Likewise, there have been many successful attempts in the past to develop software agents with the intent of playing Atari games like *Breakout*, *Pong*, and *Space Invaders*.

Each of these programs follows a ML paradigm known as reinforcement learning (RL). The following is a straightforward analogy for how RL works.

Consider the classic 1978 Atari game, *Breakout*. The object of this game is to clear all the bricks at the top of the screen by bouncing a ball back from the screen's bottom. You control a paddle at the bottom of the screen, which bounces a ball. Each time a brick is hit, it will disappear and the score increases, that is, there is a reward given. Figure 9-1 shows a series of *Breakout* screenshots illustrating how the game functions.

© Donald J. Norris 2020
D. J. Norris, *Machine Learning with the Raspberry Pi*,
https://doi.org/10.1007/978-1-4842-5174-4_9

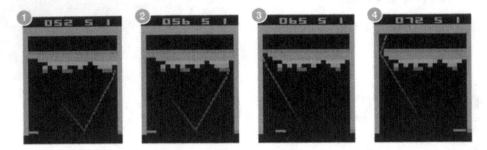

Figure 9-1. *Atari Breakout game screenshots*

Now let's consider how an ANN could be taught to play this game. One way would be to input a series of screenshots and provide an output such as move paddle right, move paddle left, or fire, meaning launch the ball. In this sense, the learning process turns into a classification problem where a given screen Image predicates taking on one of three actions. This appears straightforward, but just consider the huge number of training examples this would require. This approach is rather naive because there should be no need for a game expert to state to do this or do that tens of thousands of times. What is needed is some type of feedback that an action taken was correct or nearly so and allow for some self-correction.

RL tries to solve this type of problem. RL is either supervised or unsupervised learning. Supervised learning has a target label for each training example, and unsupervised learning has no labels. RL has sparse "labels" which are time-delayed and called rewards. The software agent has to learn behavior based only on rewards.

In reality, there are numerous challenges in the way of implementing a RL algorithm for the *Breakout* game. It turns out that the award given may have little to do with the actions immediately taken prior to the reward being given. The reward happens when a brick is hit by a ball, but the paddle must have been positioned correctly and the fire button hit at the proper time. The disconnect between the immediate reward and any and all necessary preceding actions is called the credit assignment problem, that is, which preceding action was responsible for the reward and to what extent?

Playing the *Breakout* and for that matter, most other games often require a strategy. Often, players will start out in a random manner playing a game but eventually evolve their playing strategy as they observe the game unfolding. For instance, in *Breakout* the balls tend to fly to the left more often than they do to the right. A simple strategy of moving the paddle more to the left-hand side often results in more points scored. But that may not be the only way to improve the score. An approach to determining an optimal strategy is called the explore-exploit dilemma and is a useful framework to consider when trying to obtain the most rewards.

The RL model is a useful way to encapsulate our human learning experiences, whether it be at school, in business, or even the government or military environments. Credit assignments and exploration-exploitation dilemmas come up every day in all our activities. RL is an important topic to explore and experiment with, and games are the perfect non-threatening sandbox.

I will further discuss how Q-learning and DL intersect after going through all the following demonstrations. At that point you should have acquired a good background with Q-learning to appreciate and understand the concluding discussion.

Markov decision process

The Markov decision process (MDP) is how RL is formalized. Let's suppose you are an agent, situated in an environment such as the *Breakout* game. The environment is in a certain state (e.g., paddle location, ball location and direction, brick count, etc.). The agent performs certain actions in this environment such as moving the paddle to the left or to the right. Actions sometimes result in a reward. Any action will transform the environment to a certain extent and will lead to a new state. The agent can then perform another action which leads to another state and so forth. The set of rules for how these actions are chosen is called policy. The environment is typically stochastic, which means the next state will be somewhat randomized. For the *Breakout* game, this means that every new ball is launched in a random direction.

Figure 9-2 is a figure that diagrams the MDP data flow.

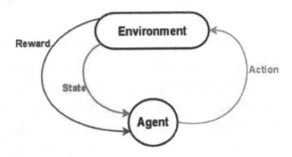

Figure 9-2. *MDP data flow*

MDP is made up states, actions, and rules for transitioning from one state to another state. An episode (game) for this process can be expressed as a finite sequence of states, actions, and rewards

$$\left(s_o, a_0, r_1\right) -> \left(s_1, a_1, r_2\right) \cdots -> \left(s_{n-1}, a_{n-1}, r_n\right) -> s_n$$

where

s_i = state

a_i = action

r_{i+1} = reward after action a_i

The episode ends with terminal state s_n. The MDP relies on the Markov assumption, which is the probability of the next state s_{i+1} depending only on the current state s_i and action a_i, but not on preceding states or actions.

Discounted future reward

For the MDP to perform well, long-term rewards must be accounted for as well as for immediate rewards. The total reward for one episode can be expressed as

$$R = r_1 + r_2 + r_3 + \cdots + r_n$$

The total future reward from time point t onward may be expressed as

$$R_t = r_t + r_{t+1} + r_{t+2} + \cdots + r_n$$

Because the environment is stochastic, there can never be a deterministic decision regarding the same reward the next time the same action is performed. The further into the future rewards are considered, the more they may diverge. To account for that uncertainty, it is common to use a discounted future reward, which is expressed as

$$R_t = r_t + \gamma r_{t+1} + \gamma^2 r_{t+2} + \cdots + \gamma^{n-t} r_n$$

where

γ = discount factor (value range of 0 to 1.0)

Because the discount factor is less than 1.0 and it is raised to a power, all future rewards are heavily reduced or discounted. A discounted future reward at time step t can be expressed in terms of the same thing at time step t+1:

$$R_t = r_t + \gamma \left(r_{t+1} + \gamma \left(r_{t+2} + \cdots \right) \right) = r_t + \gamma R_{t+1}$$

If the discount factor γ is set to 0, then the strategy will have no long-term involvement and will only depend on immediate rewards. The balance between immediate and future rewards should have a discount factor such as $\gamma = 0.9$. In case the environment is unlikely deterministic and the same actions always result in same rewards, then the discount factor can be set to 1.0.

A good strategy for an agent would be to always choose an action that maximizes the (discounted) future reward.

Q-learning

In Q-learning a function $Q(s_t, a_t)$ is defined as that function that represents the maximum discounted future reward when action a_t is performed in state s_t and continues optimally from that point on.

$$Q(s_t, a_t) = max\ R_{t+1}$$

One way to think about $Q(s_t, a_t)$ is that it is "the best possible score at the end of the game after performing action a_t in state s_t." It is called the Q-function, because it represents the "quality" of a certain action in a given state.

At first glance, the Q-function appears to be a puzzling definition. How can the final score at game's end be estimated? Future states and actions are simply not known. But assuming such a function exists is essential to support a hypothesis for maximizing possible future rewards.

Next consider the implications of having such a function would be. Suppose there is a state with two possible actions. The action that results in the highest score at the end of game should be selected. But, which action should be selected? The answer becomes simple once you have a Q-function. Just pick the action with the highest Q-value. The following equation represents this strategy:

$$\pi(s) = argmax_a\left(Q(s,a)\right)$$

where

π = policy (rule on how an action is chosen in a given state)

The question now is how is the Q-function defined given the previous discussion? I will first focus on just one transition (s, a, r, s'), where s' represents the next state after s. The Q-value of state s and action a may be expressed in terms of the Q-value of the next state s' by

$$Q(s,a) = r + \gamma max_{a'} Q(s',a')$$

This equation is called the Bellman equation. It is quite straightforward concept where the maximum future reward for the current state and action is the immediate reward plus the maximum future reward for the next state.

The principal concept in Q-learning is that it is possible to iteratively approximate the Q-function using the Bellman equation. In the simplest case, the Q-function can be implemented as a table, with states as rows and actions as columns.

A flowchart of the Q-learning algorithm is shown in Figure 9-3.

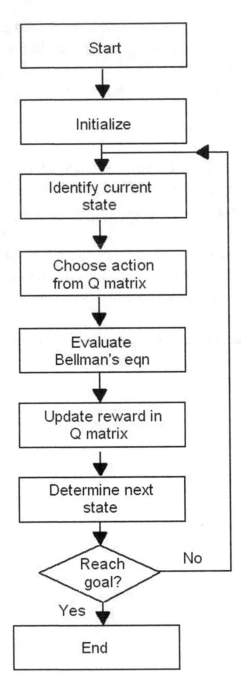

Figure 9-3. *Q-learning flowchart*

The Q-learning algorithm starts with identifying the current state *s* from an input. After the identification of the state, an action will be chosen from the action list, either by searching for the maximum reward or, if stochastic, by accepting a greedy probability ε. With all the values initialized in the previous steps, the Q-value for the action taken in state *s* is calculated using the Bellman equation. The Q-value will then be stored in the Q-table. In other words, the experience of the agent is captured within the Q-table. The rewards and penalties of the proposed Q-learning are evaluated by a set of simple rules set for the reward functions (policy). The next state *s'* for the Q-learning algorithm will be determined after the selected action *a* is executed. The stopping criteria for the Q-learning algorithm will then be checked when the next state s' has been determined. If the next state *s'* is the final goal of the Q-learning, then the process will end or else the next state *s'* will become the current state *s* for another iteration. This process continues until either the goal is reached or a stopping criterion is met.

The following is a worked out example, which should help clarify the Q-learning process.

Q-learning example

I will first credit several bloggers for great posts which inspired this example. They were also inspired by others who have tackled the complex issues of explaining Q-learning in order for the AI community to better understand this topic. The blogs are:

"Reinforcement Learning: A Simple Python Example and a Step Closer to AI with Assisted QLearning" by Manuel Amunategui

```
https://l-ing.ru/watch/Reinforcement-Learning--A-Simple-Python-
Example-and-A-Step-Closer-to-AI-with-Assisted-QLearning/
```

"Getting AI smarter with Qlearning: a simple first step in Python" from *The Beginner Programmer*

```
http://firsttimeprogrammer.blogspot.com/2016/09/getting-ai-
smarter-with-q-learning.html
```

```
http://mnemstudio.org/path-finding-q-learningtutorial.htm
```

This example starts by displaying plan view of a building with five rooms as depicted in Figure 9-4.

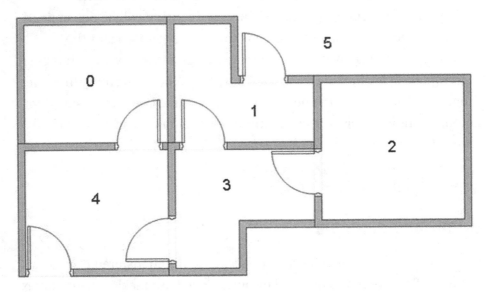

Figure 9-4. *Plan view of example building*

Each room in the building has a door through which a bot or agent can travel in either direction. Notice in the figure that doors in rooms 1 and 4 lead to the outside, which is depicted as "room" 5 for purposes of this example. However, the goal to be achieved is to have the agent enter room 5, the outside. The agent can be placed in any room to start. Reward values will be assigned to every door, and the ultimate goal will have a very large reward in comparison to door rewards which do not directly lead to the goal.

Figure 9-5 is a nodal graph depicting all the possible paths between rooms and which ones are the likely successful paths.

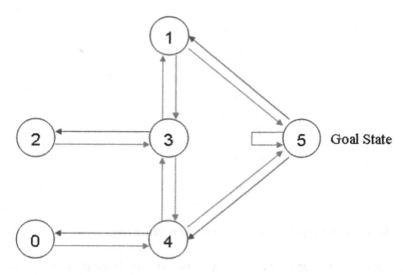

Figure 9-5. *Nodal graph*

As previously stated, the agent can be placed in any room to start and, from that room, go outside the building (this is target room 5). To set this room as a goal, a reward value is associated to each door. The doors that lead immediately to the goal have an instant reward of 100. Other doors that are not directly connected to the target room have 0 rewards. Two arrows are assigned to each room because doors are two-way (0 leads to 4, and 4 leads back to 0). Each arrow contains an instant reward value, as shown in Figure 9-6.

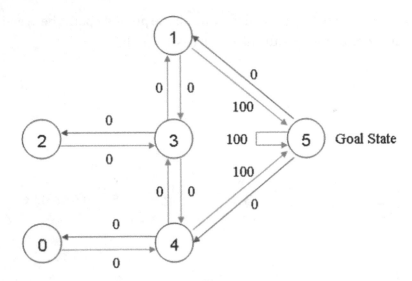

Figure 9-6. *Nodal graph with rewards annotated*

Notice in the figure that a path in room 5 loops back to itself with a reward of 100, while all the other links to the target room have a reward of 100. In Q-learning, the goal is to reach the state with the highest reward, so that if the agent arrives at the goal, it should remain there forever. This goal type is named an "absorbing goal."

Imagine our agent as a virtual bot that can learn through experience. The agent can pass from one room to another but has no knowledge of the environment, and it doesn't know which sequence of doors leads to the outside.

The objective is to determine the path for the agent from any room in the building to the outside. For the next part of the discussion, assume that the agent starts in room 2 and tries to reach the outside of the building, designated as room 5. Figure 9-7 nicely encapsulates this initial environment.

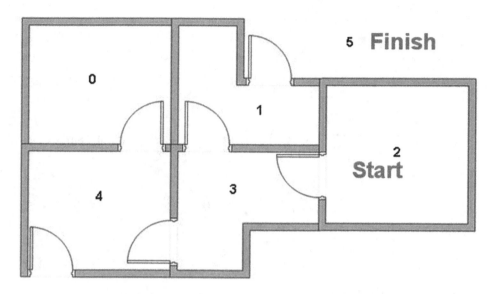

Figure 9-7. *Initial environment*

In Q-learning terms, each room, including the outside, is a "state," and the agent's movement from one room to another is an "action." Thus, in the preceding nodal figures, a "state" is depicted as a node, while "action" is represented by the arrows.

Refer to Figure 9-8 for the following discussion.

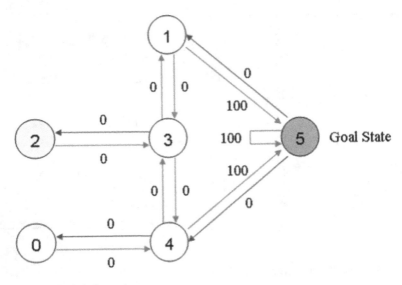

Figure 9-8. *Initial actions*

As stated previously, the agent begins in state 2. From state 2, it can only go to state 3 because state 2 is only connected to state 3. From state 3, it can go either to state 1 or 4 or back to 2. If the agent is in state 4, there are three possible actions, which are to go to state 0, 5, or 3. If the agent is in state 1, it can go either to state 5 or 3. From state 0, it can only go back to state 4.

A matrix "R" (for rewards) can be constructed to capture the state diagram and the instant reward values. Figure 9-9 shows this matrix.

$$
R= \begin{matrix} & & \textbf{Action} \\ & \textbf{State} & \begin{matrix} 0 & 1 & 2 & 3 & 4 & 5 \end{matrix} \\ \begin{matrix} 0 \\ 1 \\ 2 \\ 3 \\ 4 \\ 5 \end{matrix} & & \begin{bmatrix} -1 & -1 & -1 & -1 & 0 & -1 \\ -1 & -1 & -1 & 0 & -1 & 100 \\ -1 & -1 & -1 & 0 & -1 & -1 \\ -1 & 0 & 0 & -1 & 0 & -1 \\ 0 & -1 & -1 & 0 & -1 & 100 \\ -1 & 0 & -1 & -1 & 0 & 100 \end{bmatrix} \end{matrix}
$$

Figure 9-9. *R matrix*

The –1s in the table represent null values (i.e., where there isn't a link between nodes). For example, state 0 cannot go to state 1.

Now a similar matrix, "Q," is added to the brain of the agent. This matrix represents the memory of what the agent has learned through experience. The rows of the Q matrix represent the current state of the agent, and the columns represent the possible actions leading to the next state, that is, the links between the nodes.

Because the agent starts out knowing nothing, the Q matrix is initialized to zero. In this example, the number of states is six, representing each of the nodes. If the number of states was unknown, the Q matrix could start with only one element. It is a simple task to add more columns and rows into the Q matrix as new states are discovered.

The transition rule of Q learning is the Bellman equation

$$Q(s,a) = r + \gamma max_{a'} Q(s',a')$$

The agent will learn through experience, without a teacher, as part of its unsupervised learning experience. The agent explores from state to state until it reaches the goal. Each exploration is called an episode. Each episode consists of the agent moving from the initial state to the goal state. Each time the agent arrives at the goal state, the script goes to the next episode.

The Q-learning algorithm may be summarized as follows:

1. Set the γ parameter and the environment rewards in the R matrix.

2. Initialize Q matrix to zero.

3. For each episode (loop):

4. Select a random initial state.

5. Iterate if the goal state hasn't been reached (loop):

- Select one of all possible actions for the current state.

- Using this possible action, consider going to the next state.

- Get maximum Q-value for this next state based on all possible actions.

- Compute - $Q(s,a) = r + \gamma \max_{a'} Q(s',a')$

- Set the next state as the current state.

The preceding algorithm is used by the agent to learn from experience. Each episode is equivalent to one training session. In each training session, the agent explores the environment, represented by the R matrix, and receives the reward (if any) until it reaches the goal state. The purpose of the training is to enhance the "brain" of our agent, represented by the Q matrix. More training results in a more optimized matrix Q as is the case for an ANN.

You should realize that the function $\max_{a'} Q(s',a')$ which is used to update $Q(s, a)$ is only an approximation, and in early stages of training, it may be completely wrong. However, the approximation improves with every episode, and if the update is done enough times, then the Q-function will converge and represent the true Q-value.

Once Q matrix has been enhanced, the agent will find the fastest route to the goal state. To use the enhanced Q matrix, the agent simply traces the sequence of states, from the initial state to goal state.

The following are several step-by-step manually worked out Q-learning experiments, which hopefully will fully explain this process.

Manual Q-learning experiments

To understand how the Q-learning algorithm works, I will go through a few episodes step by step.

The first episode starts by setting the value of the learning parameter γ to 0.8, and the initial state as room 1.

The Q matrix is also initialized to all 0s as shown in Figure 9-10.

$$Q = \begin{matrix} & \begin{matrix} 0 & 1 & 2 & 3 & 4 & 5 \end{matrix} \\ \begin{matrix} 0 \\ 1 \\ 2 \\ 3 \\ 4 \\ 5 \end{matrix} & \begin{bmatrix} 0 & 0 & 0 & 0 & 0 & 0 \\ 0 & 0 & 0 & 0 & 0 & 0 \\ 0 & 0 & 0 & 0 & 0 & 0 \\ 0 & 0 & 0 & 0 & 0 & 0 \\ 0 & 0 & 0 & 0 & 0 & 0 \\ 0 & 0 & 0 & 0 & 0 & 0 \end{bmatrix} \end{matrix}$$

Figure 9-10. *Initialized Q matrix*

Next examine the second row (state 1) of the R matrix shown in Figure 9-9. There are two possible actions for the current state 1:

- Go to state 3.

- Go to state 5.

Now, say by random selection that 5 is selected as the action.

Next, imagine what would happen if the agent were in state 5. Look at the sixth row of the R matrix. It has three possible actions:

- Go to state 1.

- Go to state 4.

- Go to state 5.

Applying Bellman's equation yields

$$Q(s,a) = r + \gamma max_{a'}Q(s',a')$$

$$Q(1,5) = R(1,5) + 0.8 * max_{a'}Q\big(Q(5,1),Q(5,4),Q(5,5)\big)$$

$$Q(1,5) = 100 + 0.8 * 0 = 100$$

Because the Q matrix is still initialized to zero, $Q(5, 1)$, $Q(5, 4)$, $Q(5, 5)$ are all 0. The result of this computation for $Q(1, 5)$ is 100 because of the instant reward from $R(1, 5)$.

Due to algorithm, the next state 5 now becomes the current state. Because 5 is the goal state, this episode is finished. The agent's brain now contains an enhanced Q matrix as shown in Figure 9-11.

$$Q = \begin{array}{c} \\ 0 \\ 1 \\ 2 \\ 3 \\ 4 \\ 5 \end{array} \begin{array}{cccccc} 0 & 1 & 2 & 3 & 4 & 5 \\ \begin{bmatrix} 0 & 0 & 0 & 0 & 0 & 0 \\ 0 & 0 & 0 & 0 & 0 & 100 \\ 0 & 0 & 0 & 0 & 0 & 0 \\ 0 & 0 & 0 & 0 & 0 & 0 \\ 0 & 0 & 0 & 0 & 0 & 0 \\ 0 & 0 & 0 & 0 & 0 & 0 \end{bmatrix} \end{array}$$

Figure 9-11. *Enhanced Q matrix*

A randomly chosen initial state begins the next episode. Let's say state 3 is the initial state.

Looking at the fourth row of R matrix you can see that there are three possible actions:

- Go to state 1.

- Go to state 2.

- Go to state 4.

Assume go to state 1 is selected by random process. Next imagine that the agent is in state 1. Examine at the second row of the R matrix for state 1. You can see that it has two possible actions:

- Go to state 3.

- Go to state 5.

The Q-value now must be computed using Bellman's equation:

$$Q(s,a) = r + \gamma max_{a'} Q(s',a')$$

$$Q(1,5) = R(1,5) + 0.8 * max_{a'} Q(Q(1,2), Q(1,5))$$

$$Q(1,5) = 0 + 0.8 * max(0,100) = 80$$

The enhanced Q matrix from the last episode contained the results of Q(1, 3) = 0 and Q(1, 5) = 100. The result of the computation is Q(3, 1) = 80 because the reward is zero. The Q matrix now becomes what is shown in Figure 9-12.

$$
Q = \begin{array}{c} \\ 0 \\ 1 \\ 2 \\ 3 \\ 4 \\ 5 \end{array}
\begin{array}{cccccc}
0 & 1 & 2 & 3 & 4 & 5 \\
\left[\begin{array}{cccccc}
0 & 0 & 0 & 0 & 0 & 0 \\
0 & 0 & 0 & 0 & 0 & 100 \\
0 & 0 & 0 & 0 & 0 & 0 \\
0 & 80 & 0 & 0 & 0 & 0 \\
0 & 0 & 0 & 0 & 0 & 0 \\
0 & 0 & 0 & 0 & 0 & 0
\end{array}\right]
\end{array}
$$

Figure 9-12. *Revised Q matrix*

The next state 1 now becomes the current state. The inner loop of the Q-learning algorithm is now repeated because state 1 is not the goal state.

So, after starting the new loop with the current state 1, there are two possible actions:

- Go to state 3.

- Go to state 5.

By random selection, let's say the action selected is 5. This is shown in Figure 9-13.

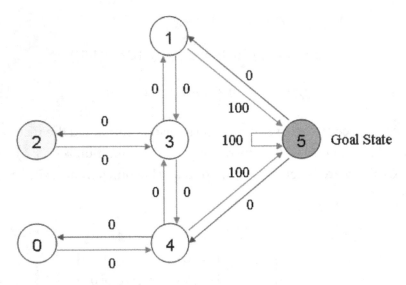

Figure 9-13. *Random selection to state 5*

Now, imagine the agent is in state 5. There are three possible actions:

- Go to state 1.

- Go to state 4.

- Go to state 5.

The Q-value is computed using the maximum value for each of these possible actions:

$$Q(s,a) = r + \gamma max_{a'} Q(s',a')$$

$$Q(1,5) = R(1,5) + 0.8 * max_{a'} Q\big(Q(5,1),Q(5,4),Q(5,5)\big)$$

$$Q(1,5) = 100 + 0.8 * 0 = 100$$

The updated entries of the Q matrix for $Q(5,1)$, $Q(5,4)$, $Q(5,5)$ are all 0. The result of this computation for $Q(1, 5)$ is 100 because this is the instant reward from $R(5, 1)$. This result does not change the enhanced Q matrix.

Because 5 is the goal state, the episode is finished. Our agent's brain now contains an enhanced Q matrix as shown in Figure 9-14.

$$Q = \begin{array}{c@{\quad}c} & \begin{array}{cccccc} 0 & 1 & 2 & 3 & 4 & 5 \end{array} \\ \begin{array}{c} 0 \\ 1 \\ 2 \\ 3 \\ 4 \\ 5 \end{array} & \left[\begin{array}{cccccc} 0 & 0 & 0 & 0 & 0 & 0 \\ 0 & 0 & 0 & 0 & 0 & 100 \\ 0 & 0 & 0 & 0 & 0 & 0 \\ 0 & 80 & 0 & 0 & 0 & 0 \\ 0 & 0 & 0 & 0 & 0 & 0 \\ 0 & 0 & 0 & 0 & 0 & 0 \end{array} \right] \end{array}$$

Figure 9-14. *Revised enhanced Q matrix*

The agent eventually learns more by completing more episodes. It will finally reach convergence values in the Q matrix as shown in Figure 9-15.

$$Q = \begin{array}{c@{\quad}c} & \begin{array}{cccccc} 0 & 1 & 2 & 3 & 4 & 5 \end{array} \\ \begin{array}{c} 0 \\ 1 \\ 2 \\ 3 \\ 4 \\ 5 \end{array} & \left[\begin{array}{cccccc} 0 & 0 & 0 & 0 & 400 & 0 \\ 0 & 0 & 0 & 320 & 0 & 500 \\ 0 & 0 & 0 & 320 & 0 & 0 \\ 0 & 400 & 256 & 0 & 400 & 0 \\ 320 & 0 & 0 & 320 & 0 & 500 \\ 0 & 400 & 0 & 0 & 400 & 500 \end{array} \right] \end{array}$$

Figure 9-15. *Final enhanced Q matrix*

The Q matrix can then be normalized by dividing all the entries by a number which will make the highest matrix value equal to 100. In this case that number is 5. This normalized matrix is shown in Figure 9-16.

$$Q = \begin{array}{c} \\ 0 \\ 1 \\ 2 \\ 3 \\ 4 \\ 5 \end{array} \begin{array}{cccccc} 0 & 1 & 2 & 3 & 4 & 5 \\ \left[\begin{array}{cccccc} 0 & 0 & 0 & 0 & 80 & 0 \\ 0 & 0 & 0 & 64 & 0 & 100 \\ 0 & 0 & 0 & 64 & 0 & 0 \\ 0 & 80 & 51 & 0 & 80 & 0 \\ 64 & 0 & 0 & 64 & 0 & 100 \\ 0 & 80 & 0 & 0 & 80 & 100 \end{array}\right] \end{array}$$

Figure 9-16. *Normalized Q matrix*

Once the Q matrix has converged, the agent has learned the most optimal paths to the goal state. Tracing the best sequences of states is as simple as following the links with the highest values at each state. This is shown in Figure 9-17.

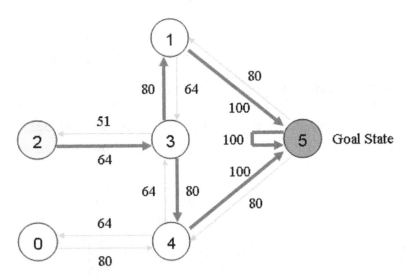

Figure 9-17. *Nodal diagram with final, normalized link values*

For example, from an initial state 2, the agent can use the Q matrix as a guide:

- From state 2 the maximum Q-values suggest the action is to go to state 3.

- From state 3 the maximum Q-values suggest two alternatives:

  - Go to state 1.

  - Go to state 4.

- Suppose the go to state 4 action is randomly chosen to be go to state 1.

- From state 1 the maximum Q-values suggest the action is to go to state 5.

- Thus, the optimal path based on Q-learning is $2 \rightarrow 3 \rightarrow 1 \rightarrow 5$.

Q-learning demonstration with a Python script

Note   I strongly recommend that you read (or reread) the previous section before reading this one. I do not repeat the step-by-step explanations in this section. Understanding the explanations will make this section much more understandable and enjoyable.

In this demonstration, I will use Q-learning in a Python script to find the shortest path between two points. The script has no prior knowledge regarding the environment and will learn only by using RL.

Figure 9-18 is a randomized point graph that was created by the script.

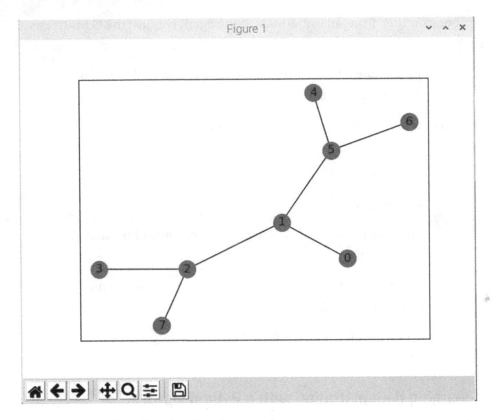

Figure 9-18. *Randomized point graph*

Point 0 will be the start position, and point 7 is the target and finish position. The objective of the script is to determine the optimal path between the start and target positions using the RL algorithm. There are obvious false paths and faux targets in the map, which will all have to be evaluated and discarded.

You will need to load one additional library to prepare to run this script. Enter the following command to load the required library:

```
pip install networkx
```

The script is named simpleRL.py, and it is available from the book's companion web site. There are no additional explanatory comments for this script because I have previously worked through several step-by-step examples for the RL process and I feel you should be adequately prepared to understand how this relatively simple script works.

```python
# Import required libraries
import numpy as np
import pylab as plt
import networkx as nx

# Map cell to cell, add circular cell to goal point
points_list = [(0,1), (1,5), (5,6), (5,4), (1,2), (2,3), (2,7)]

# Set target node
goal = 7

# Create and display graph
G=nx.Graph()
G.add_edges_from(points_list)
pos = nx.spring_layout(G)
nx.draw_networkx_nodes(G,pos)
nx.draw_networkx_edges(G,pos)
nx.draw_networkx_labels(G,pos)
plt.show()

# Define points in graph
MATRIX_SIZE = 8

# Create matrix (MATRIX_SIZE * MATRIX_SIZE)
R = np.matrix(np.ones(shape=(MATRIX_SIZE, MATRIX_SIZE)))
R *= -1
```

```python
# Assign zeros to paths and 100 to goal-reaching point
for point in points_list:
    print(point)
    if point[1] == goal:
        R[point] = 100
    else:
        R[point] = 0

    if point[0] == goal:
        R[point[::-1]] = 100
    else:
        # Reverse of point
        R[point[::-1]]= 0

# Add goal point round trip
R[goal,goal]= 100

# Create Q matrix
Q = np.matrix(np.zeros([MATRIX_SIZE,MATRIX_SIZE]))

# Set learning parameter gamma
gamma = 0.8

# Set initial start point
initial_state = 1

# Define available_actions method
def available_actions(state):
    current_state_row = R[state,]
    av_act = np.where(current_state_row >= 0)[1]
    return av_act

# Create variable to hold possible actions
available_act = available_actions(initial_state)
```

```python
# Define method to randomly select next action
def sample_next_action(available_actions_range):
    next_action = int(np.random.choice(available_act,1))
    return next_action

# Create variable to hold the randomly selected action
action = sample_next_action(available_act)

# Define method to update state if needed
def update(current_state, action, gamma):

  max_index = np.where(Q[action,] == np.max(Q[action,]))[1]

  if max_index.shape[0] > 1:
      max_index = int(np.random.choice(max_index, size = 1))
  else:
      max_index = int(max_index)
  max_value = Q[action, max_index]

  # Bellman's equation
  Q[current_state, action] = R[current_state, action] + gamma *
  max_value
  print('max_value', R[current_state, action] + gamma *
  max_value)

  if (np.max(Q) > 0):
    return(np.sum(Q/np.max(Q)*100))
  else:
    return (0)

# Update the state based on selected action
update(initial_state, action, gamma)

# Training starts now
scores = []
```

```python
for i in range(700):
    current_state = np.random.randint(0, int(Q.shape[0]))
    available_act = available_actions(current_state)
    action = sample_next_action(available_act)
    score = update(current_state,action,gamma)
    scores.append(score)
    print ('Score:', str(score))

# Display the rewards matrix
print('\nRewards matrix R\n')
print(R)

# Display the enhanced Q matrix
print('\nEnhanced Q matrix\n')
print(Q/np.max(Q)*100)

# Testing starts now
current_state = 0
steps = [current_state]

# Loop to determine optimal path
while current_state != 7:

    next_step_index = np.where(Q[current_state,] ==
    np.max(Q[current_state,]))[1]

    if next_step_index.shape[0] > 1:
        next_step_index = int(np.random.choice(next_step_index,
        size = 1))
    else:
        next_step_index = int(next_step_index)

    steps.append(next_step_index)
    current_state = next_step_index
```

```
print("Most efficient path:")
print(steps)

plt.plot(scores)
plt.show()
```

Running the script

The script is run by entering the following command:

```
python simpleRL.py
```

Figure 9-19 is a plot of the converging score vs. number of episodes completed.

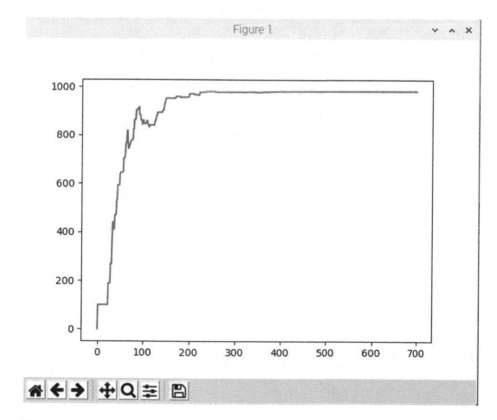

Figure 9-19. *Scoring convergence plot*

You can clearly see that the maximum scoring is reached after approximately 400 episodes have been completed. The script was hard-coded to run 700 episodes. The additional time required to run 300 episodes beyond the 400 mark was miniscule.

Figure 9-20 shows the terminal window after the script completed its run.

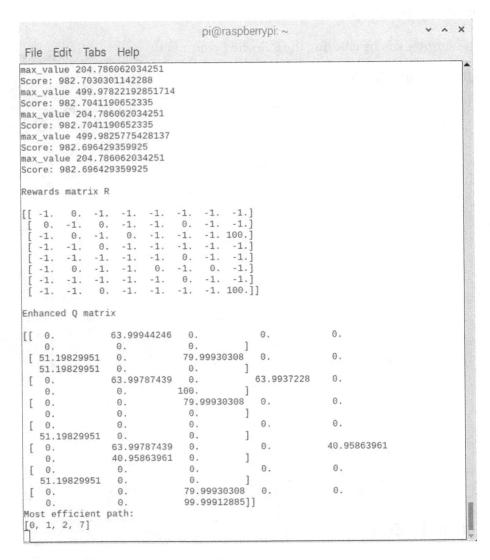

Figure 9-20. *Final script results*

There are bunch of interesting things to discuss in this figure. First is the remaining portion of the interim episode results shown at the top of the figure. Here you can see the Q-function maximum value as well as the score. The score shown is the unnormalized optimal path value.

The rewards matrix R is shown below the interim episodic results. There are two items to note regarding this matrix. There are two 100 reward values located at the R(2, 6) and R(6,6) locations. The first reward (R(2,6)) is for the direct path between node 2 and node 7. The second one (R(6,6)) is the self-absorbing link or the target node loop-back. The next item to note is that there are 0 values for existing links and –1 values for non-existing links.

The enhanced and normalized Q matrix is displayed below the R matrix. Unfortunately, the Python 3 print statement wraps the rows a bit, and it is a bit hard to read. I tried unsuccessfully to have it print out the rows, one row at a time. The matrix values are also displayed in a floating point, which is another unnecessary distraction.

The last item in the figure is a display of the optimal path which turned out to be 0 to 1 to 2 to 7.

In the next demonstration, I will be showing you how to handle hostile environment factors in a path determination.

Q-learning in a hostile environment demonstration

Sometimes, the environment in a RL project is not always amicable to an agent trying to navigate the paths. To make it obvious in this demonstration, I will assume that the agent is a group of bees trying to get to their beehive located at node 7. Now, bees don't like smoke and will avoid it all costs. In fact, beekeepers (formal name is apiarists) use a smoke gun to calm bees as they harvest honey from the beehive. I have added smoke to several nodes in the randomly generated environment as you can see in Figure 9-21. The agent will always try to avoid taking those links, which lead to smoke.

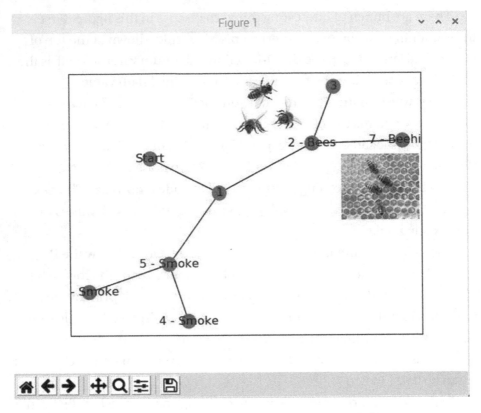

Figure 9-21. *Randomly generated environment with bees*

The following script is named beeRL.py and is available from the book's companion web site:

```
# Import required libraries
import numpy as np
import pylab as plt
import networkx as nx

# Map cell to cell, add circular cell to goal point
points_list = [(0,1), (1,5), (5,6), (5,4), (1,2), (2,3), (2,7)]
```

```python
# Set target node
goal = 7

bees = [2]
smoke = [4,5,6]

gamma = 0.8

G=nx.Graph()
G.add_edges_from(points_list)
mapping={0:'Start', 1:'1', 2:'2 - Bees', 3:'3', 4:'4 - Smoke',
5:'5 - Smoke', 6:'6 - Smoke', 7:'7 - Beehive'}
H=nx.relabel_nodes(G,mapping)
pos = nx.spring_layout(H)
nx.draw_networkx_nodes(H,pos, node_size=[200,200,200,200,200,
200,200,200])
nx.draw_networkx_edges(H,pos)
nx.draw_networkx_labels(H,pos)
plt.show()

# Define points in graph
MATRIX_SIZE = 8

# Create matrix (MATRIX_SIZE * MATRIX_SIZE)
R = np.matrix(np.ones(shape=(MATRIX_SIZE, MATRIX_SIZE)))
R *= -1

# Assign zeros to paths and 100 to goal-reaching point
for point in points_list:
    print(point)
    if point[1] == goal:
        R[point] = 100
```

```python
    else:
        R[point] = 0

    if point[0] == goal:
        R[point[::-1]] = 100
    else:
        # Reverse of point
        R[point[::-1]]= 0

# Add goal point round trip
R[goal,goal]= 100

def available_actions(state):
    current_state_row = R[state,]
    av_act = np.where(current_state_row >= 0)[1]
    return av_act

def sample_next_action(available_actions_range):
    next_action = int(np.random.choice(available_act, 1))
    return next_action

def collect_environmental_data(action):
    found = []
    if action in bees:
        found.append('b')

    if action in smoke:
        found.append('s')
    return found

# Create Q matrix
Q = np.matrix(np.zeros([MATRIX_SIZE,MATRIX_SIZE]))

enviro_bees = np.matrix(np.zeros([MATRIX_SIZE, MATRIX_SIZE]))
enviro_smoke = np.matrix(np.zeros([MATRIX_SIZE, MATRIX_SIZE]))
```

```
initial_state = 1

# Get available actions in the current state
available_act = available_actions(initial_state)

# Sample next action to be performed
action = sample_next_action(available_act)

# This function updates the Q matrix according to the path
selected and the Q
# learning algorithm
def update(current_state, action, gamma):

    max_index = np.where(Q[action,] == np.max(Q[action,]))[1]

    if max_index.shape[0] > 1:
        max_index = int(np.random.choice(max_index, size = 1))
    else:
        max_index = int(max_index)
    max_value = Q[action, max_index]

    Q[current_state, action] = R[current_state, action] +
    gamma * max_value
    print('max_value', R[current_state, action] + gamma *
    max_value)

    environment = collect_environmental_data(action)
    if 'b' in environment:
        enviro_bees[current_state, action] += 1
    if 's' in environment:
        enviro_smoke[current_state, action] += 1

    if (np.max(Q) > 0):
        return(np.sum(Q/np.max(Q)*100))
```

```
    else:
        return(0)

update(initial_state,action,gamma)

# Training starts
scores = []
for i in range(700):
    current_state = np.random.randint(0, int(Q.shape[0]))
    available_act = available_actions(current_state)
    action = sample_next_action(available_act)
    score = update(current_state,action,gamma)
    scores.append(score)
    print ('Score:', str(score))

plt.plot(scores)
plt.show()

print('Bees found')
print(enviro_bees)
print('Smoke found')
print(enviro_smoke)
```

Running the script and evaluating the results

The script is run by entering the following command:

```
python beeRL.py
```

Figure 9-22 is a plot of the converging score vs. number of episodes completed.

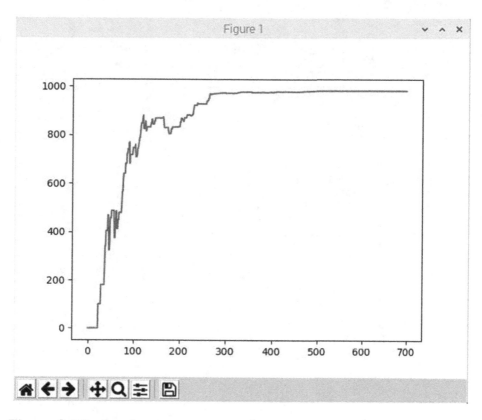

Figure 9-22. *Scoring convergence plot*

You can clearly see that the maximum scoring is reached after approximately 400 episodes have been completed. The script was hard-coded to run 700 episodes. The additional time required to run 300 episodes beyond the 400 mark was miniscule.

Figure 9-23 shows the terminal window after the script completed its run.

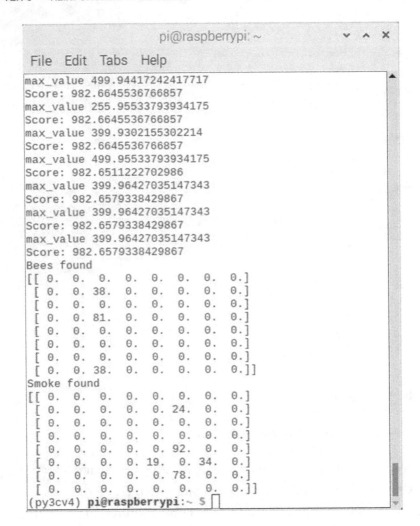

Figure 9-23. *Final script results*

The environmental matrices in the figure show how many bees and smoke the agent found during its journey while searching for the most efficient path to the hive. There were two assumptions made in order to simply this demonstration. These are

- Bees have a positive coefficient on finding hives.

- Bees have a negative coefficient on encountering smoke.

These are not unreasonable assumptions, but it does require a priori knowledge regarding the agent's behavior. A natural question now arises: can this a priori knowledge be used to improve the Q-learning performance? The answer to that question can be found in the following demonstration.

Q-learning in a hostile environment with a priori knowledge demonstration

This demonstration will show you how to use available a priori knowledge to improve how an agent performs in a path-finding task. A group of bees will still be the agent, and the goal is still to get to the beehive. However, a realistic approach is now taken where the agent dynamically looks at the new environment and assigns environmental biases as they are encountered. Links that lead to smoke filled nodes will be discounted and links that are bee-friendly are encouraged.

The significant change between this new script and the previous script is that the update method has been modified to include a scoring matrix for all attempted paths. If the attempted path leads to a smoke-designated node, then a matrix value will be decremented. Conversely, if an attempted path leads to a bee-designated node, then a matrix value will be incremented. The matrix holding all these bias values is continuously used in the training loop to guide the agent in path selection.

The following script is named beeRLenv.py and is available from the book's companion web site:

```
# Import required libraries
import numpy as np
import pylab as plt
import networkx as nx

# Map cell to cell, add circular cell to goal point
points_list = [(0,1), (1,5), (5,6), (5,4), (1,2), (2,3), (2,7)]
```

```
# Set target node
goal = 7

bees = [2]
smoke = [4,5,6]
gamma = 0.8

G=nx.Graph()
G.add_edges_from(points_list)
mapping={0:'Start', 1:'1', 2:'2 - Bees', 3:'3', 4:'4 - Smoke',
5:'5 - Smoke', 6:'6 - Smoke', 7:'7 - Beehive'}
H=nx.relabel_nodes(G,mapping)
pos = nx.spring_layout(H)
nx.draw_networkx_nodes(H,pos, node_size=[200,200,200,200,200,
200,200,200])
nx.draw_networkx_edges(H,pos)
nx.draw_networkx_labels(H,pos)
plt.show()

# Define points in graph
MATRIX_SIZE = 8

# Create matrix (MATRIX_SIZE * MATRIX_SIZE)
R = np.matrix(np.ones(shape=(MATRIX_SIZE, MATRIX_SIZE)))
R *= -1

# Assign zeros to paths and 100 to goal-reaching point
for point in points_list:
    print(point)
    if point[1] == goal:
        R[point] = 100
    else:
        R[point] = 0
```

```python
        if point[0] == goal:
            R[point[::-1]] = 100
        else:
            # Reverse of point
            R[point[::-1]]= 0

# Add goal point round trip
R[goal,goal]= 100

def available_actions(state):
    current_state_row = R[state,]
    av_act = np.where(current_state_row >= 0)[1]
    return av_act

def sample_next_action(available_actions_range):
    next_action = int(np.random.choice(available_act, 1))
    return next_action

def collect_environmental_data(action):
    found = []
    if action in bees:
        found.append('b')

    if action in smoke:
        found.append('s')
    return found

# Create Q matrix
Q = np.matrix(np.zeros([MATRIX_SIZE,MATRIX_SIZE]))

# Create matrices to hold the bees and smoke totals
enviro_bees = np.matrix(np.zeros([MATRIX_SIZE, MATRIX_SIZE]))
enviro_smoke = np.matrix(np.zeros([MATRIX_SIZE, MATRIX_SIZE]))

# Subtract bees from smoke. This gives smoke a negative bias
enviro_matrix = enviro_bees - enviro_smoke
```

```
initial_state = 1

# Get available actions in the current state
available_act = available_actions(initial_state)

# Sample next action to be performed
action = sample_next_action(available_act)

# This function updates the Q matrix according to the path
# selected and the Q learning algorithm.
def update(current_state, action, gamma):

    max_index = np.where(Q[action,] == np.max(Q[action,]))[1]

    if max_index.shape[0] > 1:
        max_index = int(np.random.choice(max_index, size = 1))
    else:
        max_index = int(max_index)
    max_value = Q[action, max_index]

    Q[current_state, action] = R[current_state, action] +
    gamma * max_value
    print('max_value', R[current_state, action] + gamma *
    max_value)

    environment = collect_environmental_data(action)
    if 'b' in environment:
        enviro_matrix[current_state, action] += 1
    if 's' in environment:
        enviro_matrix[current_state, action] -= 1

    if (np.max(Q) > 0):
        return(np.sum(Q/np.max(Q)*100))
    else:
        return(0)
```

```python
# Do an update
update(initial_state,action,gamma)

# Make a transactional matrix copy for use with the enviro_help
# method.
enviro_matrix_snap = enviro_matrix.copy()

def available_actions_with_enviro_help(state):
    current_state_row = R[state,]
    av_act = np.where(current_state_row >= 0)[1]
    # if there are multiple routes, dis-favor anything negative
    env_pos_row = enviro_matrix_snap[state,av_act]
    if (np.sum(env_pos_row < 0)):
        # Can negative directions be removed from av_act?
        temp_av_act - av_act[np.array(env_pos_row)[0]>=0]
        if len(temp_av_act) > 0:
            print('going from:',av_act)
            print('to:',temp_av_act)
            av_act = temp_av_act
    return av_act

# Training starts
scores = []
for i in range(700):
    current_state = np.random.randint(0, int(Q.shape[0]))
    available_act = available_actions_with_enviro_help(current_
    state)
    action = sample_next_action(available_act)
    score = update(current_state,action,gamma)
    scores.append(score)
    print ('Score:', str(score))

plt.plot(scores)
plt.show()
```

Running the script and evaluating the results

The script is run by entering the following command:

`python beeRLenv.py`

Figure 9-24 is a diagram of the randomly generated environment used in this demonstration.

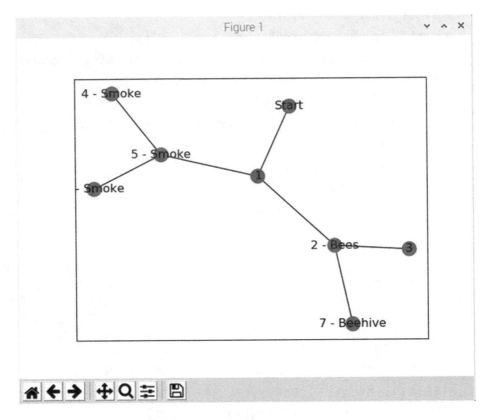

Figure 9-24. *Randomly generated environment*

Figure 9-25 is a terminal window showing the paths evaluated. The last one listed is the optimal selected path. This should not come as a surprise if you examine Figure 9-24. However, you must remember that the agent does not have this bird's-eye view of the environment and must systematically test every available link emanating from the start node.

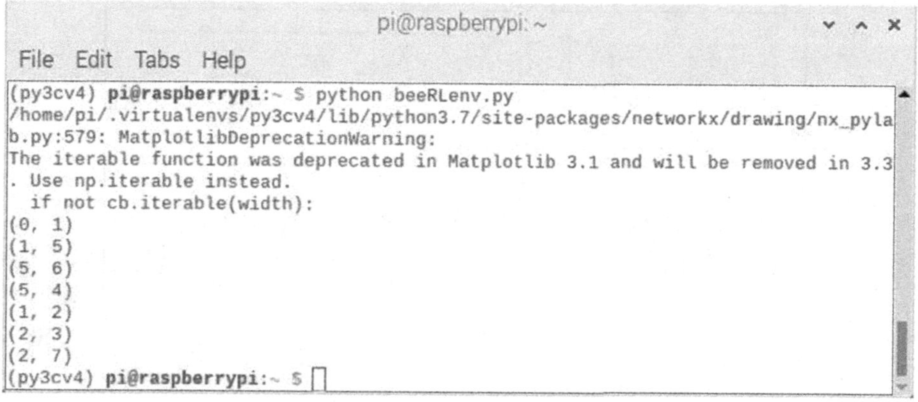

```
pi@raspberrypi: ~

File  Edit  Tabs  Help

(py3cv4) pi@raspberrypi:~ $ python beeRLenv.py
/home/pi/.virtualenvs/py3cv4/lib/python3.7/site-packages/networkx/drawing/nx_pyla
b.py:579: MatplotlibDeprecationWarning:
The iterable function was deprecated in Matplotlib 3.1 and will be removed in 3.3
. Use np.iterable instead.
  if not cb.iterable(width):
(0, 1)
(1, 5)
(5, 6)
(5, 4)
(1, 2)
(2, 3)
(2, 7)
(py3cv4) pi@raspberrypi:~ $ 
```

Figure 9-25. *Terminal window showing evaluated paths*

The final figure in this results section is Figure 9-26, which shows the scoring convergence. This is the sole performance measure for this demonstration and is the key piece of evidence, which will prove if this dynamic approach worked.

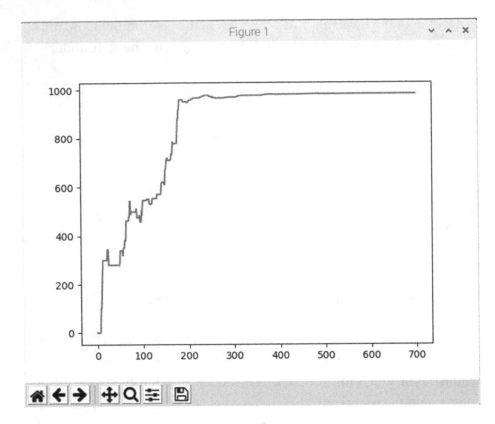

Figure 9-26. *Scoring convergence plot*

You can see from the plot that the final scoring value is effectively
reached by episode 180. Compare this plot with the one shown in
Figure 9-22 where the final scoring value converged at approximately
episode 400. The dynamic approach converged much earlier proving that
it is a much better performer than the approach which does not factor in
environmental conditions. This result would be somewhat akin to tuning
an ANN or CNN using bias values for performance improvements.

Q-learning and neural networks

The environment states in the *Breakout* game are only defined by the location of the paddle, location, and direction of the ball and the presence or absence of an individual brick. This intuitive representation however is only specific to each specific game. Is there anything more universal that would be suitable for all the games? The obvious choice is to use screen pixels because they implicitly contain all of the relevant information about the game situation, except for the speed and direction of the ball in the case of the *Breakout* game. However, two or more consecutive screens would have the ball state adequately described.

If DeepMind preprocessing is applied to game screens, which is to take the four last screen Images, resize them to 84 × 84, and convert them to grayscale with 256 gray levels. This would result with $256^{84 \times 84 \times 4} \approx 10^{67970}$ possible game states. That would mean there would be 10^{67970} rows in the Q-table, which is more than the number of atoms in the known universe – clearly an impossible situation. This vast number of states could be drastically reduced by only including the states visited. Even so, most states are rarely visited and it would take the lifetime of the universe for the Q-table to converge – again, not an ideal situation. The solution lies with developing an estimate for Q-values for states never seen.

At this point DL will definitely help. Neural networks are exceptionally good performers at extracting useful features from highly structured data. A neural network could represent a Q-function that takes the state (four game screens) and action as input and outputs the corresponding Q-value. As an alternative, the game screens could be used as an input and a Q-value output for each possible action. The latter is the approach taken by the DeepMind team. Using either approach has the advantage that only one forward pass through the network is required to perform a Q-value update or pick an action with the highest Q-value.

Figure 9-27 shows the "naive" approach of inputting four states to a neural network and obtaining a single Q-value output.

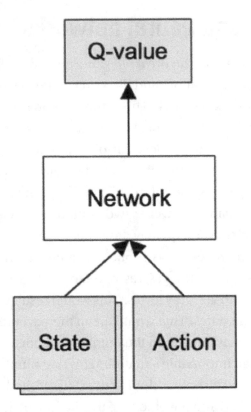

Figure 9-27. *Naive approach to using DL and Q-learning*

In contrast, Figure 9-28 shows the approach taken by the DeepMind team where a single state is input and multiple Q-values are output.

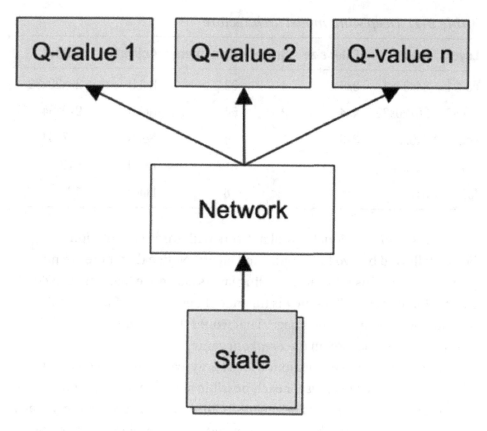

Figure 9-28. *DeepMind approach to DL and Q-learning*

For a purely informational step, Table 9-1 shows the architecture used in the DeepMind model.

Table 9-1. *DeepMind model architecture*

Layer	Input	Filter size	Stride	Num filters	Activation	Output
conv1	84x84x4	8x8	4	32	ReLU	20x20x32
conv2	20x20x32	4x4	2	64	ReLU	9x9x64
conv3	9x9x64	3x3	1	64	ReLU	7x7x64
fc4	7x7x64			512	ReLU	512
fc5	512			18	Linear	18

This is a convolutional neural network with three convolutional layers, followed by two fully connected layers. Notice that there are no pooling layers. This is because pooling layers cause the features to become translation invariant. This means the model becomes insensitive to the location of an object in the Image. That would destroy the model's ability to track the ball location in the *Breakout* game.

Inputs to the network are four 84 × 84 grayscale game screens. Outputs of the network are Q-values for each possible action, of which there are 18 for the *Breakout* game. Q-values are real values, which consequently make it a regression task, which can be optimized using simple squared error loss (L).

$$L = \frac{1}{2}\left(r + max_{a'}Q(s',a') - Q(s,a)\right)^2$$

where
$r + max_{a'}Q(s',a')$ = target
$Q(s, a)$ = prediction
Given a transition (s, a, r, s'), the classic Bellman's equation Q-table update rule must be replaced with the following process:

1. Do a feedforward pass for the current state s to get predicted Q-values for all actions.

2. Do a feedforward pass for the next state s' and
    calculate the maximum overall network outputs
    $max_{a'}Q(s',a')$.

3. Set Q-value target for action to $r + \gamma max_{a'}Q(s',a')$
    (use the max calculated in step 2). For all other
    actions, set the Q-value target to the same as
    originally returned from step 1, making the error 0
    for those outputs.

4. Update the weights using back propagation.

The preceding process shows you how to estimate the future reward
in each state using Q-learning and approximate the Q-function using a
CNN. However, it turns out that approximating Q-values using non-linear
functions is unstable. There are many tuning techniques that must be
used to make it converge. It also takes a long time, almost a week using a
computer with a single GPU board.

The most important tuning technique is to use experience replay.
During gameplay, all the experiences (s, a, r, s') are stored in a replay
memory. When training the network, random mini-batches from the
replay memory are used instead of the most recent transition. This breaks
up any similarity existing in training samples, which might inadvertently
drive the network into a local minimum. Also, using experience replay
makes the training task similar to usual supervised learning. This
simplifies debugging and further algorithm testing.

Using DL with Q-learning attempts to solve the credit assignment
problem, which I mentioned at the beginning of the chapter. This solution
happens because a reward is propagated back in time, until it reaches
the crucial decision point. That point is the actual cause for the obtained
reward.

The other major issue is the exploration-exploitation dilemma, also mentioned at the chapter's beginning. You should realize that when a Q-table or Q-network is initialized randomly, its predictions are initially random as well. If an action is chosen with the highest Q-value, then the action will be random and the agent performs a naive exploration. As the Q-function converges, it returns more consistent Q-values and the amount of exploration decreases. It may be stated that Q-learning incorporates the exploration as part of the algorithm. But this exploration is "greedy" because it selects the first effective strategy it finds.

A simple and effective fix for the preceding problem is ε-greedy exploration with probability ε choosing a random action; otherwise, go with the "greedy" action with the highest Q-value. The DeepMind system decreases ε over time from 1 to 0.1. When the DeepMind system starts, it makes completely random moves to completely explore the state space and then it settles down to a fixed exploration rate.

All of the preceding discussion can be encapsulated by some pseudo-code based on the DeepMind model, which provides a relatively easy-to-understand algorithm.

```
initialize replay memory D
initialize action-value function Q with random weights
observe initial state s
repeat:
    select an action a
        with probability ε select a random action
        otherwise select a = argmaxa'Q(s,a').
    carry out action a
    observe reward r and new state s'
    store experience (s, a, r, s') in replay memory D
```

```
sample random transitions ( ss, aa, rr, ss' ) from replay
memory D
calculate target for each mini-batch transition:
    if ss' is the terminal state, then tt = rr
    otherwise tt = rr + γmaxa'Q(ss',aa')
train the Q-network using (tt - Q(ss,aa))² as loss
s = s'
until terminated
```

There are more tuning techniques that the DeepMind team used to actually make it work such as using a target network, error clipping, reward clipping, and so on. I will leave it to the interested reader to pursue those topics.

It is amazing that this algorithm actually learns anything at all. Consider that the Q-function is initialized randomly; it will naturally output garbage data when it first starts. Now the algorithm uses this initial garbage (the maximum Q-value of the next state) as targets for the network, only occasionally recording a tiny reward. From a large-scale perspective, that approach appears nonsensical. How could the algorithm learn anything meaningful? The strange fact is that it does eventually learn.

It has been stated by some very smart people that AI is something we haven't figured out yet. Once AI has been figured out, it may not seem so intelligent any more. However, Q-learning with DL is still an amazing topic. Observing it figuring out a new game is truly an awe-inspiring event.

Index

A

© Donald J. Norris 2020
D. J. Norris, *Machine Learning with the Raspberry Pi*,
https://doi.org/10.1007/978-1-4842-5174-4

F

G

H

Printed in the United States
By Bookmasters